Reversing Sail
A History of the African Diaspora

Second edition

Beginning with antiquity, *Reversing Sail: A History of the African Diaspora* captures the essential political, cultural, social, and economic developments that shaped the black experience. In this second edition, Michael A. Gomez updates the text of the previous edition to be current with the most recent research on the African Diaspora. Continuing to pay particular attention to the everyday lives of the working classes, the second edition expands its temporal boundaries to include developments into the twenty-first century, as well as integrating women and feminist perspectives more thoroughly. It also widens the geographical span to include Latin America, while incorporating more material on African experiences in Europe, North Africa, and the Persian Gulf. Assessing the impact of religion, global trade, slavery and resistance, and the challenges of modernity, Gomez's second edition further connects the histories and experiences of Africans and their descendants over time and space, attending to both convergences and divergences, while explaining how the deep past informs subsequent developments.

Michael A. Gomez is Silver Professor of History and Middle Eastern Studies and Islamic Studies at New York University, and Director of NYU's Center for the Study of Africa and the African Diaspora (CSAAD). He is also editor of the *Cambridge Studies on the African Diaspora* series at Cambridge University Press. In addition to the first edition of *Reversing Sail: A History of the African Diaspora* (2004), he is the author of several books, including *African Dominion: A New History of Empire in Early and Medieval West Africa* (2018) and *Black Crescent: African Muslims in the Americas* (2005).

Cambridge Studies on the African Diaspora

General Editor:
Michael A. Gomez, *New York University*

Using the African Diaspora as its core defining and launching point for examining the historians and experiences of African-descended communities around the globe, this series unites books around the concept of migration of peoples and their cultures, politics, ideas, and other systems from or within Africa to other nations or regions, focusing particularly on transnational, transregional, and transcultural exchanges.

Titles in the series

Rashauna Johnson, *Slavery's Metropolis: Unfree Labor in New Orleans during the Age of Revolutions*

Daniel B. Domingues da Silva, *The Atlantic Slave Trade from West Central Africa, 1780-1867*

Jorge L. Giovannetti-Torres, *Black British Migrants in Cuba: Race, Labor, and Empire in the Twentieth-Century Caribbean, 1898–1948*

Michael A. Gomez, *Reversing Sail: A History of the African Diaspora, Second Edition*

Reversing Sail

A History of the African Diaspora

Second edition

Michael A. Gomez
New York University

CAMBRIDGE
UNIVERSITY PRESS

Shaftesbury Road, Cambridge CB2 8EA, United Kingdom

One Liberty Plaza, 20th Floor, New York, NY 10006, USA

477 Williamstown Road, Port Melbourne, VIC 3207, Australia

314–321, 3rd Floor, Plot 3, Splendor Forum, Jasola District Centre, New Delhi – 110025, India

103 Penang Road, #05–06/07, Visioncrest Commercial, Singapore 238467

Cambridge University Press is part of Cambridge University Press & Assessment, a department of the University of Cambridge.

We share the University's mission to contribute to society through the pursuit of education, learning and research at the highest international levels of excellence.

www.cambridge.org
Information on this title: www.cambridge.org/9781108498715
DOI: 10.1017/9781108595643

First edition © Michael A. Gomez 2005
Second edition © Michael A. Gomez 2020

First published 2005
Second edition 2020 (version 5, October 2023)

Printed in Great Britain by CPI Group (UK) Ltd, Croydon CR0 4YY, October 2023

A catalogue record for this publication is available from the British Library

ISBN 978-1-108-49871-5 Hardback
ISBN 978-1-108-71243-9 Paperback

Additional resources for this publication at www.cambridge.org/Gomez2ed

In memory of the strong love of my mother,
Mary Williams Gomez, 1936–1999,
the first to help me see
the beauty, suffering, and promise of the African diaspora.

Contents

LIST OF FIGURES   *page* xi
LIST OF MAPS   xiii
ACKNOWLEDGMENTS   xv

Introduction   1

PART I "Old" World Dimensions and the First Wave   7

1 Antiquity   9

Egypt   11
Egypt and the South   13
Nubian Ascendancy   14
Africans in the Graeco-Roman World   15
Suggestions for Further Reading   19

2 Africans and the Bible   21

Egypt and Nubia in the Bible   21
Africans and Origins   23
The Queen of Sheba   26
Beta Israel   28
The "Ethiopian" Eunuch and the Call to Christianity   29
Suggestions for Further Reading   31

3 Africans and the Islamic World   32
Golden Lands   33
Pilgrims and Scholars   37
The Enslaved   38
Iberia   43

India and Pakistan   47
Turkey and Iran   48
The Image of the African in the Islamic World   50
Slavery's Aftermath   55
Suggestions for Further Reading   57

PART II "New" World Realities and Diaspora's
            Second Wave (to 1945)   61

4 Transatlantic Moment and the Dawn of Modernity   63

Reconquista   65
Scope of the Trade   67
African Provenance   70
Belly of the Whale   78
Suggestions for Further Reading   87

5 Enslavement   90

Africans in Renaissance Europe   91
Enslavement in the Americas   94
Suggestions for Further Reading   119

6 Asserting the Right to Be   123

Armed Revolt and Autonomous Space   124
Everyday/way Resistance   136
Facing the Enemy   149
Slavery's End?   161
Games People Play   171
Freedom's Tease   174
Another Way   178
Suggestions for Further Reading   181

7 Reconnecting   186
Boats and Trains   187
Organizing Black Labor   193
Faiths New and Renewed   195
Conceptualizing the Solutions   200
Blacks and Science   211
Efflorescence   215
Suggestions for Further Reading   222

PART III Empire's Dismantling and the
            Third Wave (since 1945)   227

8 Movement People   229

Freedom and Fire   231
Developments in the Caribbean, Latin America, and Europe   239

   Cultural Innovations   244
   Suggestions for Further Reading   258

9 Global Africa in the Era of Mandela and Obama   263
   The Fight Against the Portuguese in Africa   266
   Dismantling South African Apartheid   270
   Further African Migration to the West   275
   Suggestions for Further Reading   282

EPILOGUE   284

INDEX   287

COLOR PLATES CAN BE FOUND BETWEEN PAGES 144 AND 145

Figures

1 Head of Taharqa   *page* 22
2 Malik Ambar   49
3 Cape Coast Castle   71
4 Slave coffle   80
5 The Africans of the slave bark *Wildfire* brought into Key West in April of 1860   84
6 Portrait of Juan de Pareja, assistant to Spanish artist Diego Velázquez and painted by him, *c.*1650   94
7 Slave market, Pernambuco   96
8 *Flagellation of a Female Samboe Slave*   101
9 Francisco de Arobe with his sons Pedro and Domingo   125
10 Female slaves in Brazil, 1830s   138
11 Dance steps and movements, Trinidad, 1830s   142
12 Queen and her court   144
13 Loading coal on a steamer, St. Thomas, 1864   147
14 *Revenge taken by the Black Army for the Cruelties practised on them by the French*   156
15 Hanging a slave, South Carolina, 1865   160
16 Thatched houses, Barbados, 1898   172
17 Black family, Beaufort, South Carolina, 1862   177
18 Children playing in Harlem, 1925   216
19 Nicolás Guillén, Afro-Cuban poet and editor of *Mediodía*, Madrid, Spain, September 1937   221
20 Group portrait of the Cincinnati Clowns baseball team with manager and business manager, 1940s   257

Maps

1 North Africa in antiquity   *page* 12
2 Major African empires, 1000–1500   34
3 Spread of Islam to 1500   45
4 West Africa in the eighteenth and nineteenth centuries   74
5 West Central Africa, 1600–1800   76
6 Latin America, 1828   95
7 Caribbean map   97
8 North America   112

Acknowledgments

I am grateful to the continued support of my wife Mary; our daughters Sonya, Candace and Jamila; and our grandchildren Nia and Alex.

Introduction

Our current century is becoming increasingly characterized by persons of varying ethnic and racial and cultural backgrounds living together in societies all over the globe. The United Kingdom, France, and Germany, together with the United States and Brazil in the Americas, are only the better-known examples. How communities of common derivation maintain their sense of connectedness in lands of destination, while also forming ties with new groups and thus giving rise to novel social formations, is a primary facet of contemporary life. But such diversity is also a major challenge, often leading to tensions arising from ignorance and fear of the unknown. The formal inclusion of the histories and cultures of everyone in the society is therefore critical to resolving misunderstanding and conflict.

This book attempts to make a contribution to that effort, as it concerns people of African descent who found (and find) themselves either living outside of the African continent, or in parts of Africa territorially distant from their lands of birth. It is also a book about critical ideas that have had a profound impact upon the African-descended, and as such the book is a history of experiences, contributions, victories, and ongoing struggles, centering mass movements and extensive relocations over long periods of time, resulting in dispersals of persons and ideas throughout much of the world, a phenomenon often referred to as the African diaspora.

To be sure, there have been other historical redistributions across land and sea. European and Asian populations (among whom the

Chinese, Japanese, Korean, and Pacific Islanders feature) have long been in motion, as have Jews, Muslims, and other religious communities. This fact underscores that persons could simultaneously belong to multiple communities, and that the African dimension is by no means the only such community. Even so, the present volume maintains, for reasons to be explored, that the African diaspora is entirely unique. It is a story, or a collection of stories, like no other.

Stories are fundamental to how we understand the human condition. It is by way of stories that we assemble information (and sometimes fictions) to make sense of our experiences, both individually and collectively. It is by way of the narrative that nations recount histories, usually emphasizing collective triumph over tribulation. And it is in the story of triumph that communities find validation and purpose. What we make of our past experience, how we fashion our collective stories, is critical to how we interpret and respond to the present.

The story of Africans and their descendants conforms to neither the popular nor official narratives of the nation-state, as their experiences are often overlooked, misrepresented, or caricatured, if not erased entirely. This is not only because those experiences are less studied and poorly understood; it is also because the black experience complicates the dominant narrative, rendering it far less flattering.

As an undergraduate text, this book is written at a time of considerable perplexity, anxiety, ambiguity, and contradiction. People of African descent – black people – can be found in all walks of life. In ancient and medieval times their achievements were in instances unparalleled, while their economic contributions to the modern world have been extensive and foundational, having introduced agricultural forms and mining techniques while providing the necessary labor. They have contributed to the sciences and the arts in spectacular ways, while their cultural influence, with individuals achieving extraordinary heights in literature, theater, painting, sculpture, dance, music, athletics, and religion, has long been celebrated. Global in scope, black musical production has featured jazz, calypso, blues, soca, reggae, and hip-hop, as just a few examples. Even so, contrasts between the individual of distinction and the popular perception of blacks as a group could not be more striking. Throughout Europe and the Americas, blacks are collectively and disproportionately associated with crime, poverty, disease, and educational underachievement. It is a perception paralleled by the view of Africa itself, a continent brimming with potential but waylaid by war, poverty, disease, and insufficient investment in human capital.

The study of the African diaspora is distinguished from the study of African Americans in the United States, or any other African-descended community in a particular country, in that the diasporic lens is concerned with at least one of two issues – and frequently both: (1) the ways in which African cultural, social, or political forms undergo transformations, yet continue a relationship with African antecedents while influencing new environments that include Europeans, First Nationers, and Asians; and (2) connections between geographically separated and/or culturally distinct communities of the African-descended.

When placed into conversation, studies of black communities reveal certain elements in common, suggesting related, even parallel conditions, if not a unified experience. These include: (1) Africa as land of origin; (2) enslavement and colonialism; (3) cultural efflorescence; (4) reifications of color and race; (5) ongoing citizenship struggles; and (6) open-ended interrogations of Africa's ongoing significance in lands of destination.

As such, the diasporic condition is often an unsettled (and unsettling) experience in which the question of "belonging" is unresolved: Africa, as land of origin, is in many ways unrecoverable; whereas it is a challenge to fully regard an oft-hostile host environment as "home." Under such circumstances, diaspora is experienced as a continuum of liminality, along which communities and individuals – linked as much by common experience as by genetic makeup – are located at various points.

Fundamental to the approach of the present study is that global watershed moments serve as the critical mechanism by which the African diaspora is progressively knitted together. That is, key historical developments, such as the 1896 Battle of Adwa in Ethiopia, serve to trigger a collective black consciousness that is, in turn, largely predicated upon such antecedent, parallel experiences as slavery, colonialism, and regimes of racialized oppression.

The present volume posits three movements or phases that comprise the Africa diaspora. The first unfolds in antiquity, and rather than the forced relocation of large numbers of Africans, begins with the dissemination of ideas that flow from Africa to other parts of the world, especially the Mediterranean. New ideas would on occasion be accompanied by substantial physical relocations to other parts of

Africa, as well as to destinations outside of the continent. But in contrast to a subsequent movement in chains, many of these Africans were moving in conquest and triumph. Yet another distinctive aspect of this first wave is that it unfolds in a period to which certain influential ideas about Africans are ascribed – even though these ideas have often developed long after antiquity's end. These concepts would prove to be both prescriptive and proscriptive in the lives of millions of Africans.

The second wave begins in the middle of the fifteenth century, with the onset of the transatlantic slave trade, and ends in the middle of the twentieth century and the Second World War. As will be explained, this periodization concurs with modernity, for which the exploitation of African labor was key. The third wave or movement, in turn, began with ever-increasing levels of immigration following the Second World War and, continuing into the present, features a series of interactions between African-descended and African-born communities. The implications of these developments are highly significant, and will be explored.

This book is therefore divided into three parts, with chapters proceeding in more or less chronological fashion. Part I: "Old" World Dimensions and the First Wave, begins with Chapter 1, "Antiquity," a discussion of ancient Egypt, Nubia, and Greece and Rome, where and when the African diasporic story factually begins. Chapter 2, "Africans and the Bible," locates the African presence in sacred text and examines the critical role Judeo-Christian traditions have played in the African experience. Chapter 3, "Africans and the Islamic World," centers Africans, sub-Saharan and otherwise, in the formation and expansion of Islam as a global force.

Part II: "New" World Realities and Diaspora's Second Wave (to 1945), begins with Chapter 4, "Transatlantic Moment." After initially treating Africans in medieval Europe and Renaissance Europe, it shifts to the transatlantic slave trade as a watershed moment for both Europe and the Americas. Chapter 5, "Enslavement," brings together similar and dissimilar experiences of slavery in the Americas. The response to the disorientation of displacement and enslavement, the various strategies of resistance and reconstitution, and the ambiguities of economic, political, and juridical conditions in the post-slavery period are the subjects of Chapter 6, "Asserting the Right to Be." The rise of global capitalism during the first half of the twentieth century would feature substantial migrations throughout the

Caribbean, the American South, and Europe, and Chapter 7, "Reconnecting," argues that such large-scale relocations also facilitated the mutual introduction of diverse populations, leading to such cultural and political developments as Pan-Africanism, the Harlem Renaissance, and Négritude.

Part III: Empire's Dismantling and The Third Wave (since 1945), consists of two chapters: Chapter 8, "Movement People," spans the period of the Second World War into the 1970s, exploring the interrelated nature of decolonization, civil rights, black power, music, sports, and literature. Chapter 9, "Global Africa in the Era of Mandela and Obama," follows the African diaspora's unfolding into the twenty-first century, focusing on how freedom struggles in southern Africa became the center of diasporic activity, followed by a discussion of increased African immigration into the northern hemisphere and its connection to the rise of Barack Obama.

Threading throughout the text are questions whose answers are not always apparent. These include: Who qualifies as a member of the African diaspora? Is such membership biologically determined? Is it culturally acquired? Is it better understood as a political statement? Can there be multiple responses to the question, and/or the answers depend upon location and/or context? If biologically premised, just how much African ancestry is required, and is phenotype a reliable measure? Is acknowledgment of African ancestry necessary to be considered part of the diaspora? Who is qualified to determine who belongs and who does not, and what in turn qualifies a person to render such judgment?

In exploring the many dimensions of the African diaspora, *Reversing Sail* issues a number of challenges. To begin, it calls into question spatial conventions, especially the nation-state, as the most useful context within which to understand the black experience. It rejects imperial privilege insofar as whose story gets to be told. It seeks to trouble cultural chauvinism, in particular of the European variety, as well as the meanings of such concepts as "the West" and "Western culture." Standards of beauty and aesthetics are interrogated, and in the discussions of race, slavery, gender, religion, capitalism, imperialism, colonialism, and the postcolonial, the study locates polarities of impoverishment and wealth within periods and formations of deep historicity.

As an interpretive history, this book is far from an exhaustive treatment of so vast a set of topics. Originally envisioned to complement a series of short introductory books to African history, *Reversing Sail* was written within those constraints, so that it is not possible to afford any geographic location the attention and detail it truly deserves. Rather, in identifying key moments within which the African diaspora unfolds, spatial emphases shift from chapter to chapter. Furthermore, and in keeping with the original series format, suggested readings rather than endnotes follow each chapter, recommending materials of most immediate assistance with undergraduate research. As such, *Reversing Sail* can be used not only for the study of the African diaspora, but as a complementary resource for African history as well.

I

"Old" World Dimensions and the First Wave

CHAPTER 1

Antiquity

Scholars of history and society have long understood that discussions of the collective black experience must begin with people and cultures and developments in Africa itself, before the rise of American slavery and the transatlantic slave trade, in order to correct, or at least debilitate the firmly entrenched view that black folk, prior to their experiences in the Americas, had no history worthy of the name, that their history begins with slavery.

Long before the rise of professional historians, black men and women were invested in uncovering Africa's deep history, and connecting it with the challenges of subsequent global displacements. Facing slavery's withering assault, independent thinkers as early as David Walker and Frederick Douglass were careful to mention the glories of the African past. When circumstances all around suggested otherwise, they found evidence of the potential and ability of black people in the achievements of antiquity. Rather than conforming to divine decree or reflecting the natural order of things, the enslavement of black people, in a context of thousands of years of African accomplishment, was but an aberration. From this perspective, black suffering and subjugation could hardly have been anticipated.

These early intellectuals, as yet uninformed about West and West Central African civilizations, invariably cited those of ancient Egypt, Nubia, and Ethiopia as exemplars of black distinction and creativity. In so doing, they presaged the subsequent writings of scholars like W.E.B. Du Bois, Carter G. Woodson, and St. Clair Drake, who similarly embraced the idea that ancient Egyptian and Nubian societies were somehow related to those toiling in American sugar cane and cotton fields. This view was not limited to black scholars in the Americas; the Senegalese scholar Cheikh Anta Diop, leader of the "Dakar" school of African historical inquiry, likewise argued for links between Egypt, Ethiopia, and West Africa. The "Afrocentrists" of the last quarter of the twentieth and early twenty-first centuries further developed these claims, but whatever the particular school of thought, certain of their ideas resonate with communities in both West Africa and the African diaspora, where the notion of a connectedness to either Egypt and Nubia or Ethiopia resides in the cultural expressions of the common, not necessarily lettered people. Whether one accepts these views or finds them extravagant, there is no avoiding the conclusion that Africans and their descendants have long pursued a conversation about their relationship to the ancients. Such intergenerational discussion has not been idle chit-chat, but rather has significantly influenced the unfolding of African American art, music, religion, politics, and societies.

A brief consideration of ancient Africa, especially Egypt, Nubia, and Ethiopia, remains important for at least two reasons. First, it contextualizes the discussion of subsequent developments that include massive trades in African captives. Antiquity reminds us that modernity could not have been predicted: that Africans were not always under the heel, but were in fact at the forefront of human civilization. Second, antiquity reminds us that the African diaspora did not begin with slave trades. Rather, the dissemination of African ideas and persons actually began long ago. In this first diasporic phase, ideas were arguably more significant than the number of people dispersed. The Mediterranean in particular benefited from Egyptian and Nubian culture and learning. This initial phase was further distinguished by the political standing of the Africans in question; Egypt was a veritable regional power, imposing its will on others, rather than the reverse. This was therefore a very different kind of African diaspora than what would follow many centuries later.

As Egypt, Nubia, and Ethiopia were powerful, illustrious states, this chapter focuses on what some regard as "high" civilizations. This is entirely appropriate in bringing attention to the fact that African societies achieved levels of exceptional distinction. But at the same time, placing the inquiry into a diasporic framework is a reminder that these societies were in mutual contact as well as with others, and that cross-cultural exchange was at times extensive. In attempting to understand these interactions, it may be that contemporary social registers do not have an equivalent in antiquity, especially within its African sector. This should be borne in mind when exploring the possible meaning of "race" among the ancients, and to the extent that it may have mirrored current notions, its overall significance may have been negligible.

Egypt

The study of ancient Egypt is a discipline unto itself, involving majestic monuments, mesmerizing religions, magnificent arts, epic wars, and the like, all of which lie beyond our purpose here. Rather, our deliberations are confined to Egypt's relations with its neighbors, especially to the south, as it is in such relations that contours of an ancient African diaspora can be demonstrated.

Ancient Egypt, located along the Nile and divided into Upper and Lower regions, exchanged goods and ideas with Sumer (in Mesopotamia, between the Tigris and Euphrates rivers) as early as 3500 BCE, and by 1700 BCE was connected with urban-based civilizations in the Indus valley, the Iranian plateau, and China. Situated in Africa, Egypt was also a global crossroad for various populations and cultures, its participation in this intercontinental zone a major feature of the African diaspora's opening chapter (see Map 1).

Just who were these ancient Egyptians? While none can reasonably quibble with identifying them as north-eastern Africans, the discussion becomes more complex when the subject turns to "race." Race, as it is used currently, may be commonly understood, but attempts to arrive at a precise, widely held definition can actually prove elusive, as its meaning is sensitive to shifting contexts. In this study, race refers to placing human beings within hierarchical categories that seem to align with phenotypic difference, supposedly reflecting fundamental distinctions as well as respective levels of ability and beauty. This concept of race lacks scientific value or basis, but as a sociopolitical concept it carries decided import and gravity.

Our understanding of ancient Egypt is therefore complicated by our own conversations about race, and by attempts to relate modern ideas to ancient times. Much more a contemporary preoccupation, race may have been of scant significance in ancient Egypt, if the

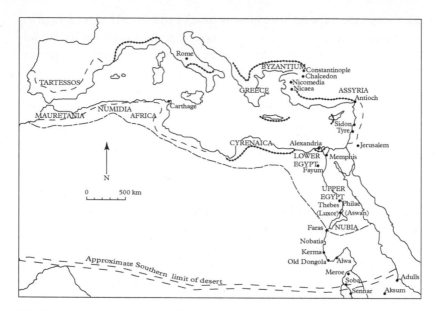

MAP 1 North Africa in antiquity

concept even existed. As an example, though some paintings depict the Egyptians as dark-skinned, it is more common to see males painted a dark reddish-brown and females a lighter brown or yellow. Such variation was not meant to simply convey physical traits, but social standing as well; a woman portrayed as light brown suggests privilege and exemption from the need to work outdoors, her actual skin tone a matter of conjecture.

While ideas about race in this region and period are therefore not readily apparent, what is clear is that ancient Egyptians were highly ethnocentric, regarding themselves as "the people" and everyone else as "uncivilized," a distinction having more to do with respective lands of birth and cultural divergence than physiognomy. Consequently, foreigners included Bedouins from Arabia, "Asiatics" from Asia Minor, Libyans from the west, and the Nehesi from the area south of Egypt, called *Nehesyu* or *Khent* ("borderland") by the Egyptians, otherwise known as Nubia or Kush. Given Egypt's extraordinarily long history, its collective gene pool would have periodically received infusions from Asia Minor, southern Europe, and the Arabian Peninsula. But that same pool would have also been affected, perhaps even more so, by populations from the south, particularly Nubia. What Egyptians may have looked like in the third millennium BCE is not necessarily how they appeared a thousand years later, let alone after another two thousand years. Swift and dramatic changes in the North American collective gene pool between the sixteenth and twenty-first centuries, only one-eighth the time of ancient Egypt's existence, effectively caution that substantial immigration can result in startling transformations.

Egypt and the South

During the Old and Middle Kingdoms (3400–2180 and 2080–1640 BCE), Egypt sought to militarily control Nubia and parts of Syria and Palestine. Under the New Kingdom (1570–1090 BCE), Egypt repeatedly invaded Palestine and Syria in its competition with Assyria and (subsequently) Babylon for control of the region. Africa was therefore a major power in what would become the Middle East for thousands of years, years that were formative, in lands destined to become sacred for millions of people.

While especially interested in Nubia's gold, Egypt also recruited the Nubians themselves for the Egyptian army, as their military prowess, especially in archery, was highly regarded (Egyptians also referred to Nubia as *Ta-Seti*, or the "land of the bow"). Nubians were sought as laborers as well, and some were even enslaved. However, with the possible exception of the Hebrews, Egypt's enslaved population was never very large, with slaves from Europe and Asia Minor often more numerous than Nubians or other Africans.

While extending its control over Nubian territory and tapping Nubian labor, Egypt also relocated select Nubians to its capital at Thebes, where an institution called the *Kap* provided a formal, exclusive Egyptian education. Nubians learned the ways of Egypt, but their presence as elites, workers, and soldiers also facilitated the spread of Nubian culture within Egypt, a phenomenon similar to much later developments in the Americas, where the convergence of African, European, Asian, and First Nation elements led to a flourishing of African-inspired cultures, among others.

One of the more fascinating aspects of the New Kingdom's eighteenth dynasty's involvement with Nubia was the determinant role Nubian women played in the royal court. Indeed, Nubian women became Egyptian royals, wielding tremendous power as queen mothers and aristocratic wives. In such capacities, they ruled at times with their husbands, at times as regents, and in instances alone. Ahmose I inaugurated the eighteenth dynasty and reigned with Nefertari, a Nubian who enjoyed immense prestige and popularity with native Egyptians. Their great-granddaughter Hatshepsut governed as both queen and regent from 1503 to 1482. Ties to Nubia were later strengthened when Amenhotep III married thirteen-year-old Tiye, another Nubian. Their seven children included sons Amenhotep IV and Tutankhamen. Renowned and emulated for her beauty, Tiye was also well educated and quite the political force; funerary sculptures depict her as an equal to Amenhotep III. She may have been responsible for affairs of state under Amenhotep IV, who changed his name to Akhenaton (from *aton*, solar symbol of the supreme deity) as part of his promotion of monotheism. As Akhenaton's wife, Nefertiti, was yet another Nubian, it is not possible to discuss the New Kingdom without acknowledging the Nubian presence and contribution.

Nubian Ascendancy

Nubia, also located along the Nile, was known as *Qevs* by its inhabitants. Of all its various names – Nubia, Qevs, Cush, Kush, Ta-Seti, Nehesyu, Khent – none refer to skin color. One can therefore surmise that whatever differences existed between Egyptians and Nubians, skin color was not one that elicited elaboration.

Like Egypt, Nubia was likewise divided into Lower and Upper regions: Lower Nubia was associated with bows, shields, and other manufactures as well as raw materials, while Upper Nubia was linked to gold, semiprecious stones, leopard skins, and cattle. In fact, a Nubian state may have existed prior to Egypt's Old Kingdom, and at least one was its contemporary. The three major Nubian kingdoms that would come later were named after their capitals: Kerma (1750–1550 BCE), Napata (750–300 BCE), and Meroë (300 BCE–350 CE).

Though Napata's specific history includes a period of political convergence with Egypt, scholars point to the overall distinctiveness of Nubian history and culture, and that Nubia was neither an outpost of Egyptian civilization nor an imitation of Egypt on a smaller scale. Indeed, under Napata's leadership, the Nubians not only freed themselves of Egyptian domination, but turned the tables and conquered Egypt. Establishing the twenty-fifth dynasty, the Nubians ruled as Egyptian pharaohs, their legitimacy in Egypt a reflection of their long mutual familiarity.

The twenty-fifth dynasty was a time of contestation between Egypt and Assyria for control of Palestine. The 674 BCE Assyrian invasion of Egypt was defeated, but three years later the Assyrians were successful in driving the Nubians south, where they eventually re-established their capital at Meroë. Rather than undertaking any serious effort to conquer Meroë, Egypt under the Ptolemies (305–30 BCE) and Rome (beginning in 30 BCE) instead elected to maintain trade relations. Commerce, along with defensible terrain, allowed Meroë to flourish and to export such commodities as gold, cotton, precious stones, ostrich feathers, ivory, and elephants (the latter for war and amusement), while producing large quantities of iron.

Meroë was a unique civilization, with majestic stone monuments of stelae and its own system of writing, Meroïtic. Nubian women continued to play major roles in government. Queen mothers were especially powerful, and together with royal wives were called *Candaces* (from *Kentakes*). The renown of the *Candaces* in the ancient Near East was such that they reappear in accounts connected with the Bible, and were a source of dramatic and powerful images, reverberating to the present day.

Africans in the Graeco-Roman World

The ancient Mediterranean world, successively dominated by the Greeks, Phoenicians, and Romans, came to know Africans from a number of places and in varying capacities. Most Africans, especially during the Roman period, entered the Mediterranean from both Egypt and Nubia. But they also came from areas south of the Nile, North Africa (from what is now Libya west to Morocco), the fringes of the Sahara Desert, and West Africa proper.

In sharp contrast to the impressions that Egyptians and Nubians had of each other for millennia, southern Europeans were struck by the African's color; the darker the color, the stronger the impression. Although stunned, southern Europeans generally did not ascribe any intrinsic value or worth to skin color, and unlike contemporary notions of race and racism, did not equate blackness with inferiority. Modern-day racism apparently did not exist in the ancient

Mediterranean world. In fact, there is evidence that just the opposite was true, that Africans were viewed favorably.

The Greeks were so taken with African pigmentation that they invented the term *Ethiopian* (from *Aethiops*). The term means "burnt-faced person," and reflects the belief that the skin color and hair of the African were caused by the sun. "To wash an Ethiopian white" was a common expression in the Graeco-Roman world, indicating enough familiarity with blackness to use it in conveying the futility of trying to change the unalterable. The term *Ethiopian* was also at times applied by the Greeks to Arabs, Indians, and others of dark hue, and is used inaccurately to refer to Nubians. It should be borne in mind that the ancient state of Ethiopia (or Axum/Aksum) did not begin until the first century CE.

Greek and Roman terms could further qualify blackness, with color gradations one scheme by which groups (rather than individuals) were distinguished. Locating such groups along a continuum from dark (*fusci*) to very dark (*nigerrimi*), the second-century CE *Geography* of Ptolemy described the population around Meroë as "deeply black" and "pure Ethiopians," while according to Flavius Philostratus (d. *c.*245 CE), those living in the border region between Egypt and Nubia were not as black as the Nubians, but darker than the Egyptians. Subjective and imprecise, such classifications nonetheless demonstrate that blackness varied in the ancient world, much as it does today.

In addition to variations in color, diet also formed the basis of European categorizations, so that the work of second-century BCE geographer and historian Agatharchides, as recorded in *On the Erythrean Sea* (and partly surviving in the writings of Diodorus, first century BCE), speaks of the *Struthophagi* or ostrich eaters, the *Spermatophagi*, consumers of nuts and tree fruit, the *Ichthyophagi* or fish eaters, and the *Pamphagi*, who ate everything. Of course, some groups were purely fanciful, as is evident by Pliny the Elder's (b. 23 CE) list that includes the *Troglodytae* (voiceless save for squeaking noises); the *Blemmyae* (headless, with eyes and mouths in their chests); the *Himantopodes*, who crawled instead of walked; and the three- and four-eyed *Nisicathae* and *Nisitae*.

Greek and Roman attempts to account for unknown parts of Africa represent an acknowledgment of the limitations of the former's knowledge. But what the Greeks and Romans did know of Africa, they tended to admire. Their attitudes toward Africans can be deduced

from their accounts of actual encounters, as well as from their literature (such as poetry and drama). Artwork is also a source of information. These views come together in yet another Graeco-Roman
division of the African population, this time along lines of civilizational
achievement; African societies deemed high in attainment were greatly
acclaimed. Egyptians and Nubians had established literate, urban-
based, technologically advanced civilizations long before there was a
Rome or an Athens, so there was every reason for African achievement
to be praised and even emulated. It is not surprising that Homer
speaks of the Olympian gods, especially Zeus, feasting with the
"blameless" Ethiopians, the most distant of men, who by the time of
Xenophanes (d. c.478 BCE) had been identified as black and flat-
nosed, and by the fifth century BCE located to the south of Egypt.
Herodotus (fl. fifth century BCE) maintained that the Ethiopians were
the tallest and most handsome of men, and the most pious. He added
that Meroë was a "great city," and that Nubians had supplied Egypt
with eighteen pharaohs. While Diodorus Siculus (fl. first century BCE)
wrote that the inhabitants of Meroë were the "first of all men and the
first to honor the gods whose favor they enjoyed," and Roman satirist
Lucian (fl. second century CE) maintained the "Ethiopians" had
invented astrology, both men asserted that many Nubian practices
and institutions were borrowed by the Egyptians. Meroë was to be
distinguished, however, from "primitive Ethiopians," who went about
"filthy" and naked (or nearly so), and who did not believe in the gods.
Celebrated sexual encounters in the Greek and Roman imagination
are yet another measure of the regard for the Nubian. Examples
include Zeus, who may have been portrayed in the *Inachus* of Sopho-
cles (c.496–406 BCE) as black or dark, and whose child by Io is
described by Aeschylus (525–456 BCE) as black, and by Hesiod
(fl. c.700 BCE) as the ancestor of the Ethiopians and Libyans. Delphos,
the founder of Delphi, was believed to be the son of Poseidon or
Apollo and a woman whose name means "the black woman." And
then there is the example of Perseus, who married the daughter of the
king of the Ethiopians, the dark-hued Andromeda.

In addition to individuals like Herodotus, who actually traveled to
Africa and gathered information, Africans also entered southern
Europe during antiquity. The context was often one of war, both
for and against the Greeks and Romans. Nubians were a part of the
Egyptian occupation of Cyprus under Amasis (569–522 BCE), and
there is the account of Memnon and his black soldiers coming to the

aid of the Greeks in the possibly mythical Trojan Wars. A large number of Nubians fought under Xerxes of Persia in the very real Battle of Marathon in 480–479 BCE. These Nubians experienced liaisons with Greek women, resulting in the "brown babies" of the Persian Wars. Carthage, founded no earlier than 750 BCE by the combination of Phoenician settlers and Berber natives referred to as Numidians, developed a society in which the Berber masses were treated harshly. Although trans-Saharan trade in the hands of the Garamantes (apparently, progenitors of the desert-dwelling Tuareg) was not very important during Carthaginian ascendancy, a sufficient number of sub-Saharan Africans made their way to Carthage, where they were inducted into military service. Frontinus (fl. first century CE) records the presence of "very black" auxiliaries among the Carthaginian prisoners taken by Gelon of Syracuse in 480 BCE. The Punic Wars (264–241, 218–201, 149–146 BCE) between Rome and Carthage also saw Maghribian (North African) "Ethiopians," possibly West Africans, employed in the invasion of Italy, serving as *mahouts* aloft elephants. Rome would also go on to conquer Egypt and occupy it from the time of Augustus to the sixth century CE. Its relations with Nubia and the south were relatively peaceful until the third century CE, when it incurred difficulties with the Beja of the Red Sea hills, called "Blemmyes" in the Roman sources.

* * *

Africans enslaved in the Graeco-Roman world were only a fraction of the total number of slaves in these territories. Enslaved Africans also only represented a portion of the overall African population living in southern Europe. A number of Africans were attracted to places like Rome for trade and occupational opportunities, working as musicians, actors, jugglers, gladiators, wrestlers, boxers, religious specialists, and day laborers. Some became famous, such as the black athlete Olympius described by sixth-century poet Luxorius. In addition to entertaining and fighting the Romans, Africans also served in the Roman armies, as was the case with the elite Moorish cavalry from north-west Africa under Lusius Quietus (fl. second century CE), him-self of possible Moroccan heritage. Black soldiers even served in the Roman army as far north as Britain.

More far-reaching than the actual presence of Africans in southern Europe was the impact of their cultural influence. Scholars debate the extent to which Egyptian science, engineering, architectural forms, and philosophy influenced developments in Greece. There can be no question, however, that Egyptian and Nubian religion was deeply influential throughout the Mediterranean world for many centuries, if not millennia, especially the worship of Isis, adopted and venerated in many places under several names. Her devotees made pilgrimage to the island of Philae, near the border of Egypt and Nubia, and Nubian specialists in Isiac worship were welcomed in various centers throughout southern Europe, where the Isiac rites were known as the Eleusinian mysteries.

From what can be determined, "racial" attitudes of the ancient Graeco-Roman world differed significantly from the contemporary West. Africans were often seen and treated as equals, the representatives of homelands both ancient and respected. Their reception in southern Europe and the Near East underscores the power and prestige of African realms and leaders, and further distinguishes this phase of the African diaspora from what takes place much later. In the ancient world, Africa and Africans were forces to be reckoned with; indeed, for thousands of years, they were the leaders of the ancient world.

Suggestions for Further Reading

A very useful companion book to the approach adopted here is Patrick Manning, *The African Diaspora: A History Through Culture* (New York: Columbia University Press, 2009). General histories of Africa include UNESCO's *General History of Africa*, 8 vols. (London and Berkeley: UNESCO, Heinemann, and University of California Press, 1981–99); Philip Curtin, Steven Feierman, Leonard Thompson, and Jan Vansina, *African History: From Earliest Times to Independence* (London and New York: Longman, 1995), 2nd ed., and J. Fage and R. Oliver, eds., *The Cambridge History of Africa* (Cambridge: Cambridge University Press, 1975–86), an eight-volume collection.

Concerning ancient Egypt, works providing general reconstructions include Ian Shaw, ed., *The Oxford History of Ancient Egypt* (Oxford: Oxford University Press, 2000); Karol My'sliwiec, *The Twilight of Ancient Egypt: First Millennium B.C.E.*, trans. David Lorton (Ithaca, NY: Cornell University Press, 2000); and Sergio Donadoni, ed., *The Egyptians*, trans. Robert Bianchi, et al. (Chicago: University of Chicago Press, 1997). Studies with foci on women, gender, and society are Lynn Meskell, *Archaeologies of Social Life: Age, Sex, Class Et Cetera in Ancient Egypt* (Oxford and Malden, MA: Blackwell, 1999); Zahi A. Hawass, *Silent Images: Women in Pharaonic Egypt* (Cairo:

American University in Cairo Press, 2000); John Romer, *People of the Nile: Everyday Life in Ancient Egypt* (New York: Crown,1982); Susan Walker and Peter Higgs, *Cleopatra of Egypt: From History to Myth* (Princeton, NJ: Princeton University Press, 2001). Regarding religion, see Dimitri Meeks and Christine Favard-Meeks, *Daily Life of the Egyptian Gods,* trans. G.M. Goshgarian (Ithaca, NY: Cornell University Press, 1996); and Aylward M. Blackman, *Gods, Priests and Men: Studies in the Religion of Pharaonic Egypt* (New York: Columbia University Press, 1993).

The issue of race in Egypt and antiquity is engaged by Cheikh Anta Diop, *The African Origin of Civilization: Myth or Reality,* trans. Mercer Cook (New York: L. Hill, 1974). St. Clair Drake's two-volume *Black Folk Here and There: An Essay in History and Anthropology* (Los Angeles: Center for Afro-American Studies, University of California, 1987–90) certainly addresses identity in ancient Egypt, but goes well beyond this period and place.

The question of Graeco-Roman indebtedness to early Egypt is taken up in Martin Bernal's controversial *Black Athena: The Afroasiatic Roots of Classical Civilization,* 2 vols. (London: Free Association Books, 1987–91), in the course of which race is considered. An oft-overlooked work making parallel arguments, but preceding Bernal by three decades, is George G.M. James, *Stolen Legacy* (New York: Philosophical Library, 1954). One of the responses to Bernal (and others) is Mary Lefkowitz, *Not Out of Africa: How Afrocentrism Became an Excuse to Teach Myth as History* (New York: Basic Books, 1996).

A rather comprehensive discussion of Nubian history is provided in P.L. Shinnie's massive *Ancient Nubia* (London and New York: Kegan Paul International, 1995). Nubia's rise and eventual takeover of Egypt is examined in Robert G. Morkot's *The Black Pharaohs: Egypt's Nubian Rulers* (London: Rubicon, 2000).

A bridge connecting Egyptian, Nubian, and Graeco-Roman societies via race are Frank M. Snowden, Jr.'s *Blacks in Antiquity: Ethiopians in the Greco-Roman Experience* (Cambridge, MA: Belknap Press of Harvard University Press, 1970), and his *Before Color Prejudice: The Ancient View of Blacks* (Cambridge, MA: Harvard University Press, 1983). Leo William Hansberry's *Africa and Africans as Seen by Classical Writers,* ed. Joseph E. Harris (Washington, DC: University Press, 1981) is also useful.

Finally, Stephen Quirke and Jeffrey Spencer, eds., allow for printed visualization of antiquity in *The British Museum Book of Ancient Egypt* (London: British Museum Press, 1992).

CHAPTER 2

Africans and the Bible

The Bible has affected the lives of Africans and their descendants in the diaspora in profound ways, perhaps more than any other document in human history, a phenomenon that can be divided into at least two spheres: the first features the roles and experiences of Africans in the Bible, while the second concerns the ways in which these roles and experiences have influenced Africans living in post-Biblical times. Because the Biblical account is seen by many as prescriptive, the interpretation of African roles in the narrative is critical, as it has often determined how post-Biblical Africans were treated, or conversely, how they have imagined themselves and understood their circumstances. The Bible has been crucial to the institution of slavery in the Americas, with both benefactors and detractors of the institution taking solace in its pages, while stories recorded in holy writ have been appropriated to explain both slavery and its aftermath. Accompanying the foregoing has also been a process of inscription *into* holy writ, whereby communities under duress understand the Scriptures as actually foretelling their own struggles.

Egypt and Nubia in the Bible

Nubian Pharaohs of the twenty-fifth dynasty appear in the Old Testament as allies against the Assyrians, and Taharqa (690–664 BCE) is mentioned by name (Isaiah 37:9; 2 Kings 19:9) (see Figure 1). Egypt and Nubia's union under this dynasty is demonstrated by the prophet

FIGURE 1 Head of Taharqa. Mario Carrieri, Milan/The Menil Foundation.
A black and white version of this figure will appear in some formats. For the color
version, please refer to the plate section.

Isaiah's conjoined messages to each (Isaiah 18–20). In language corresponding to Herodotus, Isaiah (18:2,7) writes of Nubia:

> Go, swift messengers to a nation tall and smooth,
> To a people feared far and wide,
> A powerful and oppressive nation
> Whose land the rivers divide.

Such esteem for Nubia is consistent with the view of states along the
Nile as powerful neighbors of Israel, ever present in regional affairs.
Indeed, the very formation of the Hebrew people is intimately associated with Egypt and Nubia. Egypt in particular features prominently in
the Old Testament, playing successive roles as asylum, oppressor, ally,
and foe. The enslavement and subsequent divine deliverance of the
Hebrews was a source of consolation and hope for enslaved Africans
and their descendants thousands of years later. But while many identified with the Hebrews, others would celebrate the connection to Egypt.

Assuming a historical basis for Hebrew enslavement, it is highly
unlikely they would have avoided sexual unions with Egyptians and
Nubians for 400 years; indeed, individual stories suggest that
Egyptian/Nubian–Hebrew interaction may have been significant.

Even before the Hebrew community in Egypt, Egyptian women figured prominently in the lives of the prophets. Abraham, father of revelatory monotheism, had a son Ishmael by the Egyptian Hagar, and Ishmael in turn married an Egyptian woman. Upon entry into Egypt, the patriarch Joseph also married an Egyptian woman, Asenath, who bore Manasseh and Ephraim, so that at least one of the twelve tribes was of partial African origin. Moses himself married a Nubian woman (Numbers 12:1). These examples suggest such women were desirable and instrumental at critical junctures, birthing clans and nations.

In addition to the question of intermarriage is that of cultural influence. The Hebrews were necessarily impacted by their long stay in Egypt – after all, Joseph was embalmed. Such influence probably remained with the Hebrews for many years, as they exited Egypt with a "mixed multitude" (Exodus 12:38). Much of the Old Testament is concerned with eradicating that influence, along with others from Mesopotamia. If the Exodus is afforded credibility, it gives pause that the Hebrews, every one of them, came out of Africa after a 400-year sojourn. The story is not unlike the human birthing process – the crossing of the Red Sea a movement through the amniotic fluids of an African mother.

Mention of individual Egyptians and Nubians in the Bible is relatively rare. Some are in servile positions, while others are associated with the military. They include the unnamed Nubian military courier or messenger, who told King David of his son Absalom's death in battle (2 Samuel 18:19–33). Then there is Ebed-melech (or "royal slave"), a Nubian eunuch in the service of Zedekiah, king of Judah. He rescued the prophet Jeremiah from certain death by interceding for him before Zedekiah; for his intervention, Ebed-melech would be spared the coming judgment (Jeremiah 38:1–13; 39:15–18). Others with possible blood ties to Egypt or Nubia include Aaron's grandson Phinehas, possibly an Egyptian name meaning "the Nubian" (Exodus 6:25); and the prophet Zephaniah, son of "Cushi" or the Cushite (Zephaniah 1:1). Perhaps the most famous involves the Queen of Sheba, a complicated story involving a King Solomon already married to a daughter of the Egyptian pharaoh (and eventually hundreds of other women, 2 Chronicles 8:11).

Africans and Origins

The question of identifying Africans in the Bible is influenced by assumptions brought to the text. The exercise of "discovering"

Africans in the Bible often presupposes that the document is essentially concerned with non-Africans. But what if the assumptions are different, and the Bible is presumed to be primarily concerned with "people of color," including Africans?

Independent of anthropological and archaeological records, the Bible has its own tradition of human origins. In the interpretation of that tradition over the centuries, the Garden of Eden story has rarely been situated in an African setting. A forced correlation between Biblical narrative and scientific findings, however, directs attention to East Africa, and would suggest to those concerned with Biblical teachings that the earliest actors were Africans. The notion of an African Eden, however, was far from the imagination of Western slaveholding societies. Instead, a very different tale condemning Africans was widely accepted.

The account concerns the prophet and ark-builder Noah (Nuh in the Islamic tradition), and is possibly the most dramatic example of how the subsequent interpretation of holy writ can have life-altering consequences. After the flood, the progenitors of the entire human family are listed in the "Table of Nations" (Genesis 10). According to a conventional reading, Ham became the father of "the black people," as his sons are listed as Cush, Mizraim, Put or Punt, and Canaan; that is, Nubia, Egypt, possibly Libya and/or lands beyond Nubia proper, and Palestine. Such a reading assumes that Noah's other two sons, Japheth and Shem, were "white" and "Asian" – or at least not black.

The term *Cush* probably derives from Qevs and is simply a place name; it bears no racial or ethnic connotations. The Greek terms *Ethiopia* and *Ethiopian* do not appear in the original Hebrew and Chaldean Old Testament, but rather the words *Cush* and *Cushite*, suggesting Nubian features were not a concern for Old Testament writers, but became one later with the rise of Alexander and the ensuing period of Hellenization, when translators of the Septuagint, the Old Testament in Greek, opted to substitute *Ethiopia* for *Cush*.

Although the physical features of the Cushites or Nubians were not a significant matter for early Jews, an incident that precedes the presentation of the Table of Nations would eventually be interpreted in a way that would affect issues of slavery and race for centuries to come. The incident concerns a drunken Noah whose "nakedness is uncovered" by his son Ham, a phrase with multiple possible meanings. When Noah awoke from his stupor and realized "what had been

done to him," he uttered words that would have profound implications for people of African descent thousands of years later:

Cursed be Canaan;
The lowest of servants
He shall be to his brothers.
           (Genesis 9:24–7)

The ambiguity of the passage lends itself to conflicting interpretations.
Who was being cursed – Ham, or his son Canaan? Did Noah's curse
carry divine sanction, or was it the innocuous expletives of an angry
mortal?

The interpretation of Noah's curse depends upon the perspective.
Believers are divided over its meaning. To the cynical, the curse was
written after the entry of the Hebrews into Palestine to justify the
appropriation of land. For the eighteenth- and nineteenth-century slaveholder, it became "the Hamitic curse," and meant that African slavery
had been providentially decreed. In this reading, the European slaveholder was simply fulfilling the will of God, as God's chosen instrument.

But even if the "curse" enjoys divine sanction, the likelihood that it
was meant to apply to all of the descendants of Ham is contradicted by
the record of the Bible itself. The only person discussed in any detail in
Genesis 10, site of the Table of Nations, is one Nimrod, son of Cush,
who "became a mighty one on the earth. He was a mighty hunter
before the Lord," and credited with establishing such cities as Babel
and Nineveh in Assyria. If anything, therefore, Nimrod represents a
tradition of imperialism and domination rather than subservience.
Another example is Egypt itself, as it was the Egyptians, descendants
of Ham, who were the slaveholders. Again, it was to the Nubians that
the Israelites turned for help against the Assyrians out of recognition of
their ascendancy. And then there is the fascinating account of Moses
and his Nubian bride (Numbers 12), a marriage opposed by Moses'
siblings Miriam and Aaron for reasons unclear. In a stunning rebuke,
Yahweh not only supports Moses, but turns Miriam's skin into a
leprous, luminous white that persists for days, an unusual punishment
laced with humor if not sarcasm.

Unfortunately, the import of the divine rebuke of Miriam and Aaron
did not endure. Scholars of the revered communication would produce additional literature to accompany the scriptures and unfold their
meaning. In contrast to the Jewish Talmud (a collection of laws and
rabbinical wisdom and the second most holy text in Judaism), another

tradition began, perhaps around the fifth century BCE, that may have characterized blackness itself as a consequence of and punishment for Ham's transgression, a tradition that can possibly be located in the fifth-century CE literature of the Midrashim, and the sixth-century CE Babylonian Talmud. Some scholars argue, however, that the idea of blackness-as-scourge actually derives from mistranslations of the fifth- and sixth-century CE texts, rather than the texts themselves.

African-born persons rarely appear in the New Testament. Jesus is said to have spent an unspecified number of his childhood years in Egypt, where in all likelihood he would have lived in the large Jewish community at Alexandria (Matthew 2:13–23). Simon of Cyrene (North Africa) is remembered for helping Jesus carry the cross (Luke 23:26; Matthew 27:32; Mark 15:21). The "Ethiopian" eunuch, who will be discussed in more detail, is prominently featured in the book of the Acts of the Apostles.

It is striking that the formation of the early Jewish state involved the literal transfer of a community from one land of Ham to another. It is therefore not possible to intelligently discuss the Old Testament without understanding the contribution of the African. It is not a question of a lone Nubian here and an odd Egyptian there; rather, the Old Testament world was awash in Africa's colors and cultures.

The Queen of Sheba

While the Hamitic curse would be used in the future with devastating effect, another account in the Old Testament forms the basis for perhaps the most significant and certainly most hallowed tradition involving Biblical Africa, linking the continent to its diaspora from ancient times to the present. In arresting defiance of, and in diametric opposition to, the damnation of Canaan, the very glory of God is held to have rested upon a favored Ethiopia. The explanation of how that happened is a fascinating journey into an African reading of the Bible, and links the continent to three separate faiths in fundamental and enduring ways.

The story begins with King Solomon (or Sulayman), who already had ties to the Nile valley by virtue of his marriage to an Egyptian princess, and possibly by way of his mother Bathsheba (Bilqis in the Muslim tradition), whose name may signify "from the house/land of Sheba." Word of his fabled wisdom spread far and wide, eventually attracting the Queen of Sheba, who journeyed to Israel with a large retinue to hear Solomon's wisdom for herself (2 Chronicles 9:1–12; 1 Kings 10:1–13). More than favorably impressed, the queen gave the king a large quantity of gold, spices, and precious stones. In exchange, Solomon gave unspecified gifts of his own.

According to the Ethiopian holy book *Kebra Nagast*, or "Glory of Kings," completed in the early fourteenth century and drawn from the Bible, the Qur'ān, apocryphal literatures, and other sources, Solomon and the queen, identified as Makeda in the Ethiopian manuscript, struck up a romance that was consummated through Solomon's guile. After nine months and a conversion to Judaism, Makeda gave birth to Menelik (literally, "son of the wise man"), who years later returned to Jerusalem. There he was acknowledged by his father and crowned the king of Ethiopia, but Solomon also implored Menelik to remain in Jerusalem to inherit the throne of Israel. Longing for home, Menelik instead returned to Ethiopia with a number of priests and the *Tabot* or the Ark of the Covenant (or Tabernacle of Zion). The Ark, symbol of Yahweh's presence and Israel's unique status, henceforth rests, according to this tradition, in Ethiopia, thereby transferring to the Ethiopians the honor of "God's chosen people." But the account also conveys the claim that the kings of Ethiopia are descendants of Solomon, each a "lion of Judah."

There are multiple layers to the story. To begin, the location of "Sheba" is in dispute: many cite Saba in Yemen as the most likely site, while some insist upon Nubia or Ethiopia. Interestingly, Jesus simply refers to the "Queen of the South," who came "from the ends of the earth" to hear Solomon's wisdom (Matthew 12:42; Luke 11:31), a characterization of space and distance in remarkable resonance with Homer's *Odyssey*, wherein the Ethiopians are described as "the most remote of men," dwelling by the streams of Ocean, "at earth's two verges, in sunset lands and lands of the rising sun." As Ethiopia did not exist during the time of Solomon, the only viable alternative to Yemen for Sheba's location is Nubia, where the queen may have been one of the *Candaces*. In the end, Sheba's precise location may not matter very much, as populations and cultural influences regularly crisscrossed the Red Sea in antiquity; in fact, southern Arabia was periodically dominated by powers on nearby African soil, particularly from 335–70 CE and 525–75 CE, when Ethiopia ruled portions of the southern Arabian Peninsula.

Another complication is the *Kebra Nagast*'s claims of an initial association with Judaism. Ethiopia is better known as a Christian state.

Founded at Aksum (or Axum) in 59 CE, Ethiopia became home to Amhara-Tigrean, Galla, Afar, Somali, and Omotic populations, distinguishing it both culturally and territorially from Nubia (which lay to the north). Christianity entered Ethiopia early; tradition links missionary activity to the apostle Matthew, but Ethiopia's definitive turn to Christianity took place in the middle of the fourth century, when King Ezana and the royal court embraced the new religion, and in the fifth century, when large-scale conversions occurred. In 1135, the Aksumite rulers were overthrown by the founders of the Zagwe dynasty, whose greatest achievement was the creation of a remarkable ceremonial center at Lalibela (or Roha, named after the dynasty's most illustrious ruler), the site of churches hewn from "living rock," fashioned deep in the earth. The Zagwes were in turn overthrown by the Solomonids in 1270, claiming descent from Solomon and Makeda.

The Solomonids drew upon traditions enshrined in the *Kebra Nagast* to legitimate their seizure of power, claiming the best of both worlds by trumpeting their alleged hereditary connections to Solomon and Israel while simultaneously championing Christianity. Led by a literate elite who wrote in Ge'ez (or Ethiopic), Christian Ethiopia experienced an efflorescence under the Solomonids, particularly from the thirteenth through the sixteenth centuries. Although severely challenged by Ahmad Granye's sixteenth-century Muslim campaign that saw widespread destruction of churches and monasteries, only to be followed by incursions of Galla and Oromo in the sixteenth through the nineteenth centuries, Ethiopia's unique Christian legacy survived. Ethiopia would become an icon in the modern African diaspora, a symbol of independence and fierce pride, and the focus of a new religion emerging out of the Caribbean, Rastafarianism.

Beta Israel

The Solomonids were not the only ones to draw from the *Kebra Nagast* for legitimation. The Jews of Ethiopia, who refer to themselves as the *Beta Israel* ("House of Israel") while taking umbrage at the term *Falasha* ("stranger, wanderer," coined by non-Jewish Ethiopians), also claim descent from Solomon and Makeda. The Beta Israel have a different account of what happened following Menelik's return to Ethiopia: with the Ark of the Covenant in tow, Menelik's entourage came to a river and separated into two companies – those who crossed eventually became Christians, while those who paused remained Jews. A marvelous allegory at the least.

Scholars and politicians have debated whether the Beta Israel are "true" Jews for centuries. Aside from the Solomon-Makeda tradition (given little credence by many scholars), there are other, competing theories attempting to explain how Jews came to Ethiopia. In 1973, for example, Israel's Sephardic Chief Rabbi recognized the Beta Israel as true Jews, a remnant of the lost tribe of Dan (one of the ten who seemingly vanished after their capture by Assyria in 722 BCE). Other scholars cite evidence of a Jewish military garrison at Elephantine Island, near the traditional border of Egypt and Nubia, between the seventh and the fifth centuries BCE. Yet others point to the proximity of southern Arabia, in which communities of Jews have lived since the seventh century BCE, with most arriving after the destruction of Jerusalem's Second Temple in 70 CE.

Whatever their origins, the Beta Israel's subsequent history in Ethiopia is also a matter of scholarly contention, with some maintaining they were persecuted and harassed for most of their existence, while others argue the relationship between Jews and the Christian state was at times complementary and cooperative. The Beta Israel took refuge in the mountain fastnesses of Ethiopia, and were cut off from world Jewry. There they continued to sacrifice animals, observe the Sabbath, follow certain religious laws and dietary proscriptions, and circumcise on the eighth day. They lost the Hebrew language, however, speaking in Amharic (a modern language) and praying (while facing Jerusalem) in Ge'ez (an ancient tongue). Armed with the Torah (the five books of Moses) but unaware of the Talmud, Ethiopian Jews managed to survive. Toward the end of the twentieth century, they participated in the general immigration of Jews to Israel (the *aliyah*) in spectacular ways: in 1984, "Operation Moses" brought 16,000 Ethiopian Jews to Israel, followed by the airlifting of thousands more in 1991. Media images of these "black Jews" arriving in Israel was nothing less than electrifying. The visualization of verifiable African Jews raised new questions about the scope of the African diaspora.

The "Ethiopian" Eunuch and the Call to Christianity

In addition to the Queen of Sheba and the Beta Israel, the account of the "Ethiopian" eunuch has also fired imaginations across time and space. The New Testament records the baptism of "an Ethiopian eunuch, a court official of Candace, queen of the Ethiopians, who was in charge of all her treasure" (Acts of the Apostles 8:27–40). As Ethiopia either did not yet exist or was just coming into being, and as a series of female rulers of the Nubian state of Meroë held the title *Candace*, this encounter probably refers to a Nubian court official who, after his baptism, "went on his way rejoicing," presumably all the way to Nubia. Christianity had certainly entered Nubia by the second century (following the establishment of the Coptic church in Egypt), but Nubia did not convert en masse to Christianity (according to area tradition) until the mid-sixth century and the arrival of missionaries from Byzantium. For the next 800 years Nubia flourished as a Christian culture, its literacy based upon Old Nubian, a language written in Greek form with Meroïtic vowelization. Meroë itself had ended by 350 CE, but Nubia continued on, splintering into Nobatia (or Nubia), Alwa, and Makuria. The rise of Ṣalāḥ al-Dīn and the Mamlūks in Egypt in 1169 began Christian Nubia's gradual decline until 1323, when a Muslim ruler took power. Nubian Christianity survived into the sixteenth century, in retreat from a growing Islamized and Arabized Nubian population and government.

Like Egypt, Nubia, and Ethiopia, North Africa also converted to Christianity, although the region's rapid embrace of Islam in the seventh and eighth centuries raises doubts about the depth of its preceding commitment. Even so, North Africa was the site of a brilliant Christian civilization, producing the likes of Saint Augustine of Hippo (354–440), born in North Africa and likely of Berber descent. Christian scholars and leaders located throughout Egypt and North Africa played major roles in the various schisms and doctrinal disputes characterizing the troubled history of the early church. However, while North Africa and Egypt provided the setting, European languages dominated the religious discourse; Latin in the North African church, and Greek in the Coptic.

An African past filled with splendor and pageantry helped to defend against the psychological onslaught experienced by the enslaved in the Americas much later, who were repeatedly told that Africa was of no historical significance. Though ancient and in a corner of the continent from which the vast majority of the enslaved did not hail, Egypt, Nubia, and Ethiopia were yet in Africa, and therefore represented the dignity of the entire continent, a place of honor bestowed largely through exposure to Christianity and Judaism. By the nineteenth century, the prophesy that "Ethiopia shall soon stretch her hands out to God" (Psalm 68:31) would be interpreted by many as a call to convert the African masses to Christianity, thereby helping to shape Africa and its diaspora in profound ways.

Suggestions for Further Reading

In addition to the some of the relevant suggested readings for Chapter 1, especially that of St. Clair Drake, works covering the general history of Ethiopia include Harold G. Marcus, *A History of Ethiopia* (Berkeley: University of California Press, 1994); Jean Doresse, *Ethiopia*, trans. by Elsa Coult (London: Elek Books, and New York: Putnam, 1959); and Sergew Hable Selassie, *Ancient and Medieval Ethiopian History to 1270* (Addis Ababa: United Printers, 1972).

Regarding the *Kebra Nagast*, the only English translation available remains, curiously, E.A. Wallis Budge's *The Queen of Sheba and Her Only Son Menyelek (Kebra Nagast)* (London and Boston: The Medici Society, Ltd., 1922). Given the date of the translation and Budge's reputation as something of a racist, a modern translation is sorely needed. Donald N. Levine's *Greater Ethiopia: The Evolution of a Multiethnic Society* (Chicago: University of Chicago Press, 1974), provides a critical reading of both the *Kebra Nagast* and the development of Ethiopian society. An excellent work on the Beta Israel is Steven Kaplan's *The Beta Israel (Falasha) in Ethiopia: From Earliest Times to the Twentieth Century* (New York: New York University Press, 1992), which can be joined with a study edited by Tudor Parfitt and Emanuela Trevisan, *The Beta Israel in Ethiopia and Israel* (Surrey: Curzon Press, 1999).

Concerning the Hamitic curse, see David M. Goldenberg, *The Curse of Ham: Race and Slavery in Early Judaism, Christianity and Islam* (Princeton, NJ: Princeton University Press, 2003) for a discussion of its development as an idea, and Stephen R. Haynes, *Noah's Curse: The Biblical Justification of American Slavery* (New York: Oxford University Press, 2002) for an indication of how the myth came to be exploited. Finally, among the most important works addressing blacks or Africans and the Bible are James Cone, *For My People: Black Theology and the Black Church* (Maryknoll, NY: Orbis Books, 1984); Charles B. Copher, *Black Biblical Studies: An Anthology of Charles B. Copher* (Chicago: Black Light Fellowship, 1993); Cain Hope Felder, *Troubling Biblical Waters: Race, Class, and Family* (Maryknoll, NY: Orbis Books, 1989) and his *Scandalize My Name: A Critical Review of Blacks in the Bible and Society* (Silver Spring. MD: Beckham House, 1995).

CHAPTER 3

Africans and the Islamic World

We tend to know more about Africans in the Americas than elsewhere in the diaspora. And yet, as this chapter makes clear, millions of Africans entered Islamic lands, where they made important contributions to extraordinary civilizations, from the heartlands of the faith to Muslim Spain. Extended discussion of this major component of the African diaspora is therefore important, as the juxtaposition of the similarities and differences between this experience and that of Africans in the Americas yields far greater insight into the condition of displacement than does a lone hemispheric focus.

What follows examines Islam's impact on African societies, including the embrace of the new religion in ways that allowed for a degree of continuity with existing cultural norms. As a faith with global claims, Islam's expansion necessitated interaction between diverse societies, resulting not only in significant genetic exchange, but also discussions of difference that included ideas approximating contemporary notions of race. The envelopment of parts of West and East Africa into the Muslim world featured African and non-African rulers relating as peers, while facilitating the acceptance of Africans fellow believers in a variety of capacities. And although Africans were also enslaved in that world, so were many more from Europe and Asia (at least until the eighteenth century).

We begin with a brief consideration of the Prophet Muhammad, born c.570 CE in the city of Mecca, an oasis important as both marketplace and site of religious shrines. Sensitive to the disparities between

rich and poor, Muhammad's meditations resulted in a series of reve-
lations beginning at the age of forty; three years later, he began
heralding a message centering on the oneness of God, his own
role as God's messenger, the Last Day, and the need for a response
of submission, gratitude, worship, and social responsibility. Encoun-
tering resistance and harassment, the Prophet and his Companions
(*as-Sahaba*) found asylum in Medina in 622, but by 630 he accepted
Mecca's peaceful surrender. By the time of his death in 632, the whole
of the Arabian Peninsula was united under his control. By 656, Islam
had expanded into Syria, Iraq, Egypt, and North Africa, and by 711,
Muslim armies had conquered parts of the Iberian Peninsula as well.

Islam's move into Egypt (or *Misr*) and North Africa (or *al-Maghrib
al-Aqṣā*, "the far West") was accompanied by a gradual Arabization of
the population (the spread of Arabs and their language and culture).
As part of a larger Muslim world that was quickly becoming an
empire, Egypt and North Africa once more became destinations for
other Africans, while simultaneously serving as sources of emigration
to such places as Portugal and Spain.

Golden Lands

Where Muslim armies spearheaded Islam's expansion into North
Africa and Egypt, Muslim traders and clerics led the religion's spread
into regions south of the Sahara. Regularized trade between North and
sub-Saharan Africa became possible in the first century CE with the
introduction of the camel from the Nile valley to the Sahara's southern
fringes near Lake Chad, after which they spread farther west. By the
fourth century, camel caravan patterns were crisscrossing the desert.

West Africa became associated with gold early in the history of
Islam; indeed, one of the earliest West African states, Ghana, became
known as "the land of the gold" through geographers writing in Arabic
between the eighth and eleventh centuries. Ghana, home to the
Soninke (northern Mande-speakers), was located in the *sāḥil* (or
Sahel, "shore") between the Sahara and the Savannah (flat grasslands)
farther south, as were Gao (on the eastern buckle of the Niger River)
and Kanem (along the north-eastern side of Lake Chad); together they
were introduced to the ninth-century Islamic world as *Bilād as-Sūdān*
or "land of the blacks." A brief review of developments within this

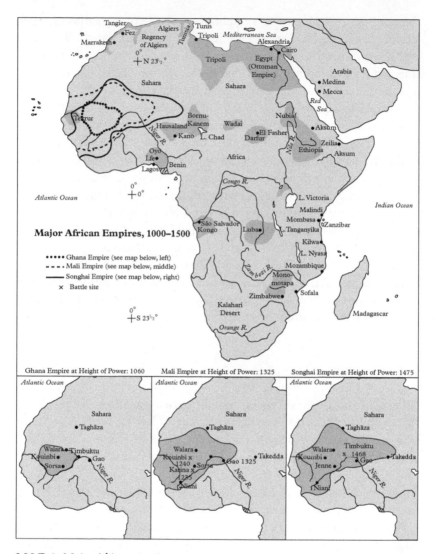

MAP 2 Major African empires, 1000–1500

region and East Africa is important, as these lands were in direct
contact with the Muslim world, constituting the origins of this component of the African diaspora (see Map 2).

West African gold was exchanged primarily for salt (from Saharan
desert mines and evaporating ponds at the mouth of the Senegal River
and elsewhere). The gold was transported to North Africa, then east to
Egypt and as far as India, where it served as payment for spices and

silks; and across the Mediterranean to pay for European goods and currency. Trade from the West African hinterland to the Sahel was organized and controlled by West Africans, who over the centuries developed an extensive network operated by Jula (a Mande term for "merchant") and Hausa traders. Once in the Sahel, gold and other commodities were transported north through the Sahara by the Tuareg, Berber-speaking desert-dwellers, along with Arab merchants. The arrangement was to the immediate advantage of West Africans, who maintained secrecy regarding the gold's sources, but ultimately to their detriment, as they did not control the trade through the desert. A pattern developed early in West Africa, whereby external powers acquired long-distance, multiregional trade experience. Those with such expertise eventually took command of the trade and dictated its terms, notwithstanding West Africa's appreciable influence.

Ghana, though still in existence in the twelfth century, was eclipsed in the thirteenth by Mali, populated by southern Mande-speakers fashioned into an empire by the Emperor Sunjata around 1230. As was true of Ghana, Mali was also associated with gold in the Muslim world, but unlike Ghana, Mali slowly became a part of that world through the early conversion of its rulers. The fourteenth-century travels and eyewitness accounts of Ibn Battuta (d. 1368) reinforced the image of Mali as a land of wealth, as did *Mansa* Mūsā's famous Pilgrimage to Mecca (reigned 1312–37). Although a diminished Mali would continue through the seventeenth century, its stature in the western Sudan (from the Atlantic Ocean to the Niger buckle) was eclipsed in the fifteenth century by imperial Songhay, whose origins go back to the seventh century and Gao. By the fifteenth century, Islam had become the religion of the court and the merchant community, while commercial towns such as Timbuktu and Jenne were transformed into centers of Islamic education and intellectual activity, a development begun under Mali's *Mansa* Mūsā. As was true of Ghana and Mali, Songhay was also known as a major source of gold, and the need to restore commerce following its disruption under *Sunni* 'Alī (1464–92) was a principal factor in *Askia* Muhammad Ture's 1492 seizure of power.

Viewed as a wealthy land, the western Sudan was increasingly incorporated into the Islamic world. North Africa, Egypt, and the western Sudan exchanged emissaries and written communication (in Arabic). Houses of wealthy merchants were often allied with leading clerical and political families through marriage. This resulted in the rise of elites in the western Sudan who were connected through

religion, marriage, and commercial interests, and who were accorded
prestige by co-religionists in North Africa and Egypt. Muslim
West Africa would therefore be differentiated from non-Muslim West
Africa, whom the Islamic world held in contempt. Stated differently,
the Muslim world entertained no single image of sub-Saharan Africa,
distinguishing its various populations on the basis of Islam and related
notions of civilization. The status of the land as opposed to the
individual was critical; a Muslim was one who practiced the religion,
but a Muslim land was one in which the religion of Islam and Muslim
rule had been voluntarily embraced. Songhay, with a majority non-
Muslim population, was a Muslim land.

Part of the central Sudan (from the Niger buckle to the Lake Chad
area) had a decidedly different trade relationship with North Africa.
The independent city states of Hausaland were apparently slower to
embrace Islam than their western Sudanic counterparts, but by the
second half of the fifteenth century cities such as Kano and Katsina
were under Muslim control, and were integrated into long-distance
trade. In contrast to Hausaland, the states of Kanem and Bornu near
Lake Chad had an Islamic pedigree with considerable historicity.
Kanem, for example, was under Muslim rulers by the tenth century,
who performed the *ḥājj* (Pilgrimage) as early as the eleventh, while
establishing Islamic offices in Kanem's government. They eventually
fled from anti-Islamic forces to the south-western edge of Lake Chad,
where they established Bornu.

Unlike their western Sudanic counterparts, Kanem and Bornu's
exports were primarily captives (who were also exported by Mali and
Songhay, but were of secondary importance there) in exchange for
cloth, firearms, and other commodities. A major trade route linked Lake
Chad to Tripoli by way of the Fezzan (in what is now south-western
Libya). The route was a notorious highway for captives well into the
nineteenth century. Captives were supposedly non-Muslims, but there
is evidence that many Muslims were taken as well. *Mai* Idrīs Alooma
(reigned 1570–1602), "the learned, just, courageous and pious Commander of the Faithful," developed quite the reputation as a slave raider.

The question of African captives arises again in East Africa, specifically along the Swahili coast, where maritime trade in the Indian Ocean is
of significant antiquity. By the second century BCE (if not earlier),
regular traffic linked East Africa to Arabia, India, and south-west Asia
by way of prevailing monsoon winds. The *dhow*, far more efficient than
the camel, sailed the Indian Ocean in one-third the time it took a

caravan to cross the Sahara, carrying the equivalent of 1,000 camel loads. Seafaring may have involved more Arabs and Indians than Africans, but coastal Africans controlled access to the East African interior, analogous to western Sudan's relations with Tuareg and Arab merchants. As such, sea and sand served as both barrier and bridge, but for the Swahili coast the bridge is the more appropriate metaphor, as the East African littoral was more fully integrated into Indian Ocean and Red Sea trade, a commercial complex both massive and lucrative. In exchange for Chinese porcelain, cowry shells, glass beads, and large quantities of cotton cloth from India and China, East Africa exported ivory, gold, mangrove poles (for housing in the Persian Gulf), and human beings. Perhaps the most dramatic demonstration of the ways in which these communities were connected took place during the career of the Chinese Admiral Zheng He, born into a Muslim (Hui) family, but subsequently captured in war and made a court eunuch during the early Ming Dynasty. He would emerge to lead an impressive fleet on seven different expeditionary voyages throughout South and South East Asia; his fourth, fifth, sixth, and seventh expeditions, from 1413 to 1433, included visits to the East African coast.

To speak of East Africa is to discuss Swahili culture and language, which incorporates Arabic and (to a lesser extent) Malagasy words and concepts. Arabs (and perhaps Persians) settling along the coast often intermarried with the local population, resulting in a fusion of genes and lifestyles. The apogee of the Swahili coastal towns lasted from the ninth through the fifteenth centuries CE, and was an age of royal courts, stone palaces, beautiful mosques, and internal plumbing in the best houses. Trade and urban growth corresponded to changes in the central Islamic world, as the political center shifted from Damascus and the Umayyad caliphate (661–750) to Baghdad and the Abbasids (750–1258), thereby elevating the Persian Gulf's importance. This period in East African history came to an abrupt halt with the arrival of Vasco da Gama and the Portuguese in 1498. Seven years later, Portuguese men-of-war returned to destroy Kilwa and inaugurate a new era of European activity in the Indian Ocean.

Pilgrims and Scholars

Many sub-Saharan Africans entered the central Islamic lands as fellow believers, usually traveling to the Middle East (and to North Africa) to make the Pilgrimage, to study, or to teach, and a number of individuals were regarded as learned and pious. Examples include the eminent scholar Aḥmad Bābā, taken captive from Timbuktu to Marrakesh in 1594 following the Moroccan conquest of Songhay, where he was imprisoned for two years, but taught classes for large numbers until his return to Timbuktu in 1608. A second example is Ṣāliḥ al-Fulānī, an obscure West African scholar from Futa Jallon (in contemporary Guinea), who headed for Cairo and finally Medina, where he studied and eventually taught from 1791 to his death in 1803/4. There are many others.

A tradition of royal pilgrimage dates back to the eleventh century in West Africa, and includes the rulers of Kanem, Mali, and Songhay. But the quintessential *ḥājj* was that of Mali's *Mansa* Mūsā in 1324. With a retinue of thousands of high officials, soldiers, and slaves, he brought so much gold to Egypt that its value depreciated for a period. Less significant for Muslim chroniclers, but more stunning in its implications and symbolism, was the manner in which *Mansa* Mūsā entered Egypt. In what must have been a sight for the ages, Mūsā and his thousands encamped around the pyramids prior to entering Cairo. For three days, the glory of imperial Mali and the wonder of ancient Egypt, two of the most iconic images of the African diaspora, merged as one.

The Enslaved

In contrast to those making the Pilgrimage, other Africans entered Muslim lands as slaves. Muslim societies made use of slaves from all over the reachable world, and Europeans were just as eligible as Africans, with Slavic and Caucasian populations, together with Asians, constituting the largest source of slaves for the Islamic world well into the eighteenth century. "Race" was therefore not a principal factor in enslavement – at least not until the eighteenth and nineteenth centuries, when European expansion in the Indian Ocean generated a closer association between blackness and slavery.

Restricting the discussion to Africa, tentative estimates for the trans-Saharan, Red Sea, and Indian Ocean slave trades are in the range of 12 million individuals from 650 CE to the end of the sixteenth century, and another 4 million from the seventeenth through the nineteenth centuries. As will be seen, more captive Africans were exported through these trades than were shipped across the Atlantic, although the latter took place within a much more compressed period (fifteenth through the nineteenth centuries). These estimates are imprecise, as it is difficult to separate the Red Sea and Indian Ocean trades, and not all who were transported through the Indian Ocean landed in Muslim lands. Even so, the number of enslaved Africans in the Islamic world clearly grew in significance over the centuries.

Slavery in Arabia was an accepted practice before Muhammad was even born, so that the Qur'ān, far from simply condoning slavery, attempts to improve the servile condition while also promoting manumission. Islam holds that freedom is the natural condition of human beings, and only certain circumstances allow for slavery. According to a strict interpretation of Islamic law, or *sharī'a*, only non-Muslims who are without a protective pact (*'ahd*) with Muslims, and who reject the offer to convert to Islam and are then captured in war (*jihād*), can be enslaved. But after the first century of Islam, reality diverged from theory, and most were in fact captured through raids and kidnapping, then sold to merchants. Stated another way, slavery in the Islamic world became a business.

Keeping in mind the theory–reality divide, Muslim slaveholders were to treat the enslaved with dignity and kindness. Slaves were not to be overworked or excessively punished, and if seriously injured were to be freed. They could marry with the slaveholder's consent, and were to be provided with material support and medical attention into old age. Though they were "property" and could be bought and sold like any other chattel, the enslaved's undeniable humanity created tensions that Islamic law attempted to resolve. Above all, slaveholders were enjoined to convert them to Islam; uncircumcised males, for example, were circumcised at the beginning of their servitude and given Arabic names. In an instructive parallel with the Americas, these names comprised a "special" category of nomenclature, reserved for the enslaved. Such appellations included Kāfār ("camphor") and 'Anbar ("ambergris") for males; and Bakhīta ("fortunate"), Mabrūka ("blessed"), and Za'farān ("saffron") for females. With the majority of the enslaved converting to Islam, some became literate in Arabic, and were taught to read the Qur'ān.

However, conversion to Islam did not obligate slaveholders to free their slaves; the Qur'ān only encouraged them to do so. The ideal arrangement was to enter into a manumission contract (*mukātaba*), whereby the enslaved could make and save enough money to purchase her or his freedom. As would be true of the Americas, such acquired freedom was qualified in that the freed person would remain a client to the former slaveholder and always in his debt, a condition passed down through several generations.

One of the most arresting aspects of the trans-Saharan, Red Sea, and Indian Ocean slave trades is that they were primarily transactions in females and children. Young girls and women were used as domestics and concubines, and often as both, as male slaveholders enjoyed the right of sexual access. As such, the concubine is referred to in the Qur'ān as "that which your right hands possess" (*mā malakat aymānukum*). Domestic work included cooking, cleaning, and wet-nursing (tasks that would become just as familiar to many African-descended women in the Americas), and there is evidence that some were (illegally) forced into prostitution. Slaveholders on occasion married enslaved females, who first had to be freed. As for concubines, the Muslim world had an order of preference, beginning with white females, many from the Balkans and lands in the south-west of what was formerly the Soviet Union, referred to as the *saqāliba*, or Slavs (although the term would come to include non-Slavs). Next in order of preference were Ethiopian, Nubian, and other women from the Horn of Africa, called the *ḥabashiyyāt* (or simply *habash*, when men were included), often found in the service of middle-class slaveholders. They enjoyed greater status and privilege than did other African women, who were allegedly the least preferred. According to Islamic law, the concubine who bore a child for the slaveholder (and thereafter became known as an *umm walad*) was automatically freed upon his death, and while he lived she could never be sold away. In contrast to what would develop in the Americas, the children of slaveholders and concubines followed the status of the fathers (when paternity was acknowledged), and were therefore free. An example of how this worked could be found in imperial Songhay, where every one of the *askias* following *Askia al-ḥājj* Muḥammad (d. 1529) was the son of a concubine. Yet another example is the 'Alawid ruler Mūlāy Isma'īl (reigned 1672–1727) of Morocco, whose mother was a black concubine.

Some concubines and female domestics were kept in large harems, where sexual exploitation was erratic and unpredictable. Women in such circumstances inhabited a world of instability, as advancing age and the failure to bear children or secure slaveholder interest could result in their sale. Central to the organization of such large harems was the eunuch or *tawāshi*, also referred to as *khādim* ("servant"), *fatā* ("young man"), and *aghā* ("chief"). The primary responsibility of the eunuch was to maintain order; his emasculation "perfected" him for such purposes, as he remained physically strong but incapable (for the most part) of posing a sexual threat. As was true of concubines, those transformed into eunuchs came from Europe and Asia and Africa, but in this instance, it was the African eunuch who appears to have been preferred (at least in the Ottoman capital of Istanbul). Because they were privy to the inner workings of the household, these individuals could amass significant influence in both the household and the society (assuming a prominent family). The authority of the *Kislar Aghā*, the Ottoman sultan's head eunuch, was legendary. In apparent violation of Islamic law, such eunuchs were allowed to own other eunuchs and concubines. According to one nineteenth-century account of the chief African eunuchs of Mecca, they were even married to enslaved Ethiopians, a most curious arrangement.

The procedures by which males became eunuchs rank among the most inhumane. Young boys were commonly forced to endure the operation, which involved either removal of the testes, or both testes and penis. Because the operation was abhorrent to Muslims, it was performed by Christians (and perhaps Jews) in such places as Baghirmi near Lake Chad, in Ethiopia, and in other locations. Accounts of the process veer toward the macabre, as young males were gelded and placed in sand up to their navels, in order to heal. Those able to urinate after some days were herded off through the Sahara; those who could not were left to die. Many who began the desert trek therefore did not complete it, expiring along the way. In addition to serving in the harems, some were chosen to serve in the mosque of the Ka'ba in Mecca and in Prophet Muhammad's mosque in Medina. The number of eunuchs in the Muslim world is difficult to estimate, but the claim that the Moroccan sultan Mūlāy Ismāʻil personally owned over 2,000 suggests their numbers were significant. Indeed, many more entered the mutilation process than exited, as a credible estimate found that only 10 percent survived the operation. In the case of Mūlāy Ismāʻil, therefore, this means that some 20,000 young males were necessary to produce the 2,000 who survived.

Africans were also used as pearl divers in the Persian Gulf, and as laborers in large agricultural ventures and mining operations. They supplied the backbreaking, bloodcurdling labor for the salt mines of Taghāza in the western Sahara, and the copper mines of Tegidda in what is now Niger. The model of exploiting sub-Saharan labor may have been provided by the Tuareg and Arabo-Berbers of the Sahara, who had a longstanding tradition of using sub-Saharan African slaves to herd animals and collect wood and water.

Agricultural projects in the Islamic world generally did not approach the magnitude of the American plantation until the emergence of clove cultivation in such places as Zanzibar in the nineteenth century, but African enslaved labor was employed in date production in Saharan oases and in tenth-century Arabia, near Bahrain. African slave labor was also used in the cultivation of sugar in the Ahwāz province of what is now western Iraq in the ninth century, together with the large-scale use of East African slave labor in nearby southern Iraq and Kuwait, in what was called the Sawād. There, captives from the interior of East Africa, the Zanj, were expended to drain vast marshlands. The conditions under which the Zanj labored were so stultifying, so deplorable, that they produced one of the most spectacular slave revolts in history. Unifying under the charismatic leadership of ʿAlī b. Muḥammad, son of an Iraqi father and a mother from Sind (the lower Indus valley), the Zanj waged insurrection for fifteen years, from 868 to 883, capturing the city of Basra and marching on Baghdad itself, capital of the Abbasid caliphate and center of the Muslim world. With their defeat, the Zanj were ruthlessly exterminated, the experiment using their labor in southern Iraq abandoned. In fact, some scholars speculate the Zanj left such a bitter taste in the mouths of the Abbasids that it influenced the brutish depiction of blacks in the *Thousand and One Nights*.

One of the more visible uses of enslaved African labor was in the military, one of the few institutions allowing for any degree of upward mobility for persons of African descent throughout the history of the entire diaspora. Slave armies were in a number of places in the Islamic world by the ninth century. The concept was to create a military that, due to its very foreignness and alienation, owed its total allegiance to the ruler. Those destined for such armies were usually acquired through purchase rather than war, and included Turks, Slavs, Berbers, and other Africans. In fact, most military slaves were non-African, and were often organized into separate units based on ethnic origin and background. Specific terms were used to identify armies as both servile and ethnically distinct: the *mamlūks*, a servile army that eventually seized power in Egypt and Syria from 1250 to 1517, were mostly from the Black Sea region; the Janissaries (or *kuls*), who took control of the Ottoman Empire in the seventeenth and eighteenth centuries, hailed from the Slavic and Albanian populations of the

Balkans. The term 'abīd, however, was apparently used exclusively for sub-Saharan African slave armies.

The 'abīd army was developed in Egypt under the Turkish governor Ahmad Tulun (d. 884), who garrisoned them separately from the mamlūk division. This particular 'abīd army was probably Nubian. The immediate successors to the Ṭūlūnids also maintained servile black troops, as did the Fāṭimids, who began in North Africa (in 909) before moving their capital to Cairo in 969, maintaining large numbers of black servile soldiers in both places. In Egypt these soldiers grew powerful, and skirmishes between them and non-black units increased in number and violence. A final conflict, the "Battle of the Blacks" or the "Battle of the Slaves," took place in 1169, when Ṣalāḥ al-Dīn led his non-black forces against some 50,000 black soldiers and drove them out of Cairo into southern Egypt. All-black units would not be used again in Egypt until the nineteenth century under Muḥammad 'Alī.

Black slave soldiers were also used in North Africa by the ninth-century Aghlabid dynasty, and thereafter under successive regimes. Further west, in what is now Morocco, the Almoravid leader Yūsuf b. Tāshīn (d. 1106) was surrounded by a bodyguard of 2,000 black soldiers, and the successors to the Almoravids, the Almohads, also used black soldiers. But the ultimate in the use of servile black soldiers took place under the aforementioned Mūlāy Ismā'īl, son of the black concubine, who along with his 2,000 black eunuchs was reported to have maintained 150,000 black troops, having ordered the seizure of all black males throughout the kingdom. The troops were provided with black females, and were forced to swear personal allegiance to Mūlāy Ismā'īl upon the ḥadīth (traditions of Muḥammad) collected by al-Bukhārī, and were therefore known as 'abīd al-Bukhārī. This 'abīd army grew enormously powerful, determining the succession to the throne for thirty years after the death of Mūlāy Ismā'īl, choosing from among his 500 sons. In 1737, the 'abīd army was brought under control by Mūlāy Muḥammad III using an Arab force. Black soldiers continue to serve in the Moroccan army to the present day, only no longer as slaves.

Iberia

Mention of the Almoravids and Almohads redirects our attention to Iberia (Spain and Portugal), site of a remarkable Muslim civilization from 711 to 1492. When Muslim forces crossed Gibraltar into Spain in

711, it was a combined army of Berbers, sub-Saharan Africans, and Arabs. The invading Muslim armies renamed the peninsula "al-Andalus" (an apparent corruption of the term *Vandal,* from the former occupiers). By 720, the Muslims laid claim to territory south of the Pyrenees and parts of southern France, and in 732 encroached further into France, where they were engaged outside of Tours and were defeated at the Battle of Poitiers by Charles Martel. Celebrated in Europe as a major victory over Islam, the event was known by the Muslims as the "Highway of the Martyrs" (*Balāṭ al-Shuhadā'*) and, from their perspective, was little more than an insignificant border raid. The "land of the Franks," as France and much of western Europe were known, was culturally unremarkable, economically unimportant, and of little interest to the Islamic world.

Portions of Iberia under Muslim control answered to the Umayyads of Damascus until 750, when the Abbasid caliphate arose and shifted the center of the Muslim world to Baghdad. A member of the Umayyad family fled to Iberia, where he restructured a version of the Umayyad caliphate, rupturing the dream of a single Muslim empire. Muslims would conquer Sicily between 827 and 902, and move into parts of southern Italy, but the eleventh century saw the return of Sicily to Christian control, as well as the slow erosion of Muslim power elsewhere in Italy and Iberia (see Map 3).

Al-Andalus was a Muslim state controlled by Arabs in command of Berbers and sub-Saharan Africans. However, conflict between Berbers and Arabs stemmed from an almost uninterrupted history of invasion and occupation of North African territory, beginning with the Carthaginians and followed by the Romans, the Vandals, the Byzantines, and lastly the Arabs. Berbers resisted Arab domination militarily, while some also embraced a different form of Islam, Kharijism, which advocated democratic and egalitarian principles. This strategy of adopting a reconfigured expression of an oppressor's religion, thus transforming it into a tool of liberation, would also be used by the African-descended in the New World. Berbers further resisted by creating politically autonomous spaces, establishing a number of Kharijite states in North Africa after 750. Kharijite societies remain in the mountains and remote areas of Algeria and Tunisia to this day, and in ways recall maroon communities in the Americas.

Yet another path of resistance was direct confrontation, an option that harkens back to ancient Ghana, as the West African savannah was crucial to the rise of the Berber Almoravid movement in the eleventh

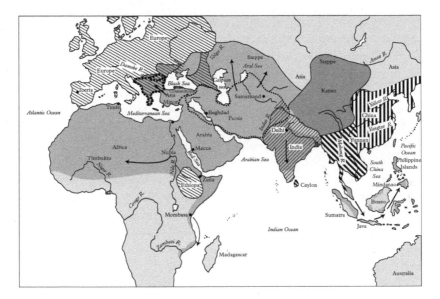

MAP 3 Spread of Islam to 1500

century. Berbers in southern Morocco noted Ghana's spectacular growth and trade, concluding it was the key to both the trans-Saharan trade and aspirations to cross into Iberia. Like Egypt's eighteenth dynasty, which secured control over Nubian resources before launching campaigns into Palestine and Syria, the Almoravids began their activities by first focusing on West Africa. Their bid for power became part of a religious reform movement, and by the mid-eleventh century the Almoravids had seized control of the southern and northern termini of the trans-Saharan trade. Financing its operation with West African gold, the Almoravids also used West African soldiers, enslaved and free. By century's end, the Almoravids had succeeded in not only bringing all of Morocco and western Algeria under their control, but al-Andalus as well, founding Marrakesh as their capital. For the first time in history, a single Berber power held sway over much of North Africa and significant portions of Iberia; Africans would rule the "kingdom of the two shores" for nearly 300 years.

The Almoravids were succeeded by the Almohads (1146–1269), who also used West African soldiers. Like Mūlāy Ismā'īl of the seventeenth century, al-Manṣūr (reigned 1184–99) was possibly of West African ancestry. Another was Abū al-Ḥasan (reigned 1331–51) of the subsequent Marinid dynasty. Earning a reputation for cruelty,

Abu al-Hasan exchanged embassies with *Mansa* Mūsā prior to the latter's death, and was a great patron of the arts. The examples of Abū al-Ḥasan, al-Manṣūr, and Mūlāy Ismāʿīl demonstrate the difficulties in distinguishing between Berbers and sub-Saharan Africans, as extensive, centuries-long interaction between these regions necessarily meant a significant sharing of genes; an ostensibly Berber-looking individual may have in fact had considerable sub-Saharan ancestral ties, and vice versa. Europeans could and did distinguish between African groups, but their tendency to label all as Moors (literally, "blacks"), suggesting all Africans represented a continuum of related characteristics, is not without warrant. Whatever the nature of their congenital relations, Africans of varying backgrounds in Iberia tended to participate in cultures connected through Islam. As such, it may be more accurate to read the designation "Moor" as a cultural rather than racial or ethnic qualifier.

Africans were present in al-Andalus throughout the 800-year period of Muslim domination, contributing to an intense period of intellectual and cultural production. It was during the Muslim domination of Iberia that science, technology and the arts, including astronomy, medicine, alchemy, chemistry, physics, mathematics, literature, and philosophy, received a tremendous boost. Indeed, the knowledge of the ancients, including Greek philosophy, had been "lost" to Europe for hundreds of years, as Latin and Greek had almost disappeared. Muslim, Jewish, and Christian scholars uncovered and translated the mostly Greek texts into Arabic, by which Europe reconnected with its past. The works of Plato, Aristotle, Ptolemy, Euclid, Hippocrates, and the physician Galen were among the many reintroduced to Europe during this period. Prominent scholars of the period include Ibn Sīnā (or Avicenna) as well as Ibn Rushd (also known as Averroës), who was born in Cordoba in 1126, and who went on to translate and comment on the works of Aristotle while establishing a reputation as a scientist, mathematician, philosopher, and poet. Made possible by the support of Almohad ruler al-Manṣūr, Ibn Rushd's work, some thirty-eight volumes, became popular largely through Spanish Jewish scholars, a circle that included Mūsā b. Maymun (or Maimonides). Students from all over Europe, including France, Germany, England, and Italy, came to study in al-Andalus, often becoming literate in Arabic. The intellectual productivity of Muslim Iberia, as well as other parts of the Muslim world, was an important foundation for the Renaissance of western Europe.

In addition to their contribution to various branches of knowledge, Muslims introduced styles of architecture resulting in stunning blends of structure and landscape, of which al-Hambra is a prime example. They founded cities that include Cordoba, Seville, Toledo, and Granada, each known for a particular quality. Cordoba was a city of libraries, while Seville was associated with music. These cities were well planned, featuring aqueducts, gardens, public baths, and fountains to embellish mosques, hospitals, and other buildings, public and private. Supplying the urban centers were fields given enhanced fertility through revamped irrigation systems and the introduction of such crops as cereals and beans. But the Muslim geographic imagination was by no means confined to land, as Muslim scholars refined geography by more accurately measuring distances (though remaining hampered by ancient models), and introduced to the Western world seafaring tools and techniques such as the astrolabe, the lateen sail, and the method of tacking. Some of these innovations were modified from their use in the Indian Ocean, and in any event proved critical to the subsequent development of European seafaring and commercial and imperial expansion.

India and Pakistan

While there are numerous scholarly works on al-Andalus or Moorish Spain, what is known about the sub-Saharan African contribution to this brilliant civilization is far from satisfactory. Research on the African presence in India is similarly in its infancy. Matters are complicated by an ancient, pre-Islamic society in which the four major castes (Brahman, Kshatriya, Vaishya, and Shudra) are hierarchically arranged in a manner corresponding with color (*varna*). Thus, the lowest, servile caste, the Shudra, is characterized in the ancient Vedic literature as "black" and "dark-complexioned," but as there are many dark-skinned populations throughout the world, attempting to locate Shudra origins in Africa may be pointless.

Given the historicity and expanse of Indian Ocean trade, Africans necessarily voyaged to the Indian subcontinent prior to the rise of Islam. But it is with that religion's movement into the subcontinent that the African presence becomes better documented. India initially experienced Islamic incursions as early as 711, and in the late tenth century Muslim forays from what is now Afghanistan and Iran resulted in considerable plunder. Islam reached its political zenith in the subcontinent under the Delhi Sultanate (1206–1526) and the Mughals (1526–1739).

Free Africans (as well as non-Africans) operated in Muslim-ruled India as merchants, seafarers, clerics, bodyguards, and even bureaucrats. Regarding slavery, African women and men assumed familiar roles as concubines and servile soldiers; in 1459, for example, some 8,000 were in the employ of Bengal's army. Called "Habshis" (from *habashiyyāt*) and "Siddis" (or "Sheedis," apparently from the title *sayyid*, afforded captains of vessels and perhaps recalling their foreign origins), Africans settled in a variety of locales. Enclaves of Siddis can presently be found in Gujarat (western India), Karnataka (south-west India), Habshiguda (a neighborhood in Hyderabad city, central India), and Janjira Island (south of Mumbai/Bombay), with the names *Habshiguda* and *Janjira* reflecting an African ancestry. They also came to what is now Pakistan, and can be found in Makran in Balochistan province (south-west), and Karachi and other towns in lower Sindh province (south-east).

During the time of the Mughals, there were a number of African Muslim rulers in the subcontinent. At least several Habshi rulers were in the breakaway province of Bengal (eastern India), including Malik Andil (or Saiffuddīn Firuz, 1487–90) and Nāṣiruddīn Maḥmūd II (1490–91). There were also several rulers in the Deccan breakaway province of Ahmadnagar of African descent, including the most famous of all, Malik Ambar (d. 1626), who supported the princess Chand Bibi (d. 1600) in her struggle against the Mughals. Malik Ambar (Figure 2), possibly Ethiopian-born, was brought to India as a slave, and eventually served as a highly educated military commander. Noted for his religious tolerance and patronage of the arts and learning, he ruled for twenty years and earned the admiration of Indians and Europeans alike.

Turkey and Iran

Given the wide expanse and deep historicity of Indian Ocean trade, discovery of an early African presence in what becomes Iran is hardly a surprise. But the research is only just beginning, and what has thus far been uncovered concerns Africans in Iran from the periods of the Qajar (1795–1925) and Pahlavi dynasties (1925–79). Trade currents brought persons captured along the Swahili coast, from such places as

FIGURE 2 Malik Ambar. A black and white version of this figure will appear in some formats. For the color version, please refer to the plate section.

(what are now) Zanzibar, Tanzania, and Kenya, along with persons from the Horn of Africa (Ethiopia, Djibouti, and Somalia) to Iran, where many were enslaved, along with similarly captured individuals from the Caucasus – including Georgians and Circassians – a region along the eastern reaches of the Black Sea. Concentrated along the Iranian southern coast (where they currently may account for 10 percent or more of the population), Africans performed agricultural as well as domestic and military services.

As for the Ottoman Empire, mention has already been made of the use of eunuchs in places like Istanbul (formerly Constantinople), whose capture by Muslim forces in 1458 officially signals the beginning of the Ottomans. But as some 362,000 Africans were imported into its heartland during the nineteenth century alone, the number of eunuchs was clearly dwarfed by those tasked with agricultural, military, and domestic service, the last of these principally provided by women and girls.

The Image of the African in the Islamic World

The Muslim view of the African was an evolutionary process, informed by changing circumstances over time. Whatever the initial attitude toward the African, the trade in slaves via the Sahara, Red Sea, and Indian Ocean had an impact. But since enslaved Europeans and Asians outnumbered enslaved Africans in the Islamic world until the eighteenth century, the slave trade could not have been the sole explanation for a less-than-complimentary view of the African. Other factors, essentially cultural, must have played a role.

There is no trace of racism in the Qur'ān. Rather, there is the assertion that difference is of divine decree:

> And among His signs is the creation of the heavens and the earth, and the diversity of your languages and colors. In that surely are signs for those who know.
>
> (*Sūra* or chapter 30, *ar-Rūm*, verse 23)

This non-evaluative acknowledgment of what is now called racial diversity is indicative of the early Muslim period in the Arabian Peninsula. There, color was both insignificant and variable, depending upon who was being compared. While Bedouins were usually described as "brown" or "olive," Arabs at times characterized themselves as "black" vis-à-vis "red" Persians; but in comparison with sub-Saharan Africans, these same Arabs became "red" or even "white." The concept of "red" could also take on metaphoric meaning with Islam's early expansion, as the hated "red" Persians were now the subjects of the Arabs, with "redness" taking on a pejorative connotation. In this way, Greeks, Spaniards, and other Mediterranean populations also became "red."

It is not surprising that the Qur'ān is devoid of racial bias, or that Arabs depicted themselves as "black" and "brown." Seventh-century Arabia was surrounded by far more powerful Sassanian (Persian), Byzantine, and Ethiopian empires, who fought each other for influence in the peninsula. The dominant peninsular power was Yemen in the south-west (previously called *Arabia Felix* by the Romans), distinct from the rest of the peninsula because of its urban-sustaining agriculture, and because of extensive ties with Ethiopia. Ethiopia had both invaded and conquered southern Arabia in the fourth century, taking control of the spice and silk trade between the Mediterranean and the Indian Ocean that passed through Arabia. With Sassanian help, the Yemenis pushed the Ethiopians out around 375, but the Ethiopians returned triumphantly in 512. The subsequent defeat of Ethiopian garrisons led to another Ethiopian expedition around 525. A few years later, divine intervention, according to the Qur'ān (*sūra* 105, *al-Fīl*, or "the Elephant"), turned back an Ethiopian assault on Mecca.

Ethiopian incursions are but one example of interaction between the Horn of Africa and Arabia that has existed for millennia; related languages and cultures are another. Such interconnectedness suggests that Ethiopians and Nubians made contributions to the Yemeni and Arab gene pool, along with other populations from the Horn. It is therefore no surprise that one of the greatest poets of pre-Islamic Arabia was ʿAntara (or ʿAntar), son of an enslaved Ethiopian or Nubian mother and an Arab father. Born in the pre-Islamic *jahiliyya* period ("time of barbarism"), ʿAntara followed his mother's status and was a slave, but earned his freedom through military prowess. His background is similar to that of another figure of the early Islamic period, Khufāf b. Nadba, son of an Arab father and enslaved black mother, who rose to become head of his (Arab) group or "tribe." On the other hand, many Arabs had "black" skin, but apparently were not descended from Africans; such was true of ʿUbāda b. al-Ṣāmit, an Arab of noble birth and a leader of the Arab conquest of Egypt.

The impression that blackness was no barrier is bolstered by the example of Muḥammad himself who, facing mounting opposition to his message, sent seventy of his followers to seek asylum with the Ethiopian ruler in 615, presaging the official *hijra* or "flight" to Medina in 622. Muḥammad's action revealed his esteem for the piety of the Ethiopians, a sentiment consistent with Homer's much earlier characterization of the "Ethiopians." There were also a number of persons of Nubian or Ethiopian descent among the Companions of the Prophet, perhaps the most famous having been Islam's first muezzin (who calls the faithful to prayer), Bilāl b. Rabāḥ, born into slavery in Mecca and an early convert to Islam. Purchased and manumitted by Abu Bakr (Islam's first caliph or successor to Muḥammad, as well as his father-in-law), Bilāl became the Prophet's personal attendant. In addition to Bilāl, notables of known African descent include the caliph

'Umar (634–44), the grandson of an Ethiopian/Nubian woman; and
'Amr b. al-'Āṣ, similarly descended from an Ethiopian/Nubian female
ancestor. The Prophet himself may have been of partial African descent, as his grandfather and paternal uncle Abū Ṭālib were both
reputed to be "black." Therefore, significant Ethiopian or Nubian
influences were circulating at the very core of Islam's foundation.
Given Ethiopia's ascendancy, if anyone felt inferior in the seventh
century, it would have been the Arabs.

And yet, there is something unsettling about these relations; one
wonders if the potential for bias was not present in pre-Islamic and
early Islamic Arabia. For despite the prominence of all of these men of
Ethiopian/Nubian descent, it is striking that so many of them descended from enslaved mothers. Perhaps free Nubian- or Ethiopian-
born males were far fewer than enslaved Nubian or Ethiopian women
in Arab society, so that the most common African figure in Arab
society was a female slave. If so, Arab society may have begun associating Africans living within their communities with slavery before the
rise of Islam. 'Antara reflects an Arab acceptance of difference, but his
own background suggests that many Africans within the Arab world
entered by way of the servile estate.

The expansion of Arab armies in the seventh and eighth centuries
may have been the period during which Arab views of Africans began
to change. Arabs were already suffering from ethnocentricity, as Islam
had been revealed to an Arab and the revelation forever sealed in his
language. Initially, it was not even clear that Islam was meant for non-
Arabs. With the world now divided into believers and infidels, the rise
of the trans-Saharan, Red Sea, and Indian Ocean slave trades did not
bode well for Africans, especially those with whom Arabs had little
experience. Their high regard for the Ethiopian and Nubian continued, but these were distinguished from other Africans, such as the
Nūba, Bujja (Beja), Zanj, and the Sūdān (from West Africa). Lack of
familiarity played some role, but since many Africans may have
entered Islamic lands as young females, the Arab view of Africans
was also informed by the perception of African women. Whatever the
answer, Muslim societies became increasingly accustomed to seeing
Africans as enslaved menials. The struggle over the meaning of blackness in early Islamic society can be seen in the poetry of "the crows of
the Arabs" (aghribat al-'Arab), men who lived during the pre-Islamic
and early Islamic periods and who were dark-skinned, but not necessarily of African ancestry. These poets alternatively bemoaned and

defended their blackness: one Suḥaym (d. 660), whose name means "little black man," wrote:

> If my color were pink, women would love me
> But the Lord has marred me with blackness.
>
> Though I am a slave my soul is nobly free
> Though I am black of color my character is white.

A century later, one of the most popular of these poets, Abū Dulāma (d. *c.*776), was a court jester for the Abbasids in Baghdad, and wrote the following in derision of his mother and family:

> We are alike in color; our faces are black and
> ugly, our names are shameful.

One hundred years later, one of the best-known composers of prose in classical Arabic literature, al-Jāḥiẓ (d. 869), also purportedly of partial African ancestry, wrote that the Zanj "are the least intelligent and the least discerning of mankind." This statement may not reflect al-Jāḥiẓ's true views of blacks as a whole, however, as he also made highly laudatory statements about them.

Some of this literature comes out of the Persian Gulf, where one of the consequences of the Zanj revolt may have been an anti-Zanj backlash of sentiment. Some scholars see the revolt as the principal cause of anti-black expressions, but the revolt did not begin until 868, well after many of these black poets were already dead. Yet another argument is that Persian Zoroastrianism and Manichaeism, with their emphasis on conflict between darkness and light, associated darkness with dark skin and light with white skin, thus influencing Muslim thinking. While this is all speculative, one source makes clear the view of the African in the Persian Gulf. *The Thousand and One Nights*, an apparent compilation of stories developed by Persian, Indian, and Chinese travelers and merchants, is associated with the early days of Baghdad's Abbasid caliphate. Black folk are mentioned frequently in the book, principally as slaves or servants of some kind. Enslaved black men also feature at the book's beginning, engaged in sexual escapades with King Shahzāmān's wife and twenty other female members of his household. Some of the most pervasive stereotypes of black folk known in the Western world were therefore already taking shape in ninth-century Iraq, and elsewhere in the Islamic world.

Those Muslims arriving at a negative assessment of the African did not do so on their own, but in dialogue with other traditions and preceding opinions. One influence was Galen (fl. 122–55), whose work on anatomy remained the seminal text in medicine for both Christians and Muslims through the medieval period. Galen was the official physician for gladiators at the Pergamum circus, and there presumably came into contact with blacks. In an interesting and fateful conjunction, it was the famous al-Mas'udī (d. 956) who introduced Galen to the Muslim world by quoting the Greek physician's observations of black men. Galen, al-Mas'udī, stated,

> mentions ten specific attributes of the black man, which are found in him and no other; frizzy hair, thin eyebrows, broad nostrils, thick lips, pointed teeth, smelly skin, black eyes, furrowed hands and feet, a long penis and great merriment. Galen says that merriment dominates the black man because of his defective brain, whence also the weakness of his intelligence.

Besides Galen, other sources interpreted Christian and Jewish texts as condemning black skin via the curse of Ham.

Not all non-black Muslim writers adopted unfavorable views of blacks. There were those who respected Africans, citing their roles as Companions of the Prophet as well as their virtues. The "defenders of the blacks" included such leading intellectuals as Jamāl al-Dīn Abū'l-Faraj b. al-Jawzī (d. 1208), who wrote *The Lightening of the Darkness on the Merits of the Blacks and the Ethiopians*; and the Egyptian scholar Jalāl al-Dīn al-Suyūṭī (d. 1505), who wrote *The Raising of the Status of the Ethiopians*. Individuals such as al-Suyūṭī had substantial experience with sub-Saharan Africans and knew a number of their scholars and political leaders personally. One must therefore be careful not to paint the entire Muslim world with the same broad stroke.

Furthermore, it is not clear that prior to the sixteenth century the Muslim view of Europeans was any better than the assessment of non-Muslim Africans. The idea that geography and climate determined group characteristics was popularized by the tenth-century Persian physician Ibn Sīnā. Because of western Europe's cold climate and cultural unattractiveness, Muslims by and large held little respect for it, enslaving many from south-eastern Europe. Arab and Persian Muslims who may have felt contempt for Africans also felt superior to Europeans, as the following quote from an Arab living in eleventh-century al-Andalus reflects:

For those who live furthest to the north ... the excessive distance from the sun in relation to the zenith line makes the air cold and the atmosphere thick. Their temperaments are therefore frigid, their humors [dispositions] raw, their bellies gross, their color pale, their hair long and lank. Thus, they lack keenness of understanding and clarity of intelligence, and are overcome by ignorance and dullness, lack of discernment, and stupidity. Such are the Slavs, the Bulgars, and their neighbors.

In view of the symmetry in opinions toward non-Muslim Africans and Europeans, any divergence may well have come after the sixteenth century, when the trade in Europeans began to diminish while its counterpart in Africans started to surge. By the eighteenth century, there was a fast association between sub-Saharan Africans and slavery in the central Islamic lands, whereas the enslavement of Europeans had largely become a thing of the past, confined to memory and books.

Slavery's Aftermath

What became of all these African slaves in the Islamic world? The answer is by no means obvious, as descent traced through the free male line obscures if not erases African maternal ancestry. A look at contemporary Arab populations in North Africa, Palestine, the Arabian Peninsula, and even the Saudi royal family reveals discernible African features, but studies are insufficient to make conclusive statements. In Mauritania and southern Morocco, the fate of sub-Saharan blacks is clearer, as the descendants of slaves, the *ḥaraṭīn* (called *bella* further east), continue in servile status to Arabo-Berber masters to the present day. These ostensibly free descendants of the *ḥaraṭīn* experience subordination and second-class citizenship, and continue to be heavily dependent upon patron families. Like their American co-sufferers, large numbers the *ḥaraṭīn* found themselves sharecropping in Mauritania and southern Morocco, along the fringes of the Sahara, effectively barred from any meaningful social mobility and virtually shut out of systems of education. But also like their American counterparts, the dispossessed of Mauritania and Morocco have experienced changes for the better with the twentieth century's progression. One famous community of blacks in Morocco are the *gnawa*, noted for their distinct musical traditions. In Morocco,

Tunisia, and Algeria, the descendants of sub-Saharan Africans (and North Africans, for that matter) practice Islam along with *bori*, a cosmology that, not unlike the *zar* of Iran, is concerned with the spirit world's interaction with the corporeal. *Bori* is a mixture of spirits – infants, nature gods, spirits of deceased Muslim leaders, Muslim *jinn* (spirits), and so forth – who cause illness, and who are appeased through offerings, sacrifice, and dance possession. West African communities practicing *bori*, such as the Songhay, Bambara, and Hausa, were distinguished in North Africa at least through the mid-twentieth century. The practice of *bori* within dominant Muslim spaces parallels a similar persistence of sub-Saharan African religions in the Christian-controlled Americas, and is a testimony to the tenacity of African culture even under duress.

In India and Pakistan, the descendants of the Habshis and Siddis no longer speak African languages, but their worship and music and dance are suffused with African content, influencing adherents of both Hinduism and Islam. Hindu Siddis in India, for example, use only Siddi priests for guidance in life, who have expertise in engaging Siddi spirits; whereas in Pakistan, the Sheedis venerate the Shi'ite leader Imam Husayn (martyred at Karbala in 680) in a way that transforms the latter into an active force. In addition to those of clear African descent are the vast millions of Dalits, with whom the former may have intermingled, along with the Shudra caste. Dalits, formerly referred to as "untouchables," were considered ritually polluting and outside of the caste system, even below the Shudra. The Shudra, Dalits, and Siddis have all experienced severe discrimination, their darker skins the reason for much of their suffering.

As it concerns Iran, the abolition of slavery began in 1828, though slavery did not completely end there for another hundred years. Divided into such families as the Durzadehs, Ghulams, and Nukars, these African-descended populations embrace an Iranian identity, and while they practice what is clearly an African-derived possession practice known as *zar*, similar to *bori*, they only have a vague sense of a connection to Africa as a land of ancestral origin.

Perhaps the greater mystery concerns the old Ottoman Empire, where the slave trade was abolished in 1857, at which point all freed persons were required to serve as domestics in designated households (presumably to preserve slaveholder interests). The contemporary Afro-Turkish population can be found in such southern coastal urban areas as Izmir, Aydin, and Mugla, as well as in the provinces of

Antalya and Adana. Communities of the African-descended can also be found in Abkhazia, north of Turkey (and Georgia). It should be noted, however, that along the western slope of the Caucasus mountains, in what is now Abkhazia and Georgia, lived a much earlier community of dark-skinned persons who were most likely Africans. Referred to as "Colchis" by the ancient Greeks, this area featured a population regarded by Herodotus as "Egyptians," as they were "black-skinned with woolly hair" who, like the Egyptians and "Ethiopians," practiced circumcision.

Suggestions for Further Reading

On the early or classical period of Islam's history, one may begin with Albert Habib Hourani, *A History of the Arab Peoples* (Cambridge, MA: Belknap of Harvard University Press, 1991). More challenging is the first volume of Marshall G.S. Hodgson's three-volume *The Venture of Islam: Conscience and History in a World Civilization* (Chicago: University of Chicago Press, 1974), and Fred Donner's *The Early Islamic Conquests* (Princeton, NJ: Princeton University Press, 1981). For Muhammad, see W. Montgomery Watt's classics, *Muhammad at Mecca* (Oxford: Clarendon Press, 1953) and *Muhammad at Medina* (Oxford: Clarendon Press, 1956). An accessible reading of the sayings and traditions of the Prophet is Alfred Guillaume, *The Life of the Prophet: A Translation of Ishaq's Rasul Allah* (Oxford: Oxford University Press, 1967).

The scholarship regarding Islam in early West and East Africa is voluminous, as is obviously true of the literature on Islam in general. One could begin with Mervyn Hiskett's *The Development of Islam in West Africa* (Boston: Addison-Wesley Longman, 1984), although it is more concerned with what becomes Nigeria. Nehemia Levtzion's *Islam in West Africa: Religion, Society and Politics to 1800* (Brookfield, VT: Variorum, 1994), and his *Ancient Ghana and Mali* (London: Methuen, 1973) are also useful, but dated. See the more contemporary work of Michael A. Gomez, *African Dominion: A New History of Empire in Early and Medieval West Africa* (Princeton, NJ: Princeton University Press, 2018); and John O. Hunwick, *Timbuktu and the Songhay Empire: Al-Sa'dī's Tā'rīkh as-Sūdān down to 1613 and Other Contemporary Documents* (Leiden: Brill, 2003). There are excellent articles in Nehemia Levtzion and Humphrey J. Fisher, eds., *Rural and Urban Islam in West Africa* (Boulder, CO: L. Rienner, 1986). More challenging but thorough are the contributions to the first volume of J.F.A. Ajayi and Michael Crowder, eds., *History of West Africa* (London: Longman, 1985), 3rd ed. Though dated, two enjoyable classics remain Félix Dubois, *Timbuctoo the Mysterious*, trans. Diana White (New York: Longmans, Green and Co., 1896) and E.W. Bovill, *The Golden Trade of the Moors* (London: Oxford University Press, 1968). For African urban areas, see Graham Connah, *African Civilizations. Precolonial Cities and States in Tropical Africa: An Archaeological Perspective* (Cambridge: Cambridge University Press, 1987). For East Africa specifically, see J.F. Safari, *The Making of Islam in East Africa* (Dar es Salaam: Benedictine Publications Ndanda-Peramiho, 1994). Biancamaria Scarcia Amoretti's *Islam in East Africa, New Sources: Archives, Manuscripts and Written Historical Sources, Oral History, Archaeology* (Rome: Herder, 2001) is a collection of data from a 1999 conference, and is helpful. For more focused studies, consider Randle L. Pouwells, *Horn and Crescent: Cultural Change and Traditional Islam on the East African Coast, 800–1900* (Cambridge: Cambridge University Press, 1987) and Frederick Cooper, *Plantation Slavery on the East Coast of Africa* (New Haven, CT: Yale University Press, 1977).

Mention of Cooper's work provides a segue into the topic of slavery. Ralph Austen's *African Economic History: Internal Development and External Dependency* (London: J. Curry and Portsmouth, NH: Heinemann, 1987) contains an important discussion of the volume and organization of the various external slave trades, while Paul E. Lovejoy's *Transformations in Slavery: A History of Slavery in Africa* (Cambridge and New York: Cambridge University Press, 1983) and Patrick Manning's *Slavery and African Life: Occidental, Oriental, and African Slave Trades* (Cambridge: Cambridge University Press, 1990) combine these insights with discussions of domestic slavery and arguments about the implications of slave trading for Africa. Moving to the actual sites of enslavement, John O. Hunwick's "African Slaves in the Mediterranean World: A Neglected Aspect of the African Diaspora," in Joseph E. Harris, ed., *Global Dimensions of the African Diaspora* (Washington, DC: Howard University Press, 1993), is an excellent overview. R. Brunschvig's "Abd," in *The Encyclopedia of Islam* (Leiden: E.J. Brill, 1960), new edition, addresses the equation of African slaves with this term. Bernard Lewis' *Race and Color in Islam* (New York: Octagon Books, 1971) and his *Race and Slavery in the Middle East: An Historical Enquiry* (New York and Oxford: Oxford University Press, 1990) are probably the most thorough discussions of the African presence in the Islamic world, although they are somewhat controversial in that translations from Arabic to English tend to favor the more pejorative of possible meanings. As such, an important counterbalance to Lewis' work is Vincent J. Cornell's translation of al-Jāḥiẓ's *Book of the Glory of the Black Race* (Los Angeles: Preston Collection, 1981). Also, compare with Murray Gordon, *Slavery in the Arab World* (New York: New Amsterdam, 1989), who emphasizes the sexual component of slavery. Important studies in various sites of the Islamic world include John Ralph Willis, ed., *Slaves and Slavery in Muslim Africa* (London and Totowa, NJ: Routledge, 1985), 2 vols.; Y. Hakan Erdem, *Slavery in the Ottoman Empire and Its Demise, 1800–1909* (New York: St. Martin's Press, 1996); Alexandre Popovi'c, *The Revolt of African Slaves in*

Iraq in the 3rd/9th Century, trans. Léon King (Princeton, NJ: Markus Weiner, 1999); Ehud R. Toledano, *Slavery and Abolition in the Ottoman Middle East* (Seattle: University of Washington Press, 1998); Leslie P. Peirce, *The Imperial Harem: Women and Sovereignty in the Ottoman Empire* (Oxford University Press, 1993). For Iran, see Behnaz Mirzai, *A History of Slavery and Emancipation in Iran, 1800–1929* (U. of Texas Press, 2017).

Graham W. Irwin's *Africans Abroad* (New York: Columbia University Press, 1977) provides translations of important documents. Information and accounts of the movement and experiences of slaves in Africa and the Middle East can be found in Martin Klein, *Slavery and Colonial Rule in French West Africa* (Cambridge: Cambridge University Press, 1998); Paul Lovejoy and Jan Hogendorn, *Slow Death for Slavery: The Course of Abolition in Northern Nigeria, 1897–1936* (Cambridge: Cambridge University Press, 1993); and John O. Hunwick and Eve Trout Powell, eds., *The African Diaspora in the Mediterranean Lands of Islam* (Princeton, NJ: Markus Weiner, 2002).

Concerning more contemporary sub-Saharan communities in North Africa and their cultures, see Chouki El Hamel's *Black Morocco: A History of Slavery, Race, and Islam* (New York: Cambridge University Press, 2014); Mohammed Ennaji, *Serving the Master: Slavery and Society in Nineteenth-Century Morocco*, trans. Seth Graebner (New York: St. Martin's Press, 1998); Émile Dermenghem, *Le culte des saints dans l'islam maghrébin* (Paris: Éditions Gallimard, 1954); Vincent Crapanzano, *The Hamadsha: A Study in Moroccan Ethnopsychiatry* (Berkeley: University of California Press, 1973); A.J.N., Tremearne, *The Ban of the Bori: Demons and Demon-Dancing in West and North Africa.* (London: Heath, Cranton, and Ouseley, 1914); and Janice Boddy, *Wombs and Alien Spirits: Women, Men, and the Zār Cult in Northern Sudan* (Madison: University of Wisconsin Press, 1989).

Context for the question of Africans in India is provided by K.N. Chaudhuri, *Asia before Europe: Economy and Civilisation of the Indian Ocean from the Rise of Islam to 1750* (Cambridge: Cambridge University Press, 1990). Joseph E. Harris was one of the first to pursue this topic in *The African Presence in Asia: Consequences of the East Asian Slave Trade* (Evanston, IL: Northwestern University Press, 1971). Fitzroy A. Baptiste's "The African Presence in India," *Africa Quarterly* 38 (no. 2, 1998: 92–126) is a fine analysis, linking the discussion to Trinidad. V.T. Rajshekhar raises vexing issues in *Dalit: The Black Untouchables of India* (Atlanta: Clarity Press, 1995), while Vijay Prashad argues for coalitions that are based on racial categories in "Afro-Dalits of the Earth, Unite!" *African Studies Review* 43 (no. 1, 2000: 189–201). The most recent literature is to be found in Edward Alpers and Amy Catlin-Jairazbhoy, eds., *Sidis and Scholars: Essays on African Indians* (New Delhi: Rainbow and New Jersey: Africa World Press, 2003).

Concerning Moorish Spain, one should begin with Jamil M. Abun-Nasr, *A History of the Maghrib in the Islamic Period* (Cambridge: Cambridge

University Press, 1987). For the adventurous with an interest in North Africa, look at Ibn Khaldun's *The Muqaddimah*, trans. Franz Rosenthal (New York: Pantheon Books, 1958) and his *Histoire des Berbères et des dynasties musulmanes de L'Afrique septentrionale*, trans. MacGuckin De Slane (Paris: P. Geuthner, 1925–56). Other references include L.P. Harvey, *Islamic Spain, 1250–1500* (Chicago: University of Chicago Press, 1990); D. Fairchild Ruggles, *Gardens, Landscape, and Vision in the Palaces of Islamic Spain* (University Park, PA: Pennsylvania State University Press, 2000); Ivan Van Sertima, *Golden Age of the Moor* (New Brunswick, NJ: Transaction Publishers, 1992); Mark D. Meyerson and Edward D. English, eds., *Christians, Muslims and Jews in Medieval and Early Modern Spain: Interaction and Cultural Change* (Notre Dame, IN: University of Notre Dame Press, 1999); Thomas F. Glick, *From Muslim Fortress to Christian Castle: Social and Cultural Change in Medieval Spain* (Manchester: Manchester University Press and and New York: St. Martin's Press, 1995); and Hugh Kennedy, *Muslim Spain and Portugal: A Political History of al-Andalus* (London and New York: Longman, 1996). Bernard Lewis' *The Muslim Discovery of Europe* (New York: W.W. Norton, 1982) and Maribel Fierro, *Judíos y musulmanes en al-Andalus y el Magreb: contactos intelectuales* (Madrid: Casa de Velázquez, 2002) provide a discussion of Europe's intellectual engagement with Muslims in Iberia and elsewhere.

II

"New" World Realities and Diaspora's Second Wave (to 1945)

———————

CHAPTER 4

Transatlantic Moment and the Dawn of Modernity

Part II of *Reversing Sail* begins with the transatlantic slave trade and the unleashing of global forces culminating in what is often referred to as "modernity." That is, transatlantic trafficking in human beings initiated processes resulting in economic, political, and cultural developments that continue to shape global relations. As such, the slave trade would fundamentally alter life on planet Earth.

The fifteenth century is the dawn of this modernity. It is the beginning of relations and hierarchies of power and privilege across race, class, and gender that started locally, then metastasized through the unfolding of colonial and empirical expansion. This expansion would prove unrelenting in a tireless search for novel ways of preserving privilege against the interests of those exploited and left marginalized in its wake. Race, class, and gender certainly existed as intertwined social and economic categories prior to the transatlantic trade, but they would acquire their distinctly contemporary significations with the transatlantic trade and slavery's spread throughout the Americas.

European engagement with the Muslim world would contribute to the former's cultural awakening, as well as to a heightened level of commercial activity with profound political transformations. An energetic Europe, bursting upon the world scene in the fifteenth century, would usher in this new era. Labor exploitation was key to this expansion, and critical to labor was the capture and enslavement of Africans. To be sure, African captives had been important and numerically significant in the Muslim world, but in addition to the transatlantic trade's exceptionally high volume and compact duration, the exploitation of Africans in the Americas stimulated forces of production in ways unknown in Muslim lands, leading to manufacturing and progressively maturing capitalist phases, each of which had as its central organizing principle the commodification of labor. Patriarchy itself would be reconfigured by industrialization, cross-racial relations, and mass migration. All of these developments began with the transatlantic slave trade, an unmitigated catastrophe for both Africa and its exiled daughters and sons.

The transatlantic slave trade is therefore unique in its relationship to global economic and political developments. Though the trade in captives through the Sahara, Red Sea, and Indian Ocean long antedates trafficking through the Atlantic, those trades did not result in the emergence of entirely novel relations of labor and power. And modernity's dawn was at great cost, as the transatlantic trade witnessed the relocation of millions of Africans from the Old to the New World, simultaneously ushering in the diaspora's second wave.

In discussing the slave trade, it is essential to view those trafficked first and foremost as human beings, with families, cultures, and sensibilities – no different from anyone else. They were neither animals nor objects, nor were they simply "slaves." They would undergo tremendous suffering, experiencing traumas prolonged and pervasive. Their calamity would generate centuries-long, intergenerational debate, existential in nature, over the reasons and purposes for their sorrows. Their internal dialogues would include fundamental questions concerning home and belonging, interrogating the precise nature of their relationship to both the New World and, especially, Africa. There would be consternation and confusion over who to blame for their predicament.

This chapter therefore initiates this long conversation by examining how certain global developments, initially independent of each other, gradually began to coalesce and, like the inner workings of a clock, gave rise to the transatlantic slave trade. In particular, four interlocking movements were foremost in creating the circumstances in which the African emerged as the principal source of servile labor, laying the foundations of the modern world: the cessation of Christian–Muslim conflict in Iberia and the Black Sea region; the expansion of sugar cane cultivation; European maritime expansion; and New World incursions.

Reconquista

Muslim forces in al-Andalus, there since the eighth century but never in control of the entire Iberian Peninsula, were continually threatened by Christian enemies during their nearly 800-year rule. The final stages of the struggle for Iberia, referred to as the "reconquest" by the Christians, unfolded at the same time as an equally momentous contest between Christian and Muslim powers raging near the Black Sea. There, Muslims fought for control of the old Byzantine or eastern Roman empire (referred to by the Muslims as *Rum*). In both Iberia and the Black Sea region, Muslims and Christians sold their captives into slavery.

The means by which war captives were marketed underscores the period's expansive commercial activity. Maritime innovations allowed the Italian city states of Pisa, Genoa, and Venice to participate in an eastern Mediterranean trade principally involving silk, spices, and sugar; but they also trafficked in captives. The Genoese, for example, sold Christian captives to Muslims, and Muslim captives to Christians, by the thousands, while the Venetians purchased captives from the Black Sea. Many, mostly women, were brought to Italy, where they performed agricultural and domestic tasks left undone by an Italian population reeling from the Black Death (peaking in the mid-fourteenth century). The newly enslaved joined the ranks of the similarly exploited in Crete and Cyprus, but especially in Sicily, southern Italy, Majorca, and southern Spain, where slavery was of considerable vintage. The enslaved in Sicily were mostly Muslim and, like Venice and other Italian sites, female.

If the fourteenth century saw increased reliance on captive labor in the Mediterranean, the fourteenth and fifteenth witnessed changes in the source of that labor. The reconquest of Portugal in 1267 signaled the beginning of the end of territorial disputes between Muslims and Christians. Muslim power in Spain also gradually declined as a result of battles and treaties, and as a result Iberia as a source of servile labor dried up, forcing Europe to turn elsewhere. By the end of the fourteenth century, the demand for slaves was largely met by captives from the Black Sea. But the struggle for Byzantium ended in 1453 with the Muslim conquest of Constantinople (henceforth Istanbul) and the consolidation of lands in Anatolia (Asia Minor) and those adjoining the Black Sea. Captives were thereafter funneled to Muslim markets. Some forty years later, in 1492, the combined forces of Castile and

Aragon defeated the Muslim's last bastion in Iberia, Granada, while also expelling the Jews and bringing the reconquest to an end.

With these reservoirs of servile labor tapped out, the northern Mediterranean was in need of workers, a demand occasioned by, among other projects, the cultivation of sugar cane. Spreading from south-east Asia to India in antiquity, sugar cane was introduced to Persians and Arabs during Islam's early years. They transferred its production to Syria and Egypt, and later to North Africa, southern Spain, Sicily, Cyprus, and Crete. European crusaders first came into contact with sugar in the Holy Lands, developing their own sugar plantations in Cyprus, Crete, and Sicily by the early thirteenth century. Europe would gradually acquire a taste for sugar (though expensive until the nineteenth century, and frequently used for medicinal purposes), having known only honey as a sweetener. Italian merchants spearheaded its production by supplying the capital and technology for its expansion into southern Iberia and (eventually) Madeira and the Canary Islands, off the West African coast.

While the Italians provided the financing, the Portuguese supplied the labor. How the Portuguese secured the labor, however, is very much connected to Indian Ocean commerce. Both the Italians and the Portuguese had long been interested in directly accessing its lucrative trade, as opposed to going through the Red Sea and Arabian Peninsula. This long-range goal of eliminating Muslim middlemen, together with such short-term objectives as securing outlets for West African gold, led the Portuguese and Italians to explore the West African coast during the first half of the fifteenth century. By 1475, the Portuguese had crossed the equator, and by 1487 they had rounded the Cape of Good Hope. By then, the Portuguese were exporting as much as 700 kilograms of West African gold in a peak year, while averaging 410 kilograms per year in the first twenty years of the sixteenth century, accounting for nearly one-fourth of all West African annual gold production. Vasco da Gama's 1497–8 voyage signaled Portugal's entrance into the Indian Ocean, and by 1520 the Portuguese were an Indian Ocean power.

Busy with gold and empire, the Portuguese were also tapping into West African labor. The Guanches, the indigenous population of the Canaries, were taken by the Portuguese and enslaved in both Madeira and the Mediterranean in the early fifteenth century. Lisbon began importing as many as 1,000 West Africans annually from 1441 to 1530, from where they were dispersed to southern Spain, Portugal, and elsewhere in the Mediterranean. But it was Madeira that emerged as the most important Portuguese possession, with its cultivation of sugar cane, initially with Guanche and then West African mainland labor (the Guanches were eventually decimated by European diseases). By the 1490s, Madeira was a wealthy Portuguese colony, exporting sugar throughout Europe and the Mediterranean, and in 1495, Madeiran planters began operations in the West African islands of São Tomé and Príncipe. Their success was such that the Old World slave trade remained numerically dominant until the middle of the sixteenth century.

The use of African servile labor to cultivate sugar cane therefore did not begin in the Americas, but in the Mediterranean and on West African coastal islands. Columbus' 1492 voyage to the "Indies" (to avoid circumnavigating Africa) set into motion a process that, among other things, transferred a system of slavery from the Old World to the New. The exploitation of African labor was consequently not the result of some far-reaching European design to demean and debilitate Africans and Africa. At least not in the fifteenth century. In a real sense, therefore, Africa was as much a casualty of geography as it was of greed.

Scope of the Trade

The trickle of African captives in the second half of the fifteenth century turned into a veritable flood by the seventeenth century. Columbus made his "discoveries," and in 1501 Pedro Cabral returned to Portugal with claims to Brazil. The movement of the Portuguese and Spanish into the New World saw the rise of mining and agricultural industries, and an increased reliance on captive African labor, due most importantly to epidemiology. In sum, Europeans introduced an entirely new disease environment into the Americas, from which indigenous peoples had no immunity. First Nation communities were subjected to smallpox, measles, influenza, diphtheria, whooping cough, chicken pox, typhoid, trichinosis, and enslavement, with catastrophic results. In central Mexico alone, an estimated pre-Columbian population of 25 million fell to 1.5 million by 1650, after which it slowly recovered; in Hispaniola, the native Taíno (viewed as either part of or separate from the Arawak) plummeted from approximately 7 million to less than 500 by the 1540s. In total, an indigenous population throughout the Americas as high as 100 million (or less than 20 million, depending on the estimate), was decimated by as much as 90 percent by the late eighteenth century, a process referred to as the Great Dying. The process of decimation would assume different guises through the nineteenth century, so that even where First Nation communities were not in decline throughout the Americas, the idea of their extinction would be used to justify their violent expulsion from (and confiscation of) their lands.

Africans, in contrast to Native Americans, shared a certain proportion of the Old World disease environment with Europeans. To be sure, African mortality rates in the Americas were alarmingly high, as were those for Europeans in places like seventeenth-century Virginia, but neither was quite as devastating as those visited upon the indigenous. The Great Dying, European familiarity with African enslaved labor in the Old World, and the cost-effectiveness of transporting Africans to the Americas explains their enslavement there, one of the most extensive mass movements in history, a displacement to beat all displacements.

Within ten years of Columbus' 1492 voyage, enslaved Africans were in the New World, along with sugar cane and experienced planters from Portugal and the Canaries. Hispaniola (present-day Haiti and the Dominican Republic), Cuba, and other Spanish-claimed territories were early destinations, and by the 1520s, Africans were replacing the indigenous Taíno in servile capacities, including gold and silver mining. From 1521 to 1594, between 75,000 and 90,000 Africans were brought to Spanish-held territories, with over half going to Mexico. Indeed, between 1521 and 1639 some 110,525 Africans entered Mexico and Peru, and by the time of formal emancipation in 1827, some 200,000 Africans had labored in Mexico alone. In 1560, Africans outnumbered Europeans in Cuba and Hispaniola, and by 1570 they equaled the number of Europeans in Mexico City and Vera Cruz.

Not all Africans entering the New World in the sixteenth century were enslaved, as some free Africans took part in military ventures alongside white conquistadores. Africans and their descendants had long resided in various Spanish towns, where some experienced a freedom qualified by substantial financial hardship. The opportunity to sail for the New World was therefore welcomed by individuals like Juan González de Léon, who among other things served as an interpreter of the Taíno language; and Juan Garrido, who came to Seville in 1496 and thereafter enlisted for service in the Americas. Garrido fought against the Taíno in Hispaniola, and both men participated in Ponce de Léon's conquest of Puerto Rico, beginning in 1508. From Puerto Rico, and with the assistance of both men, Ponce de Léon raided the Caribs in Santa Cruz, Guadeloupe, and Dominica. González de Léon and Garrido even accompanied Ponce de Léon to Florida in 1513 and 1521, where they mined for gold.

Notwithstanding these black explorers and conquerors (dubious distinctions to say the least), slavery in sixteenth-century Spanish-claimed lands was far more significant, and even more so in Portuguese-held Brazil. Sugar cane was planted as early as the 1520s in the north-eastern region of Pernambuco, and with the arrival of planters from Madeira and São Tomé, the industry steadily grew. Portuguese activity in Kongo and Angola saw a dramatic increase in the importation of African captives, and by 1600 Brazil had out-stripped Madeira as the world's leading sugar producer. Brazil was the port of call for the vast majority of captive Africans in the Americas for the whole of the seventeenth century, accounting for nearly 52 per-cent of the total.

The early African presence in the Americas was but the beginning of woes. The export figure remains a matter of debate, with some arguing for estimates that trend toward 100 million (including losses in Africa). The scholarly consensus, however, is that over 12.5 million Africans were exported from Africa, out which 10.7 million arrived alive, translating into a loss during the Middle Passage of about 15 percent. Nearly 65 percent of the total were males, and at least 26 percent children. The transatlantic slave trade spanned some 400 years, from the fifteenth through the nineteenth centuries; nearly 60 percent of all Africans imported into the Americas made the fateful voyage between 1721 and 1820, while 82 percent were transported between 1701 and 1850. In comparison with the trade in Africans through the Sahara, Red Sea, and Indian Ocean, the bulk of the Atlantic trade took less than one-tenth of the time.

Many European nations were complicit. Britain, France, Sweden, Denmark, and Holland would all join Spain and Portugal at different points in time, as did Brazil and the United States. From the fifteenth century through the middle of the seventeenth, Spain and Portugal controlled the trade; Spain transported relatively few captives under its own flag, relying instead upon foreign firms to supply its territories under a licensing system called the *asiento*. From the mid-seventeenth century, various European entities entered the slaving business in addition to those previously mentioned, including the Brandenburgers, Genoese, and Courlanders. Throughout the eighteenth century and into the first decade of the nineteenth, at the height of the trafficking, British and French involvement accounted for at least 50 percent of the trade.

Of all the voyages for which there are data from between 1501 and 1866, some 88 percent of these captive Africans wound up in Brazil and the Caribbean (including Cuba and Puerto Rico); indeed, Brazil alone imported 45 percent of the total trade. That part of the Caribbean in which the English and French languages became dominant – yet transformed through African inflections, syntaxes, and vocabularies – received 32 percent of the total, with the "British" Caribbean taking in twice as many as the French. Spanish-claimed lands accounted for 12 percent of the Africans (with Cuba alone receiving 7 percent of the entire trade), after which North America took in less than 4 percent.

African Provenance

A consideration of where Africans actually came from is critical to understanding the unfolding of histories in the Americas. That is, while it is obviously important to note the specific derivation of European influences, and to more fully acknowledge and take into consideration already existing First Nation societies, it is equally important to appreciate that Africans themselves emerged out of specific cultural spheres and historical contexts, and that simply viewing them as "Africans" (or worse, as "slaves") tells us virtually nothing about them.

The quest to learn something therefore begins with the observation that approximately 83 percent of those exported through the Atlantic came from one of only four regions: West Central Africa (45 percent), the Bight of Benin (16 percent), the Bight of Biafra (13 percent), and the Gold Coast (9 percent). The busiest ports in these regions were Cabinda and Luanda (West Central Africa), Cape Castle and Anomabu (Gold Coast), Bonny and Calabar (Bight of Biafra), and Whydah (Bight of Benin) (see Figure 3). Slavers (slave ships) often took on their full complement of captives in single regions of supply, and Africans emanating from the same regions tended to be transported to the same New World destinations. Captives from West Central Africa comprised 43 percent of those who disembarked in Saint-Domingue (present-day

FIGURE 3 Cape Coast Castle. Werner Forman Archive / HIP / Art Resource, NY. A black and white version of this figure will appear in some formats. For the color version, please refer to the plate section.

Haiti), 40 percent of those brought to "Spanish" America, and an astounding 70 percent of all Africans imported into Brazil. The Bight of Benin, in turn, was a significant contributor to Bahia and Pernambuco (north-eastern Brazil), as well as the "French" Caribbean, accounting for 30 percent of all Africans brought to northern Brazil, and 26 percent of those trafficked to the Francophone Antilles. As for what would become the British Caribbean, some 26 percent of all Africans came from the Gold Coast (contemporary Ghana and Ivory Coast), but even more – nearly 32 percent – hailed from the Bight of Biafra (what is now south-eastern Nigeria and western Cameroon), with each region equally contributing 29 percent of those brought to Jamaica. Sierra Leone (a region that includes the Windward Coast in this discussion) provided almost 6 percent of the total export figure, followed by Senegambia and South East Africa at 6 percent and 4.3 percent, respectively.

Once Africans were brought to an initial port of call, they could be subsequently shipped – either immediately or after some years – to another location; tracking these transshipments (which in instances could be substantial) remains a challenge for scholars.

Notwithstanding such redistribution, initial destination data remain very useful in determining the broad contours of settlement patterns. As yet another illustration of how these patterns could differ from location to location, the Senegambian total contribution of 6 percent to the trade obscures the fact that in what became the United States they accounted for nearly 24 percent of the Africans brought there. As would be true throughout the Americas, this specific demographic pattern is crucial to understanding the unfolding of cultural expressions and political developments in North America (see Map 4).

A review of these regions reveals considerable complexity, not only with respect to language and culture, but also as it concerns forms of government, agriculture, regional and transregional commerce, and technologies relating to each of these categories. Stated differently, while there were many similarities, there were appreciable differences of every kind among the captives.

West Central Africa was a vast region dominated by the states and populations of Kongo and Angola. Life conformed to the four ecological zones (river, swamp, forest, and savannah) of the Congo River basin, the people further linked by closely related Bantu languages. Statecraft in the region ranged from kingdoms to villages, with Kongo, Ndongo, Kasanje, and Loango representing states of substantial size and elaboration. Agriculture, the material basis for these societies, was usually performed by women, although men usually cleared the land, in addition to hunting and tending fruit and palm trees.

Communities throughout West Central Africa believed in a supreme deity, often referred to as Nzambi a Mpungu, and related spiritual entities. Since the fifteenth century, a tradition of Christianity was established in the region, the result of Portuguese commercial activities. The social history of seventeenth- and eighteenth-century Kongo arguably revolved around the exchange between Christianity and Kongolese religion, giving rise to an Africanized Christianity spectacularly symbolized by the life of Dona Beatrice Kimpa Vita (1682–1706), leader of a religious movement that sought to reconstruct a Kongo reeling from war. A prophet and priest, or *kitomi*, her claim to be the incarnation of St. Anthony, combined with her teachings that Jesus, Mary, and the prophets were all Kongolese, are examples of the ways in which Christianity was reconfigured to accommodate West Central African sensibilities. She would be burned at the stake for heresy.

Reinterpretations of Christianity in West Central Africa were influenced by preexisting beliefs, and one of the more arresting was the view that the departed spirits of those who had led good lives on earth go on to live in *mpemba*, a subterranean realm separated from the living by a large body of water, or *kalunga*. Within ten months of entering *mpemba*, the deceased change color, becoming white. It is therefore no surprise that Europeans were initially viewed as departed spirits, having crossed the *kalunga* of the Atlantic (see Map 5).

The Bight of Benin, the second leading source of captives, was the land of the Fon, Ewe, and Yoruba groups. The Ewe (concentrated in present-day Togo and south-eastern Ghana) were organized into more than 100 autonomous states, whereas the Fon of Dahomey (contemporary Benin) absorbed Weme, Allada, and Whydah to form a single centralized power in the eighteenth century. The Yoruba of what is now south-western Nigeria also witnessed expansionist polities, but were much more centered on their respective towns, and thereby much more urban than others. There are many exceptional features of Fon-Ewe-Yoruba cultures, not the least of which are the bronzes and sculptures of Benin and Ife. But the deities of the Fon-Ewe (*vodun* or *loas*) and the Yoruba (*orishas*) are so numerous and unique that they further distinguish the region. The Yoruba *orishas* include Olodumare (high god), Oshun (goddess of fresh water and sensuality), Ogun (warrior god of iron), Eshu-Elegba (or Ellegua, trickster god of the crossroads), Shango (god of thunder and lightning), and Yemanja (mother of all *orishas* and goddess of the oceans), and correspond in some instances to the Fon-Ewe *loas* of Mawu-Lisa (high god), Aziri (a riverain goddess), Gu (god of iron, warfare), and Legba (god of the crossroads, keeper of the gate). Mawu-Lisa, for example, is a composite of female and male characteristics, representing the Fon-Ewe ideal. These beliefs would become central to practices in such places as Haiti, Brazil, and Louisiana.

One of the more fascinating aspects of Dahomey society were its female warriors, the *ahosi*. Possibly formed in the early seventeenth century from a society of female hunters called *gbeto*, these soldiers would serve with exceptional valor as the palace guard, and were technically the king's wives (though they were never intimate with him). Under King Gezo (ruled 1818 to 1858), their numbers expanded from around 600 to 6,000, during a time of intense military conflict. They were far less in number by the end of the nineteenth century and Dahomey's conflict with the French, but they continued to demonstrate exceptional ferocity. The *ahosi* may well serve as a model for the "Dora Milaje" of the 2018 film, *Black Panther*.

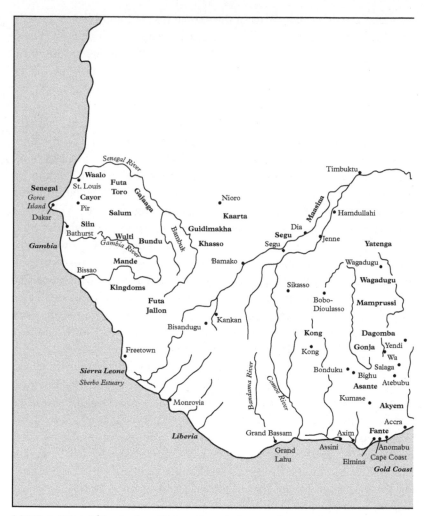

MAP 4 West Africa in the eighteenth and nineteenth centuries

In contrast to the Yoruba, most of the Igbo, Ibibio, Igala, Efik, Ijo, Ogoni, and other groups of the Bight of Biafra, the third leading source of captives, were organized into villages. The Igbo, Ibibio, and Ijo were the largest, and the Igbo in particular were marked by dense populations and agrarian economies. For the most part, they featured independent "village democracies," in which important decisions were made by a male peasantry individually distinguished by varying statuses of achievement. Men conducted long-distance

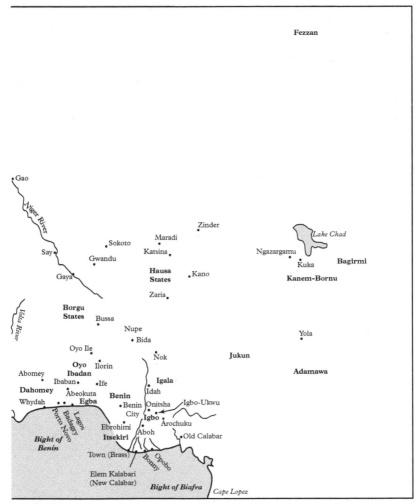

MAP 4 *(cont.)*

commerce, but women controlled local trade, keeping any money they earned in communities that were mostly patrilineal (tracing descent and inheritance through the male line). Though not trained in the same way as Dahomean female soldiers, women nonetheless also regularly fought to defend their villages. But above all else, they were revered as mothers, wives, and keepers of the soil. Regarding land, they enjoyed a special connection to Ala (or Ana) the earth mother; Ala and the land (*ala*) were highly esteemed and inextricably

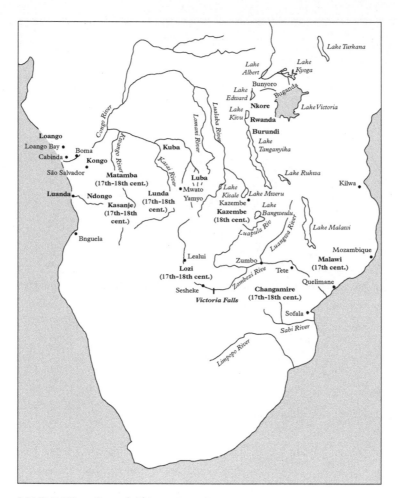

MAP 5 West Central Africa, 1600–1800

interwoven, forming the basis of Igbo law. Though functionally the most important deity in Igbo society, Ala was not the high, creator god. That honor was held by Chineke, or Chukwu, who like the Fon-Ewe's Mawu-Lisa was a blend of male and female components (*chi* and *eke*), and from whom sprang powerful spiritual forces known as the *alusi* or *agbara*, as well as the personal guardian spirit or *chi* of each individual. The ancestral dead, the *ndichie*, added to the realm of the disembodied.

According to Igbo beliefs that included reincarnation, the individual in pre-birth consultation with his or her *chi* undertook a plan of action designed to result in high individual achievement, and was guided by a philosophy and value system that stressed success – known as *ikenga*. The individual drive of the Igbo, together with their regard for the earth and belief in destiny, would clearly influence the direction of African-derived cultures in the Americas.

As for the fourth leading source of trafficked Africans, Gold Coast's southern half was dominated by Akan and Ga speakers, with the former divided into the Twi and Baule languages. Like the Igbo, women were prominent in Akan societies, as is evident in the belief that their ancestresses came from the sky, or earth, to found the first Akan towns in the forests. Matrilineal for the most part, Akan clans each claimed descent from a common mother. Each clan had a male and a female head, and women played critical roles as advisors and heads of the matriclans. Similar to the Igbo, the Akan espoused belief in an earth mother Asase Yaa, who together with the high god Onyame (or Onyankopon) created the world. In keeping with most African theologies, the Akan high gods are remote, but the next order of deity, the *abosom* (numbering in the hundreds), are accessible.

Akan societies contributed to the wide variety of political contexts out of which captives were taken, and the Akan were either part of the expansionist Asante empire (established around 1680), or they lived in its shadow. Asante was a vast realm ruled by the *Asantehene* (king), together with a bureaucracy intent on maximizing trade with both the African hinterland and with Europeans on the coast. Gold, in addition to captives, was a key export, and gold dust was the standard currency of Asante. One of the most militarily powerful and structurally complex states in all of Africa, Asante's political union was symbolized by the *Sika Dwa*, the Golden Stool.

This brief consideration of the African context concludes with Sierra Leone, a region whose interior was dominated by the large Muslim theocracy of Futa Jallon, and by a series of independent, small-scale villages along the coast composed of multiple groups. Discussion of the coast underscores the lifestyles of a majority who were farmers, fishers, and hunters. Although many groups were patrilineal, women could wield extraordinary influence as expert agriculturalists as well as leaders of "secret societies." Concerning the former, women cultivated rice, cotton, and indigo, skills that would be coveted in North America. Secret societies, in turn, were instrumental in intervillage diplomacy and commerce, and were critical to the maintenance of social order. The Sande or Bundu society of

women was one of the better-known organizations, but women also
played leading roles in such male societies as the Poro. What therefore
emerges from coastal Sierra Leone are traditions of proscribed,
limited government – in contrast to such centralized, powerful states
as Asante – in conjunction with gender relations that were possibly
more egalitarian than elsewhere.

Though located in Sierra Leone's hinterland, Futa Jallon was
also vitally connected to the Senegambian region. We have already
discussed Islam in Africa, so it is sufficient to observe that from the
seventeenth through the nineteenth centuries, militant or reformist
Islamic states were founded in Senegambia (and indeed throughout
West Africa), with Futa Jallon among them. Muslims captured non-
Muslims in wars, but were themselves also captured, with captives
from both sides finding themselves transported to the Americas –
and in such places as Natchez, Mississippi. Muslims captured in the
interior would have been taken to the coast and exported from
several regions, especially Senegambia, Sierra Leone, and the
Bight of Benin. Muslim captives from the Bight of Benin mostly
came from conflict between Muslim Hausa-Fulani (related groups
in contemporary northern Nigeria) and Yoruba combatants (some
of whom were Muslims themselves), and many would find themselves in Brazil – particularly in Bahia and Pernambuco. Muslims
were also exported from the Gold Coast, but to a lesser extent.
A number of Malagasy and Swahili captives from the coast of South
East Africa were also brought to the Americas, and some were
probably Muslim, though many were from the interior and
therefore non-Muslim.

Belly of the Whale

The transatlantic transport of all of these various Africans to the
Americas qualifies as the quintessential moment of transfiguration,
the height of human alienation and disorientation. It is a phenomenon
unlike any other, with millions uprooted from family and friends and
deposited in lands and under conditions constituting an alternate
universe. It cannot be compared with the millions of Europeans who
voluntarily crossed the Atlantic, a journey which for all of their
troubles was their collective choice. Words will never convey the
agony, despair, and bewilderment of these innocents, the depth of

their suffering, the pain of their separation. The transatlantic voyage, the so-called the Middle Passage, was an unspeakable horror.

The movement across the Atlantic necessarily began on African soil, where those captured in the hinterland were brought to coastal holding stages, or barracoons. Between initial capture and the barracoon, anything was possible, including escape. Alternatively, they could have been taken north to the trans-Saharan trade, or retained and enslaved within Africa, where eventual export to the Americas (or the Mediterranean) was a continual possibility. Welcome to a realm of heightened uncertainty and fear, gateway to lands of the macabre.

Reference to "captives" points to the debate over the capture itself. Do scholars who maximize African involvement in the abduction and sale of other Africans do so for the purpose of minimizing Western culpability? Are those who are appalled by the very suggestion of African participation in the slave trade motivated by the same logic, only in reverse? The truth of the matter may be more nuanced than straightforward. There can be no doubt that European and American demand for slave labor drove the entire enterprise. It is also the case that Europeans entered Africa and hunted humans like prey, especially in the case of the Portuguese in Angola and Mozambique. But it is equally undeniable that, as was true of the trans-Saharan trade, there were African groups and governments involved in the capture of other Africans, together with instances of cooperation between European and African traffickers. For example, at Bonny, in the Bight of Biafra, and points along the Gold Coast, Europeans used "boating," sailing small vessels upriver to purchase captives from villages along the banks, a practice also found along the Windward Coast. While other African states and groups resisted slaving, and in instances were successful, clearly their efforts were unable to save over 12.5 million others.

To understand the foregoing, the notion of "African unity" at this point in history must be debilitated, as it was alien to the continent until relatively recent times. As has been discussed, Africa was inhabited by communities of differing cultures, religions, and political agendas, and these differences were exacerbated (or created) to feed the slave trade. Raids, kidnapping, and warfare produced most captives, while individuals found guilty of crimes, or sold into bondage to pay debts, were also taken. Indeed, with the acceleration of the slave trade came a corresponding surge in the number of persons convicted

FIGURE 4 Slave coffle. Pictures from History / Granger, NYC – All rights reserved. Image No. 0607705.

of crimes. Can African participation in the slave trades be divorced from the engines of European and American demand? Culpability was shared, but was it symmetrical? Does the answer matter?

Captured Africans, in their forced march from the hinterland to the sea, could cover substantial distances, anywhere from 100 to 700 kilometers, depending upon place and time, and could take four months or longer to reach the coast (see Figure 4). Loss of life during the trek is conservatively estimated to have averaged from 10 to 15 percent, while in Angola sometimes approximating an obscene 40 percent. Captives reaching the shore could remain there for months, due to poor health and the need to convalesce, or to wait for the next slaver (slave ship). Ports with established traffic attracted larger numbers of slavers with greater frequency and differed, along with the various kinds of barracoons, in type and size. Some barracoons were simply pens exposed to the elements, sometimes adjacent to European factories (trading posts). Others ranged from weather-protected dwellings to fortified castles. Still others, according to Mungo Park's late eighteenth-century observation along the Gambia, were compounds attached to nearby communities, for "if no immediate opportunity offers them to advantage, they are distributed among the neighbouring villages until a slave ship arrives, or until they can be sold to black traders who sometime purchase on speculation."[1] Park described their circumstances, stating that "the poor wretches are kept constantly fettered, two and two of them being chained together, and employed in the labours of the field; and I am sorry to add, are very scantily fed, as well as harshly treated."

The Angolan experience paralleled that of the Gambian. The former involved coffles averaging 100 captives from the interior. They were fed the cheapest food – often rotten – which they were also forced to carry. Bound and brutalized, they were taken to the Luanda port, where conditions remained deplorable, and there branded three times: on the right breast with a royal coat of arms, on the left breast or arm to indicate individual ownership, and on the chest with a small cross, as captives were baptized before embarking for Brazil. They might then wait for weeks, if not months, chained and exposed, with little to eat and little to wear, eating, sleeping, and eliminating in the most intimate of spaces. As many as 12,000 captives arrived annually in Luanda for export, with 6,000–7,000 surviving for eventual ship-ment. The "putrid miasmas" of human filth, disease, and death filled the air, circulating throughout the city.

The boarding of captives did not therefore necessarily mean the voyage was underway. There were often further delays of weeks, if not months, as a slaver sailed from barracoon to barracoon before reach-ing the ship's full complement. As such, a direct Middle Passage of two or three months, while horrific enough, does not represent the entire trafficking experience. Adding to that trauma was the period during which the slaver slowly filled, as well as the period from initial capture to eventual embarkation – the barracoon stage – which alone could last the better part of a year.

Examples include the *James*, which departed England on April 5, 1675, but did not arrive in Barbados until May 21, 1676. Having reached Assini (on the Gold Coast) on August 30, the *James* exchanged commodities for both gold and captives at several points along the coast until January 11, 1676, when the vessel arrived at the

---

[1] Mugo Park, *Travels in the Interior Districts of Africa* (London: Evert Duyckinck, 1799; reprint, New York: Arno Press, 1971), p. 18.

English factory near Wyemba. There the slaver boarded captives each day for about a week, most of whom were described as "very thin ordinary slaves," indicative of the preceding ordeal onshore. The *James* made yet another stop at Anomabu before setting sail for Barbados on March 8, 1676.

Similarly, the Dutch slaver *St. Jan* began loading captives at Ardra in the Bight of Benin, also called Slave Coast, on March 4, 1659. The ship continued east, picking up additional captives and supplies in the Bight of Biafra. By the time the *St. Jan* left the Biafran area for the Cameroon River on May 22, it had boarded 219 Africans. From that time until August 17, the vessel journeyed along the coast in search of food as far as Cape Lopez (just south of the equator). The search for provisions was a major preoccupation for slavers, with the captain of the *James* complaining that his search for food was a "great trouble." His concern was echoed by the captain of the *Arthur*, operating in the Biafran Bight, in February of 1678: "This day we sentt our Boat att Donus to see whatt might be done there, wee findinge negroes to be Brought on Board of us fast enough but wee nott free to deale in many fearing lest wee should take in negroes and have noe provisions for them." It was Barbot's calculation (at the beginning of the eighteenth century) that a "ship that takes in five hundred slaves, must provide above a hundred thousand yams; which is very difficult, because it is hard to stow them, by reason they take up so much room."[2]

Once purchased by European slavetraders, captives were often branded with the company's coat of arms. These became their only coats, as they were usually stripped of all clothing. In 1699, Bosman recorded that "they came aboard stark naked as well women as men; in which condition they are obliged to continue, if the master of the Ship is not so charitable (which he commonly is) as to bestow something on them to cover their nakedness." Some 128 years after Bosman, Mayer noted in 1827 that, two days before loading captives onto the slaver, the heads of both males and females were shaved. And then:

> On the appointed day, the *barracoon* or slave-pen is made joyous by the abundant "feed" which signalizes the negro's last hours in his native country. The feast over, they are taken alongside the vessel in canoes;

---

[2] Elizabeth Donnan, *Documents Illustrative of the History of the Slave Trade to America* (Washington, DC: Carnegie Institute, 1930), vol. 2, p. 15.

and as they touch the deck, they are entirely stripped, so that women as well as men go out of Africa as they came into it – *naked*. This precaution, it will be understood, is indispensable; for perfect nudity, during the whole voyage, is the only means of securing cleanliness and health.
(Brantz Mayer, *Captain Canot, or, Twenty Years of an African Slaver*, New York: Appleton, 1854, p. 102)

Slavetraders may have been concerned with hygiene, but they were not oblivious to the psychological implications of forced nakedness. Contrary to popular ignorance, most Africans did not go about butt naked, swinging through trees, but in fact placed great value on textiles, the primary commodity for which captives were traded to Europeans in the first place. The humiliation of prolonged exposure before captors and the opposite sex, as well as children, seared an overwhelming sense of vulnerability into the psyche (see Figure 5).

But captives did not suffer silently. To the contrary, they often rebelled. To prevent mutiny and escape, male slaves were chained together at the wrists and ankles in groups of two as soon as they were boarded. Women and girls were physically separated from the males and usually unfettered, an arrangement that became standard procedure by the last quarter of the eighteenth century. The segregation of the sexes was maintained throughout the voyage except when permitted on deck. Such precautions reflect the fact that Europeans had learned to prepare for rebellion as early as 1651, when captain Bartholomew Haward was told that "there is put aboard your Pinck *Supply* 30 paire of shackles and boults for such of your negers as are rebellious and we pray you be veary carefull to keepe them undr and let them have their food in due season that they ryse not against you, as they have done in other ships."[3]

The separation of male and female captives facilitated the long, sordid history of the rape of African women and girls by European men, a humiliation that began long before they were ever sold to New World planters (who promptly went out and did the same thing). Though crews were given sexual access to captive females as a matter of policy, it was not simply for their sexual gratification. Rape, as an implement of power and domination, has also been wielded throughout human history as a weapon of war, a means of debilitating an

---

[3] Donnan, *Documents Illustrative*, vol. i, p. 130.

FIGURE 5 The Africans of the slave bark *Wildfire* brought into Key West in April of 1860. From *Harper's Weekly* (June 2, 1860), vol. 4, p. 344. Library of Congress, Prints and Photographs Division, LC-USZ62-41678.

adversary's resolve. In this way, even a small number of females, violated infrequently, was sufficient to establish the captive population's vulnerability.

Captain Bartholomew Haward's admonition to keep captives below deck, in the hold of the slaver, until the African shoreline was no longer in sight was usually heeded. This was done to discourage revolt, for the African maintaining visual contact with her homeland was sorely tempted to return. The *Hannibal*'s Captain Phillips poignantly records the African response: "The negroes are so wilful and loth to leave their own country, that they have often leap'd out of the canoes, boat and ship, into the sea, and kept under water till they were drowned to avoid being taken up and saved by our own boats, which pursued them; they having a more dreadful apprehension of Barbadoes than we have of hell."[4]

That the Africans were in such dread of the New World was related to their fear that Europeans were cannibals. Barbot records that it "has been observ'd before, that some slaves fancy they are carry'd to be eaten, which make them desperate; and others are so on account of their captivity: so that if care be not taken, they will mutiny and destroy the ship's crew in hopes to get away."[5] In seeing whites for the first time, Olaudah Equiano became "persuaded that I had got into a world of bad spirits, and that they were going to kill me ... When I recovered a little, I found some black people around me ... I asked them if we were not to be eaten by these white men with horrible looks, red faces, and long hair."[6] Equiano's concerns were consistent with those in West Central Africa (Equiano may have been Igbo, from what is now south-eastern Nigeria), where Europeans were perceived as spirits, their advent a portent of death. Such was the fear of the New World, so overwhelming was the sense of separation from family and land, that many chose to starve themselves; refusing to eat was an option so pervasive that crews often force-fed their captives, giving them a "cat," or flogging. In the face of their past capture, present suffering, and bleak future, many chose suicide by other means. Those who could went over the side; those who could not often went insane.

But many did not go insane or over the side. And because the slave trade was, in the final analysis, a business transaction, the African had to be maintained in some fashion. Captives were therefore usually fed twice a day aboard the slavers. Their diet included horse beans, rice, yams, limes, lemons, ground Indian corn, and

---

[4] Frederick Dalcho, *An Historical Account of the Episcopal Church in South Carolina* (Charleston: E. Thayer, 1820; reprint, New York: Arno Press, 1972), p. 104.

[5] Donnan, *Documents Illustrative*, vol. 1, p. 462.

[6] Robert J. Allison, ed., *The Interesting Narrative of Olaudah Equiano, or Gustavus Vasa, the African* (London: printed for the author, 1789), in Philip D. Curtin, ed., *Africa Remembered* (Madison: University of Wisconsin Press, 1967), pp. 91–4.

palm oil. And though fish caught along the voyage was occasionally provided, meat was extremely rare. Obviously a necessity, water was rationed.

Practitioners called surgeons were often included among the crew to attend the medical needs of the captives. Of dubious ability and questionable reputation, these "surgeons" were further restricted by the few resources available to them. They monitored the health of the captives on a regular basis, segregating those with serious illnesses while treating them with such physics as wine or sago, a starch-like substance. Surgeons examined captives on African coastal shores to determine their fitness, and again helped to prepare them for market once the New World was reached.

The consequences of the surgeons' limitations, together with the cramped, filthy conditions aboard the slavers, were nothing short of ruinous. Diseases assailing the captives included dysentery (the "flux" or the "bloody flux"), measles, scurvy, and "fever." Ophthalmia, a condition leading to blindness (possibly related to river blindness), was widespread. Yaws (bacteria-induced, infectious skin lesions that may also affect cartilage and bone) was as prevalent and potentially fatal. Intestinal worms added to the collective misery. Aside from the bloody flux, contracted from food and water contamination, smallpox was of greatest concern; whole ships were quarantined upon reaching New World destinations until "the pox" had run its course and was no longer contagious.

Spacing also contributed to the collective misery. Scholars may disagree over the frequency of "tight packing" and its impact on the captives' health, but there can be no question that tight packing contributed to suffering, and suffering is definitely a health issue.

In addition to those who did not survive the Middle Passage, many perished in Africa itself. Depending upon the specific region in question, from 10 to 40 percent of those captured in the interior died en route to the sea, at which point at least another 10 percent are estimated to have expired while awaiting export – the barracoon phase. When mortality rates from points of capture through the Middle Passage are combined (rates which do not take into consideration those initially killed in slaving raids and wars), from 35 to 65 percent of those captured for eventual export to the Americas never arrived; that is, as many as 17.7 million people (and possibly many more) were forced into a process that eventually yielded 10.7 million Africans exiled to the New World. Mutinies and shipwrecks would add to the hosts of the dead.

Slave ships, in the Dutchman Bosman's words, were "always foul and stinking"; the "stench of a slave ship could be scented for miles," its deck "so covered with blood and mucous that it resembled a slaughter-house."[7] So miserable were the conditions that the surgeon Isaac Wilson believed two-thirds of the 155 who perished aboard the *Elizabeth* (out of 602) died from "melancholy," observing that once the captives were taken aboard, "a gloomy pensiveness seemed to overcast their countenances and continued in a great many." The sounds emanating from slavers usually included a "howling melancholy noise."[8] To combat this mother of all blues, captives were brought on deck and forced to dance and sing, and were sometimes beaten to make them comply. Arguably minstrelsy's forerunner, such feigned animation in the midst of so much sorrow demonstrates the deep and complicated history of black performance, its relationship to coercion both complex and disturbing.

From the belly of the whale, Africa's sons and daughters were distributed throughout the New World, occupying every conceivable place, performing every imaginable task. The terror of the Passage would be seared into their consciousness, and they would pass on the memory of their trauma to progeny. But for all of the transatlantic slave trade's horror, it did not completely rupture ties to the homeland. Africa would remain a central consideration in the hearts and minds of many, with the dream of reconnecting, of reversing sail, one of the diaspora's central challenges.

Suggestions for Further Reading

The best place to begin examining the volume of the transatlantic slave trade is the database compiled by David Eltis, Stephen D. Behrendt, David Richardson, and Herbert Klein entitled *The Trans-Atlantic Slave Trade: A Database on CD-ROM*, www.slavevoyages.org (Cambridge: Cambridge University Press, 1999), which contains records for over 36,000 voyages, the most comprehensive response to Philip D. Curtin's groundbreaking *The Atlantic Slave Trade: A Census* (Madison: University of Wisconsin Press, 1969). Works mentioned in the preceding chapter's suggested reading section, such as those of Patrick Manning and Paul E. Lovejoy, are applicable here as well. The literature on

[7] Donnan, *Documents Illustrative*, vol. I, p. 442.
[8] Donnan, *Documents Illustrative*, vol. I, pp. 290–1.

the transatlantic slave trade, exploring the economic, political, and social implications for all or segments of those involved, is in fact vast; one would want to include, however, Joseph E. Inikori's *Forced Migration: The Impact of the Export Slave Trade on African Societies* (New York: Africana Pub. Co., 1982); Joseph E. Inikori and Stanley L. Engerman, *The Atlantic Slave Trade: Effects on Economies, Societies, and Peoples in Africa, the Americas, and Europe* (Durham, NC: Duke University Press, 1992); and Joseph C. Miller, *Way of Death: Merchant Capitalism and the Angolan Slave Trade, 1730–1830* (Madison: University of Wisconsin, 1988).

John K. Thornton, *Africa and Africans in the Making of the Atlantic World, 1400–1800* (Cambridge: Cambridge University Press, 1998), 2nd ed., and David Brion Davis, *Slavery and Human Progress* (New York: Oxford University Press, 1984), have excellent chapters on the emergence of the trade in the Mediterranean and Iberia. Also see John Thornton, *A Cultural History of the Atlantic World, 1250–1820* (Cambridge: Cambridge University Press, 2012). The work of A.J.R. Russell-Wood, especially *A World on the Move: The Portuguese in Africa, Asia, and the Americas, 1415–1808* (Manchester: Carcanet Press and New York: St. Martin's Press, 1992) provides keen insight into Iberian developments as they relate to the slave trade. Ruth Pike's *Aristocrats and Traders: Sevillian Society in the Sixteenth Century* (Ithaca, NY and London: Cornell University Press, 1972) is also pertinent, while Eric R. Wolf's *Europe and the People Without History* (Berkeley: University of California Press, 1982) remains a path-clearing contribution.

For the Middle Passage, see Olaudah Equiano, *The African: The Interesting Narrative of the Life of Olaudah Equiano* (London: Black Classics, 1998) for a first-hand account, though Vincent Carretta argues Equiano was probably born in South Carolina, not West Africa, in his *Equiano, the African: Biography of a Self-Made Man* (Athens: University of Georgia Press, 2005). Elizabeth Donnan's *Documents Illustrative of the History of the Slave Trade to America* (Washington, DC: Carnegie Institute, 1930–5) remains an important source of information on this and other aspects of the slave trade. For interpretative analyses, see Herbert S. Klein, *The Middle Passage: Comparative Studies in the Atlantic Slave Trade* (Princeton, NJ: Princeton University Press, 1978).

A discussion of the Middle Passage as well as the origins and cultures of transported Africans can be found in Michael A. Gomez, *Exchanging Our Country Marks: The Transformation of African Identities in the Colonial and Antebellum South* (Chapel Hill: University of North Carolina Press, 1998). The slave ship itself is the focus of Marcus Rediker's *The Slave Ship: A Human History* (New York: Viking, 2007); and Sowande' M. Mustakeem, *Slavery at Sea: Terror, Sex, and Sickness in the Middle Passage* (Urbana-Champaign: University of Illinois, 2016). An interesting and at times technical study of the impact of Old World migrations into the New is located in Guy A. Settipane, ed., *Columbus and the New World: Medical Implications* (Providence,

RI: Oceanside, 1995). For an important discussion of the ways in which "Indian distinction" was mythologized as a means to appropriate land and justify murder, see Yuko Miki, *Frontiers of Citizenship: A Black and Indigenous History of Postcolonial Brazil* (New York: Cambridge University Press, 2018). Finally, treatment of these and other issues is contained in Joseph E. Harris, *The African Diaspora*, ed. Alusine Jalloh and Stephen E. Maizlish (College Station, Texas: Texas A&M University Press, 1996).

CHAPTER 5

Enslavement

Africans experienced the most painful of introductions to the New World. The forced voyage through the sea represents the birth of not only the modern African diaspora, but modernity itself. Europe's rise and expansion were undergirded by slavery, its economic prosperity fundamentally related to the exploitation of Africans, an argument initially championed by Trinidadian scholar Eric Williams. The vast wealth, considerable privilege, and seemingly limitless opportunities associated with American elites were all achieved on the backs of impoverished Africans and subjugated Native Americans. To be sure, a peasantry and working class from all points of the globe would eventually find themselves in the Americas, where they would also make contributions under exploitative conditions. Even so, it was enslaved African labor that paved the way for all to come.

Focus on the introduction of Africans as enslaved workers does not obviate the possibility of a pre-Columbian African presence. Artifacts, archaeological remains, linguistic evidence, Native American traditions, and European explorer accounts render possible the idea that Africans crossed the Atlantic prior to Columbus, as do references in West African sources to transatlantic voyages under imperial Mali in the fourteenth century. But even if they indeed reached the Americas, there is little scholarly agreement as to how they may have impacted First Nation communities.

This chapter begins with a brief consideration of the African presence in Renaissance Europe, as it antedates the American experience and serves as one context. The chapter then moves on to African enslavement in the Americas. It explores their quotidian experiences, which both converged and diverged throughout the western hemisphere, while emphasizing their gendered dimensions. Though the subject of resistance is taken up in subsequent chapters, it should be borne in mind that Africans resisted their captivity from the start. Coercion was certainly a major mechanism by which Africans were kept subjugated, but there were other methods by which their defiance was debilitated, which will be considered.

Africans in Renaissance Europe

The beginning of the transoceanic trade in African captives in the fifteenth and sixteenth centuries was also the period of Europe's Renaissance. As discussed, the African presence in Europe is as old as antiquity, with references dating as far back as the early third century, when Rome sent "division of Moors" to help defend Hadrian's wall. That presence continued throughout the period of Muslim control over parts of Iberia, from 711 to 1492, during which time Arabs, North Africans, and West Africans undertook a variety of roles, including those of magistrate, merchant, scholar, student, performer, athlete, and soldier. In fact, most of the Africans residing in Europe during the Renaissance were in Portugal and Spain. But along with many non-Africans, some Africans were also enslaved as a result of the struggle over what would become Portugal and Spain.

Between 1441 and 1530, Portugal alone imported some 1,000 West Africans per annum, from where they were dispersed to southern Spain, Portugal, and elsewhere in the Mediterranean. By 1532, some 32,000 were enslaved in Portugal alone, some 3 percent of a total population of about 1 million. The enslaved in Portugal were concentrated in Lisbon, comprising 10 percent of its mid-sixteenth-century population. Many hailed from Senegambia, and many of these were Muslim, variously referred to as *negros de jalof* or *gelofes* (Wolof from the state of Jolof, along with the Fulbe or Fulani) and *mandingas* (Mande-speakers). Captives from West Central Africa (the Congo region) were labeled *bantus*. Those achieving some facility in Portuguese were called *ladinos*, while those who did not were regarded as *boçales* or *bozales* (Portuguese and Spanish designations for "raw").

Slave trafficking into Portugal was coterminous with the previously discussed rise of Madeira (off West Africa's coast) as its most important and wealthiest colony, followed by the late-fifteenth-century emergence of São Tomé and Príncipe. By 1462, the Portuguese were veritable slavetrading entrepreneurs, and in 1479 the Treaty of Alcáçovas granted Portugal the right to supply Spain with African captives. West African captives were brought into Cádiz and Barcelona, as well as Valencia and Seville. Importation estimates are uncertain, but Valencia may have received some 5,200 captives between 1477 and 1516, while a 1616 census in Cádiz reveals West African captives outnumbered North Africans by more than 20 percent. By 1565, however, Seville had the largest concentration of enslaved Africans – some 6,327 out of a municipal population of 85,538, accounting for 6 percent of an estimated 100,000 total number of enslaved persons in Spain. The slave trade was clearly a factor in Seville becoming a thriving city – Spain's largest at the time.

Slavery was multifaceted in Portugal and Spain, and indeed throughout Europe. Men worked in mines and on farms, and served as butlers, coachmen, and footmen, but they could also be artisans. Yet others were purchased by the Crown and used in the galleys in various construction projects, and although not all galley slaves were West Africans, many were.

Women were also used in domestic service, and along with men represented symbols of wealth for the European upper crust. As just one example, upon marrying the Portuguese King João in 1526, Catherine of Austria was attended by enslaved Africans performing all sorts of tasks – court jesters, musicians, chefs – but the preference was for young women and children, some of whom would be trained to sew clothes for the royal wardrobe, or to attend to the queen personally. Others were assigned to clean her horse stables, but some acquired levels of literacy.

As would be true elsewhere, enslaved Africans were at times manumitted. But their post-emancipation lives could be difficult, especially if they were menial laborers lacking marketable skills. In sixteenth-century Seville, for example, manumitted West Africans worked alongside both free and enslaved *moriscos*, Muslims who under duress ostensibly converted to Christianity during the Reconquista. They were all were impoverished, performing similar tasks and working in close proximity.

But not all Africans were enslaved, and arguably the most famous individual (from either North or West Africa) was actually a fictive character, Shakespeare's *Othello*, possibly written in 1603 and arguably adapted from *Un Capitano Moro* ("A Moorish Captain"), written by the Italian Giovanni Battista Giraldi (nicknamed "Cinthio," d. 1573). Othello is depicted as a "Moor," a term inconsistently applied to North Africans, West Africans, and Arabs. As such, it connotes both dark skin and cultural difference, and tends to convey an association with Islam. Paul Robeson would most famously perform as Othello in a 1943 American production, the first African American to do so.

As a "Moorish" general in the service of Venice, Othello's regal bearing may have been informed by African royals and their ambassadors, who on occasion visited European courts and were received with honor and respect. This is consistent with Renaissance portraits that depict Africans in a dignified manner. That these Africans tend to be adorned in European-styled clothing suggests class and cultural bias, but at the same time arguably represents an embrace of a common humanity in this age of reason.

Africans could be found in many places in Renaissance Europe, and in addition to the fictive Othello was the very real Alessandro de Medici, born in Urbino (Italy) in 1511. The son of an unknown Medici father and an African peasant woman, Alessandro was appointed Duke of Florence at the age of nineteen, only to be assassinated by a cousin at the age of twenty-six – apparently in protest against his absolutism (during a time of rising republicanism). Written descriptions of his physical appearance accompany his portraits, and though he was unmistakably African-descended, none of these representations reveal racial bias or animosity (see Figure 6).

Alessandro de Medici's contemporary, Juan Latino (born around 1518) would emerge as a university-educated scholar in Grenada, Spain. Juan Latino's trajectory is striking in that he was born a slave (to an enslaved African mother), and may not have even been manumitted when he married the daughter of the Duke of Sessa, with whom he had a family. Renowned as a teacher of Latin grammar at the University of Granada, Juan Latino (consistently described as a "full-blooded African") also wrote poetry, and apparently translated Virgil into Spanish. He is best known for his *Austrias carmen* (written in Latin and published in 1573), an epic poem describing the 1571 Battle of Lepanto, between the Christian Holy League (the Vatican, Venice, and Spain) and the Ottoman Empire.

FIGURE 6 Portrait of Juan de Pareja, assistant to Spanish artist Diego
Velázquez and painted by him, c.1650. New York, Metropolitan Museum of Art,
Inv. 1971.86. A black and white version of this figure will appear in some formats.
For the color version, please refer to the plate section.

For all of Juan Latino's considerable accomplishments, his origins
point to the condition of enslavement so prevalent for Africans in Renaissance Europe. With the decline of captives from the aforementioned
Muslim–Christian conflict in Iberia and the Black Sea in the fifteenth
century, slavery in Europe became more and more identified with "black"
Africans, a process of racialization that would gain tremendous momentum with the exponential expansion of the transatlantic slave trade.

Enslavement in the Americas

Renaissance Europe certainly had its share of enslaved Africans,
whose collective presence registered most prominently in the cities
of Lisbon and Seville. But the vast majority of captive Africans were
trafficked to the Americas, and as Brazil accounted for some 45 percent of all such captives, consideration of American slavery can begin
there (see Map 6). This vast, Portuguese-claimed territory has a

MAP 6 Latin America, 1828

diverse economic history that can be divided into four periods. North-eastern Brazil was the destination of most of Africans from the second half of the sixteenth century through the whole of the seventeenth, with the captaincies (provinces) of Bahia and Pernambuco receiving the lion's share of a workforce cultivating sugar cane. From the late seventeenth century through the mid-eighteenth, gold and diamond mining redirected as many as two-thirds of all Africans to the captain-cies of Minas Gerais, Mato Grosso, and Goiás in central Brazil, but with the collapse of the mining boom by the 1770s the majority

FIGURE 7 Slave market, Pernambuco. From Maria Graham, *Journal of a Voyage to Brazil* (London, 1824), opposite p. 107. Library of Congress, Prints and Photographs Division, LC-USZ62-97202. A black and white version of this figure will appear in some formats. For the color version, please refer to the plate section.

returned to Bahia and Pernambuco to produce sugar cane and tobacco. Coffee would become king from the 1820s onward (though cotton production also became significant early in the nineteenth century), resulting in the growth of African slavery in central and southern Brazil, particularly Minas Gerais, Rio de Janeiro, and São Paulo.

The various agricultural regimes, fluctuating demographics, differing climates, and changing rates of captive importation meant that slavery in Brazil was multifaceted and complex. However, two aspects of Brazilian slavery stand out: first, the number of Africans imported into Brazil was enormous; and second, two-thirds of the Africans brought to Brazil were male (see Figure 7).

Concerning what would become the English-speaking Caribbean, the British arrived in Jamaica in 1655, having established a presence in St. Kitts (St. Christopher) in 1624, Barbados in 1627, Nevis in 1628, and Montserrat and Antigua in the 1630s. Limited arable land in St. Kitts, Nevis, Montserrat, and Antigua meant that these islands could not compete with Barbados, the wealthiest and most densely populated of the English colonies in the seventeenth century. Originally covered by thick tropical growth with neither mountains or rivers, Barbados had a high percentage of cultivable land, and was cleared

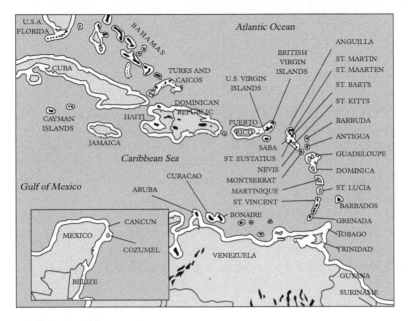

MAP 7 Caribbean map

for sugar cane within the first forty years of foreign occupation. However, the exactions of sugar cane, combined with territorial limitations, eventually exhausted the soil (see Map 7).

Jamaica was also relatively abundant in arable flat land. The Spanish maintained a minimal presence for 150 years before 1655 and the English incursion. English-speaking Jamaica was "founded in blood," seized from the Spanish by a motley crew of unruly soldiers. For the remainder of the seventeenth century it was the principal site of buccaneering operations against the Spanish. The end of the century, however, saw a transition from pirating and small-scale farming to large-scale plantation agriculture, in concert with a dramatic rise in the number of black slaves, soaring from 514 in 1661 to 9,504 in 1673. Between 1671 and 1679 another 11,816 Africans arrived, and by 1713 the enslaved population had reached 55,000, larger than that of Barbados. The year 1817 saw the largest number of slaves in Jamaica, some 345,252, but by that time many of African descent were no longer slaves. The island developed a reputation as the preserve of Akan speakers from the Gold Coast, but just as many were imported from the Bight of Biafra. These two regions account for the origins of almost 60 percent of all Africans arriving in Jamaica, and enjoyed considerable cultural and social influence.

In addition to amassing the largest group of slaves in the British Caribbean, Jamaica also had one of the most diversified economies of the region. By 1832, slightly less than one-half of all the enslaved worked on sugar plantations, 14 percent worked on coffee plantations, 13 percent in "livestock pens," 7 percent inhabited minor staple plantations, 8 percent lived in towns, and 6 percent performed general labor. Owing to environmental needs, sugar cane plantations were concentrated along the island's northern coast, but could also be found elsewhere.

European occupation of Trinidad began in July of 1498, and for the next 300 years the island languished under Spanish domination and neglect. This changed with the *cédula* (decree) of 1783, by which migration and slavery's expansion were encouraged through the offer of land. Any purported Roman Catholic from a nation friendly to Spain could swear an oath and receive free land; additional land was provided for every slave imported. The *cédula*'s terms essentially excluded all but the French, along with the Irish and others of various backgrounds, who would be later be joined by those fleeing the French Revolution. This group included wealthy planters, and by 1784 the island was effectively a French colony, with the French outnumbering the Spanish twenty to one. Immigrants arrived that year from Grenada, Martinique, Guadeloupe, St. Lucia, and Cayenne, speaking French and Creole languages (a mixture of African and European tongues). Their numbers would be augmented by Royalist planters fleeing the Haitian Revolution (1791–1804).

In contrast to Jamaica, Barbados, and other Caribbean islands, the arrival of substantial numbers of enslaved Africans in Trinidad was relatively late. The absence of both gold and significant Spanish interest in agriculture meant that Trinidad's pre-1783 population was never more than a few thousand; for example, in 1777, there were 200 enslaved blacks, 870 free "mulattoes," and 340 whites in Trinidad. But by 1789 the population had increased to 18,918, including 2,200 indigenous, 10,100 enslaved persons, 4,467 free "coloreds," and 2,151 whites. The African distribution in Trinidad reveals that 44 percent arrived from the Bight of Biafra, followed by 21 percent from the Gold Coast and 15 percent from West Central Africa.

The British seized Trinidad in 1797, by which time the island had over 150 sugar estates. Sugar cane had become the island's most important crop, and by 1832, 90 percent of the total value of Trinidad's exports was provided by sugar and its by-products, requiring some 70 percent of the enslaved labor. The impact of the 1783 *cédula* was the swift peopling of the island and the emergence of a bustling export economy.

While the sugar industry was important in Trinidad, cocoa, coffee, and cotton were also grown. Cocoa production had continued from the Spanish period, expanding even more rapidly during sugar's spectacular rise. Cocoa, however, was a smallholder's specialty, principally cultivated by the free colored and black populations and therefore not as dependent on slave labor. Even so, at least 20 percent of Trinidad's population was free and colored by 1810, and they owned 37.3 percent of all estates and 31.5 percent of all slaves. That African-descended persons could be slaveholders is a subject to be explored, but the fact that they were overwhelmingly smallholders partially accounts for cocoa's mere 6.2 percent of the total value of exports in 1832, together with the observation that demand for cocoa only became very significant in the 1860s, when the taste of the drink *chocolat* was improved by the addition of the powderized extract.

Slavery in the Caribbean was distinguished from its North American counterpart by the presence of large plantations and the widespread absence of plantation owners. By convention, a North American plantation was an enterprise of twenty or more slaves, whereas Caribbean plantations featured at least a hundred slaves, and often considerably more. Absentee ownership of Caribbean plantations increased toward the end of legal slavery in the British West Indies, and underscores the relatively small number of whites in the islands. In Jamaica, for example, the black population already constituted 90 percent of the total by 1734.

As was true of Brazil, approximately two-thirds of the Africans imported into the Anglophone Caribbean were males, and taking the Anglophone Caribbean as a whole, life and labor were extremely arduous. Early in the history of the Caribbean, the relatively low costs of procuring captives from Africa made it less expensive to simply replace exhausted workers with new recruits rather than promote stable families and strategies of reproduction in the islands. Imbalanced sex ratios and appalling working conditions resulted in a life expectancy of less than ten years upon disembarkation. In Barbados, for example, the importation of some 85,000 captives between 1708 and 1735 raised the enslaved population from 42,000 to only 46,000.

As was true throughout the Americas, newly arriving Africans, referred to as "fresh" or "salt-water" blacks, often underwent a painful period of adjustment known as "seasoning," lasting up to three years. It was during this time that captives became enslaved, whereas prior to disembarkation anything was possible, including mutiny. Seasoning involved acclimating to a new environment, new companions, strange languages and food, and new living arrangements. But above all, seasoning involved adjusting to life and work under conditions cruel and lethal. As a result of brutal treatment, the shock of the New World, disease, and the longing for home, between 25 and 33 percent of the newly arrived did not survive seasoning.

Slavery required force – coercion – or it simply could not operate. The whip was therefore everywhere employed, supplemented by an assortment of tortures and punishments in the Caribbean chamber of horrors. The unimaginable included burning body parts with varying degrees of heat, chopping off limbs, placement in stocks, and solitary confinement. Women, many pregnant, were whipped on their bare behinds, after which salt and pepper were often poured into the wounds along with melted wax, a reflection of slavery's sadistic nature (Figure 8).

Throughout the English-claimed Caribbean, women worked in many of the same capacities as men, particularly on large plantations. During harvest, between October and March, they worked eighteen hours or more in the sugar cane fields and in the sugar mills, and by the early nineteenth century, three-quarters of the enslaved throughout the Caribbean were working on sugar cane plantations. These plantations required greater female participation in the fields than did coffee due to the disproportionate use of males in processing the cane, and it was the sugar cane plantation, generally an unhealthy place, that had the highest rates of slave mortality, morbidity, and infant mortality rates (followed by coffee plantations, then cocoa and cotton plantations). In addition to working as hard as men, women and girls were susceptible to sexual exploitation in ways and at rates that did not apply to men (though the subject of males as victims of sexual assault has received far less scholarly attention, with the exception of lynching and its attendant castration ritual). Absentee owners had to rely on managers and overseers, both white and black, who viewed sexual access as their right. Many enslaved children resulted

Flagellation of a Female Samboe Slave.

FIGURE 8 *Flagellation of a Female Samboe Slave*. James Ford Bell Library, University of Minnesota. A black and white version of this figure will appear in some formats. For the color version, please refer to the plate section.

from these unions; the question of how these interactions should be understood is a matter of debate. The rewards of voluntary cooperation could have included a relatively easier life, but avoidance of violation may not have always been possible, especially when enslaved women (and their families) risked serious reprisal for refusing advances. The element of coercion was therefore present in every case, even in romanticized unions of "consent." Enmity between black and white women was a by-product, the latter often as harsh in their treatment of slaves as white males.

Before 1765, the official value of the Caribbean's slave-produced exports to England was fourteen times that of exports from North American colonies north of the Chesapeake, after which time their value only dropped to ten times as great. Indeed, the value of exports to Britain from the Anglophone Caribbean led that of commodities from Asia, Africa, Latin America, and the whole of North America from 1713 to 1822, while the same Anglophone Caribbean was the principal importer of British goods in comparison with Africa, Asia, and Latin America. Clearly, the British-held Caribbean was of enormous value and importance to Britain, premised on the backs of African labor.

With slavery throughout the Americas as context, developments in Haiti merit special attention. In 1697, Hispaniola was formally divided into Spanish-held Santo Domingo and French-controlled Saint-Domingue (which later became Haiti, reuniting with Santo Domingo from 1822 until 1844, when the latter declared its independence as the Dominican Republic). As important as the British Caribbean was to Britain, the French-held territory of Saint-Domingue was, by 1789, the wealthiest of all West Indian colonies. The French national economy benefited from slavery in Saint-Domingue as much as did the rich planters, but events on the island, particularly the Revolution of 1791–1804, were arguably of even greater significance to the African-descended throughout the Americas, and were certainly influential in France's decision to cede vast territories to the United States in the Louisiana Purchase of 1803.

Engagés, or white indentured servants of peasant and working-class backgrounds from France, were originally called upon to provide labor in Saint-Domingue. Under three-year contracts, these *engagés* were eventually working alongside small numbers of Africans. The move to indigo production by 1685 was a definitive turn in Saint-Domingue's history, as the importation of Africans increased geometrically. With the introduction of sugar cane twenty years later, Africans became the overwhelming source of labor, and the *engagés* became the overseers and tradesmen. Between 1676 and 1800, over 770,000 Africans were brought to Saint-Domingue, producing a population of nearly half a million by 1789. Of that figure, some two-thirds were African-born, which is significant in light of the Haitian Revolution. West Central Africans, following the earlier arrival of small groups from Senegal through Sierra Leone in the sixteenth century, would eventually account for 46 percent of the total number imported, followed by 25 percent from the Bight of Benin.

As was true of places like Jamaica, Saint-Domingue's plantations were characterized by increasing absentee ownership, with some owners never having seen the island. Absentee interests were represented by agents or managers – *procureurs* – who acquired a kind of power of attorney and enjoyed all of the advantages of the absentee owner. Both absentee and in-country owners were known as *grands blancs*, as were French merchants and colonial officers in the cities. Other whites were labeled *petits blancs*, many descendent from seventeenth-century *engagés*, while others were such townspeople as barristers, shopkeepers, carpenters, criminals, and debtors. The *petits blancs* were sometimes called *faux blancs*, or even *nègres blancs* by blacks, an indication of low esteem. But is this "white trash" characterization convincing as an expression of derision, or does it ultimately rest upon the disparagement of blacks?

The concept of race, the notion that human beings can be clearly differentiated into basic, hierarchically arranged categories based upon certain combinations of shared physical characteristics, evolved in tandem with the institution of slavery in the Americas. The concept emphasizes difference rather than commonality, and as a tool of power and privilege has few rivals. The specifics of race would vary throughout the Americas, but the essence of the idea was consistent: whites and blacks, as categories of contrasting mythical purity, also represent contrasting polarities of power, wealth, and beauty. Located along a continuum between these polar opposites were First Nation communities, Asians, and persons of interracial heritage. In some societies, "mixed" groups achieved a stable intermediary status, whereas in others they shared economic and social disabilities similar to those of blacks. White elites used race to their personal advantage; poor whites accepted race because it ennobled them, granting them a status that could never be challenged by darker people, and with whom they denied any semblance of circumstance. On the other hand, some of African descent also came to embrace the concept of race, as they suffered as a group and saw benefit in collective resistance. However, as will be discussed concerning Brazil in the nineteenth and twentieth centuries, race could be kaleidoscopic in variation among those born in the Americas, while the African did not always accept associations based upon skin color, preferring cultural and linguistically based identities instead.

Race was certainly complex in Saint-Domingue. In addition to whites and the enslaved were the *affranchis*, or free blacks, and *gens de couleur* ("persons of color" or mixed ancestry). The *affranchis*, mostly women, numbered about 27,500 in 1789, equaling the number of whites and owning about 25 percent of the enslaved. Some 15 percent of this group lived in urban areas, including Cap-Français and Port-au-Prince, and accounted for 11 percent of the total urban population. Two-thirds of the *affranchis* were *gens de couleur*, largely the consequence of liaisons between white slaveholders or their managers, and enslaved females, a system of concubinage in which ties between slaveholder/manager and enslaved often carried the understanding that children from such unions would be free. As a result, there developed a sizable free colored population by the beginning of the eighteenth century, and by 1789 their numbers were greater than their counterparts in the whole of the British- and remaining French-claimed Caribbean combined. *Affranchis* took advantage of the rapid rise in coffee cultivation, and by the middle of the eighteenth century were planters in their own right. A few even joined the exclusive, *grands blancs* club of sugar cane planters, but most were excluded by their inability to inherit or own money (or its equivalent in land) beyond a specified amount, thus explaining their concentration in coffee as well as various trades and commerce.

Because the *affranchis* were dominated by *gens de couleur*, they constituted a third racial category and were used as a buffer group between whites and the enslaved masses. Striving to be accepted by whites, the *affranchis* adopted their tastes and habits, and because many were slaveholders, they identified with powerful, white property interests. However, although at least 300 planters were married to women of color by 1763, there was no reciprocation of policy in kind. *Affranchis* could not hold public office, vote, practice law or medicine, or participate in certain trades. By the 1770s, they could not take the names of their former owners, they could not enter France for any reason, and they were subject to sumptuary laws. However, they were required to render militia duty to protect the colony, serving in their own units commanded by white officers. *Affranchis* exclusively comprised the *maréchaussée*, whose chief function was to hunt down runaway slaves, a role played by poor whites in the United States (where they were called patrollers, or "patty-rollers" by blacks). By making the *maréchaussée* exclusively "colored," the whites in power drove a deep wedge between them and the vast majority of Africans and their descendants. But by refusing to grant them full rights and privileges, whites denied the *affranchis* access to full freedom. They therefore became a subject caste, with serious implications for the future of Saint-Domingue.

By 1789, Saint-Domingue was the site of more than 3,000 indigo plantations, 2,500 coffee plantations, nearly 800 cotton plantations, and fifty cocoa plantations. Such was the island's coffee production that it became the world's leader after 1770. But it was Saint-Domingue's dominance in sugar production that distinguished it. By the time of the Haitian Revolution in 1791, Saint-Domingue's sugar cane industry was operating at peak capacity, with almost 500,000 enslaved laborers on nearly 800 plantations producing 79,000 metric tons of sugar, compared with the 60,900 metric tons of Jamaica's 250,000 enslaved population. France re-exported rather than consumed most of the sugar crop from its colonies, thereby supplying 65 percent of the world's market in sugar by 1791, 50 percent of which came from Saint-Domingue. In contrast, Britain consumed most of its Caribbean-produced sugar, and only re-exported 13 percent to the world market between 1788 and 1792. The divergence between France and Britain is partially explained by wine and rum; the French were far more interested in the former, whereas Saint-Domingue sugar was used in the rum production of various colonies due to its higher sucrose content and lower production costs.

The riches of Saint-Domingue were built on the backs of black suffering. The context for that suffering was a shortened lifespan; in the eighteenth century, half of all newly arriving Africans only lived another three to eight years. As for those born into slavery in Saint-Domingue, the so-called creoles, they could expect a working life of fifteen years. As was true of the early British strategy in the Caribbean, the French determined it more cost effective to simply replace worn-out, no-longer-useful, or dead slaves with new arrivals.

By the 1780s, the male-to-female ratio in Saint-Domingue stood at 120:100, down from the high of 180:100 in 1730. Both women and men were organized into work groups or *ateliers*, and both sexes performed heavy labor in the fields that included tilling, weeding, clearing trees, brush, and stones, digging trenches and canals, and planting and picking. Work days averaged eighteen hours, with some working twenty-four-hour shifts. For those on sugar cane plantations, the grinding season between January and July followed the harvest and was just as arduous, whereas coffee plantation workers labored under a seasonal system that was different, yet taxing. Field hands were the backbone of the labor regime, but enslaved workers were also boiler-men, furnacemen, carpenters, masons, coopers, wheelwrights, and stockmen. Males dominated such jobs, while women and girls per-formed most agricultural tasks; in the 1770s and 1780s, some 60 per-cent of the field hands were female. Females were also dominant as washerwomen, house servants, and seamstresses, tasks that would inordinately feature women of African descent throughout the twenti-eth century in various parts of the Americas. Most cooks were males, while valets and coachmen were always so. Creoles rather than the African-born filled most domestic jobs, as whites were more comfort-able with those who could speak their language and were, in many instances, of partial European descent.

Like their counterparts in the British-claimed Caribbean, the enslaved in Saint-Domingue maintained their own provision grounds, small plots of land upon which they cultivated crops for personal consumption. The enslaved had to squeeze in time to tend their gardens, usually on Sundays, holidays, and around noon during the week, when they had a two-hour respite. Surpluses from their provi-sion grounds were sold in nearby towns on Sundays and holidays, an activity dominated by women. Women-controlled markets may have resulted from restrictions placed upon men by slaveholders, but such markets are strikingly similar to West African practices in which women were often in charge of local markets. The provision grounds and market days of the Caribbean are often cited as features further distinguishing the experiences of blacks there from their co-sufferers in North America.

Provision grounds and markets notwithstanding, the enslaved of Saint-Domingue were, generally speaking, perpetually hungry and consistently malnourished. This should not have been the case, since the institution under the French (like slavery in the Islamic world) was regulated, at least in theory, by a body of rules known as the *Code Noir*, first promulgated in 1685. The idea was to minimize the brutality of the slave regime as a whole and the slaveholder in particular by requiring certain minimum standards of treatment. The hours worked by the enslaved, the amount of food they received, and types of permissible punishments were all covered by the *Code Noir*. But as was also true in the Islamic world, there was often a chasm between theory and reality, with the enslaved regularly overworked and underfed.

They were also severely abused, and in ways as inhumane and shocking as could be found anywhere in the New World. In addition to the tortures mentioned as part of the British Caribbean experience, slaveholders in Saint-Domingue added such measures as hurling humans into blazing ovens; cramming their orifices with gunpowder and igniting the powder; transforming their bodies into human fireballs; mutilating their body parts (especially the genitalia, male and female); burying victims alive after forcing them to dig their own graves; burying individuals up to the neck, allowing for the slow dismantling of sugar-covered heads by insects and animals; and so on. This was savagery, and it had nothing to do with Africa.

Given Saint-Domingue's prominence in the production of sugar, the Haitian Revolution instigated a "dramatic transformation" of the world sugar market, occasioning an upsurge in sugar cane production elsewhere. Jamaica and the British Isles were the initial beneficiaries of Saint-Domingue's demise, with Jamaican sugar production doubling between 1792 and 1805. Jamaica's production continued to be substantial if not quite so prodigious, but it would be replaced as the leading sugar producer by Cuba in the 1820s. Brazil would compete, but its market share was hampered by outdated technology and inadequate transport. Cuba continued to dominate world sugar production in the second half of the nineteenth century, though suffering a decline in sugar prices from the rise of the French beet sugar industry between 1827 and 1847. The implication and consequence of the shift in sugar production from Haiti to Cuba constitutes the most bitter of ironies, however, as the demise of slavery in the former directly stimulated its rise in the latter. In fact, the expansion of slavery in Cuba, Brazil, and the United States in the nineteenth century was so dramatic as to constitute a "second slavery" in the estimation of some scholars.

In considering Spanish-held territories, Hispaniola was probably the first site to which enslaved Africans were brought early in the sixteenth century, and *ladinos* (Africans with some command of either Spanish or Portuguese) were the first to be imported. But as early as 1503, Nicolás de Ovando, Hispaniola's first royal governor, petitioned Spain to stop sending *ladinos* because they were suspected of inciting revolt. Instead, de Ovando requested the importation of *bozales*, unacculturated Africans directly from West Africa. The governor did not appreciate, however, that *ladinos* and *bozales* were coming out of the same region, Senegambia, and that the former's familiarity with European culture was mitigated by their shared cultural ties with the latter, with Islam as an important factor. The revolts therefore continued, and it was not until 1513 that the Spanish began to import Africans from West Central Africa. By 1514, there were some 1,000 *ladinos* and *bozales* in Hispaniola, along with 689 Europeans.

De Ovando may have also been responsible for introducing Africans to Puerto Rico in 1509, when he brought them from Santo Domingo. By the following year, an unspecified number of Africans were on the island, along with 200 Europeans. The 1516 appeal of Dominican friar Bartolomé de Las Casas to prohibit the enslavement of Native Americans and instead enslave Africans and Europeans reinvigorated the African trade. Charles I restarted the shipment of Africans in 1517, an important decision for Puerto Rico, whose *boricua* or native population was in decline, as was its gold supply. Colonists, faced with the choice of either abandoning the island or developing an alternative source of income, chose the latter and planted sugar cane. The first *ingenio* (sugar mill and surrounding lands) was established on the grasslands of San Germán (contemporary Añasco in the western part of the island) in 1523. In addition to Hispaniola and Puerto Rico, there was also a Senegambian presence in early sixteenth-century Costa Rica and Panama.

Regarding Venezuela, initially a "poverty-stricken outpost" of Spanish imperialism, Africans had arrived there by 1529 in small numbers. By the eighteenth century, Venezuela had become a leading source of cacao (from which chocolate is derived). The slave trade, insignificant before the eighteenth century, accelerated between 1730 and 1780, providing labor for the production of cacao, sugar, indigo, and hides. Pearl divers of African descent were also used in Venezuela (and Colombia, as they were also used in the Persian Gulf). The end of the "cacao boom" around the turn of the century led to the eventual cessation of the slave trade in 1810, by which time there were some 60,000 enslaved persons in Venezuela. As for

Colombia and Peru, Africans destined for Lima, Santo Domingo, and Puerto Rico in the late fifteenth/early sixteenth centuries arrived initially in Cartagena. Those headed for Peru voyaged another nine to ten days to Portobelo, where they made a difficult two-day crossing through the isthmus. Africans reached Peru as early as 1529, where they were put to work in the silver mines high up in the Andes, and by mid-century the African population in Lima was near 3,000. By the mid-seventeenth century, there were probably 20,000 Africans in Lima, one-half of the city's population and two-thirds of all of the Africans in Peru.

The Peruvian economy in general and agriculture in particular benefited from the increase in African numbers. Olives, plantains, oranges, sugar cane, wheat, and barley were all cultivated by Africans, who also produced sugar and wine. They tended the cart-pulling oxen and mules, and fulfilled various roles in trade and shipping along the Pacific coast. They were prominent as masons, carpenters, shipwrights, bricklayers, blacksmiths, and tailors, and were employed as *jornaleros*, or day-wage workers hiring out their labor. Africans were also domestics in the urban areas, especially Lima, where they were on conspicuous display as symbols of slaveholder wealth. In 1791, there were 40,000 enslaved and 41,398 free blacks and persons of mixed ancestry in Peru; by the time of slavery's abolition in 1854, there were about 17,000 slaves in Peru. The 1876 census estimated the black population at 44,224.

Briefly concerning the Rio de la Plata (the estuary formed from the combination of the Uruguay and Parana Rivers), early nineteenth-century Montevideo (Uruguay) was the port through which southeastern slave trafficking was required to pass before going on to Buenos Aires (Argentina), Paraguay, and Bolivia. Some remained in Uruguay, and from 1770 to 1810 about 2,691 Africans were imported. From 1742 to 1806, perhaps half of the slaves entering the Rio de la Plata came from Brazil, the other half hailing directly from Africa.

We end the discussion of Spanish slavery by returning to Cuba. Except for Havana, there were no large concentrations of Africans in Cuba prior to the eighteenth century. The slave trade was irregular, and captives who arrived were employed in diverse tasks. The island's planter class would be encouraged, however, by England's transformation of Barbados into a sugar colony, the English seizure of Jamaica in the mid-seventeenth century for the same purpose, and the corresponding establishment of the French in Saint-Domingue.

The cultivation of sugar cane was unevenly developed until the 1740s, when the Spanish crown lifted all taxes on Cuban sugar entering Spain at a time when the world market was paying more for sugar. From 1750 to 1761, the number of *ingenios* (sugar mill and surrounding lands) increased from sixty-two to ninety-six, a portent of things to come.

The period between 1763 to 1838 brought dramatic change to Cuba. In 1763, the English occupied Havana for ten months, effectively ending the *asiento* system. This intervention, together with Cuban planter initiative, opened up the island to greater numbers of Africans. From 1761 to 1790, some 23,000 entered the island, only to be followed by more than 211,000 between 1791 and 1820, a nearly one hundredfold increase. The proverbial floodgates were now open, with another 504,000 Africans arriving between 1821 and 1860. These dramatic increases were in response to several developments. First, as previously observed, the Haitian Revolution created a tremendous void in the production of sugar and coffee, sparking a sharp rise in the price of sugar in Europe. Second, some of the planters fleeing Saint-Domingue resettled in the eastern parts of Cuba, bringing the enslaved with them; their ranks would be joined by planters from Louisiana after the 1803 Purchase. Coupled with technological improvements, these developments led to skyrocketing sugar production in Cuba, with the number of *ingenios* tripling from 529 in 1792 to 1,531 by 1861. A concomitant rise in coffee production also drew heavily upon enslaved labor, their numbers swelled by a slave trade officially abolished in 1820, but which nonetheless proceeded unabated through the 1860s. By 1838, Cuba had been transformed from a land of few towns, scattered ranching (*potreros*), and tobacco farms (*vegas*) to a huge sugar cane and coffee complex. By 1862, when there were more people of African than European descent in Cuba, the island held 368,550 enslaved persons, 60 percent of whom were male, working on sugar cane and coffee plantations as well as small-scale farms (*sitios*), ranches, and tobacco fields. By the end of the slave trade, the total number of Africans shipped to Cuba, some 778,541 people, had surpassed the 773,542 brought earlier to Saint-Domingue.

Taking the slave trade to Cuba as a whole, approximately 31 percent and 24 percent of the captives came from West Central Africa and the Bight of Biafra, respectively, followed by the Bight of Benin (14 percent), Sierra Leone (11 percent), South East Africa (9 percent), and Senegambia (3 percent). Over 80 percent of all Africans imported during the nineteenth century wound up on a plantation as opposed to a town (where they were domestics, tradespersons, or *jornaleros*). By the late 1860s, nearly 50 percent of all the enslaved worked on *ingenios* under white overseers (*administradores*) and their assistants (*contra-mayorales*), some of whom were black. Whites also occupied "skilled" positions on these plantations, while semi-skilled jobs were performed by Asian indentured servants, so-called Chinese coolies, nearly 125,000 of whom entered Cuba between 1853 and 1874 and labored under slave-like conditions.

Like other Caribbean societies, Cuba also developed a free mixed race or *pardo* category of individuals who tallied 33,886 in 1791, a figure that nearly tripled fifty years later to 88,054, when the number of the enslaved of mixed ancestry is estimated to have been 10,974. Altogether, those of mixed ancestry represented almost 10 percent of the total 1841 population of 1,007,624. The free *pardo* group, together with free blacks (or *morenos*), were concentrated in the towns and eastern provinces.

Like the French *Code Noir*, the Spanish *Siete Partidas*, originally developed in the thirteenth century, was a series of regulations that included slave codes. The *Siete Partidas* served as the basis for slave laws developed in 1680 and revised in 1789, 1812, and 1842, but in many if not most cases these laws constituted an exercise in semantics, as they were either not implemented or, in the case of the 1789 revision, not even read in Spanish-held territories.

As was true in the British and French Caribbean, slaves in early Cuba were worked to death and replaced with new recruits from Africa. The *zafra* (crop-time) and *tiempo muerte* (dead season) of the agricultural cycle were both regulated by the whip, stocks, and shackles. Females, outnumbered by males on the plantations 2:1, were required to return to work forty-five days after giving birth, having labored alongside males into their ninth month of pregnancy. As expected, infant mortality soared. A key indicator of the deplorable plight of the African-descended (enslaved and free) comes from a decline in their population, from 596,396 in 1860 to 528,798 in 1887, a shift from 43.7 to 32.5 percent of the total population. The decline suggests an inability to maintain their numbers absent a slave trade abolished in the 1860s, a picture inconsistent with claims that slavery in Cuba was more benign than in North America.

And North America was no picnic (see Map 8). The proverbial twenty Africans who landed in Jamestown in 1619 are usually cited as

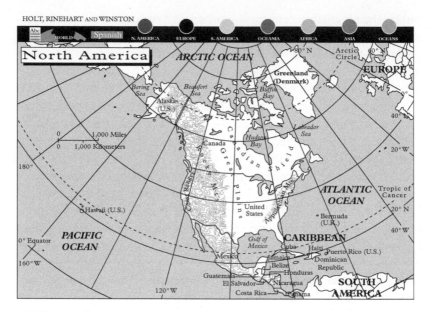

MAP 8 North America

the first to set foot in North America, but as early as 1526 a contingent of African captives was brought to South Carolina by the Spanish. Furthermore, the Jamestown Twenty were initially indentured servants who would eventually become enslaved, as it was only in the second half of the seventeenth century that the fast association between African ancestry and slavery was legislatively achieved. By 1756 the total African population had increased markedly, numbering some 120,156 and nearly matching the white population of 173,316. Slavery spread quickly, with Virginia, South Carolina, Maryland, Georgia, and Louisiana serving as its foundational colonies in the South, where the enslaved initially cultivated rice and indigo with skills and techniques developed in Africa by women, and subsequently introduced to whites.

But captive Africans were also as far north as New England, though not as numerous. Colonial New England primarily invested in slavery as a commercial enterprise; a number of slavetraders were there, as the slave trade was a major economic engine for New England until 1776. Slavetraders exchanged fish and rum for Africans, molasses, and sugar, and while some Africans remained in New England to help build its ports, many were shipped elsewhere, including the Caribbean. Conversely, captives originally enslaved in the Caribbean were often shipped to New England in small parcels. By 1776, Massachusetts had the largest number of blacks with 5,249, but Rhode Island boasted the heaviest concentration, with 3,761 blacks to 54,435 whites. The mid-Atlantic colonies of New York, New Jersey, and Pennsylvania were also slaveholding, but after the war with England the percentages of the enslaved fell; by 1790, only 28 percent of some 50,000 blacks were enslaved, and half were in the state of New York. Slavery was dying out in New England even more rapidly, so that only 3,700 out of 13,000 blacks were enslaved by 1790. While rural for the most part, the total North American black population of 750,000 in 1790 also featured an urban component, principally in New York City, where there were 3,252 (of whom 2,184 were enslaved) and Philadelphia, where only 210 out of 1,630 were in formal bondage. In contrast to New York City, all 761 black Bostonians were free.

Toward the end of the eighteenth century, the South shifted from indigo, rice, and tobacco production to cotton, made possible by the cotton gin and the introduction of the upland, short staple variety. The area under cultivation increased dramatically, and with it the demand for servile labor. In contrast to the early pattern elsewhere in the Americas (with the exception of Barbados), North American planters pursued pronatalist policies that supported conditions in which the enslaved could sustain their numbers. The strategy worked, because by 1860 an importation of no more than 400,000 had produced a population of slightly less than 4.5 million people, more than 10 percent of whom were no longer formally enslaved.

Nearly 48 percent of Africans arriving in what would become the United States originated in West Central Africa and Senegambia (24 percent each). Next came Sierra Leone and the Windward Coast (17 percent), the Bight of Biafra (also 17 percent), the Gold Coast (14 percent), and the Bight of Benin (2 percent). Those from the Bight of Biafra were numerically dominant in Virginia, whereas West Central Africans were the majority in South Carolina and significant in Georgia. Senegambians, together with those from Sierra Leone and the Windward Coast, were substantially represented everywhere, but Senegambians were numerically superior in Maryland and Louisiana, followed (in Louisiana) by those from West Central Africa and the Bight of Benin. Comparable to Brazil and the Anglophone Caribbean, males constituted nearly 68 percent of all those imported, while 23 percent were prepubescent children.

The legal importation of captive Africans ended in 1808, but a clandestine trade directly from Africa, together with transshipments from the Caribbean (especially Cuba), continued to the outbreak of the Civil War. The domestic slave trade became very important, facilitating the westward expansion of white settlers and their enslaved workers by 1815. Planters relocated from the seaboard states to Alabama, Mississippi, and Louisiana, and then on to Texas. Manifest Destiny came at a high price, paid largely by Africans, Native Americans, and (later) Asians.

Although there were 8 million white Southerners in 1860, only 384,884 were slaveholders. This would suggest that the vast majority of whites had no vested interest in slavery, but just the opposite was true. Particularly after 1830, the vast majority of whites supported slavery, and the regional economy was entirely dependent upon it. The large white population was in stark contrast with the demographic picture in the Caribbean, as was the fact that some 88 percent of slaveholding families each held less than twenty enslaved persons, with the vast majority of slaveholders living on their plantations. While blacks may not have been concentrated on large, Caribbean-style plantations, over 50 percent lived on holdings of twenty-five slaves or more, while some 25 percent lived on properties with fifty or more. They furthermore tended to be "clustered" on farms and plantations along rivers, in the Tidewater of Virginia, in the Georgia-South Carolina Low Country, and on the Gulf Coast, representing veritable "black belts" of people and soil. Within such concentrations, individuals from different holdings maintained a regular commerce, so that the physical configuration and frequency of interaction allowed the enslaved to somewhat approximate the intimacy of the larger Caribbean setting. Clustering not only characterized the South, but New England as well, helping to explain significant African influences in its culture.

Unlike Spain with its *Siete Partidas* or France with its *Code Noir*, neither the British Caribbean nor North America developed a single system of laws governing slavery. What emerged instead was a hodge-podge of rules and regulations developed in each of the slaveholding states and colonies, in North America collectively known as the Slave Codes, which were in many ways complementary. As opposed to the French and Spanish notions of providing protections for the enslaved, the Slave Codes were more concerned with protecting the rights of the slaveholder. As such, the enslaved were considered to be chattel, property to be bought and sold like cows and horses. As property, the enslaved could not participate in legal proceedings (unless those deliberations involved other blacks), make a contract, defend themselves against whites, buy or sell, and so on. Punishments included the infamous whip. But of course, all of this assumes an application of the law, such as it was, to cases involving slaves, when in fact whites were often a law unto themselves, treating black folk as they saw fit.

In 1850, there were 3.2 million enslaved persons in the United States, of whom 1.8 million worked on cotton plantations, while others performed a variety of tasks, including raising sugar cane in places like Louisiana. The calculation in general was that one slave was needed for every three acres of cotton. During harvest, adults were expected to pick 150 pounds of cotton per day, sunup to sundown. Given the emphasis on cash crops, little time was available for subsistence farming. In contrast to parts of the Caribbean, some of the larger plantations featured a central kitchen where food was prepared for all, and even when there was no central facility, many received regular rations of meal and salt pork, supplemented at times with peas, rice, syrup, sweet potatoes, and fruit. It is possible to venture interpretive comparisons between this North American distribution system and the provision grounds of the Caribbean, and to assert that the different arrangements engendered docility and passivity in the recipients of the former, while encouraging independence and entrepreneurship in the participants of the latter. A difficulty with such an analysis is the "collapsing" of history – the failure to consider intervening periods of time that also affected later developments. The post-emancipation period in the United States, for example, saw freedpersons more self-reliant than ever. Furthermore, many slaves in North America maintained gardens and livestock, and regularly hunted and fished. North American slave gardens did not approach the scope of the Caribbean provision ground, but too much can be made of the differences.

In addition to cultivating cash crops, the enslaved in North America were carpenters, coopers, wheelwrights, painters, seamstresses, tailors, shoemakers, masons, etc., and were hired out by slaveholders to earn additional income. The hiring out process, more vigorous during the "lay-by" period between harvest and new planting, was similar to the Spanish *jornal* system, although the latter appears to have afforded more autonomy. In urban areas there were other uses for slaves, such as working on the docks as porters. While most of the enslaved in the various towns were used in domestic capacities and as common laborers, others built southern railways, or found themselves in the iron and lead mines of Kentucky, or in textile mills from Florida through Mississippi.

The issue of nonagricultural, vocational skills raises the question of literacy among the enslaved. Through the nineteenth century many people – white, black, or First Nation – could not read or write in the American South (or anywhere else, for that matter). Given that the overall rate of literacy was low, it comes as no surprise that the Slave Codes often included laws against educating the enslaved; the ability to read and write could be employed against slaveholder interests. Despite these concerns and the overall abysmal level of literacy among slaves, there are numerous instances of their learning to read and write. In fact, slaveholders themselves sometimes taught those they claimed to own; Frederick Douglass, for example, was taught by his mistress. But beyond the realm of the exceptional experience, and contrary to expectation, there were even a few schools in the South established for the education of black children, or in which a few black children were enrolled along with white children.

Literacy among the enslaved did not depend exclusively upon receiving education in American schools or at the feet of a slaveholder. Many slaves, perhaps thousands, entered North America already literate, some having learned Portuguese, Spanish, or French, and others Arabic. Recent research has shown that the number of Muslims entering North America from West Africa was much higher than formerly believed. Individuals such as Umar b. Said (d. 1864), who wound up in North Carolina, and Bilali, who lived on the Georgia sea island of Sapelo during the early nineteenth century, were just two of a number of individuals who left written documents, and represent the many literate in Arabic.

Differing skills and varying sorts of responsibilities meant that, while most were enslaved, not all experienced the institution in the same way. While too much can be made of the divide between so-called house and field negroes – as there are many instances of cooperation and collaboration between the two categories – they nonetheless represent different levels of material comfort, exposure to abuse, and even status (however relative). In the same way, the enslaved who were hired out in urban areas, or who enjoyed skills beyond the agricultural, had the potential to pass through enslavement in a fashion less brutalizing than the average field hand. Such distinctions provided one of the bases for eventual class distinctions within the African-derived community. Another basis was color differentiation, a phenomenon that would evolve into subsequent notions of "colorism," but this factor had to be teamed with some vocational distinction to make a difference. Stated another way, there were plenty of lighter-complexioned persons who remained field hands and who made common cause with their darker-hued brethren, but individuals selected to learn other trades, or put to work as domestics, were disproportionately lighter-skinned persons.

Those who acquired additional skills were in instances able to save money and purchase their freedom. Likewise, those whose fathers were white (the 1850 census states there were 246,000 mixed race persons out of 3.2 million enslaved) were in a better position to acquire their freedom, although this was far from guaranteed. As a result, the acquisition of freedom was another basis for eventual class divisions within the black community, and was related to vocational training. In 1790, there were 59,000 free blacks in the United States, with 27,000 in the North and 32,000 in the South. By 1860 there were 488,000 free blacks, 44 percent of whom lived in the South. Of course, the concept of a "free" black in a slaveholding society had many limitations, and there were any number of laws issued for the purpose of inhibiting such freedom, in the North as well as the South. But in spite of heavy repression, the African-descended were able to register modest gains. In 1860, black folk owned over 60,000 acres of land in Virginia, with urban properties worth $463,000; in Charleston, 359 blacks paid taxes on properties valued at more than $778,000. In Maryland, they paid taxes on properties exceeding $1 million in value. But New Orleans represented the pinnacle, as African-descended persons owned properties worth more than $15 million in 1860.

One of the more interesting anomalies of North American slavery was the black slaveholder. He or she was usually someone who purchased his or her spouse, or some other relative, to deliver them from slavery. However, there were blacks who were clearly slaveholders in the grandest sense, such as Cyrian Ricard of Louisiana, a slaveholder of ninety-one persons. It can be observed in his personal, written communications with neighboring white planters that he fancied himself a peer. As such, Monsieur Ricard joins the company of many in places like Trinidad, Saint-Domingue, and Brazil, who also saw no contradiction in the observation that they, as descendants of Africans, claimed to own others of similar descent.

To be sure, in the long annals of history, Europeans have held other Europeans in bondage, as have Asians held other Asians, and Africans other Africans. That the Ricards of North America appear an oddity underscores the degree to which slavery in the New World had become racialized. But the example of Ricard, as unsavory as it seems, cannot be interpreted to mean that anyone in America could become a slaveholder (assuming the desirability of such a goal). As such, does the example of Cyrian Ricard have any implications for contemporary society, where success stories of African Americans are often employed as an argument against the existence of systemic barriers, over which so many of African descent have yet to vault?

Although scholarly debate continues, the essence of the thesis raised by Eric Williams concerning the relationship between slavery, the transatlantic slave trade, and the economic development of Europe and North America remains viable. While scholars may bicker over the profitability of the slave trade, there can be little doubt that participation in it provided a boost to such port cities as Lisbon, Nantes, Liverpool, and Bristol, stimulating a commercial expansion that resulted in the rise of such related industries as shipbuilding, port expansion, the establishment of businesses to service the ports, etc. These secondary and tertiary economic benefits were important, and are not unlike the central role played by slavery and the slave trade in the economy of the United States. The tentacles of both the trade and the institution were far-reaching, touching if not enveloping the lives of many. Even leading universities like Brown, Harvard, and Yale were the beneficiaries of the nefarious enterprise. Brown University was founded in part by slavetraders John and Nicolas Brown, while the founder of Harvard Law School endowed the school with money from slavetrading in Antigua. As for Yale University, its first professorship was endowed by one of the most notorious slavetraders of his day, Philip Livingston, and the school's first scholarships were derived from the profits of slaveholder George Berkeley's New England plantation. We could go on.

By 1840, the American South was cultivating some 60 percent of the world's cotton, representing more than 50 percent of the value of all exports from the United States. In other words, the goods and capital imported to develop the United States was largely paid for by slaves. Ports such as Charleston and New Orleans were not only paid for with cotton grown by slaves, but were also literally dug out of the earth by the enslaved, as was true of a significant proportion of the country's colonial and antebellum infrastructure. New York City was itself a major and direct beneficiary of enslaved labor, as cotton was distributed and exported from there in exchange for fees and services connected to insurance, interest, commissions, shipping and handling charges, and so on. As such, it is not at all surprising that Wall Street, site and symbol of the world's leading financial markets, was originally the site of a slave market. The argument can even be extended, as 70 percent of the cotton grown in the American South was used by Britain's textile industry, and it was by means of textile exports that Britain financed its empire. The statement, "We built this country," commonly heard in African American casual conversation, is no groundless assertion; indeed, not to take anything away from the millions of European and Asian immigrants who also labored in the United States, the statement is more accurate than not. In fact, it leads to the following query: Just who were the founding fathers, and what about the founding mothers?

A bloody apocalypse would bring the institution of slavery to an end in the United States. But neither did that war, nor myriad emancipatory actions throughout the Americas, simply materialize out of thin air. Rather, all such actions developed out of a context of long and bitter struggle waged by people of African descent, a struggle to which Chapter 6 turns.

Suggestions for Further Reading

The literature on slavery in the Americas is enormous, examining general trends and specific regions and locales, the treatment, cultures, and societies of the enslaved, the lives of slaveholders, relations with other societal components, the economies impacted, the role of ideologies, and so on. One could begin with Eric Williams, *Capitalism and Slavery* (Chapel Hill: University of North Carolina Press, 1944) for a discussion of its impact on capitalist development, and contrast it with David Eltis, *The Rise of African Slavery in the Americas* (Cambridge and New York: Cambridge University Press, 2000). Regarding the idea of a second slavery in the Americas, see Dale W. Tomich, *Through the Prism of Slavery: Labor, Capital, and World Economy* (Lanham, MD: Rowman and Littlefield, 2004). David Brion Davis' *The Problem of Slavery in Western Culture* (Ithaca, NY: Cornell University Press, 1996) and *The Problem of Slavery in the Age of Revolution, 1770–1823* (Ithaca, NY: Cornell University Press, 1975) remain valuable contributions, although they are not so much concerned with the slave experience as with the implications of slavery for Western society.

As for Caribbean slavery, Carolyn E. Fick's *The Making of Haiti: The Saint Domingue Revolution from Below* (Knoxville: University of Tennessee Press, 1990) is a wonderful introduction to Haitian slavery and is a response to the pioneering contribution of C.L.R. James, *The Black Jacobins: Toussaint Louverture and the San Domingo Revolution* (New York: Dial Press, 1938). These works also inform Chapter 6 of this book. For the English-speaking Caribbean, consider Randy M. Browne, *Surviving Slavery in the British Caribbean* (Philadelphia: University of Pennsylvania Press, 2017); Vincent Brown, *The Reaper's Garden: Death and Power in the World of Atlantic Slavery* (Cambridge, MA: Harvard University Press, 2008); Verene Shepherd, *Livestock, Sugar and Slavery: Contested Terrain in Colonial Jamaica* (Kingston: Ian Randle, 2009); Verene Shepherd and Hilary McDonald Beckles, *Caribbean Slavery in the Atlantic World: A Student Reader* (Kingston, Jamaica: Ian Randle; Oxford: James Currey; Princeton, NJ: Markus Weiner, 2000). Others include Orlando Patterson, *The Sociology of Slavery: An Analysis of the Origins, Development and Structure of Negro Slave Society in Jamaica* (London: MacGibbon and Kee, 1967); Richard S. Dunn, *Sugar and Slaves: The Rise of the Planter Class in the English West Indies, 1624–1713* (Chapel Hill: University of North Carolina Press, 1972); B.W. Higman, *Slave Populations of the British Caribbean, 1807–1834* (Baltimore, MD: Johns Hopkins University Press, 1984); James Millette, *Society and Politics in Colonial Trinidad* (Curepe, Trinidad: Omega, 1970); Gabriel Debien, *Les esclaves aux Antilles françaises, XVIIe–XVIIIe siècles* (Basse Terre: Société d'histoire de la Guadeloupe, 1974); Sidney Mintz, *Sweetness and Power: The Place of Sugar in Modern History* (New York: Viking, 1985); Carl Campbell, *Cedulants and Capitulants: The Politics of the Coloured Opposition in the Slave Society of Trinidad, 1783–1838* (Port of Spain, Trinidad: Paria Publishing Co., 1992); and Bridget Brereton, *A History of Modern Trinidad, 1783–1962* (Port of Spain, Trinidad: Heinemann, 1981). For the cocoa industry in Trinidad, see Kathleen E. Phillips Lewis, "British Imperial Policy and Colonial Economic Development: The Cocoa Industry in Trinidad, 1838–1939" (PhD thesis, University of Manitoba, Winnipeg, 1994).

Works focusing on women and gender in the Caribbean include Sasha Turner, *Contested Bodies: Pregnancy, Childrearing, and Slavery in Jamaica* (Philadelphia: University of Pennsylvania Press, 2017); Jennifer L. Morgan, *Laboring Women: Gender and Reproduction in the Making of New World Slavery* (Philadelphia: University of Pennsylvania Press, 2004); Verene Shepherd, *Livestock, Sugar and Slavery: Contested Terrain in Colonial Jamaica* (Kingston: Ian Randle, 2009); Verene Shepherd, Bridget Brereton, and Barbara Bailey, eds., *Engendering History: Caribbean Women in Historical Perspective* (Kingston: Ian Randle and London: James Currey, 1995); and Hilary McDonald Beckles, *Natural Rebels: A Social History of Enslaved Women in Barbados* (London: Zed Books, 1989). Lucille Mathurin-Mair, *The Rebel Woman in the West Indies During Slavery* (Kingston: Institute of Jamaica, 1975); Lucille Mathurin-Mair,

A Historical Study of Women in Jamaica, 1655–1844 (Kingston: University of the West Indies Press, 2007). Darlene Clark Hine and David Barry Gaspar, eds., *More than Chattel: Black Women and Slavery in the Americas* (Bloomington: Indiana University Press, 1996), expands the scope of the discussion.

For Latin America and Brazil, see Gonzalo Aguirre Beltrán, *La población negra de México: estudio ethnohistórico* (Mexico, DF: Fondo de Cultura Economica, 1972), 2nd ed.; Frederick P. Bowser, *The African Slave in Colonial Peru, 1524–1650* (Stanford: Stanford University Press, 1974); Colin Palmer, *Slaves of the White God: Blacks in Mexico, 1570–1650* (Cambridge, MA: Harvard University Press, 1976); Leslie B. Rout, Jr., *The African Experience in Spanish America: 1502 to the Present Day* (Cambridge: Cambridge University Press, 1976); Franklin W. Knight, *Slave Society in Cuba During the Nineteenth Century* (Madison: University of Wisconsin Press, 1970), and *The African Dimension in Latin American Societies* (New York: Macmillan, 1974); Rolando Mellafe, *La introducción de la esclavitude negra en Chile: tráfico y rutas* (Santiago, Chile: Editorial Universitaria, 1984); Manuel Moreno Fraginals, *El ingenio: complejo económico social cubano del azúcar*, 3 vols. (Havana: Editorial de Ciencias Sociales, 1964, 1978); Laird W. Bergard, Fe Iglesias García, and María del Carmen Barcia, *The Cuban Slave Market, 1790–1880* (Cambridge: Cambridge University Press, 1995); Stuart Schwartz, *Sugar Plantations in the Formation of Brazilian Society: Bahia, 1550–1835* (Cambridge and New York: Cambridge University Press, 1985); Mary C. Karasch, *Slave Life in Rio de Janeiro, 1808–1850* (Princeton, NJ: Princeton University Press, 1987); Katia M. de Queirós Mattoso, *To Be a Slave in Brazil, 1550–1888*, trans. Arthur Goldhammer (New Brunswick, NJ: Rutgers University Press, 1986); Herman Bennett, *Colonial Blackness: A History of Afro-Mexico* (Bloomington: Indiana University Press, 2009); Flávio dos Santos Gomes, *Histórias de quilombas: mocambos e comunidades de senzalas no Rio de Janeiro, século XIX* (Rio de Janeiro: Arquivo Nacional, 1995); Kathryn R. Dungy, *The Conceptualization of Race in Puerto Rico, 1800–1850* (New York: Peter Lang, 2015); Yuko Miki, *Frontiers of Citizenship: A Black and Indigenous History of Postcolonial Brazil* (New York: Cambridge University Press, 2018).

For what becomes the United States, there are myriad studies. For the experience of slaves, John Hope Franklin and Alfred A. Moss, Jr., *From Slavery to Freedom: A History of African Americans* (New York: McGraw Hill, 1994), 7th ed., is always a helpful place to start. Some of the more important recent publications include Walter Johnson, *River of Dark Dreams: Slavery and Empire in the Cotton Kingdom* (Cambridge and London: Belknap of Harvard University Press, 2013), and his *Soul by Soul: Life Inside the Antebellum Slave Market* (Cambridge, MA: Harvard University Press, 1999); Edward E. Baptist, *The Half Has Never Been Told: Slavery and the Making of American Capitalism* (New York: Basic Books, 2014); Sven Beckert, *Empire of Cotton: A Global History* (New York: Knopf Doubleday, 2014); Rashauna Johnson,

Slavery's Metropolis: Unfree Labor in New Orleans during the Age of Revolutions (Cambridge: Cambridge University Press, 2016); Ira Berlin, *Many Thousands Gone: The First Two Centuries of Slavery in North America* (Cambridge, MA: Belknap of Harvard University Press, 1998), or his more accessible *Generations of Captivity: A History of African-American Slaves* Cambridge and London: Belknap of Harvard University Press, 2003); David R. Roediger, *The Wages of Whiteness: Race and the Making of the American Working Class* (London and New York: Verso, 1991).

Critical inquiries centering on gender include Thavolia Glymph, *Out of the House of Bondage: The Transformation of the Plantation Household* (Cambridge: Cambridge University Press, 2008); Tera W. Hunter, *Bound in Wedlock: Slave and Free Black Marriage in the Nineteenth Century* (Cambridge and London: Belknap of Harvard University Press, 2017); Daina Ramey Berry, *The Price for Their Pound of Flesh: The Value of the Enslaved, from Womb to Grave, in the Building of a Nation* (Boston: Beacon Press, 2017); Brenda E. Stevenson, *Life in Black and White: Family and Community in the Slave South* (New York: Oxford University Press, 1996); Kathleen M. Brown, *Good Wives, Nasty Wenches, and Anxious Patriarchs: Gender, Race, and Power in Colonial Virginia* (Chapel Hill: University of North Carolina Press, 1996). There is, of course, the classic work of Deborah Gray White, *Ar'nt I a Woman: Female Slaves in the Plantation South* (New York: W.W. Norton Company, 1985).

Among older yet beneficial monographs are John W. Blassingame, *The Slave Community: Plantation Life in the Antebellum South* (New York: Oxford University Press, 1972); Eugene D. Genovese, *Roll, Jordan, Roll: The World the Slaves Made* (New York: Pantheon Books, 1971); Kenneth M. Stampp, *The Peculiar Institution: Slavery in the Ante-Bellum South* (New York: Knopf, 1956); Nathan I. Huggins, *Black Odyssey: The Afro-American Ordeal in Slavery* (New York: Pantheon, 1977). A classic remains Winthrop D. Jordan, *White Over Black: American Attitudes Toward the Negro, 1550–1812* (Chapel Hill: University of North Carolina Press, 1968).

CHAPTER 6

Asserting the Right to Be

The achievement of freedom throughout the Americas, however qualified, was very much a consequence of the myriad struggles of the African-descended. Their efforts would be supported by well-meaning whites and some indigenous groups. The American War of Independence and the French Revolution would contribute concepts and language to the struggle, but the enslaved did not need theoretical principles, developed to facilitate a breakaway republic in North America or the resolution of class conflict in Europe, to know more definitively than any enunciation of Enlightenment rationality could ever approximate, the depth of their anguish and yearning for deliverance.

The fight against slavery would assume any number of shapes, and was waged in a thousand theaters of war, both literal and figurative. Activities from large-scale revolt to marronage to absconding to work slowdowns to poisoning were employed throughout the period of legal enslavement. However, as the anti-slavery struggle progressed, it became clear that the African was not only combating a nefarious system of inequitable labor extraction, but was also up against a force arguably even more insidious: the conviction that African ancestry was an immutable mark of inferiority. Slavery was to leave an indelible imprint upon the attitudes and opinions of all who lived in the Americas, particularly those of European ancestry, who by and large came to view the African and her descendants as intellectually and morally deficient. Various ideas would come along to buttress this view, including social Darwinism and the rise of pseudoscientific racism in the nineteenth century, by which time African inferiority was held as a certainty. Given the rise of racism, the destruction of slavery did not end the woes of African-descended people. Freedom was not the absence of slavery and, in any event, did not automatically follow abolition. Even whites who supported abolition did not necessarily subscribe to its full implications – that black folk should enjoy complete, broadly defined freedoms with rights and privileges identical to those of whites. White opposition to black enslavement did not mean white acceptance of black equality; the phenomenon of racism would prove to be an even more intractable foe than the planter class.

What this meant for the African-descended is that the fight against slavery, while obviously crucial, was at the end of the day only one component of a more complex combat, a lone (though major) battle in a larger campaign for freedom. Forces of oppression assumed temporal, ever-shifting guises, and the vanquishing of one target, such as slavery, often led to discouragement and bewilderment as racism, seemingly defeated, simply morphed into a subsequent form, such as North American segregation. In view of the changing face of oppression, freedom came to mean different things to different people of African descent. We must keep in mind the variable, relative nature of freedom if we are to understand the African's fight for freedom, beginning with the struggle against slavery.

Armed Revolt and Autonomous Space

It did not take long for Africans to revolt. Rebellion began at the initial point of capture within Africa itself, continued in the barracoons, and often mutinously erupted aboard the slavers. Once in the New World, Africans were as quick to seize upon any opportunity to reverse their circumstances. As early as 1503, Hispaniola's governor Nicolás de Ovando complained that African *ladinos* were colluding with the Taíno population and fleeing to the mountains to establish maroon or runaway communities. Two decades later, in 1522, some twenty slaves abandoned an *ingenio* (sugar mill and adjacent lands) owned by the governor of the island, Admiral Diego Columbus, son of the famed explorer and himself a substantial slaveholder. Anticipating events on the same island some 300 years later, the insurrectionists mobilized an equal number of co-conspirators on neighboring

FIGURE 9 Francisco de Arobe with his sons Pedro and Domingo – Francisco de Arobe was the leader of a Central American maroon community, c.1599. Museo de América, Madrid. A black and white version of this figure will appear in some formats. For the color version, please refer to the plate section.

establishments and, machetes in hand, literally dismembered planta-tion personnel and livestock, leaving burned houses and crops in their wake. A mixed force of Europeans and Taíno effectively ended the revolt; when the dust settled, at least fifteen people were dead, at least nine of whom were Europeans. Diego Columbus reflected that if the uprising had not been quelled quickly, many more "Christian" lives would have been lost. Thus began the first collective insurrection of Africans in the Americas, a movement largely composed of Senegambians, some of whom were probably Muslims. Senegambians would continue to lead revolts in Hispaniola through the middle of the sixteenth century, after which they disappear from the record there.

But Hispaniola was not the only New World site of rebellion in the early sixteenth century. Revolts broke out everywhere: Puerto Rico in 1527; Santa Marta, Colombia in 1529; the Panamanian town of Acla in 1530; Panama City in 1531; Mexico City in 1537; the Venezuelan towns of Coro in 1532 and Buría in 1555; and San Pedro, Honduras in 1548 (see Figure 9). White colonists in Panama had complained about maroon (runaway) communities prior to 1556, but by that year the threat fully surfaced. Ballano, an African-born leader of royal descent, led one of these communities, a mixture of *ladinos* and *bozales*. He was lured into attending peace talks at a banquet site and, eerily fore-shadowing Haitian leader Toussaint Louverture's experience with

Napoleon, was immediately captured and eventually taken to Spain; unlike Toussaint, Ballano was given a royal pension, living out the rest of his life in Seville (where there was already a considerable African presence, as previously mentioned).

In 1553, the enslaved rose up in Peru and fought the Spaniards for more than a year. They again took up arms in Santiago de Chile in 1647, when an earthquake provided the occasion for some 400 slaves to rebel under a leader known as the "King of Guinea." Venezuela experienced a series of slave uprisings, such as the 1732 revolt at Puerto Cabello and Capaya; the 1747 revolt led by Miguel Luengo in Yare; the uprisings in Caucagua and Capaya in 1794; the rebellion of Maracaibo in 1799; and the insurrection in Sierras de Coro in 1795, probably the most significant of all, led by José Leonardo Chirinos.

Maroon formation was a central feature of Cuban slavery as well. Those fleeing the institution took refuge in the mountains, where they formed *palenques*, or *cumbes*. Life in the *palenques* was supported by a combination of agriculture and trade. Manioc and sweet potatoes were grown, while cattle were confiscated from neighboring estates. Honey and virgin wax were sold to outsiders in exchange for weapons, gunpowder, tools, sugar, and clothing. Transactions often required third parties, such as slaves on nearby plantations, who went to town and made the purchases.

The *palenques* were a constant source of concern, as they inspired rebellion and defiance among the enslaved. The government tried to eradicate *palenques* in Cuba between 1848 and 1853, but was only partially successful as there were literally hundreds of *palenques* throughout the island. The more permanent, better defended ones were located in the eastern mountains, including Bumba, Maluala, Moa or El Frijol, and Tiguabos, all of which lasted until the first War of Independence in 1868, when *palenque* members joined the Cuban Liberation Army in large numbers. The 1868 decree of the victors recognized the right of the *palenques* to continue to exist; some eventually faded from existence, while others became towns or rural neighborhoods and were joined by Cubans of all backgrounds. One of the most famous *palenque* leaders was Ventura Sánchez, whose nineteenth-century community was near Santiago de Cuba.

One pattern of resistance is therefore clear: if the enslaved could flee to an inaccessible place beyond the reach of authorities, he could live in a manner more of his choosing. It was not Africa, but barring repatriation, it was as close as he was going to get. Success depended upon a number of factors, including the reception of the indigenous population. If he could reach an understanding with them, whereby he would not be returned to white authorities, he had a chance of surviving. The understanding sometimes involved forming settlements close to but independent of indigenous communities, and at other times it meant becoming an integral part of those communities, including intermarriage.

Creating a maroon society was one thing; keeping it free of colonial control or interference was another. The former was an act of resistance, an affirmation of human dignity, whereas the latter often saw those values compromised. The preservation of autonomy sometimes meant yielding to the pressures of slaveholding interests to return runaway slaves in exchange for continuing non-interference. Quite the dilemma, it epitomizes a series of predicaments confronted by the slave seeking freedom. Indeed, the choices facing the enslaved were severely proscribed, and the adoption of any one of them usually carried some element of excruciating sacrifice. Freedom was never free.

Perhaps the greatest example of maroon communities was Palmares. Established as early as 1605 and lasting until around 1695 in Pernambuco, north-eastern Brazil, Palmares ("palm forests") was actually much more than a community of runaways, and it is more accurate to think of this "black republic" as an independent state; as such, it was the first created by non-native peoples in the New World. In the parlance of the Brazilian context, Palmares was one of ten major *quilombos* or *mocambos* (terms derived from African languages and equivalent to the *palenques* or *cumbes* of Spanish-claimed lands) in colonial Brazil, and of the ten, it was by far the most significant. Two others, one in Minas Gerais and the other in Mato Grosso, lasted from 1712 to 1719 and from 1770 to 1795, respectively, while the other seven were wiped out within a few years of their founding. Some of these *quilombos* were in fact combined settlements of Africans and First Nation societies, and at least two were led by African women. In contrast, Palmares practically spanned the whole of the seventeenth century, with a peak population of at least 5,000, and possibly as high as 30,000. Palmares was such a threat that it endured successive military attacks from the Portuguese between 1672 and 1694, at a rate of one every fifteen months, assaults costly in lives and resources.

Palmares was in reality a composite of federated political units or *palmars*, each of which owed ultimate allegiance to the sovereign, the *Ganga-Zumba* ("great lord"), the greatest of whom was Zumbi.

Initially founded by African-born runaways, distinctions between those from Africa and those born in Brazil, the *crioulos*, became less significant over time; indeed, given the lengthy history of Palmares, a point was reached at which many of its citizens knew nothing of Africa or slavery first hand, having been born in the *quilombo*. Friction between the Portuguese and Palmares intensified as individuals increasingly fled the surrounding *engenhos* (sugar mills and adjacent lands) for the *quilombo*. The final destruction of Palmares came after a siege of forty-four days, after which the Palmares ruler was captured and decapitated, his head publicly displayed to dispel belief in his immortality.

In addition to those mentioned, Brazil was inundated with smaller *quilombos* throughout much of its slave history, including those in lands surrounding Bahia in north-east Brazil, of which Salvador was the principal port and city. A major source of sugar cane production between 1570 and 1680, Bahia registered the existence of a *quilombo* as early as 1575. By the turn of the seventeenth century there were reports of maroons (*quilombolas*) living in the mountains, having inter-married with the local population. The tradition of the maroon in Bahia continued through the nineteenth century, when it met with Portuguese opposition and the resulting destruction of such *quilombos* as the Buraco de Tatú, just outside Salvador. Even so, some 3,500 *quilombos* still exist in Brazil, where descendants of enslaved ancestors continue to live, to some of whom land titles have been granted.

The maroons of Jamaica have also attracted considerable interest. With the instability of the transition to British rule in 1655, some 1,500 of the enslaved struck out on their own, forming three distinct groups, only two of which have been written about. One group settled in the mountains under the leadership of Juan Lubola, and the other gathered at Los Vermejales (or the Vermahalis), on a plateau in the interior of the island. The maroons under Lubola sided with the remaining Spanish settlers against the British until 1658, when the Spanish were defeated. Lubola promptly entered into an alliance with the British that recognized the legitimacy of his 150-person community, but it also called for him to fight with the British against other maroons; this policy of forming impermanent alliances made sense, but its defects would soon be revealed. Lubola was killed in a raid on the maroons of Los Vermejales, who managed to retreat to the north-east part of the island. Los Vermejales was eventually joined in the last quarter of the seventeenth century by some 200 runaways,

mostly Africans from the Gold Coast (so-called Coromantee or Kro-
manti, after the Gold Coast port, otherwise known as Akan speakers)
and Malagasy captives from a shipwreck. Together in the hills of
eastern Jamaica, they established communities informed by African
cultures and folkways. They became known as the Windward group,
with Nanny Town as their center, named after a woman skilled in war
and *obeah* (the practice of manipulating spiritual forces to inflict
harm). In the meantime, another group of Gold Coast rebels settled
in the mountainous areas in the island's center, where they became
known as the Leeward group.

Around 1720 the First Maroon War broke out between the
maroons and the British who, moving into the north-east coast to
establish new plantations, suffered continuous assault and
harassment. Cudjoe, an adept of guerrilla warfare, led the Leeward
group, while the Windward sector, initially under Nanny's control,
was now marshaled by Cuffee following Nanny's planter-instigated
murder in 1733. The Maroon War dragged on, with Nanny Town
changing hands several times, and in 1735 the Windward group splintered into two. One of the two factions, some 300 women, men, and
children, walked more than a hundred miles to join Cudjoe and the
Leewards. In a defining decision that revealed the complex and contradictory nature of the Leeward leader as well as the dilemma of
maroon life, Cudjoe essentially rejected the Windward refugees, only
accommodating them for several months until they could return to the
north-east. Cudjoe, for all of his bravery and skill, was reluctant to
unduly anger the British; the defense of his freedom included avoiding
unnecessary confrontation.

Unfortunately for the maroon community and the enslaved,
Cudjoe's war weariness, or perhaps his treachery, became apparent
in March of 1739 when he agreed to a treaty with the British. Its terms
recognized his community as free and owners of the land adjoining
their towns, some 1,500 acres. The treaty further allowed the maroons
to hunt within three miles of a white-held establishment, to pursue
their own form of justice with the exception of administering capital
punishment, and to sell their produce in local markets. For such
liberties, however, Cudjoe sold the store. He agreed to create roads
linking his settlements to coastal plantations to promote "friendly
correspondence"; he agreed to allow two white men to live among
the maroons for purposes of surveilling them; but most egregious of
all, he agreed to fight Britain's external enemies, to kill and destroy

all in rebellion to British authority, and to return all runaway slaves to their slaveholders for compensation. Prior to the signing of the treaty, Cudjoe reportedly fell to his knees and kissed the feet of the British officer, begging forgiveness.

Certain of Cudjoe's generals could not accept this turn of events, but their attempts to organize a response were discovered; Cudjoe himself put two of them to death. Others in opposition to the treaty tried to develop strategies throughout the island, especially in Spanish Town, but the authorities responded with brutal repression. The end of the First Maroon War in 1739 saw the Windwards, their numbers depleted and facing eminent war with the Leewards, sign a treaty similar to that of Cudjoe's. However, the spirit of rebellion would resurface some twenty years later, directly inspired by the early maroon example.

In Antigua, maroons preceded the rapid, late seventeenth-century advance of sugar cane. By 1678 there were about 4,500 residents on the island, more or less equally divided between Africans and Europeans, but already there were significant problems with runaways, especially in the south-west, in the Shekerly Hills of St. Mary's Parish. Records show that the maroons were a hodgepodge of African groups, including Akan, Igbo, "Angolans," and Malagasy. These strongholds threatened British planters, but the latter had time on their side, as the gradual deforestation of the island eventually led to the termination of the maroon threat.

In the islands controlled by the French, maroons were divided into *petit* and *grand marronage*. The former involved small groups who abandoned the plantation for several days, only to return. Grand marronage could also involve small numbers, but was characterized by the fairly permanent nature of the stay, and therefore of greater concern. One of the first to come to the attention of the French was a group of about 400 to 500 in Martinique who, under the leadership of Francisque Faboulé in 1665, stirred such trouble that the authorities negotiated a short-lived agreement with them. Faboulé was granted his freedom and 1,000 pounds of tobacco, while his followers were given immunity from punishment. Faboulé would form another group of runaways, but was eventually captured and sent to the galleys.

Guadeloupe also had its share of maroons, one group an amalgam of Africans and the autochthonous population led by one Gabriel as early as 1707. Gabriel viewed his community as independent, and preferred to be called "Monsieur le Gouverneur." Though they raided for livestock, the maroons in Guadeloupe were even more notorious for taking enslaved women, a reflection of imbalanced sex ratios. By 1726 some 600 maroons were living in four distinct communities in Guadeloupe.

In Saint-Domingue, maroons were famous for frequently raiding nearby plantations and netting livestock while leaving fields ablaze, suggesting an interest not only in survival, but in the destruction of slavery altogether. The French responded with vigorous campaigns, and although leaders of the various maroons were captured and punished, the communities themselves continued under new leaders. In the area around the northern coastal town of Le Cap, for example, leaders such as Noël wreaked havoc until his capture in 1775, only to be replaced by Télémaque Conga and Isaac and Pyrrhus Candide, who pursued the triple objectives of livestock confiscation, female abduction, and field torching. The most famous of all Saint-Domingue's maroon societies was Le Maniel. Established at some point before the end of the seventeenth century, Le Maniel successfully defended against repeated attacks throughout the eighteenth century and witnessed the dawn of Haiti. Le Maniel owed much of its success to its location on the border with the Spanish-held eastern part of the island, from which it received support against the French. Indeed, together with the southern mountainous area, the Spanish-held section of the island was the preferred destination of most maroons, where some 3,000 are estimated to have settled by 1751.

In general, the maroon communities of Saint-Domingue were overwhelmingly male, with women accounting for no more than 20 percent of the population. Most were born in West Central Africa, and had labored in the fields. Although removed from the plantation, the maroons stayed in touch with those who remained, receiving provisions and news of slaveholder activities and intentions. The maroons also kept open lines of communication with free blacks who gave some assistance, a reminder that interaction within Saint-Domingue society could be fluid.

François Makandal is probably the most famous of the maroon leaders. His background is rather curious, as he is said to have been born in an Islamic society in West Africa, raised as a Muslim, and literate in Arabic. Captured at the age of twelve and shipped to Saint-Domingue, his grounding in Islam may have been incomplete, for by the time we encounter him on the island, Makandal is a full-blown voodoo priest. Voodoo, *vodu*, and *vodun* are terms that derive from

Dahomean words for "gods"; the religion as practiced in Haiti, Martinique, Louisiana, and Mississippi, represents both a transformation and amalgamation of various religions from West and West Central Africa, specifically Fon-Ewe-Yoruba influences from the former and Bakongo elements from the latter. Due to either an amputated hand from sugar mill machinery, or a dispute with a slaveholder over a black woman, Makandal set off on an independent course. An eloquent man with extensive knowledge of both medicinal and injurious properties of plants and herbs, he developed a following of undetermined size. In concert with those who systematically pillaged estates, but unlike others content to live in isolation, Makandal developed a conspiracy to destroy slavery as an institution, and recruited followers from the plantations. The blow for freedom was to begin with a general poisoning of the water in the town of Le Cap, highlighting poisoning as a weapon of choice among the enslaved in Saint-Domingue. As would be true in many conspiracies, carelessness led to his arrest in early 1758, before the revolt could begin, and after a brief but sensational escape, he was recaptured and burned at the stake. Makandal's career was an indication, however, of epic events soon to come. The Revolution that would arrive some thirty years later saw the forces of marronage combine with those on the plantation to effect sweeping change.

In various places throughout the Caribbean, Africans and Native Americans engaged in a complex series of relations. Not unlike the dilemma facing the Jamaican maroons, the Arawak and Carib confronted the issue of runaways in their efforts to defend their freedoms from European colonial powers. The Arawak and Carib were formidable forces in the eastern and southern Caribbean, and unlike their indigenous counterparts in the larger islands (or Greater Antilles), they used their considerable naval capabilities to both defend themselves and to counterattack Spanish positions in the sixteenth and seventeenth centuries. Runaways often reached their territories, where they either merged or formed associated but independent communities. Some merged communities reportedly began with seventeenth-century shipwrecks, such as the "Black Caribs" of St. Vincent, whose descendants were later taken to Belize, Guatemala, and Honduras, where they would form the Garifuna nation (or Garinagu, as they prefer to name themselves); and the "Zambos Mosquitos" of Nicaragua's Mosquito Coast. Reasons for not forming single communities included either party's desire to preserve their cultural integrity.

But the African was also aware that the Carib and Arawak had their own version of slavery, and sometimes re-enslaved runaways for their own purposes, or returned runaways to Europeans. Runaways were especially vulnerable following peace treaties between native groups and Europeans, a provision of which invariably called for returning the absconded. For example, runaways were brought back to the French in the mid-seventeenth century as part of a treaty, but apparently not fast enough, as token Carib compliance caused the French to oust them from Martinique in 1658. The Black Caribs of St. Vincent momentarily stopped returning runaways to the English after 1680, having come to regard runaways as societal members. Runaways from the neighboring islands of Guadeloupe, Barbados, and Martinique reached such numbers, however, that the threatened and overextended St. Vincent Caribs relented and agreed to return the later arrivals.

The territory that would become the United States also had maroon communities; at least fifty existed in the swamps, forests, and mountains of Florida, Louisiana, Mississippi, Alabama, Georgia, Virginia, and the Carolinas between 1672 and 1864. Often ephemeral and numerically smaller than their counterparts elsewhere in the Americas, these maroons were frequently related to the frontier, beyond which white settlement was sparse and indigenous reception a possibility. Enslaved blacks often struck out for the backwoods to seek refuge in otherwise inhospitable, inaccessible, mountainous terrain. One early retreat center was St. Augustine in Florida, founded as a Spanish position around 1565. Beginning in the late seventeenth century, Carolina slaves fled to St. Augustine and the neighboring village of Gracia Real de Santa Teresa Mose, or Fort Mose, for asylum; those involved in the famous Stono Rebellion of 1739 may have also been headed for St. Augustine, where they could acquire their freedom due to Spanish–English hostility. St. Augustine continued as a problem for English planters through the colonial period, after which their focus shifted to the growing challenge of runaways among the Seminoles (a term meaning "runaways"). Like the Carib and Arawak, blacks either intermarried with or established separate but linked villages among the Seminoles. Africans and Seminoles became culturally fused, establishing a fortified position of their own, Fort Blount. The number of runaways among the Seminoles rose so dramatically that Carolina and Georgia planters demanded a federal response, especially after a Georgia army was repulsed in 1812.

The United States government intervened, and none other than Andrew Jackson himself led the charge, attacking Fort Blount in July of 1816. Confronted by the Americans, some Seminoles switched sides and became slavetraders, but this is only part of a more complicated story. When the United States claimed Florida in 1821, Africans and Native Americans responded by retreating even further into the swamps and forests of Florida. The so-called Seminole Wars ensued, lasting until 1842.

In colonial Louisiana, maroon communities were established in the cypress swamps, *la siprière*, where they grew their own crops, gathered berries and nuts, and sold baskets and squared cypress logs to outsiders. Like their counterparts elsewhere, the maroons also raided nearby establishments to supplement their provisions. By the end of the American War of Independence, maroons controlled virtually the whole of the Bas du Fleuve, the area between the mouth of the Mississippi River and New Orleans. As the maroons were in defensible terrain and the white population minimal, there was not much the latter could do for a significant period of time. But the dynamics of the area began to change by the middle of the eighteenth century, such that in 1784 St. Malo, leader of the maroons, was captured and hanged along with many of his followers, signaling the beginning of the end of an era.

There were also maroon communities in the Dismal Swamp, between Virginia and North Carolina, where at one point nearly 2,000 runaways lived. In South Carolina and Georgia, maroons both traded with whites and raided their establishments. White fear of insurrection led to a number of laws being passed, calling for the destruction of these communities and the killing of their leaders. Maroons invariably enjoyed relations with the enslaved on farms and plantations, and planters frequently complained that maroon influence was corrupting their slaves, inspiring them to rebel. As a result, expeditions were launched all over the South to rein in the maroons. Their numbers were reduced here and there, but on the whole maroons continued through the Civil War.

A major feature of North American society, not necessarily true elsewhere in the Americas, was the bifurcation of the republic between slaveholding and free states. The existence of the latter presented another option for the enslaved, arguably another sort of marronage. The organized procession of escaping to the North, referred to as the Underground Railroad, was therefore a means to another kind of

existence. Those who escorted and facilitated the runaways, the con-
ductors or operators, numbered at least 3,200. The greatest of all,
Harriet Tubman, would actually hire herself out as a domestic servant
for several months to support her work. An extraordinary individual,
she was alone responsible for conducting at least 300 persons to
freedom, threatening to shoot any who succumbed to fear and
attempted to turn back. The Underground Railroad was so effective
that 100,000 persons may have escaped between 1810 and 1850,
creating such a problem that in 1850 the country passed the Fugitive
Slave Act, granting slaveholders the right to arrest and return runaways from any state in the Union.

An important station in the Underground Railroad was Canada,
which in instances served as the last stop in the escape from slavery.
There was indeed African slavery in Canada, but the numbers were
relatively small; in New France (which before 1763 included Acadia
and the Canadian provinces of Quebec, Montreal, and Three Rivers;
in 1763 Acadia and Canada would be sold to England), there were
never more than several hundred enslaved blacks, at a time when most
of the enslaved were Native Americans. From 1763 until 1834 and the
abolition of slavery throughout British-claimed territories, the institution continued to be relatively insignificant, from several thousand
to perhaps tens of thousands enslaved (estimates vary), largely used in
domestic work and on small farms, but who also worked as sailors,
fur traders, fishers, miners, and as artisans in various capacities.

As abolitionist sentiment gained momentum in Canada in the latter
decades of the eighteenth century, it became increasingly attractive as
a refuge from slavery. Nova Scotia and Ontario (in Upper Canada)
were particularly distinguished as reception centers. With the
1850 passage of the Fugitive Slave Act, Canada became an even more
important destination for those escaping slavery, a number of whom
now had to leave US territory altogether. This does not mean, however, that in running from slavery they found Canada to be free of
racism. They did not.

Finally, the ultimate maroon formation developed in the Guianas.
Maroons in French and British Guyana were eradicated by the end of
the eighteenth century, but those in Suriname continue to the present,
representing a legacy of more than 300 years. Formerly called "Bush
Negroes," this group escaped the littoral plantations of Suriname in
the late seventeenth and early eighteenth centuries and moved into the
interior, where they fought long and hard against a colonial military.

Treaties were signed and broken, but the Surinamese maroons continued on, living in states of self-sufficiency save for their reliance on such manufactured goods as firearms. Principally informed by African cultures, various cultural groupings emerged out of the maroons, with the Juka (Djuka) and the Saramaka as the most prominent. Their lifestyles have been the subject of significant anthropological investigation.

Everyday/way Resistance

Somewhere between forming maroon communities and collectively taking up arms to dismantle the slaveocracy were vast numbers of slaves who found other ways to resist, and did so on a regular basis. Some eventually joined the maroons, while others ultimately took up the gun (or some other implement transformed into a weapon). But many did neither, and instead employed other methods to contest both the substance and the implications of slavery.

Although this section concerns resistance to slavery, it must be acknowledged that there were many blacks who did not resist. Some would indeed internalize racism, accepting the idea that their fate was determined by the Hamitic curse and that they could expect no better outcome. In tandem, there were certainly those who yearned for any degree of recognition from whites. This is to say that not everyone resisted, and that some indeed capitulated. The seemingly endless betrayals of conspiracies are evidence of this.

But many, perhaps most, did resist, and resistance assumed many forms, covert and overt, sporadic and continuous, direct and indirect. It is probably a mistake to think of resistance as a continuum, ranging from "sassing massa" in the lower register, to maroons and organized revolution in the highest. First of all, individuals who experienced any substantial length of life may have made any number of decisions, over time exhibiting various behaviors that were different, even contradictory. While there were surely those whose actions were consistent, some who resisted at certain points in their lives may have cooperated at other times. Second, any demonstrable action of resistance was the product of not only the individual's will and disposition, but also the result of several calculations. In addition to determining the likely success of any given action, the individual had to define the meaning of success itself. What of consequences for family and

friends? What of separation from family and friends? What of other
options less risky and without the drama? These were only some of the
meditations of folk engaged in rebellion, and it may be unfair to
conclude that those who remained with family were less opposed to
slavery, or less valiant, than those who ran away.

In many ways, simply surviving with most of your body and mind
intact was an act of resistance, especially where Africans were
imported and worked to death within a few years. To beat the odds,
to start a family, to see your sons and daughters develop and mature,
to impart to them something of your guidance and wisdom – these
were all acts of defiance, and though difficult, must have taken place,
as the considerable population of the African-descended in the
contemporary Americas attests.

On the other hand, accounts of mothers choosing to not have
children (or sex), or even allegedly killing their young infants, suggests
that not all saw survival as resistance, and underscores the relative and
mutable nature of opposition. Infanticide remains an open question;
scholars disagree over the evidence and the degree to which it was
practiced. Less open to debate is the use of birth control, often accomplished by prolonging lactation through breastfeeding; and the incidence of abortion, practiced throughout the Americas and especially
in the Caribbean, where knowledge was largely derived from African
procedures and involved the use of herbs, shrubs, plant roots, tree bark,
lime, mango, papaya, yam, manioc, frangipani, and the less popular
option of sharp sticks and stalks. Caribbean planters were convinced
that enslaved women were inducing miscarriages, and were turning to
older women and *obeah* practitioners for assistance. The use of aborti-
facients may have been a deliberate strategy to deny the slaveocracy
the labor it needed; it may also have constituted the recognition of a
very high infant mortality rate, in the Caribbean largely the result
of such diseases as peripneumonic fevers and infant tetanus, or the
"jawfall." In the United States, scholars have offered sudden infant
death syndrome as an alternative explanation to infanticide, especially
where mothers were said to have accidently rolled over and suffocated
their infants during sleep. Whatever the causes of miscarriage and infant
mortality, it would seem that the protection of young life, as well as its
termination, were both viewed as viable options.

That preservation and destruction of life may have both been
viewed as consistent with resistance underscores that slavery, above
all else, was a theater of the absurd, and that the enslaved faced an

FIGURE 10 Female slaves in Brazil, 1830s. From Jean Baptiste Debret, *Voyage Pittoresque et Historique au Bresil* (Paris, 1834–39), vol. 2, plate 22. Print Collection, Miriam and Ira D. Wallach Division of Art, Prints and Photographs, The New York Public Library, Astor, Lenox, and Tilden Foundations. A black and white version of this figure will appear in some formats. For the color version, please refer to the plate section.

almost impossible navigation in seas of perpetual dilemma. Indeed, *the predicament* characterized the enslaved condition; any action, be it adversarial or compliant, would likely engender unpleasant consequences. If she runs, she will suffer the loss of her family, who may well be punished as co-conspirators; but if she stays on the plantation, there is the certainty of unending ignominy at the end of a whip.

Women were probably more familiar with the dilemma than men; it was most likely their constant companion (see Figure 10). Women throughout the Americas were more valued as producers than reproducers, but this observation cannot obscure the fact that they were also women (and girls), and that they were objectified sexually.

The rape of African women and girls is well established in the literature throughout the Americas, and was necessarily violent in nature. Untold numbers were made to endure the violation, sometimes repeatedly, and this fact alone may help explain the incidence of abortion and infanticide. But what about the woman who was not subjected to physical coercion, but rather felt psychological and social pressure to yield in exchange for an improved lifestyle? What if she could alleviate the backbreaking monotony of fieldwork for both herself and her children, or her aged mother, by agreeing to compromise? Was it always a compromise? What if she were already free, of mixed ancestry, and lived in a place like New Orleans, where she would have been more valued than women not of mixed ancestry, and where her status would be considerably elevated by entering into *plaçage*, a socially recognized relationship in which she lived as a homemaker with a white suitor and in a marriage-like condition (not quite marriage, as the suitor was likely married to a white woman in France or on some plantation)? Her children would receive a decent education, and perhaps even travel to Paris to further it. Given such circumstances and options, was there a "right" course of action? Was there one consistent with "resistance?" And in the final analysis, is it really possible to extract the element of coercion, in whatever form, from such relations? Was it possible for such unions to have been "consensual?" These queries have particular relevance in the case of Sally Hemings, described as "mighty near white ... very handsome, long straight hair down her back," who according to DNA results most likely had at least one child, and possibly as many as six, by her master, the illustrious Thomas Jefferson.

Ultimately, many problems flowing out of some fundamental predicament were related to the question of family. And in the end, although some made decisions and conducted their lives as individuals, so many more proceeded out of a familial context. It was the African family, therefore, that informed the decision to resist, the modalities of that resistance, the when, where, how, and degree of that resistance. People often acted in concert, they moved in groups, they fought in units. Some discussion of the family is therefore in order, before attention can be turned to other dimensions of resistance.

The literature on African families, as historical variables in transition, remains one of the least understood aspects of the heritage of the African diaspora. There is a tendency to overgeneralize about "the African family," glossing over important ethnolinguistic and even regional differences within Africa. Not all African families were matrilineal (tracing identity and inheritance through the female line); many were patrilineal, and some were bilineal. While polygyny was a possibility in West and West Central African societies, the likelihood of substantial numbers of men having more than one wife was small, since men needed time to build sufficient resources to support multiple wives and their children, which in turn usually meant that men were significantly older than the women they tended to marry, especially a second wife. This also meant that younger men did not always have access to women, given the hurdles of economic preparation and competition from older, established men. Polygyny was therefore a function of status in much of West and West Central Africa, and in every circumstance a relationship of mutual responsibilities rather than unbridled license. Polygyny's seeming continuation in the Americas was therefore much more the result of New World circumstances than Old World traditions. That is, other factors influenced the formation of African families in the Americas. Indeed, the disproportionate importation of males to females could only heighten feelings of frustration and competition.

Planters in the Caribbean and Latin America were for a long time unconcerned with the African family, or at least with the ability of the enslaved to replicate their numbers. To be certain, the *Code Noir* and the *Siete Partidas* contained provisions encouraging the maintenance of families, and with the support of the Catholic church discouraged the dismemberment of families through individual sales. But the reality on the ground was different; planters were solely preoccupied with the bottom line prior to 1790, when pressures to abolish the transatlantic slave trade forced planters to enact measures more favorable to child-bearing. New pronatalist policies were therefore embraced at the end of the eighteenth century, such as lightening the workloads of pregnant women as their "time" drew near, and the construction of special houses or plantation hospitals for expectant mothers, efforts less successful than envisioned.

A strategy to produce a self-sustaining, enslaved population was also adopted in North America. However, the sanctity of the African family was hardly a consideration; North American planters were interested in their slaves procreating for the purpose of augmenting the labor force. "Family" beyond the mother–child bond was unimportant to these planters; indeed, slave marriages did not enjoy any legal standing, although circumstances in Catholic regions may not have been so antagonistic. Consistent with the objective of maximum exploitation, and in stark contrast to Muslim prescription by which the children of a free man and an enslaved woman followed the status of the father (if paternity was acknowledged), a very different concept, derived from ancient Roman law, would substantially impact the "Africanness" of black families. For in the Americas, the principle of *partus sequitur ventrum* ("that which is brought forth follows the womb") was followed, such that the children of free fathers and enslaved mothers inherited the condition of the mother.

Like their counterparts in the Caribbean and Latin America, the enslaved in North America had to struggle to create some semblance of family life, a struggle informed by what the African knew of family prior to the Middle Passage. Therefore, the African family in America tended to be extended; that is, relations of significance went well beyond the nuclear arrangement. Uncles and aunts and cousins became very important, as did the reverence for elders. Fictive kinship was also critical, and familial ties were formed based upon experiences of common suffering, such as those created among survivors of the Middle Passage, who became relatives for life, even practicing exogamy. Slave marriages were as stable as conditions allowed, but because those conditions frequently changed, partners sold far away from one another often remarried. Such serial marriages point to the importance the enslaved attached to the institution of marriage, rather than the reverse. "Abroad marriages," where partners attempted the difficult task of sharing their lives while belonging to neighboring plantations and farms, were widespread. Enslaved women were therefore often abroad wives and single mothers, while the male presence in the lives of his wife and children was inconsistent and variable through no fault of his.

Families also participated in cultures, and scholars continue to discuss how African cultures engaged those of Europe and Native America. Africans had to learn aspects of European culture to survive, but they also continued to practice aspects of their own cultures. And while the results of such interaction varied with time and place, it was generally the case that European forms adopted by the African-descended were heavily influenced by African antecedents. From religion to music to literature to clothing, European sensibility was Africanized and then re-embraced, in many instances by those of European as well as African descent. This is arguably the essence of American culture (see Figure 11).

Religion was a cultural fundamental, and African religions all posited belief in a generally unapproachable supreme being, with whom were associated more accessible, lesser deities as well as the spirits of departed human beings who remain active in the world. Many African religions also practice spirit possession, not unlike the *bori* practices in North Africa. As culture bearers, Africans throughout the Americas transformed the Christianity of whites by bringing such beliefs and practices into its adoption, precisely what whites had done in Euro-peanizing a faith originating in the Middle East. In North America, for example, the African-descended gradually adopted a form of Protestant

FIGURE 11 Dance steps and movements, Trinidad, 1830s. From Richard Bridgens, *West India Scenery*. Trinidad (London, 1836), plate 22. General Research Division, The New York Public Library, Astor, Lenox, and Tilden Foundations.

Christianity consistent with their own conceptual framework. The concept of a Trinity was not shocking or beyond consideration, nor was the idea of an indwelling Holy Spirit. But the stiff, placid liturgical styles of the various churches were altered substantially to accommodate the full expression of the Holy Ghost, within which dance and ceremony was in every way consistent with African notions of spirit possession. The ring shout, featuring worshipers moving counterclockwise in an ever-quickening circle, was derivative of West Central and West African observance, and was widespread in North America. In these and other ways, Christianity itself was first converted, facilitating the subsequent conversion of the African to its main tenets.

Africans also entered the Americas speaking their own languages which, like religion, both altered European languages and were altered by them. For the most part, complete African languages were gradually silenced in the Americas, although significant portions remained in areas where groups were isolated, or where the preservation of African religions required linguistic familiarity. More widespread, however, was the tendency for Africans to take European languages and infuse them with African structure, cadence, and terms, a process that began with Portuguese and continued with Spanish, English, French, Dutch, and other such tongues. The degree of Africanization depended upon several factors, but the end result spanned a continuum, from speaking the European language with an African accent, to changing the syntax of what remained an essentially European idiom, to so altering the language and infusing it with African content that it became unintelligible to Europeans, achieving a "creole" or *patois* status, at which point it was as much African as European, if not more. There is debate as to whether this last stage represents a whole new language (as opposed to a *patois*), but in places like Haiti, Kreyòl is broadly accepted as such. The Africanization of non-African languages occurred all over the diaspora, such that "black English" or "ebonics," with which North Americans are most familiar, is not necessarily an indication of social disadvantage, as it is also the product of identifiable historical processes.

One of the more fascinating and complicated aspects of African-derived cultural practice during slavery were the various processions and coronations that took place annually throughout the Americas. Perhaps one of the best known was Jonkonnu or Jankunu or Junkanoo, also called John Canoe. Re-enacted in Jamaica, the Bahamas, Virginia, North Carolina, and elsewhere in the Caribbean, this Christmas-season festival featured masked dancers and drumming, and was at its height in the eighteenth and nineteenth centuries. The term Jonkonnu may simply derive from the French *les gens inconnus*, or it may relate to an apparently important African merchant named John Kenu or January Conny (there are multiple variations of the name) who, in the eighteenth century, operated both in conjunction with and, at times, against the interests of European traders along the Gold Coast at Axim. Because "Kenu" is an Akan name, the Jonkonnu festival is often associated with this ethnicity; however, the festival's masking feature bears strong resemblance to similar Igbo practices, and the Igbo were heavily represented in places like Jamaica. One tradition maintains that Jonkonnu began in Jamaica in 1708, when word of John Kenu's defeat of the Germans (and others) at Axim reached the island around Christmas. Jonkonnu's observance included the selection of a "royal court," with a king and queen.

The Jonkonnu royal court may well have been influenced by the example of the English monarchy, with the naming of a king and queen a play on white authority, but could it have represented something more than simple mimicry? The celebration of Pinkster may shed additional light. Pinkster (*Pinksteren* in Dutch) refers to the Dutch observance of Pentecost (or advent of the Holy Spirit), held seven weeks after Easter.

FIGURE 12 Queen and her court. Bridgeman-Giraudon / Art Resource, NY.
A black and white version of this figure will appear in some formats. For the
color version, please refer to the plate section.

This was a major holiday for black folk in New Jersey and New York
during the eighteenth and first part of the nineteenth centuries. Assem-
bling in large numbers in such places as Albany and Brooklyn, the
enslaved would select a king to officiate at the festivities. Instructively,
Albany would ban the gathering by 1813, out of concern for unbridled
celebration, but also out of fear that such assemblies could mask sedition.

The common element of the royal court in both Jonkonnu and
Pinkster would suggest it was not simply patterned after European
models, and that African cultural and political forms also served as
sources of inspiration. This thesis is strengthened by the existence of
similar royal courts – with kings and queens and courtiers – throughout Latin America since the sixteenth century, all associated with
elections and processions and festivals (see Figure 12). Though identified with specific ethnicities, the common thread connecting these
traditions – especially in Brazil – is the considerable West Central
African presence and widespread regard for the ruler of Kongo. In
light of the (previously discussed) widespread phenomenon of
African-led maroon communities, as well as the examination of open

FIGURE 1 Head of Taharqa. Mario Carrieri, Milan/The Menil Foundation.

FIGURE 2 Malik Ambar

FIGURE 3 Cape Coast Castle. Werner Forman Archive / HIP / Art Resource, NY.

FIGURE 6 Portrait of Juan de Pareja, assistant to Spanish artist Diego Velázquez and painted by him, c.1650. New York, Metropolitan Museum of Art, Inv. 1971.86.

GATE & SLAVE MARKET AT PERNAMBUCO.

London. Published by Longman & C°. & J. Murray. 3 April 1824.

FIGURE 7 Slave market, Pernambuco. From Maria Graham, *Journal of a Voyage to Brazil* (London, 1824), opposite p. 107. Library of Congress, Prints and Photographs Division, LC-USZ62-97202.

Flagellation of a Female Samboe Slave.

London, Published Dec.r 2.d 1793, by J. Johnson, S.t Paul's Church Yard.
38

FIGURE 8 *Flagellation of a Female Samboe Slave.* James Ford Bell Library, University of Minnesota.

FIGURE 9 Francisco de Arobe with his sons Pedro and Domingo – Francisco de Arobe was the leader of a Central American maroon community, c.1599. Museo de América, Madrid.

FIGURE 12 Queen and her court. Bridgeman-Giraudon / Art Resource, NY.

revolt (in the next section), even the most playful royal re-enactments during seasons of celebration would have contained elements of subversion, evincing visions of a very different political configuration.

To be sure, for the enslaved to insist upon practicing their own culture was not necessarily, in and of itself, resistance to enslavement. Many pursued African-derived cultural forms because it was all they knew; it was the substance of their lives, and it was not necessarily laden with political content. But the close identification of the African with slavery, such that by the nineteenth century the overwhelming majority slaves were of African descent, combined with their dehumanization and the rejection of Africa as a site of civilization, meant that resistance for the enslaved was multidimensional. One resisted not only the physical apparatus of slavery, but also the devaluation of the African person, which is also about culture in the final analysis. As it became impossible to separate slavery from the African, so the fight against slavery and the insistence on African cultural forms became one and the same struggle for many. But, of course, not for all. Some blacks had become enamored of European ways and saw little value in anything African. For them, deliverance from slavery required a simultaneous rejection of African culture, which they came to regard as the primary source of their woes.

From a sense of who they were in relation to each other and to Africa, therefore, many of the enslaved engaged in all manner of resistance. Slaveholders and overseers were sometimes killed, often through the use of poison, or they were seriously injured and maimed. Work slowdowns and stoppages, misinterpreted throughout the Americas as exemplifying the "innate laziness of the Negro," were common. Sabotage was a related mechanism of resistance, as enslaved workers deliberately torched fields and destroyed equipment. Food and provisions were regularly confiscated, often through the offices of domestics working in the big house, who never forgot their co-sufferers and were constantly on the lookout for opportunities to collude. Blacks acquiring their freedom often aided those remaining in slavery. Persons hired out by slaveholders did their best to shield their actual earnings. Those allowed to sell produce in the markets, such as black market women in eighteenth-century Charleston, monopolized certain goods and controlled the prices, charging as much as 150 percent more than their initial outlay, thereby extorting additional revenues from their white customers while keeping the extra money for themselves and their fellows. So well had they mastered the

essentials of capitalist entrepreneurship, so expansive was their sense
of autonomy, that these women, as many as several hundred by the
mid-eighteenth century, reached a point where they were unafraid to
tell whites just what they thought of them. Regarded as "insolent" and
"impudent," these market women dared to openly sass and make fun
of their white customers. The charge of insolence resonates with the
very same characterization of enslaved women elsewhere, providing an
extraordinary moment in American history (see Figure 13).

But perhaps the most fundamental expression of resistance was
absconding. Running for freedom was widespread throughout the
Americas. As there could be no maroons without this initial step,
flight was essential to the development of an alternative, independent
community. Escape to marronage can be viewed as the ultimate form
of absconding, but there was yet another, far more unalterable voyage
from which there was no return – suicide, common throughout the
diaspora, men as well as women, African-born as well as creole. The
former understood suicide as a return voyage to Africa, a means of
reversing sail. There are collections of stories in the United States and
in the Caribbean (and doubtless in Latin America as research will
uncover), that make reference to "flying Africans," who became fed
up with slavery and took wings and "flew back to Africa" or, in other
folklore, marched in groups to the seashore, where they mounted
the sky and flew away, back to their homeland. The commission of
suicide was no light matter, as it was an abominable act worthy of the
greatest condemnation in many African societies; recourse to this
form of resistance was a direct indication of the depth of suffering
and despair.

Sometimes abscondees stayed away for only a few days, or a few
weeks, just enough time to clear their heads or experiment with the
idea of escape. Specific incidents, rather than the overall circumstance
of slavery, may have triggered the decision to leave: a particularly
brutal beating, the sale of a spouse or child, or some other unbearable
humiliation. Perhaps the runaway simply wanted to obtain better
working conditions, or some other concession, and temporary flight
drove the point home. But often the design was much more permanent, the decision much more final. In such instances the enslaved stole
away under various scenarios and traveled under every imaginable
arrangement. The old fled as well as the young, though in far fewer
numbers. Persons belonging to the same ethnolinguistic grouping ran
away together; persons belonging to differing groups did the same.

FIGURE 13 Loading coal on a steamer, St. Thomas, 1864. From John Codman, *Ten Months in Brazil* (Boston, 1867), facing p. 20.

The African-born joined the creole, and from the runaway
slave advertisements it is not always clear which of the two was in
command. A few individuals from the same family disappeared, while
whole families would on occasion risk the danger. Very dark-
complexioned persons conspired with very light-skinned ones,
whereas other bands were exclusively composed of persons from
either category. While statistically there were more males than females
in flight (at least in North America), there are plenty of instances
in which groups were all female, some with small children in tow,
many still nursing. It was the support of women, who remained to care
for the children and who maintained the family, that often enabled
men to run in the first place, and it was frequently a network of women
who kept them alive as they moved from safe haven to asylum. In sum,
there was no circumstance under which the enslaved would not bolt.

For those intending a more permanent stay, the question of destination generates a number of responses. While many headed for
maroon communities, others made their way to towns and cities,
where they had a better chance of blending in, a possibility enhanced
by vocational skills. In these and many other instances, those absconding were often seeking to reconnect with family and friends, with
runaway advertisements frequently describing persons "escaping" to
another plantation, where it was believed they had relatives. Flight to
urban areas and neighboring farms makes the point that although
marronage is usually associated with inaccessible, defensible terrain
(mountains, swamps, forests), it was also possible to cloak one's
presence in either anonymity (in towns and cities) or familiarity
(in the case of adjacent operations). Instances of the latter could even
include planters offering protection to persons claimed as slaves by
someone else in exchange for their labor, but absent responsibility for
their care.

Some of the more striking cases of absconding involved newly
arrived Africans heading for the coast, or toward some body of water,
with the apparent intention of returning to Africa or some other place,
as was true of Jamaica during the last quarter of the eighteenth century, when runaways sought to escape to Cuba by way of canoe. Taken
together, these and other vignettes create a more complete picture of
an enslaved world on the move, in constant motion. It is the portrait of
a hemisphere engaged in an enormous enterprise of industry, agriculture, and commerce largely fueled by enslaved labor, whose restless-
ness constituted an ever-present threat to these vast, interwoven

operations. The African was never comfortable or complacent in slaveholding America – she could never sit still.

Facing the Enemy

The decision to confront the very fount of oppression directly, rather than create spaces of autonomy, stirs the imagination like no other. In sixteenth-century Hispaniola and elsewhere in Spanish-claimed territories, Africans revolted with regularity, actions which often resulted in the first American maroons. In Antigua, a 1736 conspiracy engulfing the whole of the island was led by Court (or Tackey), along with Tomboy. An Akan speaker and a creole, respectively, they were assisted by Obbah (Aba) and Queen, both Akan women who provided critical leadership in facilitating the "Damnation Oath," a ceremony derived from Akan traditions in which the insurrectionists committed themselves by drinking rooster blood, cemetery dirt, and rum, among other elements. Court had been crowned by 2,000 of the enslaved as the "King of the Coromantees," the basis of which was the Akan *ikem* ceremony, a tradition preparing participants for war. Queen, in turn, may have been Court's principal advisor, playing the same role as the queen mother or *ohemaa* in Akan society. While the conspiracy was exposed before it could be executed, planters were astonished that not only the enslaved, but many free blacks and so-called mulattoes were also implicated. Some eighty-eight enslaved males were executed, and forty-nine expelled from the island.

A few decades following Tackey's insurgency in Antigua, conspiracies and revolts erupted throughout the Caribbean: Bermuda and Nevis in 1761; Suriname in 1762, 1763, and 1768–72; British Honduras in 1765, 1768, and 1773; Grenada in 1765; Montserrat in 1768; St. Vincent in 1769–73; Tobago in 1770, 1771, and 1774; St. Croix and St. Thomas in 1770; and St. Kitts in 1778. Yet another Tackey led a revolt in Jamaica in 1760, two decades after the British–Maroon peace treaty. With Abena presiding as the Akan queen mother in Jamaica, over 1,000 slaves raised havoc for six months; some sixty whites died, as opposed to 600 of the enslaved after Tackey was killed by the Windward maroon leader Captain Davy of Scotts Hall. Well organized and widespread, the revolt was Akan based, incorporating participants from a number of parishes. Taking an oath similar to the 1736 Antiguan Damnation Oath, the Akan sought to destroy slavery and replace it with a society based upon West African models. They found succor in the example of the Windward and Leeward maroons, and sought to extend the freedoms the maroons enjoyed. But as irony would have it, it was the Leewards and Windwards who, in compliance with the 1739 treaty, fought alongside the planters to end the 1760 revolt; they would do the same in the revolts of 1761, 1765, and 1766, all Akan-led conspiracies betrayed by informants. The Leewards, particularly the Accompong and Trelawny Town groups, were rewarded with twice as much money as were the Windward groups of Scotts Hall, Moore Town, and Charles Town, whose participation was considerably less enthusiastic.

Maroon opposition to these revolts would eventually return to bite them in the behind. The enslaved could not help but feel ambivalent, at best, toward the maroons, unsure if they were friend or foe. Conversely, some maroons may have become contemptuous of the slaves, but they were never comfortable in their role as treaty partners with the British. Wary of the planters and the colonial government, the maroons were concerned about the latter's continual encroachment and attempts to bring them under colonial jurisdiction. Tensions came to a boil in 1795, at the height of the Haitian Revolution, when conflict erupted between the Trelawny Town maroons and the local government of Montego Bay of St. James Parish. The Trelawny Town War ensued until the following year, with minimal slave support for the maroons. Indeed, the other Leeward group, the Accompong, fought against the Trelawnys on the side of the British, whereas the Windwards, as a whole more distrustful of the planters and more independent, offered the British little in the way of assistance. In the end, the Trelawnys were defeated and some 568 were deported, first to Nova Scotia (Canada) in June of 1796, and ultimately to Sierra Leone. Their land, some 1,500 acres, was seized by the British.

The war against slavery in Jamaica continued, but the end of the eighteenth century saw an important development in the insurrection movement. An uprising led by Cuffy, another Akan speaker, was this time composed of several ethnolinguistic groups in addition to the Akan. This represented a heightened awareness of similarities among the enslaved, and suggests they were moving away from specific African groups to a broader sense of African-derived commonality. The zenith of this new corporate expression took place in 1831–2, when some 20,000 slaves from all ethnolinguistic backgrounds, together with the Jamaican-born or creoles, waged a widespread war against the slaveocracy. This was the best organized of all of Jamaica's slave revolts, a critical factor in the eventual collapse of slavery in the British Caribbean, and was also the most costly to repress.

The 1831–2 Jamaican uprising was preceded by developments in Barbados and Demerara (what is now Guyana). In the former, the African-born Bussa, together with John and Nanny Grigg, led a three-day rebellion of some 400 enslaved persons in 1816, the largest in Barbadian history. Evidence suggests it was actually Nanny Grigg, a creole domestic, who provided the intellectual fodder for the revolt. Bussa would be killed in battle with fifty other insurrectionists, and when the fighting ended, another 300 were put on trial in Bridge-town, resulting in the execution of 144 and the expulsion from the island of another 132. Bussa's Rebellion lives on as a powerful symbol of defiance, but the 1823 Demerara Rebellion involved many more – some 10,000 enslaved persons – who under the leadership of John Gladstone (and possibly his father Quamina) challenged authorities for two days before being put down. John Gladstone would be deported to St. Lucia, but up to 250 other insurrectionists were killed in battle and another twenty-seven executed, including the English cleric John Smith, who would inspire England's William Wilberforce and become a "martyr" for the abolitionist movement. Though repressed, the revolts in Barbados, Demerara, and Jamaica succeeded in raising the costs of maintaining slavery, and just two years after the Jamaican revolt, formal slavery in the Caribbean came to an end.

Similar kinds of disturbances, again attributed to the Akan, were taking place in eighteenth-century New York City. The port had a significant slave population during the period: between 1700 and 1774, at least 6,800 slaves were imported, 41.2 percent of whom were African-born. Before 1742, 70 percent came from Caribbean and American sources, with thousands arriving from Barbados and Jamaica, underscoring the interconnectedness of enslaved populations throughout the Americas. After 1742, however, 70 percent came directly from Africa. This turnabout was related to the revocation of the *asiento* after 1750, when Spanish markets were closed to English slavers and traders flooded New York and other English colonies with captives. The enslaved loaded and unloaded at docks, slips, and warehouses along the East River, worked in shipbuilding and con-struction industries, ferried between Long Island farms and the city, labored in public works, served as domestics, and sold so much produce in the city streets that the Common Council curbed their activities in 1740.

Those from Jamaica and other Caribbean locations would have been aware of slave revolts and unrest in the islands; some had in fact been shipped to New York precisely because of their participation. It is not surprising, then, that the Akan played prominent roles in the New York City rebellion of 1712, when "some Negro slaves of ye Nations of Carmantee and Pappa plotted to destroy all the White[s] in order to obtain their freedom."[1] Nine were killed and five or six wounded before the uprising ended; twenty-one were executed by hanging, burning, or being broken at the wheel. Six ended their own lives. The conspiracy of 1741 involved similar participation from these and other ethnolinguistic groups, when it was believed (partially informed by white paranoia) that some 2,000 slaves were poised to torch the city. Sixteen blacks and four whites (judged co-conspirators) were hanged, thirteen blacks were burned at the stake, and another seventy-one were expelled from the island following mass hysteria and a sensational trial.

Turning to Latin America, Brazil experienced many slave insurrections that, like Jamaica and to a lesser extent New York City, tended to be organized along ethnolinguistic lines. In particular, the northeastern province of Bahia was a hotbed of discontent, notorious for slave revolts in the first half of the nineteenth century, and it is there that a multiplicity of identities arising from the intersection of racial intermixing, free versus slave statuses, urban versus rural settings, and religious adherence can be discerned. The Hausa, Muslims from what is now northern Nigeria, had been implicated in a revolt in Bahia dating back to 1607; 200 years later, the Hausa near the city of Salvador were again accused of a conspiracy to capture ships and reverse sail to West Africa. Enslaved and free Hausa plotted together, and the two leaders of the conspiracy were executed. Two years later, in January of 1809, almost 300 slaves, again mostly Hausa, attacked the town of Nazaré das Farinhas in search of food and weapons. The attack was beaten back and eighty-three captured, women and men. The 1809 revolt saw increased non-Hausa participation, in the form of "Jêjes" or Aja-Fon-Ewe from Dahomey, and "Nagôs," or Yoruba from what is now south-western Nigeria. There were three more

---

[1] Quote in Thomas J. Davis, *A Rumor of Revolt: The "Great Negro Plot" in Colonial New York City* (New York: The Free Press, 1985), pp. 18–20, 79–80.

revolts of significance between 1810 and 1818, the second of which involved Nagôs under Hausa leadership headed by a *malomi* or *malām*, a Muslim religious leader. These revolts continued with regularity from the 1820s to 1835.

That year, a major insurrection of the so-called *malês* took place, a term referring to African Muslims who were by then mostly Nagôs rather than Hausa. Islam had become an important religion in Bahia, though it was not the dominant religion among blacks, nor were all Nagôs Muslim. In January of 1835, up to 500 Africans, mostly Muslim, enslaved and free, took to the streets of Salvador under Muslim leadership. The plan called for the conspirators to link with the enslaved in the surrounding plantations, but betrayal forced them to begin the uprising prematurely. Brutally repressed with over seventy killed, the *malê* revolt revealed the importance of Islam and an impressive level of Arabic literacy among participants who wore distinctive clothing, maintained their own religious schools, and observed Islamic rituals such as fasting Ramadan. The 1835 revolt also suggests that participating Africans rejected the notion of race, preferring their own ethnolinguistic identities. The rebels sought to kill not only whites, but also "mulattoes" and *crioulos* (creoles or Brazilian-born blacks), and further intended to re-enslave Africans from Congo and Angola, associating them with either ancestral practices or Christianity. The 1835 *malê* revolt was therefore more than a straightforward slave revolt, as it reflected cultural divergence, racial ambiguities, and an alternative sense of social order. In the end, hundreds were sent to the galleys, imprisoned, lashed, or expelled from Bahia, with some even returning to West Africa. In this context, there was no such thing as a single, all-inclusive definition of blackness.

In the uprisings already mentioned as well as ones to come, those in revolt often wielded implements both intended for battle as well as refashioned for that purpose. But some in revolt also made use of martial arts originating in Africa and further refined in the Americas. These forms included the *engolo* (or *n'golo*) of southern Angola's Kunene community, techniques most famously characterized by head butts, leg sweeps and kicks that arguably formed the basis for Brazil's *capoeira* – a mesmerizing tradition that blends fighting and dance moves; the *mgba* wrestling tradition of the Igbo, practiced by males and females; and the *ladja* (or *danmyé*) observed in Martinique and seemingly related to *capoeira* techniques.

The number of people involved in nineteenth-century South American and Caribbean uprisings was enormous – tens of thousands. But these rebellions were both preceded and partly inspired by revolution in Saint-Domingue, the single most far-reaching revolt in the New World. The former uprisings were certainly critical to the eventual abolition of slavery, but the Haitian Revolution stands apart as the only insurrection to militarily defeat the slaveocracy and colonialism, and it is the only one that ended slavery directly. That the enslaved and their free black allies liberated themselves sent shock waves throughout the Americas, striking horror in the hearts and minds of slaveholders all around. Word of the Revolution also reached the ears of co-sufferers from Virginia to Bahia, and served as a model for one of the most important conspiracies in North America – the Denmark Vesey Conspiracy of 1822. News traveled not only through slaveholder conversations and newspapers but also through black seamen, underscoring the fact that blacks regularly plied the seas in ships other than slavers. But in addition to the spread of news were enslaved individuals themselves, either expelled from Saint-Domingue or in the company of slaveholders fleeing the island. So it was that on the island of Curaçao, as one example, several of the enslaved from Saint-Domingue joined Tula in his 1795 revolt against the Dutch.

The repercussions of the 1789 French Revolution were far-reaching, to say the least. In Saint-Domingue, white planters took advantage of the new situation to agitate and maneuver for greater autonomy. Although there were serious political differences among them over developments in France, they became one in resisting attempts of *affranchis* (free blacks and persons of "color") to join their ranks and enjoy equal liberties. The enslaved, observing the dissension and rancor, began to realize that all this talk of freedom and liberty, combined with the unstable situation on the ground, was a unique opportunity to do something about their own circumstances. The enslaved on several plantations in the north began holding clandestine meetings in the woods, initially broken up by the *maréchaussée* (hunters of runaway slaves) and the execution of leaders. The meetings nevertheless continued, and by August 22, 1791, the date of the Revolution's commencement, leaders from northern plantations had been meeting for weeks, planning wide-scale revolt. At the Lenormand de Mézy plantation in Morne-Rouge, they finalized plans to set it off.

The leaders of the conspiracy included Boukman Dutty, a voodoo priest, Jean-François, and Georges Biassou; the first two apparently had some maroon experience. In an instructive example of how relatively privileged persons were not necessarily narrowed by that privilege, but could instead see the larger picture, Toussaint Louverture, the eventual leader of the Revolution, was a black *affranchi* and a coachman. He was in the background in the early days, serving as a link between the leaders. Women played important roles as well, including Cécile Fatiman, a voodoo high priestess or *mambo* described as a "green-eyed mulatto woman with long silken black hair." In the dense forest of Bois-Caïman, she and Boukman officiated a solemn voodoo ceremony for conspirators that was not unlike the Damnation Oaths in Antigua and Jamaica, again demonstrating the centrality of African religions.

At ten o'clock on the morning of August 22, 1791, the enslaved, two-thirds of whom were African-born, began torching plantations in the north, destroying everything in their path. By the eighth day of the insurrection, some 184 sugar plantations had been destroyed in seven parishes, rising to 200 sugar and 1,200 coffee plantations by September's end. By the end of November, some 80,000 out of 170,000 enslaved in the north had burst their chains, attacking both symbol and substance of power. This initial eruption was soon channeled into more manageable military order, as the insurrectionists were organized into bands under officers answering to Jean-François, who assumed the generalship following Boukman's capture and decapitation by the French, his head impaled on a pole and displayed in Le Cap's public square. After initially indicating a willingness to settle for less than full freedom, the Revolution's leadership was forced by the masses to persevere in the fight.

The Haitian Revolution would take a number of unpredictable, bewildering shifts and turns. Unlike the North, the enslaved in the South and West of the island were not as organized or cohesive, and were overshadowed by the politics of the free blacks and *gens de couleur* (persons of color or mixed ancestry). Matters spun out of control, with free blacks and *gens de couleur* teaming up to fight white planters in the south. The enslaved were enlisted to fight on both sides, and therefore fought each other. Further developments, and the realization that the *gens de couleur* were also slaveholders, even more so than whites, led the enslaved in the south to come together and fight for their own interests (see Figure 14). The combination of insurrection and conflicts with Britain and Spain led France to abolish slavery throughout

FIGURE 14 *Revenge taken by the Black Army for the Cruelties practised on them by the French.* Private Collection/Bridgeman Images.

Saint-Domingue on October 31, 1793. But for the most part, little changed for the ex-slaves. Although they could no longer be whipped or tortured, they were still landless, legally bound to the plantations of former slaveholders. Many continued to run away, or commit acts of sabotage.

In the meantime, Toussaint had emerged as leader of the forces in the north, under whom served his brother Paul, his adopted nephew Moïse, and future rulers Dessalines and Henri-Christophe. By 1798, after further intervention by the British, Toussaint had taken control of both the north and the west, with the south under the control of Rigaud, leader of a mixed race elite. Civil war (or perhaps better labeled fratricide) ensued, with Rigaud and those under his command suffering defeat. By 1801 and the termination of the civil war, Toussaint was the single leader of a slaveless Saint-Domingue, but it remained a French colony. Continuing conflict with France eventually led Toussaint to accept an invitation to a meeting to negotiate a settlement. Like Ballano in Panama in 1556, he was promptly arrested and shipped to France. Unlike Ballano, he would remain isolated in the French Alps for the rest of his life, dying of consumption. His lieutenant Dessalines, now commander of a unified black and mixed race army, would go on to defeat the French and to declare independence on January 1, 1804. The island would henceforth be called Haiti, from the original Arawak name Ayiti.

The Haitian Revolution stands as a crowning achievement of those Africans determined to deliver themselves from American slavery. In the short term, however, the fall of slavery in Saint-Domingue ironically led to the expansion of the institution elsewhere, especially in Cuba, in the attempt to replace the island as a leading sugar producer. As for Haiti itself, those who struggled so valiantly against tyranny have only met with US-led policies of ostracism and indifference well into the twenty-first century. The island's poverty endures.

The struggle in Haiti was joined by forces to the north, on the North American mainland, where there were a number of revolts. One of the more striking examples was the preceding Stono Rebellion of 1739, when a contingent took up arms twenty miles west of Charleston, South Carolina and marched through the countryside wreaking havoc. South Carolina at this time had a black population of some 39,000 (compared with 20,000 whites), and like Saint-Domingue, 70 percent of them were African-born – in this case from West Central Africa. The revolt was put down after several days and the deaths of thirty whites and forty-four blacks.

Another North American development was the response of the African-descended to the American War of Independence, a conflict financed by black labor. Blacks fought on both sides with the hope of ensuring their freedom, so it is not inaccurate to characterize their participation as a slave revolt coinciding with, or taking advantage of, an anticolonial struggle. Those who fought with the colonies, some 5,000 out of 300,000, were mostly from the North and only entered American ranks after considerable vacillation by the Continental

Army, which under George Washington had initially forbade the participation of blacks, only to amend that policy later. Most of the colonies also reversed themselves and allowed for both enslaved and free blacks to serve (with the exceptions of Georgia and South Carolina). The cause of the colonies' reversal was the November 7, 1775 declaration of Lord Dunmore, governor of Virginia, freeing all slaves and indentured servants who bore arms on the side of the British. As a result, it is estimated that Georgia lost 75 percent of its enslaved population (of 15,000), while Virginia and South Carolina combined may have lost some 55,000 slaves; it is not clear precisely how many of these actually fought for the British, but even if they only ran away and did not formally join the British, their actions represented a significant defection.

Blacks who fought for the British had every right to do so. Indeed, the Declaration of Independence, that oft-quoted articulation of a desire for freedom and equality, absolutely ignored the plight of the enslaved. This comes as no surprise, since many of the Declaration's signatories were themselves slaveholders. In a surreal echo of the second-century Greek physician Galen, Thomas Jefferson, primary architect of both the Declaration and the Constitution, reveals his deep-seated reservations and overall racist sentiments concerning the African in his *Notes on the State of Virginia* (1781–2):

> The first difference which strikes us is that of colour ... And is this difference of no importance? Is it not the foundation of a greater or less share of beauty in the two races? Are not the fine mixtures of red and white, the expressions of every passion by greater or less suffusions of colour in the one, preferable to that eternal monotony, which reigns in the countenances, that immoveable veil of black which covers all the emotions of the other race? Add to these, flowing hair, a more elegant symmetry of form, their own judgment in favour of the whites, declared by their preference of them, as uniformly as is the preference of the Oranootan for the black women over those of his own species ... They are more ardent after their female: but love seems with them to be more an eager desire, than a tender delicate mixture of sentiment and sensation. Their griefs are transient. Those numberless afflictions, which render it doubtful whether heaven has given life to us in mercy or in wrath, are less felt, and sooner forgotten with them. In general, their existence appears to participate more of sensation than reflection ... Comparing them by their faculties of memory, reason, and imagination, it appears to me, that in memory they are equal to the whites; in reason much inferior, as I think one could scarcely be found capable of tracing and comprehending the

investigations of Euclid; and that in imagination they are dull, tasteless, and anomalous ... This unfortunate difference of colour, and perhaps of faculty, is a powerful obstacle to the emancipation of these people. Many of their advocates, while they wish to vindicate the liberty of human nature, are anxious also to preserve its dignity and beauty. Some of these, embarrassed by the question "What further is to be done with them?" join themselves in opposition with those who are actuated by sordid avarice only. Among the Romans emancipation required but one effort. The slave, when made free, might mix with, without staining the blood of his master. But with us a second is necessary, unknown to history. When freed, he is to be removed beyond the reach of mixture.

(*Notes on the State of Virginia*, New York: W.W. Norton and Co., 1972, pp. 138–43)

This distillation of racism into its two core components – the rejection of African somatic form and the dismissal of African intelligence – is notable for both its inimitable style and devastating effect. For Jefferson, the racial chasm was unbridgeable, a certitude that could only encourage rebellion.

Smaller revolts followed the American War of Independence, but in August of 1800, Gabriel Prosser and Jack Bowler met with an army of over 1,000 of the enslaved six miles outside of Richmond, Virginia. Having planned their assault for months, they marched on the city only to be thwarted by a powerful storm and the previous betrayals of two slaves, by whom the governor, fully informed of the conspiracy, called out the militia. Many were arrested and thirty-five executed; Prosser himself was captured in late September and also killed.

The Denmark Vesey conspiracy of 1822 also developed in an urban setting – Charleston – and demonstrates the interconnectedness of the African diaspora by the early nineteenth century. Vesey, born either in the Caribbean or Africa, was a fifty-five-year-old seafarer who had purchased his freedom in 1800. Like Toussaint, he lived relatively well as a carpenter in Charleston, but became persuaded by the suffering of the masses that there was more to life than his personal comfort. Organizing a revolt that took into consideration differences among the enslaved, he formed columns of distinct groups, such as the Igbo and Gullah (West Central Africans and/or Gola from West Africa). African religious practices and Christianity were both observed out of respect for diversity. Vesey evoked the Haitian Revolution, predicting that help would arrive from that island, and from Africa itself, if only those in and around Charleston would take the initiative. All of this suggests that Vesey's followers, possibly as many as 9,000, could grasp his vision of a black world, in which the cause of freedom transcended divisions of birthplace and language. But the refrain is all too familiar: made aware of the conspiracy by informants, white authorities preempted the revolt and arrested suspects; thirty-five blacks were hanged, and forty-three deported to either Africa or the Caribbean.

David Walker may have been in Charleston during the time of the Vesey conspiracy; something certainly inspired him to pen his famous anti-slavery *Appeal* in 1829, in which he called for a general uprising in clear language. Walker died in Boston under very suspicious circumstances the following year, but Nat Turner attempted to answer his summons, launching a large-scale revolt in August of 1831 in Southampton, Virginia. A religious mystic, Turner interpreted that February's solar eclipse as a divine signal to begin the apocalypse, and launched the revolt on August 21. Within twenty-four hours, some sixty whites were killed, including Turner's owner and family. When the smoke cleared, over a hundred of the enslaved had been killed in combat, and another thirteen were hanged (along with three free blacks) (see Figure 15). Captured on October 30, Turner was

FIGURE 15 Hanging a slave, South Carolina, 1865. From *Harper's Weekly* (Sept. 30, 1865), p. 613.

executed on November 11. The revolts would continue in less dramatic fashion, only to flare up one more time just before the Civil War, when John Brown's company of less than fifty men, including several blacks, raided the federal arsenal at Harpers Ferry, Virginia on October 16, 1859. John Brown's leadership, reminiscent of the Zanj revolt in ninth-century Iraq under 'Alī b. Muḥammad, points to the fact that whites were involved in a number of these uprisings, usually in supportive roles. Federal and state troops overwhelmed Brown's small force, killing many and hanging others. On December 2, John Brown was also hanged, but only after his self-sacrifice and complete identification with the enslaved had caused a sensation.

Slavery's End?

The cumulative effect of all of these acts, large and small, was to undermine the institution of slavery throughout the Americas. Resistance increased slavery's costs, affecting the bottom line while raising the level of danger. Resistance also emboldened the oppressed, making the entire system increasingly unmanageable. Slavery expired with a whimper in some places, while in others it required herculean efforts to subdue. In the end, the anti-slavery struggle of the enslaved themselves was fundamental to abolition.

But abolition was a long process, informed by other factors as well. Throughout the Americas there were those, black and white, who opposed the slave trade or slavery and who fought for their destruction by way of anti-slavery publications (pamphlets, newspapers, novels, slave narratives) and government petitions, seeking legislative means to this end. In North America, anti-slavery sentiment became significant following the American War of Independence, as whites struggled with Enlightenment ideas and the Bible. Manumission and anti-slavery societies, first organized by the Quakers in 1775, were in every state from Massachusetts to Virginia by 1792, in tandem with similar forces in Britain. A direct consequence of their agitation was the passing of legislation in 1807 (effective in 1808) by both Britain and the United States, outlawing the transatlantic slave trade. The trade continued illegally and without significant efforts on the part of the United States to enforce the ban, but the story with Britain was different. While maintaining its slave-based colonies in the Caribbean, Britain gradually committed its naval capabilities to interdicting the trade. They met with some success, but it was not possible to police all nations and parties trafficking through such a vast ocean. Not unlike the implications of the Haitian Revolution for slavery's expansion in Cuba, the real effect of the ban in the United States, where the westward expansion of commercial agriculture required labor, was the acceleration of the domestic slave trade.

Anti-slavery literature included the important 1789 publication of Olaudah Equiano's *The Interesting Narrative of the Life of Olaudah Equiano, or Gustavus Vassa*. Anti-slavery sentiment in the United States intensified after 1815, resulting in such papers as white abolitionist William Lloyd Garrison's *Liberator*, first appearing in January 1831, and religious treatises such as James G. Barney's *Letter to the Ministers and Elders* in 1834, and Theodore Weld's *The Bible Against Slavery* in 1837. Black abolitionists had their own newspapers, including the first black newspaper, *Freedom's Journal*, published in 1827 by John Russwurm and Samuel Cornish. Others included the *National Watchman*, published by Henry Highland Garnet and William G. Allen, and the *North Star*, begun by Frederick Douglass in 1847. Important slave narratives included Douglass' own story, first published in 1845 and subsequently revised, while the most prominent anti-slavery novel was Harriet Beecher Stowe's 1852 *Uncle Tom's Cabin*. Selling more than 300,000 copies in its first year of publication, its description of the horrors of slavery was also dramatically translated to the stage. Whether in print or theater, the effect was electrifying.

Abolitionism in the US was also directly related to what some scholars refer to as the first of several waves of feminism. This is to say that a number of women involved in the fight against slavery would, following that fight, refocus on the plight of women, in particular the struggle for the right to vote. The American suffragette movement would be led by such individuals as Elizabeth Cady Stanton, Susan B. Antony, Lydia Maria Child, Lucretia Mott, and the sisters Sarah and Angelina Grimké, who in advocating for abolitionism (and temperance) learned critical communication and organizing skills that they would employ in the struggle for women's equal rights. These were all white women, but there were also black women abolitionists, including Maria Stewart, Mary Ann Shadd Cary, Frances Ellen Watkins Harper, Sojourner Truth, and Charlotte Forten Grimké (married to the nephew of the Grimké sisters). Perhaps most emblematic of how abolitionism and women's rights could combine is Sojourner Truth's 1851 "Ain't I a Woman" speech, delivered at the Akron, Ohio Women's Rights Convention. Called the "Libyan Sibyl" by Harriet Beecher Stowe, there is controversy over whether Truth actually made the speech, and how, as she grew up speaking Dutch. If the 1848 Seneca Fall Convention is viewed as the beginning of the suffragette movement, the ratification of the Nineteenth Amendment in 1920, granting women the franchise, was a tangible outcome.

Brazil also witnessed the development of a significant abolitionist movement. Before 1850, independence leader José Bonifácio de Andrada e Silva spoke out against slavery, although his protests were rejected by Brazil's ruling class. In the late 1860s, a number of anti-slavery societies were created, consisting for the most part of persons of mixed ancestry and relative privilege. Perhaps the most important was Antônio Frederico de Castro Alves, who recited his poetry before large gatherings and was involved with two abolitionist societies in Salvador and Recife prior to his death in 1871. José do Patrocínio of Rio de Janeiro, whose father was a Portuguese priest, was a former slave who achieved his freedom and went on to purchase two newspapers, turning them into anti-slavery organs. In 1880, Patrocínio would be instrumental in the creation of an anti-slavery umbrella organization called the Abolitionist Confederation, and was crucial in making the debate over slavery much more public. The more elite Brazilian Anti-Slavery Society was founded in 1880 by Joaquim Nabuco and intellectual André Pinto Rebouças, and was the organization through which *The Abolitionist* newspaper began. A final example of leading Brazilian abolitionists was Luís Anselmo da Fonseca, a medical professor who published *Slavery, the Clergy, and Abolition*, the most influential critique of slavery of the period, in which he took both the Catholic church and free black Brazilians to task for their complicity in slavery.

One of the more arresting developments to come out of the anti-slavery campaign was the movement to repatriate African descendants to Africa. These efforts reveal how participants in what appeared to be the same enterprise could be animated by entirely different assumptions and motivations. For Africans and their descendants, the opportunity to return to Africa represented the possibility to reverse sail and reconnect, to escape the oppressive, racist atmosphere of the Americas and start over as pioneers, or to fulfill a missionary zeal to bring the Christian gospel to "benighted heathens" (reflecting the extent to which they themselves had internalized the West's denigration of

Africa). Whites who supported repatriation were divided. Those in Britain were interested in relocating the "black poor" (indigent blacks and some Asians, most of whom had been brought to London as slaves, indentured servants, or sailors) to Africa, where they could both improve their lives and facilitate British interests in "legitimate" (non-slave) trade. Whites in the United States, on the other hand, were mostly cynical in their approach, advocating the project to rid the land of free blacks, thereby actually strengthening slavery. Men like Thomas Jefferson and Abraham Lincoln (at least early in his political career) were convinced that Africans could never become the equal of whites, and that repatriation to Africa, or deportation to the Caribbean, was the best solution for resolving "the freedman question." This is consistent with the fact that whites could be opposed to the slave trade but not slavery, or if they were opposed to slavery, did not necessarily advocate full citizenship rights for blacks, attitudes evident in the US North and Canada where blacks, though technically free, suffered from a range of discriminatory laws, practices, and even violence.

Whatever their various impulses, repatriation to Africa from Britain and Canada, the latter the destination for Jamaican maroons and a refuge for blacks who fought for the British during the American War of Independence, began in 1787 and centered on the British settlement at Sierra Leone. These initial groups would be joined, beginning in the nineteenth century, by captives taken from slavers bound for the Americas, the result of the British effort to outlaw the trade. Sierra Leone received thousands of such recaptives, reaching a peak in the 1840s. As for the United States, repatriation assumed the form of an organized, state-sanctioned enterprise in 1817 with the founding of the American Colonization Society, which in 1822 began a colony in what would become Monrovia, Liberia. Money was raised to finance voyages, and by 1830 some 1,420 persons had sailed to Liberia. All told, nearly 15,000 blacks participated in the return, to which can be added recaptives liberated from slavers by the American navy. The scheme was opposed by abolitionists, white and black, but in both Sierra Leone and Liberia, the return of Africans and their descendants from the Americas would have a profound effect upon the future course of those nations. Fundamentally, the cultures of the returnees had been altered by the experience in the Americas; they did not necessarily identify with Africans who had never left the continent. Stratification developed largely along lines of cultural differences between the returnees and the indigenous, with the former arrogating privilege and power for themselves. It was a recipe for disaster, the consequences of which continue to reverberate.

While many Africans and their descendants returned to the continent by way of American and British government and private assistance, others financed their own way. In North America, Paul Cuffe, possibly of Akan (but also of Native American) descent, personally carried thirty-eight persons back to Africa in 1815, financing the entire enterprise himself. Perhaps even more spectacular was the return of people from Brazil and Cuba to West Africa, particularly to what is now south-western Nigeria and Benin, but also to Ghana. A number of those found guilty of conspiracy in the Americas, if not executed, were shipped back to Africa, a reverse trajectory joined by members of *cabildos* (in Cuba) and *irmandades* (Brazil), fraternal organizations based upon purported membership in ethnolinguistic groups. These brotherhoods pooled their resources to pay for such return voyages, among other things. Rather than blending in upon their return, however, persons originally taken from the Bight of Benin (many of whom were Yoruba, Fon, and Ewe) often formed their own settlements along the coast, where they became known as *amaros*. Similarly, some of the Yoruba and Fon-Ewe rescued at sea by the British and brought to Sierra Leone later returned to south-western Nigeria and Benin, where they were referred to as *saros*. Perhaps the captive and New World experience had changed them, like it had the "Americo-Liberians." There is great irony here: people who voluntarily returned to Africa wound up distancing themselves from Africans – or perhaps it was the indigenous who rejected the returnees, though rejection and self-containment may have both been in operation. In any case, the recovery of a life prior to the slave trade proved challenging, but perhaps more importantly, these reverse sailings underscore how the history of Africa itself is informed by the American experience; that early cultural influences were not simply one way – from Africa to the Americas – but that they flowed in both (and even multiple) directions.

One by one, and over a long stretch of time, the various polities throughout the Americas dismantled the machinery of slavery. The people of Haiti freed themselves in 1791. Next came many of the colonies under Spanish control, where wars of independence were organized as early as 1808. As would be true of the United States and Cuba, black soldiers made their own contributions to the independence efforts, fighting as well for an end to slavery. General José de San

Martín, who led much of South America in its struggle against Spain, was authorized by both Argentina and Chile to grant freedom to slaves enlisted in his armies, resulting in the mobilization and manumission of thousands. The scope of these manumissions was limited, as those who would become freedmen or *libertos* could only do so after serving extended terms in the army; one condition, for example, required that they continue to serve for two years after all hostilities had ended. While some deserted, others stayed the course; in the invasion of Chile in 1816 to fight the Spanish, half of San Martín's army were ex-slaves, recruited from Buenos Aires and western Argentina and serving in all-black units. These soldiers paid dearly; they fought with San Martín in Chile, Peru, and Ecuador between 1816 and 1823, returning to Argentina with only 150 of the original 2,000. But some had risen to the rank of officer, a feat duplicated in Mexico, where African-descended leaders José Maria Morelos and Vicente "El Negro" Guerrero provided important leadership. In what is now Colombia and Venezuela, the "great liberator" Simón Bolívar favored abolition, though he was ambivalent about freed Africans becoming full members of society. Abolition was opposed by Colombia's and Venezuela's mining interests, for whom 55 percent of the 38,940 enslaved still toiled as late as 1830. As a result, slavery was officially abolished in Chile, the countries of Central America, and Mexico in 1823, 1824, and 1829, respectively, but not until 1852 in Colombia. Ecuador followed suit that year, then Argentina and Uruguay (1853), Peru and Venezuela (1854), Bolivia (1861), and Paraguay (1869).

The great irony of South America's fight for liberation from Spain is that its efforts were aided by none other than Haiti. At a critical juncture, when Simón Bolívar faltered against the Spanish in 1815 and 1816 following a series of defeats, he and his soldiers twice took refuge in Haiti, where he not only convalesced, but where he received both men and guns to renew the fight in South America. Not only did Bolívar benefit materially and directly from Haiti, but in forming Bolivia's government and Venezuela's constitution, there is evidence that he borrowed a number of ideas from Haitian models. In return for Haiti's support, Bolívar was asked to free the slaves in South America, but not only did he fail to do that, he also turned his back on the black republic in 1826, when under US pressure he chose not to invite Haiti to the Panama Congress, which he headed. When presented with opportunities to repay Haitian charity and solidarity, the "great liberator" instead succumbed to racist sentiment.

Emancipation in the British Caribbean, achieved through the resistance of the enslaved, was supported by British abolitionists under William Wilberforce's leadership in the late eighteenth and early nineteenth centuries. Initially waging a campaign of "amelioration" to improve the conditions of the enslaved, these abolitionists soon lobbied for the interdiction of the transatlantic trade and the end of slavery itself. Prominent among them were Olaudah Equiano and Ottobah Cugoano, who published his *Thoughts and Sentiments of the Evils of Slavery* in 1787. The cumulative effect of anti-slavery forces was the passing in Parliament of the Emancipation Act of 1833, ratified the following year, which ushered in the Apprenticeship period in the English-speaking Caribbean. With the exception of Barbados and Antigua, both of which transitioned directly into emancipation, the Apprenticeship provided that children under six years of age were now free, but that all others were to work for their former slaveholders for another four years, after which all would be emancipated in 1838. For their losses, slaveholders received significant compensation.

The relatively modest institution of slavery in Canada was also destroyed by the British Parliament's 1833 Emancipation Act, following its demise in Upper Canada (now Ontario) in 1793. Slavery in what remained of the French- and Danish-held Caribbean was abolished in 1848, while the Dutch afforded the same to their colonies (Aruba, Bonaire, Curaçao, St. Maarten, St. Eustatius, and Saba) in 1863. It would take a major civil war, however, for the institution to be abolished in the United States. Some 186,000 blacks enlisted in the Union Army, 93,000 of whom came from seceding states, and over 38,000 died in the war. Reminiscent of the pattern during the American War of Independence, the Union initially opposed using black troops, but changed its policy in August of 1862, more than a year after the war began. The enslaved also advanced their liberation by crossing Union Army lines and offering to work for wages. On the other side, the Confederacy used slaves for much of the vital infrastructural work, such as repairing railroads and bridges, manufacturing firearms and powder, constructing fortifications, and burying the dead. They were the cooks for the Confederate Army, and attended wealthy soldiers, cleaning their clothes, polishing their swords, and running errands. A few blacks even fought with the South, a last-ditch effort resulting from an act of desperation on the part of the Confederate government, enacted in March of 1865, by which time all was lost – the Confederacy surrendered at Appomattox the following month.

But before placing the South in too cynical a light, we should recall that President Abraham Lincoln preceded the Confederacy in embracing expediency. In issuing the Emancipation Proclamation, initially floated on September 22, 1862 but not put into effect until January 1, 1863, Lincoln sought to deny the Confederacy its labor base and main support for the war. The Proclamation only applied to those in the Confederacy, and did not emancipate the enslaved in states loyal to the Union or in territory under Union occupation. It was not until the war's end and the ratification of the Thirteenth Amendment on December 18, 1865 that the formerly enslaved were officially freed.

The American Civil War was so intensely fought that it can be described as a veritable bloodbath, an apocalypse in every sense of the word, the likes of which were never before nor since recorded in the annals of American history. Interpreted by some as divine retribution for the institution of slavery, some 650,000 persons perished, 620,000 of them soldiers, more than the number of American soldiers who died in two world wars, the Korean War, and the Vietnam War – combined.

The Civil War's culmination brought into focus the remaining Spanish-held territories of Puerto Rico and Cuba as slaveholding societies. A military junta seized power in Spain in 1868, and issued a Cuba-directed decree freeing children born to enslaved mothers. The abolitionist Segismundo Moret, appointed minister of the colonies in 1870, convinced the Spanish legislature to pass the Moret Law that same year, which in effect reinforced the 1868 decree. The Moret Law impacted the fortunes of Puerto Rico, whose enslaved population by 1872 was less than 2 percent of its labor force; the Spanish legislature abolished slavery in that island in 1873 without compensating slaveholders.

The exponential growth of slavery in Cuba, which saw some 715,000 Africans imported between 1791 and 1860, combined with the successful, massive insurrection in neighboring Haiti, would prove to be explosive. A conspiracy led by the free black carpenter and artist José Antonio Aponte in 1812, inspired by the Haitian Revolution, set Cuba ablaze in a series of revolts, collectively called the Aponte Rebellion. During his trial, Aponte was required to explain his series of drawings in his now famous (but yet to be recovered) "Book of Paintings," which included Toussaint and Dessalines as subjects. Aponte would be hanged and decapitated, but in 1825 Cuba would again experience a serious, African-led revolt in Matanzas, in western Cuba, involving some 200 enslaved persons that spread to twenty-five plantations, killing fifteen whites. The eruption of three more major slave revolts in 1842–3, followed by the repression of an 1844 conspiracy known as *La Escalera* ("The Ladder," where those charged with insurrection were customarily tied and beaten), further underscored the level of unrest in the island. But the fatal blow to Cuban slavery was struck during the Ten Years' War (1868–78), when Cuba attempted to throw off the Spanish colonial yoke. As was true of both the American War of Independence and the American Civil War, whites fought for their reasons and blacks fought for those same reasons as well as their own, particularly for freedom. Slavery became more of an issue as the war progressed, but initially the war was fought in the name of Cuban nationalism. These two different yet related issues would coalesce to place Cuba's greatest military leader, Antonio Maceo, on the horns of yet another dilemma. The son of a free African Cuban, Maceo delivered stellar service to the Cuban struggle for independence, but he was suspected by white revolutionaries of harboring secret plans to establish a black republic on Cuban soil, à la Haiti, a fear encouraged by the Spanish. Maceo was joined by such men of African descent as Quintín Bandera, Guillermo Moncada, and Policarpo Pineda (or Rustán) as military leaders in the Ten Years' War, and they were joined by thousands of enslaved infantry. The war ended with the Pact of Zanjón and the defeat of the nationalists, and Spain manumitted 16,000 slaves to quell further trouble, but Maceo rejected the pact precisely because it did not manumit all slaves. The Guerra Chiquita ("Little War") ensued in eastern Cuba from 1879 to 1880, in part waged by blacks and those of mixed ancestry over their lack of power and slavery's continuation. Quickly suppressed due to a lack of support by white Cubans, Spain further undermined the spirit of the rebellion by declaring the end of slavery in 1880 and the start of the *patronato* or apprenticeship which, like the policy in the British Caribbean, required former slaves to work for former slaveholders for the next eight years. Because there were few *patrocinados* left in Cuba by 1885, Spain declared the end of the apprenticeship in 1886. The enslaved's fight for freedom from both slavery and colonial rule would deeply influence the concept of race in Cuba.

Working in tandem with the rise in violent resistance were efforts to use the courts to achieve manumission. This is counterintuitive as slaves were generally without rights, yet as the nineteenth century unfolded, women in particular made use of the courts, whenever possible, to obtain their freedom. In Cuba and Brazil, women and children were disproportionately successful (relative to men) in petitioning the courts for their manumission, and similarly those in urban settings were more successful than those in rural areas. In most instances, they sought to either take advantage of the failure of slaveholders to fulfill their obligations as such, or they sought the implementation of "free womb" laws – the Spanish Moret Law (passed by the Spanish government in 1870) and the equivalent Brazilian Rio Branco Law (passed the following year) – mandating that children subsequently born to enslaved women would be free. These activities, in conjunction with other antislavery efforts, had the effect of severely eroding the institution of slavery.

Brazil was the last to abolish slavery. In contrast to both Cuba and the United States, there was no all-consuming conflagration within which the enslaved fought for multiple purposes, with the possible exception of the Paraguayan War of 1865–70. It was during that war, waged against Paraguay by Brazil, Argentina, and Uruguay, that Brazil offered freedom to those who enlisted. Although this war was important to the demise of Brazilian slavery, more critical was the steady diminution in the slave population stemming from resistance, mechanization, and the abolitionist campaign in that country. The ban on the transatlantic trade, initially agreed to in 1817 by the Portuguese, was finally enforced after 1850, although the clandestine trade continued. The 1860s through the 1880s saw a significant increase in the number of slaveholders killed by the enslaved, the number of (mostly small-scale) uprisings, and the number fleeing from slavery, particularly in the coffee regions around Rio de Janeiro and São Paulo. The surge of activity pressured the government to pass the aforementioned Rio Branco Law of 1871, or Law of Free Birth, and a sexagenarian law passed in 1885 granting freedom to those reaching sixty years of age. The effect of resistance and legislation was the precipitous decline in the percentage of the enslaved, from 50 percent of the total population in 1822 to 5 percent in 1888. In that year, the Golden Law was enacted, officially abolishing a slavery in Brazil that had been practically ended by the enslaved themselves.

The close of the nineteenth century saw the end of an institution throughout the Americas, but by the time slavery was finished in Cuba and Brazil, another chapter had begun elsewhere in the Caribbean and the northern mainland. The question for all concerned was: How "free" would freedom be?

Games People Play

The most arresting, startling, disturbing, and indisputable fact concerning the whole of the Americas and their respective processes of emancipation was that, whether slaveholders were compensated for their losses or not, the enslaved themselves received virtually nothing. It is therefore the case that both past and present development in the Americas is based upon an institution whose labor came free of charge. Many contemporary African countries may be presently indebted, but the Western world is indebted historically and ironically so, as it extracted free labor in exchange for incalculable suffering from Africans and their descendants, stolen from Africa. Does this historical debt require some contemporary resolution from those in the Americas and Europe, who obviously were not "there" from the sixteenth through the nineteenth centuries, but whose lives and fortunes continue to benefit from an economic foundation based upon slavery?

A review of post-emancipation societies, beginning with the British Caribbean, demonstrates a certain continuity of experience between slavery and freedom. The Apprenticeship, 1834 to 1838, began the process by which the status of some 80 percent of the British Caribbean population changed. During the four-year transition period, former slaves were still required to work for former slaveholders in exchange for wages, and were bound to the plantations by means of so-called pass laws that restricted their mobility. It became clear, therefore, that the apprentices themselves would have to take action to transform the meaning of freedom from an abstraction of colonial decree to the substance of lived experience. This they did by asserting as much control over their labor as possible; they used their free time (a quarter of the week) as they saw fit, often withholding it from desperate employers. They also refused to work in some instances, resorting to sabotage in others. While wary of the legal system, they yet sought to clarify their freedom in the courts.

Following apprenticeship, blacks were keen to negotiate a freedom that afforded the conditions of their labor as much flexibility as possible, while providing their families with as much autonomy as possible, including the opportunity to relocate, both within the island of their residence as well as to different islands. Many vocationally skilled and semi-skilled workers moved to urban areas, while others migrated from lower-wage areas such as Barbados and the Leeward and Windward islands to higher-wage sites, such as Trinidad and British Guianas. Negotiations, work stoppages or strikes, and violence accompanied efforts to receive equitable, acceptable salaries. Conflict with employers determined to reduce wages produced major strikes in Jamaica in 1838–9 and 1841, Guianas in 1842, and Trinidad in 1843. While wages were important, the African-descended also fought for task work and jobs that did not require contracts, both of which maximized their choices and enhanced their liberty. They could better control their schedules on the plantations, and have more time to cultivate their own provision grounds and participate in the market, or pursue supplemental economic endeavors. They insisted on shorter weeks for women and children than men, allowing women more time to work the provision grounds and pursue huckstering in the market.

Attempts to define the terms of freedom, severely handicapped by the absence of any meaningful compensation for slavery, was resisted within ten years of emancipation by former slaveholders. They responded by seizing the courts and imposing a series of restrictions on movement, squatting, and the use of plantation property (see Figure 16). They succeeded in lowering wages and reestablishing their ownership of provision grounds. Increased educational access represented a glimmer

FIGURE 16 Thatched houses, Barbados, 1898. From Robert T. Hill, *Cuba and Porto Rico* (New York, 1898), facing p. 396.

of hope, but was severely restricted to a few privileged families and individuals, sharpening class divisions among blacks.

The backlash from former slaveholders resulted in a period of renewed oppression, contiguous with enslavement. The African-descended responded in ways similar to their resistance during slavery; cultural opposition took the form of a reinvigorated embrace of African-influenced religions, while the folklore, memorials, and the language itself evinced a deep-seated anger. The cultural worked in tandem with the political, and violent revolts against reconfigured oppression broke out all over the Caribbean. These included the 1844 Guerre Nègre in Dominica, the Angel Gabriel Riots of British Guiana in 1856, the 1862 Vox Populi Riots of St. Vincent, the 1876 Belmanna Riots of Tobago, and the Confederate Riots of Barbados of the same year. Perhaps the most representative of these uprisings were the Morant Bay Disturbances of 1865 in Jamaica, led by the lay preacher Paul Bogle.

In 1865, the people of Stony Gut, a St. Thomas Parish farming village located on land leased by blacks following apprenticeship, faced desperate economic times, a condition exacerbated by royal and colonial government indifference. Refusing to continue paying rent to the magistrates of Morant Bay, these black farmers claimed squatters' rights. The local planters tried to evict them, and Bogle, leader of the Stony Gut community, called for revolt. Following the rescue of a fellow farmer on trial in Morant Bay, members of Stony Gut violently resisted the arrest of the rescuers. In a response bearing clear resemblances to Akan-based uprisings during slavery, Bogle and his followers took an oath and administered it to others, and on October 10 they marched into Morant Bay with drums beating and conch shells blaring, crying "Cleave to the black, color for color." Vowing to kill repressive whites while saving white sympathizers, they took control of St. Thomas Parish for three days. After death and destruction, Bogle was captured with the assistance of – wait for it – the maroons, and was hanged on a British gunboat on October 24, along with over 1,000 other blacks.

By the 1870s, then, many in the British Caribbean had been forced to return to dependence on the plantations as a consequence of both planter countermeasures and the disruption of trade resulting from the American Civil War. They suffered rates of unemployment, lowered wages, and a surge in food prices that placed them in conditions not far removed from those characterizing slavery. Their continued resistance, however, establishes this response as a major theme in the history of the African diaspora. Their experience would be echoed in the mainland of the United States.

Freedom's Tease

The close of the Civil War ushered in Reconstruction (1865 to 1877), the quintessential saga of the rise and fall of a people's dreams and aspirations, as promising and progressive social policies introduced during Reconstruction were ultimately reversed and crushed by the period's end. Some 4 million people had been emancipated, but as was true of the British Caribbean, the precise significance of their emancipation was undefined and contested. A war-torn South, struggling to regain an economic footing while wrestling with the implications of this new freedom, initially attempted to resolve both by controlling black labor. Again, not unlike the Caribbean, southern whites adopted legislation collectively known as the Black Codes, seeking to ensure black worker availability. The Black Codes were similar to the antebellum South's Slave Codes in that they proscribed black movement, limiting where they could rent or own property, and forcing them to work for white employers by means of vagrancy laws. Black life in the workplace and society in general was regulated, and opportunities for blacks' participation in the political process denied. The dawn of Reconstruction was fairly bleak.

Determining that Andrew Johnson, Lincoln's successor following the latter's assassination in April of 1865, was content to allow white home rule in the South, Congress intervened in December of 1865 and wrested control of Reconstruction from the executive branch, inaugurating the sub-period known as Radical Reconstruction. With the exception of a cooperative Tennessee, the South was divided into five military districts governed by martial law; no southern state would be admitted into the Union until it ratified the Fourteenth Amendment granting blacks citizenship. In March of 1865 the Bureau of Refugees, Freedmen, and Abandoned Lands was established. Better known as the Freedmen's Bureau, the agency oversaw efforts to relieve not only blacks but whites of intense suffering. To that end, the Bureau created forty-six hospitals by 1867, and by 1869 dispensed food rations to 5 million whites and 15 million blacks. The Bureau intervened in disputes between black workers and employers, and helped thousands resume work under better conditions. "Freedmen's" courts were created to adjudicate cases deemed inappropriate for local tribunals. Perhaps more importantly, the Bureau promoted the education of freedpersons, and created day, evening, Sunday, and vocational schools. The African-descended of all ages sat in the same classroom, eager to finally read the Bible for themselves. Colleges were also established with Bureau assistance during this time, including the Hampton Institute and Fisk, Howard, and Atlanta Universities. Hundreds, if not thousands of whites from the North volunteered as teachers, and by 1870 there were some 247,333 students in over 4,000 schools.

In addition to such measures, the Reconstruction Act of 1867 enfranchised southern blacks and loyal whites while disfranchising a large number of disloyal whites. Constitutional conventions were held in 1867 and 1868 in which blacks participated, constituting the majority in South Carolina while equaling the white delegation in Louisiana. Black delegates helped craft the most progressive state constitutions the South has ever known, with such features as the abolition of property qualifications for the franchise and elective office. Blacks went on to hold public office, especially in South Carolina, where they controlled the lower house of the legislature for a period, contributed two lieutenant governors, and served in the state supreme court from 1870 to 1876 in the person of Jonathan Jasper Wright. Between 1868 and 1896, Louisiana saw thirty-eight black senators and ninety-five representatives elected to the state legislature; of its three black lieutenant governors, P.B.S. Pinchback served as acting governor for forty-three days. At the national level, of the twenty blacks elected to the House of Representatives between 1869 and 1901, South Carolina supplied the largest number with eight. There were also two black senators, Blanche K. Bruce and Hiram R. Revels, both of Mississippi; no African descendant would again serve in that capacity until the election of Edward Brooke of Massachusetts in 1966.

Although these developments were significant, they did not address the fundamental economic difficulties of freedpersons. The notion of "forty acres and a mule" for every black family stems from an 1865 military order by General Sherman, by which certain sea islands and a thirty-mile tract of coastal land south of Charleston were designated for freedperson settlement. Households were assigned forty-acre plots and a pack animal (if no longer needed by the Union army), and by 1865 some 40,000 freedpersons had received 400,000 acres of land. But in February of 1865, Congress stripped the Freedmen's Bureau of the authority to assign such lands, and President Johnson soon rescinded all such land titles. Some of the many displaced were helped by the Southern Homestead Act of 1866, which provided those in five southern states, black and white, the opportunity to secure homesteads. By 1867, blacks owned 160,960 acres in Florida, while acquiring over 350,000 acres in Georgia by 1870.

In the larger scheme of things, however, the vast majority of the 4 million freedpersons received nothing and, as was true of the Caribbean, were forced by economic necessity to return to the same plantations they had worked prior to the war, lands owned by former slaveholders. They were then required to work for either monthly wages or as sharecroppers; in the former instance, the wages in 1867 totaled less than what had been paid to enslaved persons who had been hired out (see Figure 17). As for sharecropping, it was a nefarious system that kept black labor in place, bound to the land like serfs, because at year's end they were always in debt to plantation and farm owners who manipulated the records or "cooked the books." Thus, the reality for too many was an economic arrangement similar to an institution that had supposedly been abolished. Sadly, but predictably, the South's production of cotton rebounded from its wartime lows, and by 1880 was higher than it had ever been.

Just as sharecropping was another form of exploitation – even slavery under a different name – so the South resurrected another "institution" echoing the activities of the antebellum "patty-rollers." The institution made the reimposition of white control possible and was, simply put, state-sponsored terrorism. In reaction to Radical Reconstruction, white southerners unleashed a widespread, unrelenting campaign of sheer horror, aimed at driving blacks, along with their white supporters, out of the political process and back to the plantations, where they were immobilized and "put in their place." As early as 1866, organizations such as the Regulators and the Black Horse Cavalry emerged, terrorizing blacks throughout the South. After 1867, the number of these clandestine societies mushroomed to include the Pale Faces, the Rifle Clubs of South Carolina, the White Line of Mississippi, the White League of Louisiana, the White Brotherhood, the Knights of the White Camelia, and the Knights of the Ku Klux Klan. Together with the Black Codes, these terrorist organizations were highly effective in intimidating a defenseless population, and worked with white

FIGURE 17 Black family, Beaufort, South Carolina, 1862. Photograph by Timothy O'Sullivan. Library of Congress, Prints and Photographs Division, LC-B8171-152-A.

politicians to resist and gradually overturn progressive legislation through murder, mutilation, rapine, and confiscation. It should be observed that such vigilantism was far from confined to the nocturnal raids of organizations in hoods, as over time many of these heinous crimes were carried out by unmasked mobs in broad daylight, often in suits and ties and dresses, decked out in in their Sunday best. Both men and women were lynched, their lifeless bodies then burned and dragged through the streets of the local black community to multiply terror's effect. With the North weary of the fight for black citizenship, the federal government's decision to remove federal troops from the South in 1876 opened wide the floodgates for white supremacists. By such requirements as the poll tax, proof of literacy and ability to understand any part of the state constitution, ownership of property, grandfather clauses, and by vulgar physical threat, blacks were removed from the polls in dramatic fashion. By 1910, state constitutions rewritten to include such requirements had disfranchised blacks in North and South Carolina, Louisiana, Georgia, Mississippi, Alabama, Virginia, and Oklahoma. "Jim Crow" laws, legislating separate and segregated spaces for blacks and whites in public and private places, became fixtures on the legal landscape, upheld by the Supreme Court itself in its 1896 *Plessy v. Ferguson* decision – they would remain the law of the land until the civil rights gains of the 1960s. By the dawn of the twentieth century, the vestiges of slavery were apparent throughout the South, home to 90 percent of all African-descended persons in the United States. For another one hundred years following slavery's abolition, black folk suffered another form of legal, state-supported discrimination and oppression, and again endured the exploitation of their labor, the destabilization of their families, and the curtailment of their potential. All of this, simply because they were black.

Another Way?

The different yet parallel experiences of the African-descended in the United States and the Caribbean suggest that de facto slavery in the post-emancipation period was a powerful factor in the development of race and racial consciousness in these societies. The denial of opportunity and pervasiveness of black suffering, white arrogation of privilege and power, and the mediating role disproportionately played by those of mixed ancestry rendered racial identity a meaningful category of social significance. Blackness, well established during slavery, acquired an even greater quality of immutability, as the end of legal slavery failed to significantly alter the very real predicament of the formerly enslaved.

A consideration of post-slavery Cuba, however, may suggest that the concept of race was neither universal nor unchanging throughout the Americas, but rather was relative to the unique circumstances of a given society. Cuba's struggle for independence from Spain, coming at the heels of the abolition of Cuban slavery, forged a collective identity in that island that attempted to merge color and nationality. That is, the African-descended felt loyal to both their blackness and their Cubanness; the two were not easily separated, and were uniquely linked to their white Cuban compatriots. Evidence for this view of racial identity can be found in the words of the black general Guillermo Moncada, military leader in both the Ten Years' War and the Guerra Chiquita, who argued for the existence of a "Cuban race." The context for Moncada's statement was war with Spain, without which Cuba's racial relations may have conformed to North American and British Caribbean patterns. The notion of a Cuban race was in conversation with the idea of a *raza de color* ("race of color") or *clase de color*, created by African-descended Cubans that sought to join *morenos* (blacks) and *pardos* (those of mixed ancestry) in a unified category, with the result that *morenos* and *pardos* were both often called *negros* (blacks). But even those who embraced the idea of a *raza de color* saw themselves as fully Cuban, and vigorously fought for their rights as such.

The end of slavery in Cuba resulted in continuing despair for the majority of the formerly enslaved. As was true elsewhere, they received nothing. Some moved to urban areas, others fled the sugar plantations of the island's western sector in search of land to farm on their own. However, most remained where they had been, on or near their former plantations, where they worked for either wages or tenancy. Wages were uncertain and their lives quite precarious, as a Cuban sugar industry in crisis suffered from competition, in addition to other factors. Laborers had also been displaced by an influx of more than 100,000 Spaniards between 1882 and 1894, most of whom wound up working in rural areas, where the devastation of two wars between 1868 and 1880 remained a formidable challenge. By the early 1890s, therefore, the situation for blacks in Cuba was not unlike their counterparts in the United States and the Caribbean.

Desperate economic conditions further fueled the flame of resistance to Spanish rule and the drive for independence. To counter the insurgency, Spain held aloft the example of Haiti, and warned that independence efforts would devolve into racial conflict. Led by the writings of José Martí, the response of Cuban intellectuals of all shades was to develop a concept of transracial nationalism in Cuba. Their work aimed at "rewriting" the black insurgent as raceless compatriot and hero rather than black, vengeful, and menacing, an effort greatly assisted by black and mixed race journalists and writers, including Juan Gualberto Gómez, Martín Morúa Delgado, and Rafael Serra y Montalvo. Through such individuals, along with black newspapers, the struggle for black civil rights was simultaneously waged, and the establishment of such organizations as the Directorio Central de las Societies de la Clase de Color allowed black and mixed race organizations to coalesce. Their creation indicates that black leaders did not necessarily agree on the best way to achieve a common Cuban identity, as some advocated black political organizations and others (such as Antonio Maceo) did not.

Led by Martí's Cuban Revolutionary Party, the independence movement again took up arms in February of 1895, for which Antonio Maceo again served as leading general, and during which black participation was again both significant and crucial. Racial equality was enunciated by independence leaders as the ideological underpinning of the movement. Achieving rapid success, the insurgents suffered a major setback when Maceo was ambushed and killed in Havana province in December of 1896. Hopes that Spain would be more amenable to Cuban independence were revived with the assassination of the Spanish prime minister in August of 1897 and the fall of Spain's conservative government. The American entry into the conflict in April of 1898 launched the Spanish-American War, ending with an American victory that August. The Americans would remain in Cuba for three and a half years, until the Cubans had satisfactorily demonstrated (to the Americans) their "fitness to rule," certified by Cuba's acceptance of the 1901 Platt Amendment (which granted the United States the right to intervene in Cuba whenever the former deemed necessary).

American interventionism was a blow to Cuba's transracial experiment, as Americans introduced Jim Crow to Havana, complete with segregated fighting units. The black Cuban's pride in both her blackness and her nationality would be tested, therefore, as some white Cubans were encouraged by North American racism to forego the principles of Martí.

The irony in the Spanish-American War is difficult to overlook. African Americans from the United States enthusiastically supported Cuban independence out of an identification with Cubans, who they viewed as largely black or of mixed ancestry and therefore members of a shared community. After all, both groups were just out of slavery. Four all-black units (known as "Buffalo Soldiers") fought in Cuba, and probably saved Theodore Roosevelt's famous "Rough Riders" from annihilation at the June 1898 Battle of Las Guasimas. Those very same black American soldiers, however, suffered shameful discrimination in a service for which they were prepared to give their lives. They could not even get to Cuba without first passing through a gauntlet of hate-filled white mobs in the American South, protesting their transit. For those black American soldiers, a raceless American nationalism was unimaginable.

The end of the nineteenth century saw the overwhelming majority of African-descended persons mired in poverty throughout the Americas. They had been "freed" from slavery but not from structural racism, with the result that their lives changed very little. The idea of "racelessness" was inconceivable to African American soldiers fighting in Cuba at the end of the nineteenth century, perhaps as "unthinkable" as the Haitian Revolution and the very notion that enslaved blacks could successfully overthrow slavery and establish their own state. What should have been celebrated as arguably the most glorious triumph of the human spirit was instead ignored, rejected, or otherwise resisted by the "democracies" of the world in the "Age of Revolution." In fact, Haiti's achievement was so unacceptable that in 1825, King Charles X sent the French navy to threaten Haiti with destruction lest it pay an "independence debt" of 150 million gold francs in indemnities and as compensation for slaveholders who had been relieved of their "properties," offering in exchange France's much-needed diplomatic recognition. In 1838, the sum was reduced to 90 million francs (roughly $19 billion), which Haiti somehow managed to pay by 1947 (which with interest and inflation was actually closer to $40 billion). In effect, rather than compensating the formerly enslaved, France effectively made Haiti pay (once more) for its freedom (and insolence), virtually ensuring a *longue durée* of poverty for the country. Nothing better represents the extent to which racism permeated all aspects of policies related to black folk in the Americas than the Haitian experience.

Suggestions for Further Reading

Resistance and emancipation literature has amassed rapidly. Michel-Rolph Trouillot introduces the idea of the Haitian Revolution as "unthinkable" in his

Silencing the Past: Power and the Production of History (Boston: Beacon Press, 1995). In addition to aforementioned works by C.L.R. James and Carolyn Fick, there is Marlene L. Daut, ed., *Tropics of Haiti: Race and the Literary History of the Haitian Revolution in the Atlantic, World, 1789–1865* (Liverpool: Liverpool University Press, 2015); Laurent Dubois, *Avengers of the New World: The Story of the Haitian Revolution* (Harvard: Harvard University Press, 2005) and *A Colony of Citizens: Revolution and Slave Emancipation in the French Caribbean* (Chapel Hill: University of North Carolina Press, 2004); David Barry Gaspar and David Patrick Geggus, eds., *A Turbulent Time: The French Revolution and the Greater Caribbean* (Bloomington: Indiana University Press, 1997); David Patrick Geggus and Norman Fiering, eds., *The World of the Haitian Revolution* (Bloomington: Indiana University Press, 2009); David Patrick Geggus, ed., *The Impact of the Haitian Revolution in the Atlantic World* (Columbia: University of South Carolina Press, 2001); Jean Fouchard, *Les marrons de la liberté* (Paris: Éditions de L'École, 1972). For a discussion of martial arts, see T.J. Desch-Obi, *Fighting for Honor: The History of African Martial Art Traditions in the Atlantic World* (Columbia: University of South Carolina Press, 2008).

For the English-speaking Caribbean, see Mavis Campbell, *The Maroons of Jamaica, 1655–1796: A History of Resistance, Collaboration, and Betrayal* (South Hadley, MA: Bergin and Garvey, 1988); Michael Craton, *Testing the Chains: Resistance to Slavery in the British West Indies* (Ithaca, NY: Cornell University Press, 1982); David Barry Gaspar, *Bondsmen and Rebels: A Case Study of Master–Slave Relations in Antigua, with Implications for Colonial British America* (Baltimore: Johns Hopkins University Press, 1985); and Thomas C. Holt, *The Problem of Freedom: Race, Labor, and Politics in Jamaica and Britain, 1832–1938* (Baltimore: Johns Hopkins University Press, 1992). An introduction to themes in the Caribbean is provided by Hilary Beckles and Verene Shepherd, eds., *Caribbean Freedom: Society and Economy from Emancipation to the Present* (Kingston, Jamaica, and London: Curry, 1993).

For Brazil and Latin America, see Anne Eller, *We Dream Together: Dominican Independence, Haiti, and the Fight for Caribbean Freedom* (Durham, NC: Duke University Press, 2016); Barbara Weinstein, *The Color of Modernity: São Paulo and the Making of Race and Nation in Brazil* (Durham, NC: Duke University Press, 2015); Emilia Viotti da Costa, *The Brazilian Empire: Myths and Histories* (Chicago: University of Chicago Press, 1985) and *Crowns of Glory, Tears of Blood: The Demerara Slave Rebellion of 1823* (New York: Oxford University Press, 1994); Rafael Duharte Jiménez, *Rebeldá esclava en el caribe* (Veracruz: Gobierno del Estado de Veracruz, 1992); João José Reis, *Slave Rebellion in Brazil: The Muslim Uprising of 1835 in Bahia*, trans. Arthur Brakel (Baltimore: Johns Hopkins University Press, 1993), and *Death is a Festival: Funeral Rites and Rebellion in Nineteenth-Century Brazil*, trans. H. Sabrina Gledhill (Chapel Hill: University of North Carolina Press, 2003); Camillia

Cowling, *Conceiving Freedom: Women of Color, Gender, and the Abolition of Slavery in Havana and Rio* (Chapel Hill: University of North Carolina Press, 2013); Flávio dos Santos Gomes, *Experiêncas atlânticas: ensaios e pesquisas sobre a escrivadão e o pós-emancipação no Brasil* (Passo Fundo: Universidade de Passo Fondo, UPF Editora, 2003); Aisha Finch, *Rethinking Slave Rebellion in Cuba: La Escalera and the Insurgencies of 1841–1844* (Chapel Hill: University of North Carolina Press, 2015); Manuel Barcia, *The Great African Slave Revolt of 1825: Cuba and the Fight for Freedom in Matanzas* (Baton Rouge: Louisiana State University Press, 2012); Rebecca J. Scott, *Slave Emancipation in Cuba: The Transition to Free Labor, 1860–1899* (Princeton, NJ: Princeton University Press, 1985); Rebecca Scott and Jean M. Hébrard, *Freedom Papers: An Atlantic Odyssey in the Age of Emancipation* (Cambridge, MA: Harvard University Press, 2012); Ada Ferrer, *Freedom's Mirror: Cuba and Haiti in the Age of Revolution* (Cambridge: Cambridge University Press, 2014) and *Insurgent Cuba: Race, Nation, and Revolution, 1868–1898* (Chapel Hill: University of North Carolina Press, 1999); Matt D. Childs, *The 1812 Aponte Rebellion in Cuba and the Struggle against Atlantic Slavery* (Chapel Hill: University of North Carolina Press, 2006); María Elena Díaz, *The Virgin, the King, and the Royal Slaves of El Cobre: Negotiating Freedom in Colonial Cuba, 1670–1780* (Stanford: Stanford University Press, 2000); Louis A. Pérez, *The War of 1898: Cuba and the United States in History and Historiography* (Chapel Hill: University of North Carolina Press, 1999); Aline Helg, *Our Rightful Share: The Afro-Cuban Struggle for Equality, 1886–1912* (Chapel Hill: University of North Carolina Press, 1995). Richard Price, *Maroon Societies: Rebel Slave Communities in the Americas* (Baltimore: Johns Hopkins University Press, 1979), remains useful, while Pierre Verger, *Trade Relations between the Bight of Benin and Bahia from the 17th to 19th Century*, trans. Evelyn Crawford (Ibadan, Nigeria: Ibadan University Press, 1976) provides fascinating insights into cultural ties between West Africa and Brazil.

As for the United States, W.E.B. Du Bois, *Black Reconstruction* (Millwood, NY: Kraus-Thomson, 1963) remains a standard and remarkable work, as is C. Vann Woodward, *The Strange Career of Jim Crow* (New York: Oxford University Press, 1955) and Leon F. Litwack, *Been in the Storm So Long: The Aftermath of Slavery* (New York: Knopf, 1979). There is a lot of work on rebellions. Herbert Aptheker, *American Negro Slave Revolts* (New York: International, 1970) has been an important source for many years. Eugene D. Genovese, *From Rebellion to Revolution: Afro-American Slave Revolts in the Making of the Modern World* (Baton Rouge: Louisiana State University Press, 1979), organizes slave revolts in a progression with which not all scholars agree, but is nonetheless valuable, especially concerning Denmark Vesey, an example of which is Douglas R. Egerton, *He Shall Go Out Free: The Lives of Denmark Vesey* (Madison: Madison House, 1999). An instructive scholarly debate on Vesey entitled, "Forum: The Making of a Slave Conspiracy" can be found in *William and Mary Quarterly*, vol. **58** (no. 4, October 2001) and vol. 59 (no. 1, January 2002). The journal *Slavery and Abolition* is also an excellent source for materials on slave insurrection. Peter P. Hinks, *To Awaken My Afflicted Brethren: David Walker and the Problem of Antebellum Resistance* (University Park: Pennsylvania State University Press, 1997) is a related, though overlooked investigation of David Walker, and suggests a possible, indirect link between him and Vesey. There is also Stephanie Camp's acclaimed *Closer to Freedom: Enslaved Women and Everyday Resistance in the Plantation South* (Chapel Hill: University of North Carolina Press, 2004), a gender-centered analysis.

Concerning abolitionism, see Ellen Carol Dubois, *Feminism and Suffrage: The Emergence of an Independent Women's Movement in America, 1848–1869* (Ithaca, NY: Cornell University Press, 1999); Jean Fagan Yellin and John C. Van Horne, eds., *The Abolitionist Sisterhood: Women's Political Culture in Antebellum America* (Ithaca, NY: Cornell University Press, 1994); Rosalyn Terborg-Penn, *African American Women in the Struggle for the Vote, 1850–1920* (Bloomington: Indiana University Press, 1998); and Nell Irvin Painter, *Sojourner Truth: A Life, A Symbol* (New York: W.W. Norton, 1997). There is also the classic, Benjamin Quarles, *Black Abolitionists* (New York: Oxford, 1969).

The movement of black sailors and their contributions to resistance can be read about in Peter Linebaugh and Marcus Rediker, *The Many-Headed Hydra: Sailors, Slaves, Commoners, and the Hidden History of the Revolutionary Atlantic* (Boston: Beacon Press, 2000); Marcus Rediker, *Villains of All Nations: Atlantic Pirates in the Golden Age* (Boston: Beacon Press, 2004); Vincent Carretta, *Equiano, the African: Biography of a Self-Made Man* (Athens: University of Georgia Press, 2005). Black mariners and revolt are also taken up in Julius S. Scott, "The Common Wind: Currents of Afro-American Communication in the Era of the Haitian Revolution," (PhD thesis, Duke University, 1986). Jeffrey W. Bolster, *Black Jacks: African American Seamen in the Age of Sail* (Cambridge, MA: Harvard University Press, 1997) also contributes to the subject of black seafarers.

Regarding culture and resistance, one should consult such works as Gwendolyn Midlo Hall, *Africans in Colonial Louisiana: The Development of Afro-Creole Culture in the Eighteenth Century* (Baton Rouge: Louisiana State University Press, 1992); Margaret Washington Creel, *"A Peculiar People": Slave Religion and Community Culture among the Gullahs* (New York: New York University Press, 1988); Albert J. Raboteau, *Slave Religion: The "Invisible Institution" in the Antebellum South* (New York: Oxford University Press, 1978); James H. Sweet, *Domingos Álvares, African Healing, and the Intellectual History of the African World* (Chapel Hill: University of North Carolina Press, 2011). Alex Bontemps, *The Punished Self: Surviving Slavery in the Colonial South* (Ithaca, NY and London: Cornell University Press, 2001) presents slavery as a predicament, an idea borrowed here. On black festivals and coronations, consider Jeroen Dewulf, *The Pinkster King and the King of Kongo: The Forgotten History of America's Dutch-Owned Slaves* (Jackson: University of Mississippi Press, 2016). The work of Sterling Stuckey, *Slave Culture: Nationalist Theory and the Foundations of Black America* (New York: Oxford University Press, 1987) has been critical to the uncovering of a resilient African culture's role in resistance to slavery and racism in the United States. Also see, Michael A. Gomez, *Exchanging Our Country Marks: The Transformation of African Identities in the Colonial and Antebellum South* (Chapel Hill: University of North Carolina Press, 1998).

CHAPTER 7

Reconnecting

Two striking aspects of the first half of the twentieth century concern the large-scale and widespread movements of the African-descended throughout the Americas, together with their persistent efforts to reconnect in meaningful ways with Africa. The former was in response to economic need and incentive, while the latter was motivated by political, philosophical, and religious considerations. Whatever the motive, rather than forgetting their African ancestry, people were endeavoring to remember and sustain it. In these ways, they were reversing sail in their minds and hearts, if not with their bodies.

While reconnecting with Africa, those of African descent were also redefining themselves as a series of communities related yet distinct from each other, a consequence of differing local circumstances and histories. Reconnections and redefinitions took place during periods of rapid industrialization, organization and theorization of labor, emerging struggles against empire, world war, women's rights movements, the rise of pseudoscientific racism, and the division of the world into Eastern and Western camps. Members of the African diaspora played significant roles in all of these developments.

From this complex period of interpenetrating influences and experiences arose a cultural efflorescence throughout the African diaspora. Notable works of art, literature, and scholarship, as well as political and religious innovations, resulted from this intercontinental cross-fertilization of ideas and experiences. The components of the African diaspora were therefore in extensive dialogue, a conversation that has only intensified until the present day.

Boats and Trains

The latter quarter of the nineteenth century had been an enormous disappointment to most throughout the African diaspora, their hopes of "full freedom" dashed by the realities of debt peonage, rural wage labor, peasant impoverishment, and either wide-ranging, systematic, state-backed terrorism, or a heavy-handed colonialism favoring a few while disparaging many. Whether on an island or on the mainland, most people were trapped, virtually incarcerated within an economic and political system from which there seemed no escape.

Changes in the international economy, combined with two world wars, created cracks in this "prison" through the demand for labor. The problem, however, was that those meeting the demand were required to relocate to places hundreds, if not thousands of miles from their lands of birth, resurrecting the dilemma of opportunity at the cost of family. Conditions were so desperate, however, that many made the sacrifice. The African diaspora during the first half of the twentieth century was therefore characterized by perpetual motion, in both hemispheres.

The peasant majority in the Caribbean remained locked in a struggle to bypass the power of planters through strategies of self-reliance. In Barbados and Antigua, they invariably continued to reside on or near former plantations, providing labor in exchange for occupancy. In Cuba, most remained in the countryside as wage laborers on sugar plantations or as squatters in new areas, and in the latter instance were not unlike many in Haiti, where many plantations had been dismantled and divided into smallholdings of one or two acres. Timber and minerals were extractive industries financed by American and European interests in various islands, but after the First World War (1914–18) the focus shifted to petroleum in Trinidad, Aruba, and Curaçao; and bauxite (for aluminum) in Jamaica and British Guiana. The region's economy was strengthened by these two exports until 1929, when the depression contributed to perennial unemployment.

As a consequence, the Caribbean emerged as the quintessential region of migratory activity. Divided into several phases, the first of the region's major redistributions took place between 1835 and 1885, when activity centered on the islands themselves. Persons from economically depressed areas, such as Barbados, sought opportunities elsewhere, especially in Trinidad and Tobago and British Guiana. About 19,000 left the eastern Caribbean for Trinidad and British

Guiana between 1835 and 1846; from 1850 to 1921, some 50,000 emigrated to Trinidad, Tobago, and British Guiana from Barbados alone. Destinations during this initial phase were not limited to the islands, as perhaps as many as 7,000 left for the goldfields of Venezuela.

Such considerable flight of labor caused concern within the sugar industry, resulting in government recruitment of workers from outside the Caribbean. In response, labor was drawn from two sources. The first were so-called "post-emancipation Africans," or persons seized from slave ships and taken to Sierra Leone and St. Helena in West Africa. Some 36,120 were subsequently spread throughout the British-held Caribbean between 1839 and 1867, where their arrival also reinvigorated cultural ties to Africa. The second source was Asia, principally the Indian subcontinent (but also China), from where approximately 500,000 indentured laborers were imported between 1838 and 1917, arriving in such places as Jamaica, Trinidad, Grenada, Martinique, St. Lucia, and St. Vincent. While resulting in some tensions, Africans and Asians have also intermarried, and have engaged in substantial cultural exchange.

A second migratory phase originating within the Caribbean between the 1880s and the 1920s was both intra-Caribbean as well as an out-migration. Destinations included Panama, Cuba, the Dominican Republic, Costa Rica, and the United States, as well as other Central American sites. But it was construction of the Panama Canal that laid the foundation for this important phase.

The United States' acquisition of the Panama Canal in 1903 was part of an imperialist expansion that began with the 1898 Spanish-American War and the US seizure of Cuba and Puerto Rico. The American presence in Panama was followed by a treaty with Haiti in 1915, giving the Americans control over the island's finances and internal security for ten years, a period that actually lasted nineteen, complete with US occupational forces. In 1916, the marines landed on the other side of the island in the Dominican Republic, guaranteeing the preservation of American economic interests there until the present day. Finally, the 1917 purchase of the Virgin Islands from the Danes effectively created an American lake in the Caribbean; de facto American colonialism was therefore extended over a significant portion of the African diaspora in the Americas. With such military and political control established, American and European economic interests proceeded unencumbered.

By 1903, some 44,000 from the Caribbean were already working on the Panama Canal, mostly from Barbados and Jamaica. By the time the canal was completed in 1914, between 150,000 and 200,000 people from the Caribbean had labored on the canal, as many as 45,000 from Barbados alone. Stated differently, those of African descent built the Panama Canal. While the contract workers were mostly male initially, they were joined by women who began arriving in Panama in increasing numbers, eventually balancing the sex ratio. They worked as domestics, cooks, and laundry women, reflecting a general surge in the percentage of women emigrating from the Caribbean through the first quarter of the twentieth century. It was on the canal site that Caribbean workers were introduced to North American Jim Crow, for although they performed every imaginable job associated with the canal's building and operation, they did so in segregated fashion, living in segregated housing. When the canal was completed, the United Fruit Company transported thousands of the unemployed to its banana and sugar plantations and railroads in Costa Rica, Honduras, Cuba, and the Dominican Republic. Cuba alone took in as many as 150,000 from English-speaking islands, together with some 40,000 Haitians between 1913 and 1928; as is true of Panama, a significant community of their descendants remain in Cuba.

Taking jobs in other parts of the Caribbean and Central America was not an entirely effective strategy, however, as the economies of these areas declined during the First World War. The United States, already a focus for many who had worked in Panama, became the destination for others. Those who had come directly from Panama paid for their and their loved ones' voyages with "Panama money," highly esteemed because of the horrific human costs associated with it – thousands had died or were permanently maimed in con-structing the canal. These workers and their families were for the most part illiterate, according to some accounts, whereas those from the Caribbean who joined them later were from a different social stratum and were either literate or in possession of marketable skills. By 1930 some 72,000 had arrived in US urban areas, including Miami and other Floridian cities, but their major port of call was New York City, where some 40,000 took up residence in Harlem between 1900 and 1930, providing a substantial proportion of the professional and entrepreneurial classes. Most were from the English-speaking islands, but they also came from Cuba, Puerto Rico, and the

Dominican Republic. The Caribbean presence and contribution to New York City, dating back to colonial times, has therefore been crucial to its development as an economic and cultural mecca.

Emigration from the Caribbean continued after the Second World War. Bauxite and petroleum were still the region's leading industries, but bananas replaced sugar as the leading export of a number of islands. The rise of large-scale agribusiness, combined with increased mechanization, resulted in the collapse of plantation agriculture and heightened unemployment, forcing people to again seek work elsewhere. Haitians went to the sugar fields of the Dominican Republic; both Haitians and Dominicans came to Florida, along with others from the Caribbean and Central America. Puerto Ricans undertook major migrations to New York City, Chicago, and Philadelphia after 1945, and in the 1960s significant numbers of Dominicans began arriving in New York City, New Jersey, and Boston. Those from the English- and French-speaking islands also relocated to the cities of Britain and France, and would find their way to Canada in a movement that became much more numerically significant in the 1950s and 1960s.

In North America, blacks already in the United States joined Caribbean immigrants. The Great Migration between 1916 and 1930 witnessed more than 1 million leave the South for the North, with over 400,000 boarding trains between 1916 and 1918. This was an intense period of relocation, involving such push factors as economic despair (related to the ravages of the boll weevil) and white racism in the South. The latter element had become particularly pernicious, as more than 4,300 people – men and women, the vast majority black southerners – are documented to have been lynched from the end of the Civil War to 1935, and it is probable that the total number includes thousands more. Pull factors centered on the high demand for labor in the North, occasioned by global war and the precipitous decline in foreign immigration from Europe, from 1.2 million in 1914 to 110,000 by 1918. The Second World War had a similar effect, and in the 1940s an additional 1.6 million black southerners are estimated to have left for the North as well as the West (especially the Los Angeles and San Francisco-Oakland areas), a figure that does not include movement to the South Atlantic and Gulf coasts, where many found jobs in defense-related industries. Such migratory activity continued into the 1950s and 1960s, when 2.9 million are estimated to have left the South. The movement north would transform the majority of African

Americans into urban dwellers, so that by 1950, some 52 percent of African Americans were living in cities and large towns (a figure that would increase to 81 percent by 1980).

Paralleling the economic experiences of those in North America and the Caribbean were those of the African-descended in Brazil. As the 1835 *malê* revolt revealed, the politics of racial identity in Brazil were complicated; by the late twentieth century, over a hundred options would appear on the Brazilian census, such was the fusion of African, European, and native elements. To speak of "black" Brazilians is to therefore employ a term that is both unstable and ever evolving. To be sure, the current percentage of Brazilians with African ancestry is undoubtedly much higher than official estimates allow, as many ostensibly white Brazilians admit to having had a "foot in the kitchen" (a reference to longstanding white male access to black female domestics). Discounting such persons, the concept of black Brazilians is used here to denote those of discernible African descent (well over half of the current Brazilian population) who may or may not have embraced the classification of *prêto* (black) or *pardo* (mixed), or who may have appropriated such categories for some purposes and not others. Reference to black Brazilians also recognizes a pervasive reality that darker-skinned people have historically been disadvantaged, however they may have defined their individuality, and that poverty, ignorance, and disease were historically concentrated in the squalor of their existence. This was true not only of Brazil, but also the entire western hemisphere.

In the sugar-producing north-east, black Brazilians remained as wage laborers and tenants on the plantations, but in the coffee region of the south-east there was considerable migration to the rapidly developing cities of São Paulo and Rio de Janeiro. There, they ran into the issue of *embranquecimento*, or "whitening," an effort to increase European immigration and thereby achieve so-called civilized status as a nation, approximating that of North America and Europe. As one example of this idea-turned-policy, some 90,000 Europeans immigrants, called *colonos*, arrived in Brazil between 1886 and 1889. The policy's implications for São Paulo were dramatic: by 1894, *colonos* outnumbered Brazilians in a variety of industries and accounted for 79 percent of all manufacturing workers. By 1940, *colonos* controlled 44 percent of the city's earned industrial capital and far outnumbered those of African descent in São Paulo, who made up only 12.6 percent of an estimated 1.3 million. Factory jobs were reserved for European immigrants, while those of African descent were forced to accept menial, low-wage jobs.

Regarding world war, black folk participated as both combatants and civilians. As an example, when the United States entered the First World War in 1917, some 400,000 blacks went into military service. Emmett J. Scott, Booker T. Washington's secretary at the Tuskegee Institute in Alabama for eighteen years, served as a special assistant to the secretary of war, advising him on matters relating to blacks. His presence, however, could not alter the deep-seated hatred of and discrimination against blacks; while represented in almost every branch of the army save the aviation corps' pilot section, they could not serve in the marines, and only as menials in the navy. Black soldiers were assaulted by white civilian mobs in a number of incidents throughout the country, resulting, for example, in a (white) riot in Houston in 1917. Those who made it overseas were largely relegated to serving as stevedores and laborers, while those who were allowed to actually fight suffered disproportionate casualties. This was certainly the experience of the army's 369th Regiment, otherwise known as the Harlem Rattlers, who actually saw combat in the European theater. At war's end, a bloody race riot in East St. Louis in 1918, in which forty blacks were killed, presaged the famous Red Summer of 1919, in which twenty-five race riots erupted from June to the end of the year. White soldiers returning home from war expected jobs, so that labor competition was a major factor precipitating the flare-ups, one of the worst of which took place in Chicago in July and August, leaving twenty-three blacks and fifteen whites dead, with 537 injured and over 1,000 (mostly black) left homeless. As for the Second World War, discrimination remained but was less of an impediment. Approximately 1 million black men and women served in the United States military, over 700,000 in the army, and perhaps a half-million overseas. One of the more dramatic developments was the formation of the 99th Pursuit Squadron of the US Army Air Corps, the famed Tuskegee Airmen, 450 black pilots who were later incorporated into the 322nd Fighter Group and flew combat missions in Europe, contributing significantly to the war effort.

Blacks from British and French colonies also participated in both world wars under the flags of the respective colonial powers. The Caribbean sent more than 20,000 soldiers to fight in the West Indies Regiment, formed by Britain in 1915, most importantly in the Middle Eastern theater. As for the Second World War, something called the

Caribbean Regiment was formed, and some 16,000 West Indians, including women, fought in it as well as in the Royal Air Force, where nearly 500 West Indians and Africans served as navigators, gunners, engineers, and even pilots.

African soldiers also fought in European theaters of war. The French were particularly active, recruiting 450,000 for the First World War, especially West Africans (*Tirailleurs Sénégalais*, "Senegalese Riflemen") and North Africans. As for the Second World War, about 1 million African soldiers fought for the Allies, although nearly 140,000 Eritrean *Ascari* ("soldiers") fought with the Italians. Both world wars were also fought on African soil, and though it was Le Clerc's all-white division that was given the honor of liberating Paris in the Second World War, more than half of de Gaulle's Free French were African or Arab.

Organizing Black Labor

Blacks in the United States had perhaps the largest percentage of industrial workers in the African diaspora in the early twentieth century; by 1910, over 350,000 of them were in factory jobs in both the North and the South. Even so, black labor was virtually banned by all-white labor unions, making it very difficult to acquire skills and experience in certain vocations. The Knights of Labor had accepted 60,000 black workers as early as 1886, but the Haymarket Square riots of the same year discredited the organization as a foreign-controlled entity. The American Federation of Labor permitted widespread discrimination against blacks, leading the latter to form their own unions, including the Associated Colored Employees of America and the Association of Afro-American Steam and Gas Engineers and Skilled Workers of Pittsburgh. Efforts at self-organization intensified following the First World War, and the American Negro Labor Congress held its inaugural meeting in Chicago in 1925 to mobilize. Perhaps the most significant union of this type, the Brotherhood of Sleeping Car Porters and Maids, or Pullman Porters, was also founded in 1925 by A. Philip Randolph. In becoming such an important labor leader, however, Randolph was careful not to publicize his homosexuality, out of concern that it would be used to undermine his overall efforts. In fact, the 1930s and 1940s would witness a broad campaign by the Congress of Industrial Organizations to unionize black workers throughout the South, resulting in the Steel Workers Organizing Committee; the International Union of Mine, Mill, and Smelter Workers; and the Food, Tobacco, Agricultural, and Allied Workers, names indicative of a wide range of industries reliant upon black labor. These efforts point to the complexity of black life in the American South, as it was not uncommon for Marxist-influenced unionization efforts to seek support from local churches and benevolent societies. Blacks who joined unions maintained their religious values, suggesting a multidimensional analysis of social realities.

In the English-speaking Caribbean, membership in industrial unions was severely limited, although there was some development between 1919 and 1929, the result of a robust regional economy based upon bauxite and oil. However, the ensuing depression wiped out these gains. Increased unemployment and seeming British indifference resulted in an activism of the 1930s interested not only in workers' rights, but the end of colonial rule. The Butler Riots of 1937 in Trinidad are an example of the period's unrest, as workers joined Grenadian Tubal Uriah "Buzz" Butler's rival union to counter the one supported by industry and colonial authority, and reacted violently to the refusal of the American-owned oil company to restore pay cuts after the company had rebounded from a momentary drop in revenues. A 1938 workers' revolt in St. Thomas Parish, Jamaica, site of Paul Bogle's 1865 assault on Morant Bay, involved some 1,400 machete- and stick-wielding persons, whose protests were likewise put down by the state. In similar fashion, sugar industry workers vehemently reacted to the loss of wages and work throughout the islands in the 1930s.

In Brazil, individual choice of identity did not shield the discernibly African-descended person from discrimination, and racial barriers to industrial jobs meant that black Brazilians found it difficult to organize labor unions. Their response was to develop trade associations focused on social security and retirement benefits, much like self-help societies. Brazilian trade associations tended to be segregated, reflecting occupational divisions along racial lines. For example, artisans and barbers were traditionally "black" occupations going back to slavery, and these professions were represented organizationally by the Artisans' Philanthropic Union Beneficent Society and the Barbers' Union Beneficent Society, both associations of *homens de côr*, or people of color. Although not a trade association, the Sociedade Protectora dos Desvalidos, or the Society for the Protection of the Needy, was critical in that it offered benefits to blacks of all trades.

Faiths New and Renewed

While those of African descent were fighting to recreate themselves as free workers, they were also developing religious traditions that can be placed into three streams. The first extended a process that began with the African's initial contact with European Christianity, whereby the religion was steadily Africanized both liturgically as well as theologically. The second stream, also continuing from previous periods, involved practices developed in Africa and transferred to the Americas, where they were renewed as well as altered, though remaining identifiably African. The third stream saw the creation of new religions, typically taken from the fabrics of Islamic-Judeo-Christian traditions and woven into entirely novel patterns, informed by a vision of Africa as a historical power and, in some instances, a future destination. While the following examples are taken from specific regions, the streams of religious tradition they represent are not territorially limited, but flow elsewhere in the Americas.

The first stream is more a river, in that Christianity contains a range of African influences often inversely proportionate to class: the higher the class, the lesser the African influence. The practices of hoodoo and voodoo, analogues derivative of West and West Central African religions, permeated the beliefs of peasant and working-class black Christians in the American South, whose religious services were in any event charged with song and dance and possession in the Holy Ghost. In the English-speaking Caribbean, Christianity was often infused with substantial African content and connected with *obeah*, the use of supernatural powers to inflict harm, and *myalism*, the employment of spiritual resources and herbs to counteract witchcraft and other evil. The religions of *convince* and *kumina* also developed, the former involving respect for the Christian deity, but also an active veneration of the spirits of African and maroon ancestors by practitioners known as Bongo men. *Kumina*, otherwise known as *pukumina* or *pocomania*, also venerates ancestors, who rank after sky gods and earth deities, but also involves ecstatic states of song and dance that could render practitioners prone for days.

The second stream is most prominently represented in Brazil and Cuba, where many were adherents of renewed African religions. Enslaved Africans entering Brazil maintained the concept of distinct ethnolinguistic groupings by pursuing, as one strategy, religious traditions peculiar to their lands of origin. In the complex society that would become Brazil, the reality was that groups intermingled, borrowing ideas from one other while retaining the concept of distinct communities, or *nações* ("nations"). As the black population became predominantly *crioulo* (Brazilian-born) and stratified along lines of color gradation during the nineteenth century (with *prêtos* or "blacks" and *pardos* or intermediate shades as the basic divisions), persons born in Bahia and elsewhere began to choose a *nação*. This was significant, as those who made such choices were also choosing an African identity and an African religion. The various *nações*, such as the Nagôs (Yoruba) and Jêjes (Aja-Ewe-Fon), maintained distinctive religious traditions, which can collectively be referred to as *candomblé*. The various African traditions, associated with specific *nações*, were centered upon sacred spaces known as *terreiros*, where rituals were held. Originating in private houses, the *terreiros* expanded to separate plots of land during the first half of the twentieth century, facilitating the pursuit of *candomblé* as a way of life with minimal outside interference. As such, the *terreiros* became epicenters of not only African religion, but African culture. Women were the principal leaders of *candomblé*, and perhaps the most famous of the *terreiros* in Bahia, Ilê Iyá Nassô or Engenho Velho, was founded around 1830 by women from the Yoruba town of Ketu. *Terreiros* were established in the late nineteenth and early twentieth centuries by women of considerable financial means, including Eugenia Anna dos Santos, or Aninha, who founded the *terreiro* of Ilê do Axe Opô Afonjá in 1910. As some *terreiros* maintained commercial and intellectual ties with Yoruba spiritual leaders in what would become south-western Nigeria, their collective story illustrates how African-influenced religion in Bahia was not only a matter of practices transported by captive Africans and transmitted over generations, but it was also informed through ongoing transcontinental interactions. Eugenia Anna dos Santos is a fascinating example of the mutability of ethnic identity in Bahia, as she was initiated into the Nagô tradition at Ilê Iyá Nassô, but her African-born parents were Gurunsi, not Yoruba.

All of these various *candomblé* houses were associated with *irmandades*, brotherhoods and sisterhoods that were mutual aid societies, providing burial benefits and unemployment assistance at a time when state relief either did not exist or was woefully insufficient. Examples include the Bôa Morte (Good Death) sisterhood and the Senhor dos Martírios (Lord of the Martyrs) brotherhood of the Nagôs, and the Bom Jesus das Necessidades e Redenção dos Homens

Prêtos (Good Jesus of the Needs and Redemption of Black Men) of the Jêjes. The affiliation of the brotherhoods or sisterhoods with specific *terreiros* underscores an important feature of *candomblé*: its connection to the Catholic church. Indeed, the multiple *orishas* or deities of *candomblé*, such as Eshu, Yemanja, Oshun, and Shango, are associated with the various saints and principal figures of Catholicism, useful when *candomblé* needed concealment.

Other African-centered religions include West Central African *macumba* near Rio de Janeiro, and elsewhere the practice of *umbanda*. Together with *convince*, *kumina*, and *candomblé*, these religions feature the common elements of African spiritual entities, sacrifice, drumming and singing, and spirit possession. They parallel the Cuban experience, where research is revealing the importance of such clandestine religious organizations as the *abukuá*, a society originating in the Cross River area of south-eastern Nigeria and Cameroon. Cuba is also a center of Yoruba or *lucumí* influence, apparent in the practice of *santería*. Divisions among the African-born and their descendants, which as in Brazil eventually became a matter of choice, were equally preserved in Cuba's system of *naciones*, supported as they were by the respective *cabildos*, the functional equivalents of the Brazilian *irmandades*. Yoruba-based religion can also be found in Trinidad in the religion of *Shango*, in which the Yoruba gods Shango, Yemanja, Eshu, and Ogun are worshiped along with deities of Trinidadian origin.

The third stream of religious expression is just as dynamic as the first two. Perhaps its most innovative example is the Rastafarian movement. The onerous economic struggle in the Caribbean not only produced emigration, labor unionism, and social unrest, but also conditions in which the sufferers re-envisioned themselves within an international context. Incessant emigration and subordination to colonial empire generated within the Caribbean a transnational perspective, contributing specifically to the belief among the downtrodden in Jamaica that there was a special connection between the diaspora and Ethiopia. Leonard Percival Howell, experienced in foreign travel, returned to Jamaica in 1932 to proclaim that black Jamaicans should no longer offer their loyalty to England, but to the emperor of Ethiopia, Ras ("Lord") Tafari Makonnen, crowned in November of 1932 and given the throne name Haile Selassie I. The idea that a black man was a sovereign ruler, at a time when most of African descent were under colonial rule in both Africa and the Americas, stirred the collective African imagination. Howell, Archibald Dunkley, and Joseph Hibbert further held that because black Jamaicans belonged to an African nation under Haile Selassie, they should not pay taxes to England.

The 1935 Italian invasion of Ethiopia was a watershed event in the history of the African diaspora. All around the world, the African-descended were scandalized by the occupation of this ancient, Biblically related land, and rallied to support the Ethiopian cause. A remarkable, formative moment, the response to the invasion demonstrated the importance of Africa to those struggling thousands of miles and hundreds of years removed from its shores. The invasion also strengthened the position of Howell and his associates. In 1937, the Ethiopian World Federation was founded by Dr. Malaku Bayen in New York City to promote Ethiopia's liberation, linking it to the fortunes of black folk everywhere. The Federation elevated Haile Selassie as the "Elect of God" and maintained that Africans were the Twelve Tribes of Israel, a claim based upon the Beta Israel and the ancient *Kebra Nagast*.

The British persecuted and imprisoned Howell and his followers, who in 1940 had established a commune at Pinnacle in the hills of St. Catherine, Jamaica. Released from prison in 1943, Howell led a process through which the tenets of the Rastafari were gradually worked out. Haile Selassie acquired divine status while the capitalist, imperialist system was identified as Babylon, its rejection symbolized by "dreads" or locking of the hair, perhaps in emulation of Kenya's Land and Freedom Army (or "Mau Mau") in the 1950s, as well as by the use of ganja and the pipe, both introduced to the Caribbean from India. Africans and their descendants were the true Israel, and Ethiopia the promised land, to which the Rasta would eventually return. The Pinnacle would be repeatedly raided by the authorities, and Howell would be placed in a mental asylum more than once. But the Rastafari movement would continue to grow, becoming an international phenomenon while influencing the anticolonial struggle, in turn giving rise to a deeply political and spiritual reggae.

While the Rastafari borrowed from Judeo-Christian traditions, innovations in the United States engaged these same traditions as well as Islam, forging movements that, while entirely novel in theory and practice, were politically similar to the Rastafari in their anticolonialism and advocacy for the black poor. Specifically, the Moorish Science Temple of America, possibly founded as early as 1913 in Newark,

New Jersey by Noble Drew Ali, offered the startling proposition that African Americans were in fact "Moors" from Morocco, and as such were part of a larger "Asiatic" community of persons that essentially included everyone except Europeans. The claim of Moorish ancestry, like the Rastafari, linked the diaspora back to Africa, but the Asiatic identification suggests a worldview not limited to Africa. Unlike the Rastafari, Noble Drew Ali never advocated a physical return to Morocco. As Moors, his followers adopted an unorthodox version of Islam, with Noble Drew Ali penning his own *Circle Seven Koran*, drawing upon metaphysical beliefs foreign to conventional Islam. Noble Drew Ali died under mysterious circumstances in 1929, by which time another Islamically related movement was taking root. The Nation of Islam, founded in Detroit by W.D. Fard Muhammad in 1930, certainly employed Noble Drew Ali's notion of an international Asiatic identity, but went much further in its denunciation of Europeans, identifying them as "devils." Indeed, the Nation rejected the principles of sanctioned religion as such, dismissing the idea of an afterlife and the conception of God and Satan as spiritual beings, positing instead that just as whites were devils, blacks were divine, with W.D. Fard Muhammad as Allah. The Nation's identification with Africa was not as strong as the Moors and the Rastas, however, for although members were given an "X" or an equivalent variable to represent the African name lost through enslavement, the original home of blacks was not Africa but Mecca, from where they later migrated to "East Asia" or Egypt, and from there to other parts of the African continent. The Nation embraced a variant of Islam in conflict with many of the latter's central tenets, including the claim that Elijah Muhammad, W.D. Fard Muhammad's successor after the latter's disappearance in 1934, was a messenger of God. With the death of Elijah Muhammad in February of 1976, the movement splintered into several factions, with some either embracing or moving toward orthodoxy.

The racialism of the Nation of Islam reversed the assumptions and values of the day. Blackness, long associated by whites with evil, immorality, filth, and worthlessness, became the embodiment of holiness, cleanliness, morality, and self-confidence. The Nation's emphasis on hard work and economic self-reliance was the means by which a disproportionate number of its members achieved middle-class status, and provided a model for black economic development. At the same time, the Nation's early years were very much influenced

by global conflict, and by its support of Japan during the Second
World War. An early form of black nationalism, the Nation saw white
racism as a phenomenon separate from capitalist venture, condemning the former while embracing the latter; indeed, the Nation was
generally opposed to leftist movements, and as such differed in quality
from the more radical Rastafari.

The Nation of Islam and the Moorish Science Temple of America
were also mutual aid societies, but there were others in the Americas
not so directly tied to religion. To be sure, Freemasonry enjoyed a
significant white following, but the Masons, Odd Fellows, Order of
the Eastern Star, and Sisters of Calanthe were parallel secret societies
with large black memberships, providing significant assistance in
times of need, while organizations such as the Ancient Sons of Israel
and the Independent Order of St. Luke issued insurance policies to
cover sickness and death. Those in and from the Caribbean often had
their own mutual aid networks, and the *sou sou*, a fund into which
members paid regularly and out of which they could draw when
necessary, was a common societal feature. Beneficial and insurance
societies such as the Young Mutual Society of Augusta, Georgia and
the Workers Mutual Aid Association of Virginia were not secret
societies, but provided similar services through the collection of
weekly dues. Hospitals, orphanages, and homes for the elderly were
also established. But as important, if not more so, was the extensive
assistance provided by black churches, efforts supported in varying
degrees by white congregants of mainline denominations, especially
concerning education. In a nutshell, black folk throughout the diaspora drew upon what meager resources they had, animated by belief
systems reaching back to an ancient African past.

Conceptualizing the Solutions

Just about everything black people did and said carried political implications. Their labor, religion, and mutual support systems all
addressed social and economic relations of power. Black folk revealed
views on social policy with their benevolent societies, they communicated their sense of community through religion, and they protested
economic conditions through strikes, riots, and stoppages. These were
all significant, but black folk also articulated political views in clear
and explicit terms. In examining political developments within the

African diaspora, greater attention is often afforded individuals as leaders of the masses, but it must be borne in mind that the participation of the latter was just as critical, if not more so.

As early as Denmark Vesey and David Walker, black leaders of the highest caliber have consistently displayed an awareness that the plight of their particular community was somehow tied to similar communities elsewhere. Eventually referred to as pan-Africanism, connections between these communities varied, but it was rare for a visionary to not have a sense of a more broadly defined, African-derived community extending beyond geopolitical boundaries. The last quarter of the nineteenth century through the first half of the twentieth saw the growth of this principle among the leadership. Their activities, in conjunction with labor migrations, advances in technology, and the reality of empire itself, helped disseminate the concept of an African diaspora among working-class blacks. Reconnecting to Africa and others in the diaspora, initially envisioned as an intellectual quest or an ideological campaign, often led to concrete action.

Early leaders of pan-Africanism, many of whom were Christian ministers, included Henry Highland Garnet, whose grandfather was Mandinka and whose immediate family escaped Maryland slavery in the 1820s. In his 1843 *Address to the Slaves of the United States*, Garnet called for armed revolt against the slaveocracy, citing Toussaint Louverture as an example to be emulated (Frederick Douglass, who initially opposed Garnet's call for revolt, later reversed his position). Garnet further revealed a diasporic perspective in predicting that the islands of the Caribbean would eventually be "ours" (a reference to blacks in the Caribbean, not North American blacks), and by his organization of the Cuban Anti-Slavery Committee in 1873. He completed the circle in his voyage to West Africa in 1882, where he died and remains buried. His contemporaries Alexander Crummell, Henry McNeil Turner, and Martin R. Delany all favored black emigration to either Africa or Central and South America, convinced that they would never receive the "full free" in the United States. Delany's views were certainly informed by his experience at Harvard Medical School in 1850, where and when he and two other black students – the first blacks to be admitted to the school – were forced to abruptly leave in the face of white student protests. Edward W. Blyden, born in St. Thomas, Virgin Islands, would in fact repatriate to West Africa beginning in the 1860s, and became a leading force in establishing educational institutions in Liberia and Sierra Leone. While Anna Julia

Cooper, born to an enslaved mother and a white slaveholder, cannot be categorized as a back-to-Africa emigrationist, her 1892 *A Voice from the South* established connections between racial and gender inequalities in the United States and downtrodden populations beyond its borders.

Perhaps the quintessential expression of diasporic political consciousness was the creation of the Universal Negro Improvement Association and African Communities League (UNIA) under Marcus Garvey. Born in Jamaica on August 17, 1887, Garvey learned the printing trade before joining the tens of thousands who left the Caribbean for work in Central America. Traveling to London in 1912, he came across the pan-Africanist ideas of the Egyptian Dusé Muhammad, editor of the *African Times and Orient Review*. Upon his return to Jamaica, he founded the UNIA in 1914, in which his wives Amy Ashwood and later Amy Jacques Garvey would play prominent roles. Venturing to the United States in 1916 to raise money for the UNIA and to meet Booker T. Washington (who, unknown to Garvey, had died the previous year), he incorporated the UNIA in New York state in 1918, establishing his headquarters in Harlem. Garvey's "back-to-Africa" movement involved much more than a simple call for repatriation. Facing colonialism in both the Caribbean and Africa, he advocated the dismantling of European and American empire and the reconstruction of black societies everywhere. His businesses, such as the Black Star Line, were launched to promote trade between black communities in the Americas. His official organ, the *Negro World*, was the most widely circulated black publication in the world, appearing in English, French, Spanish, and Portuguese, and was edited from 1923 to 1928 by T. Thomas Fortune, former editor of the New York *Age*. By 1921, Garvey had achieved international recognition, his parades through Harlem, along with his annual August conventions, attracting thousands from all over the world. His initial backers included labor leader A. Philip Randolph (who would later withdraw his support) and Ida B. Wells Barnett, champion of the anti-lynching campaign, while Madame C.J. Walker, cosmetics entrepreneur and multimillionaire, provided some financial backing. Centered in Harlem, the UNIA was the literal embodiment of pan-Africanism, and in time established 996 branches in forty-three countries, including Cuba, South Africa, Europe, and even Australia. Its membership is difficult to calculate, but it conceivably numbered in the hundreds of thousands at its apex.

Familiar with racism and light skin privilege, Garvey instilled pride in dark skin, thick lips, broad noses, and nappy hair. He originated the Red, Black, and Green flag of pan-Africanism and black nationalism, and taught that hard work and discipline were the keys to success. His overall message was a much-needed balm, but there were problems in the organization. Succinctly put, his advisors were not up to the task, and his investments were poorly guided. There were also elements within the American black community appalled by his back-to-Africa message, at his ability to raise substantial sums of money, and at his rapid ascent. Some were sincerely concerned that Garvey was a charlatan, but others were driven by the politics of xenophobia and personal ambition. For them, Garvey was an outsider "with an accent," a dark-skinned West Indian who had come to Harlem, the center of the black world, and virtually "taken over." His critics became even more alarmed after Garvey met with the Ku Klux Klan in 1922, their anxiety converging with that of the federal government, the latter concerned about the implications of Garvey's antiracist, anticolonial activities. Britain also was uneasy with Garvey, and together with the United States covertly opposed the UNIA's attempt to acquire land and establish a base in Liberia. The "Garvey Must Go" campaign resulted in his indictment on mail-fraud charges in 1921 and conviction in 1923. In 1925, he began serving a five-year term at the federal penitentiary in Atlanta, Georgia. His sentence was commuted in 1927 by President Coolidge following a campaign for his release by the national black press. Garvey would return to Jamaica, and from there to London, where he died in 1940. The UNIA still exists, though in much truncated form, as Garvey's efforts at revitalizing it were largely unsuccessful.

One of Garvey's principal critics and veritable nemesis was W.E.B. Du Bois. Born in Great Barrington, Massachusetts and of partial Haitian ancestry, Du Bois' long lifespan (1868 to 1963), his training at Fisk, Harvard, and Berlin, and his unparalleled intellect positioned him to make incredible contributions to the struggle of black folk and the downtrodden globally, and he continues to serve as an exemplar of the scholar-activist. As early as 1897, he founded the American Negro Academy with other black intellectuals, including Alexander Crummell. Between 1896 and 1914 he led the annual Congress on Negro Problems at Atlanta University. In 1903, he published *The Souls of Black Folk*, challenging, among other things, Booker T. Washington's emphasis on vocational training, his de-emphasis of the struggle for social and political equality, and his extraordinary influence in the decision-making process affecting black people, otherwise known as the "Tuskegee Machine." Instead, Du Bois proposed a vigorous campaign for full citizenship led by a black "talented tenth," in whom he would express great disappointment later in life.

Du Bois, at the head of a similarly minded group, met in Niagara Falls, Canada in June of 1905. Four years later, the Niagara Movement became institutionalized in the founding of the National Association for the Advancement of Colored People (NAACP), whose leaders included Ida B. Wells Barnett (but not Monroe Trotter, publisher of the Boston *Guardian*, who disagreed with the inclusion of whites). In 1911, the National Urban League was founded, likewise a multiracial organization dedicated to improving the social and economic plight of blacks. It was within such a context, with national organizations already in place and fighting to improve conditions for black people, that Marcus Garvey entered the picture.

Du Bois concluded that Garvey did not understand North American race relations, and saw him as a menace. It did not help that both men engaged in personal invective. They differed from each other in a number of ways, but one of the greatest ironies of the period is that both were committed to the struggles of black people on an international scale. As long-time editor of the *Crisis*, official organ of the NAACP, Du Bois published articles and information that covered the whole of the African diaspora, and in that way paralleled the range of Garvey's *Negro World*. A series of several Pan-African Congresses, begun in 1900, saw Du Bois' organizational involvement in 1919, 1921, 1927, and 1945. These congresses, convened to marshal opposition to colonialism and racism, were not unlike Garvey's annual conventions, and the two men's efforts were often confused in the media. Du Bois would go on to incorporate a Marxist analysis into a powerful critique of capitalism, while Garvey remained an unabashed capitalist enthusiast. Disillusioned with developments in the United States, Du Bois would relocate to Ghana in 1961, join the Communist Party, and renounce his American citizenship; he died in Ghana on the eve of the August 27, 1963 March on Washington. Tensions between Du Bois and the Garvey camp lessened when Amy Jacques Garvey and Du Bois collaborated in organizing the 1945 Manchester Pan-African Congress. The tempestuous reality of Du Bois and Garvey as pan-Africanist pioneers was symbolically reconciled on African soil under Kwame Nkrumah, independent Ghana's first president. Having studied in the United States at Lincoln University, Nkrumah's pan-Africanist vision for Africa was directly inspired by both men.

Based solely upon the foregoing, the Caribbean contribution to pan-Africanism and the concept of the African diaspora was clearly significant. But in addition to Garvey and Blyden, Trinidadian Henry Sylvestre Williams called the first Pan-African Congress in London in 1900, and collaborated with Dr. Robert Love of Jamaica to establish branches of the Pan-African Association in Jamaica in 1906. Deeply disturbed by the 1935 Italian invasion of Ethiopia, Jamaican Harold Moody transformed his League of Coloured Peoples from an educational organization to a decidedly political one, while the response of Trinidadians George Padmore and C.L.R. James, along with the future president of Kenya, "Burning Spear" Jomo Kenyatta, was to found the International African Service Bureau in London in 1937. Padmore, born in 1902, had attended Fisk and Howard universities, dropping out of the latter's law school in 1928 and joining the US Communist Party to combat imperialism. A gifted writer, Padmore became editor of the influential *Negro Worker*, rising to prominence in the Communist International, for which he wrote *The Life and Struggles of Negro Toilers*. But four years before establishing the Bureau with James, he exited the Communist Party over differences concerning race. Padmore would control the Bureau until it became the Pan-African Federation in 1944, and was instrumental in recruiting many of the organizers for the Manchester Congress the following year. Having published the insightful *How Britain Rules Africa* in 1936, he continued to write articles for a number of publications, including the *Crisis*, the *Chicago Defender*, and the *Pittsburgh Courier*, demonstrating the international dimension of the black media during this period. Padmore's influence as a journalist writing on labor strikes in Trinidad and the Caribbean in 1937 and 1938 was far-reaching, exposing the relationship between foreign capital and colonial rule in the increasingly desperate plight of the peasant turned wage laborer. He would precede Du Bois in Ghana, where in the 1950s he served as an advisor to Nkrumah.

C.L.R. James, another towering scholar-activist whose work continues to influence, left Trinidad in 1932 with only a high-school education. In 1938 he published *The Black Jacobins*, the seminal work on the Haitian Revolution, simultaneously igniting a scholarly revolution by inaugurating a movement in which history is written "from the bottom up," or from the perspective of the working and downtrodden classes. His 1938 *History of Negro Revolt* centered people of African descent in world history, emphasizing the vital role they must play in future global struggles. As was true of *Black Jacobins*, James demonstrated how the African-descended could take ownership of ideas originating in Europe and forge them into meditations on liberation with his 1963 *Beyond a Boundary*, which ostensibly concerns cricket.

No less important was North American Paul Robeson, born at a time (1898) when the memory of slavery was quite fresh, his father having escaped it at the age of fifteen. Raised in Princeton, New Jersey, Robeson graduated from Rutgers and then Columbia Law School after stellar accomplishments, both academically and athletically. While his acting and singing careers began during law school, he traveled to London in 1927 to study at the London School of Oriental Languages. There he met James, Padmore, Kenyatta, and Nnamdi Azikiwe, first president of Nigeria, and would later recall, "I discovered Africa in London." Robeson studied African languages and read widely on Africa, adding to his understanding of black art and spirituality. His 1934 publication, *What I Want from Life*, is one of the most incisive inquiries into the collective psyche of the African-derived, emphasizing the importance of retrieving an African-centered identity. During his travels to the Soviet Union and Spain in the 1930s, he developed a deeper appreciation of the plight of the downtrodden, and began to stress the need to coordinate anticolonial and antiracist struggles throughout Africa, the African diaspora, and Asia. He became increasingly radical as his singing and acting careers soared, helping to establish in 1937 what became the Council on African Affairs (CAA), serving as its chair for most of its existence after 1942.

Perhaps the CAA's most important work was in South Africa, where it supported the African National Congress. Robeson's anticolonial activities intensified after the Second World War, but following the CAA's "Big Three Unity" rally in June of 1946 at Madison Square Garden in New York City, attended by 19,000 people and led by Robeson, Du Bois, and Mary McLeod Bethune (and others), Cold War politics caused a major split in African American leadership. As early as 1942 the FBI had begun investigating the CAA as subversive, and by 1948 a previously receptive white media joined the NAACP under Walter White in denouncing Robeson (and Du Bois, who was dismissed from the NAACP that same year). Concerned with the influence of Robeson and Du Bois in West Africa and elsewhere, the US government revoked Robeson's passport in 1950. Robeson would suffer a fate similar to that of Du Bois, virtually forgotten by his people who owed him so much, reaching the end in 1976.

As the examples of Amy Ashwood Garvey, Amy Jacques Garvey, and Ida B. Wells Barnett suggest, women of the period were as participatory in radical politics as men. West Indian women radicals included Elma Francois, born in St. Vincent in 1897 but who, in search of work, relocated to Trinidad in 1919. Working as a domestic, she would join the Trinidad Workingman's Association, then later co-found the Negro Welfare Cultural and Social Association (NWCSA), a decidedly Marxist organization that fought for workers and mobilized the unemployed for a series of "hunger marches" in 1934 and 1935. Francois was her own person, and would deliver open-air speeches in Port of Spain's famous Woodford Square (as later would Trinidad and Tobago's first prime minister, Eric Williams). Having galvanized support for Ethiopia in the face of the 1935 Italian invasion, the NWCSA would support striking oil workers during the 1937 Butler Riots. Francois was the first woman in Trinidad's history to be tried for treason, though she was later acquitted.

Perhaps more famous than Francois was Claudia Jones, born Claudia Vera Cumberbatch in 1915 in Trinidad, relocating with her family to New York City in 1924. Dropping out of high school to help support her family after her father's passing, the squalor of her living conditions would contribute to her contracting tuberculosis at the age of twenty-seven. Intellectually gifted, she persevered and penned a column ("Claudia's Comments") for what would become the Urban League, but the 1931 Scottsboro Boys case, in which nine black teenagers were falsely convicted of raping two white women on a train, sparking an international uproar and efforts to exonerate the defendants, accelerated her political trajectory, and in 1936 she joined the Youth Communist League USA. Fighting the southern legacy of all-white juries, a collection of organizations, including the NAACP and the Communist Party USA (CPUSA), were eventually successful in getting the convictions dropped in four of the nine Scottsboro cases; even so, seven would serve considerable prison time, with all either escaping or being released by 1946. Jones would later become a leading official in the CPUSA, in 1949 writing "An End to the Neglect of the Problems of the Negro Woman," a seminal work connecting race and gender. Because of her high profile in the CPUSA (during the height of McCarthyism), Jones would be arrested several times, spending eight months in prison after being found guilty of "un-American activities." In 1955, she was deported to the UK, where she continued fighting for worker and civil rights, founding the *West Indian Gazette* in 1958 and, in the same year, launching what would become the London Notting Hill Carnival in response to Britain's heightened xenophobia.

Though born in 1883 in Georgia, Grace P. Campbell's father was Jamaican. Like Claudia Jones, Campbell moved to New York City in 1927, where she became an activist for unwed mothers while working in the women's division of New York's Tombs Prison. Also like Jones but preceding her, Campbell would become the first African American woman to join the CPUSA around 1919. However, by 1921 she had become disaffected with the CPUSA, and helped launch the African Blood Brotherhood along with Cyril Briggs (himself from Nevis), a shadowy organization with black nationalist aspects, though openly hostile to Marcus Garvey. In 1919 and 1920 she would unsuc-cessfully run for the New York State Assembly on the Socialist Party ticket, receiving support from A. Philip Randolph. She would later seek to conjoin her interests in the rights of women, blacks, and workers by becoming a member of the Mao Zedong-influenced Com-munist Workers Party in the United States.

Other black women radicals of the time include Louise Thompson Patterson, born in 1901 in Chicago; and Esther Cooper Jackson, born in 1917 in Virginia. But perhaps two of the more magnetic figures were Queen Mother Audley Moore, born 1898 in Louisiana; and Shirley Graham Du Bois, born in 1896 in Indianapolis. Living until 1996, Queen Mother Audrey Moore's longevity actually spanned multiple periods, and her activities reflect this. She would relocate to New York City in 1922, moved by Marcus Garvey's words, and there join the UNIA. Encouraged by the CPUSA's fight on behalf of the Scottsboro Nine, she later joined the Communist Party in 1931, but would exit in 1950, disappointed with the racism she experienced within the party. That same year she would found the Universal Association of Ethiop-ian Women in 1950, and in 1963 she launched the Committee for Reparations for Descendants of U.S. Slaves in 1963. It was in 1972 that she received, in Ghana, the title of Queen Mother.

In contrast to Queen Mother Moore, who dropped out of school in the fourth grade due to the death of both parents, Shirley Graham Du

Bois was well educated and accomplished, having studied at the Sorbonne, with undergraduate and master's degrees from Oberlin College. She was a playwright (penning seven plays), composer, singer, and educator. Her interest in African culture is captured in her master's thesis, "The Survival of Africanisms in Modern Music," and she wrote several biographies, including those of George Washington Carver, Phillis Wheatley, and Frederick Douglass. An avid supporter of leftist causes, Shirley Graham had been in touch with W.E.B. Du Bois since the early 1930s, when they began reading each other's work. Though nearly thirty years younger, she would marry Du Bois in 1951, his first wife having passed away the previous year (Shirley Graham had also been married decades earlier). Just days before their departure for Ghana in 1961 (to begin the "Encyclopedia Africana" project under Kwame Nkrumah), Du Bois declared his official membership in the Communist Party – apparently, Shirley Graham was already a member. Du Bois would die in Ghana in 1963, and Shirley Graham would move to Tanzania, acquiring citizenship under Julius Nyerere. She would die in Beijing, China in 1977.

Radical black women saw the struggles of race, gender, and class as closely related, but they were not the only black women concerned with such matters. The black women's club movement stands in some contrast to the efforts of radical black women, and was part of a larger women's club movement of the Progressive Era (1890s to 1920s). Like radical black women, club black women were concerned for the poor, but they were invested in different strategies toward a different outcome. Capitalist formation was not necessarily a problem, nor was class struggle a central concern. Rather, the key idea to understanding the movement, at least in its earlier phases, was "uplift"; that is, middle-class black women were to join their efforts in ameliorating the circumstances of poor black women and families, and this was to be accomplished through teaching such values as thrift, self-reliance, sexual propriety, and better care of home and family. In other words, the objective was to alter the perceived culture of the black poor, as this was viewed as the key challenge. In identifying the "culture of poverty" as the principal culprit in the efforts of back people to advance, proponents participated in a form of "respectability politics," agreeing in some ways with whites that blacks had a "problem," but disagreeing that the problem was congenital. Rather, the solution was to effect behavioral change, whereby values and practices considered "mainstream" could be assimilated. As the context was the struggle to

achieve full citizenship, to find acceptance as an American, respectability politics – arguably the forerunner to the "pull up your pants"
approach – had its appeal. And although racism was rejected within
this particular vision for social change, patriarchy and Victorian
gender conventions were not. Supporting schools and orphanages,
the National Association of Colored Women was founded in 1896,
under the leadership of Mary Church Terrell. Over the next several
decades a faction would emerge within the club movement, no doubt
partly in response to more radical alternatives, that would eschew the
conservative emphasis on uplift and instead advocate for changes in
social policies, thereby identifying structural problems as critical
impediments. In 1935, Mary McLeod Bethune founded the National
Council of Negro Women to lead this fight.

Turning to Latin America, and notwithstanding the complexities of
racial identity in Brazil, consciousness of a larger black world
developed there as well. In São Paulo, black newspapers such as
A Liberdade, *O Menelick*, and *O Alfinete* ("The Pin"), published
early in the twentieth century, initially featured community news
and information, social commentaries, and reports concerning racial
discrimination. These earlier newspapers gave way to *O Clarim da
Alvorada* ("The Clarion of Dawn") and *Progresso* in the 1920s, and
A Voz da Raça ("The Voice of the Race") in the 1930s. Under the
leadership of co-founder José Correia Leite, *Clarim* sought to unify
the African-descended community through examining the challenges
of the day and by emphasizing African Brazilian history. At the same
time, the first African Brazilian activist organization in São Paulo was
founded, the Centro Cívico Palmares, its name a tribute to the famous
quilombo. Correia Leite was a member of the Palmares organization,
and connected *Clarim* to both an activist agenda and a diasporic
vision, as *Clarim* published articles from both the *Chicago Defender*
and Garvey's *Negro World*. Robert Abbott, publisher of the *Defender*,
visited Brazil in 1923, and subsequently began sending his paper to
Clarim and to *Progresso*. The Garvey influence apparently came
through an English teacher in Bahia named Mario de Vasconcelos,
who sent translations of *The Negro World* to the offices of *Clarim*.

Black Brazilian consciousness took a momentous step forward in
September of 1931, when the Frente Negra Brasileira, or the Black
Brazilian Front was founded under the leadership of Arlindo Veiga
dos Santos and others. A civil rights organization as well as a benevolent society, the Frente Negra launched *A Voz da Raça*. However,

schisms between the Frente Negra and other sectors of the African Brazilian community arose due to Veiga dos Santos' autocratic style of leadership and embrace of fascism. Dissolved (along with all political parties) by the imposition of the Estado Novo ("New State") under Getúlio Vargas in November of 1937, the Frente Negra nevertheless remains a critical turning point in the effort to both unify the African-descended in Brazil and to connect them with blacks elsewhere.

A similar movement developed in Cuba, where the Partido Inde-pendiente de Color ("Independent Party of Color") was established in 1907 by Evaristo Estenoz and Pedro Ivonet. Fighting for equality of treatment from a government under heavy American influence, they were opposed by others of African descent, including Juan Gualberto Gómez, who saw their race-based efforts as divisive and anti-Cuban. The party was outlawed in 1910, Estenoz and Ivonet arrested, and the ensuing revolt by aggrieved party members brutally repressed by President José Miguel Gómez (with American backing). Unlike members of the Frente Negra, thousands of party members were slaughtered, including women and children. The aspirations of Afri-can Cubans would suffer for many years to come.

Blacks and Science

Black folk have always maintained a dynamic and vibrant life of the mind. Not even slavery, Reconstruction's failure, and the rise of state-sponsored terrorism in the American South could stamp out their creativity and scientific genius. Individuals of distinction followed in the footsteps of the mathematician, astronomer, almanac maker, and surveyor Benjamin Banneker (d. 1806), discovering how to intellec-tually transcend the impediments of racism. While Banneker, greatly responsible for the design of the District of Columbia, had been freeborn, the slave-born George Washington Carver (d. 1943) developed hundreds of applications for such plants as soybeans, sweet potatoes, and peanuts, and was instrumental in aiding the South's flagging agriculture, working in his laboratories at the Tuskegee Institute. Elijah McCoy (d. 1929) was also familiar with slavery, his parents having fled the institution in Kentucky for Canada, Elijah's birthplace. Eventually settling in Detroit, McCoy accumulated nearly sixty patents, his steam engine lubricator so celebrated that it became "the real McCoy," a standard by which such machinery would be measured. Freeborn Granville T. Woods (d. 1910) also held over sixty patents, and played a major role in the development of rail by creating a telegraph system that allowed communication between trains and stations. Likewise, Norbert Rillieux (d. 1894), son of a slave woman and a planter in Louisiana, received an education in France and made contributions to industry with his invention of an evaporating process to refine sugar. Perhaps as significant was the accomplishment of Rebecca J. Cole (d. 1922), the second black female physician on record in the United States, having received her medical degree in 1867. Edward A. Bouchet (d. 1918) was also highly educated, receiving a PhD in physics from Yale in 1876. Lewis Latimer (d. 1929) held patents for an electric lamp and a carbon filament for light bulbs, and was a member of Thomas Edison's laboratory. Madam C.J. Walker (d. 1919) became wealthy as an innovator of female hair care techniques.

The preceding are just some of the African-descended who made significant contributions to science and industry. They would be accompanied or succeeded by such individuals as Roger Arliner Young (d. 1964), the first black woman to receive a PhD in zoology in 1940 from the University of Pennsylvania, and who went on to publish significant research; Dr. Daniel Hale Williams (d. 1931), who performed the first known successful open heart surgery in 1893; Dr. Ernest E. Just (d. 1941), noted zoologist; Howard Medical College professor Ruth Ella Moore (1903–94), the first African American woman to earn a doctorate in bacteriology from Ohio State University in 1933; and Dr. Charles Drew (d. 1950), a leading expert in blood plasma and pioneer in the creation of blood banks.

Then there are the remarkable women who worked at the Langley, Virginia research facility of the National Advisory Committee for Aeronautics (or NACA, replaced in 1958 by the National Aeronautics and Space Administration, or NASA). They were part of a larger group of women, in the hundreds if not the thousands, who beginning in 1935 worked as "computers" in flight and space initiatives (long before technological advances would surpass human capacity for such work in the 1970s). It was not until the 1940s, following President Franklin D. Roosevelt's 1941 Executive Order 8802 (in response to A. Philip Randolph's threat to march on Washington, DC), that racial discrimination in the federal government or defense industry was made illegal, opening the door for black women to join the effort in Langley. Reflecting segregated working conditions, black women were known as the "West Computers," and notwithstanding Executive Order 8802, continued to experience significant discrimination based upon their race and gender. Even so, these college-degreed mathematicians made critical contributions to the space initiative, their mathematical calculations most famously facilitating the 1961 and 1962 pioneering space flights of Alan Shepard and John Glenn, respectively. Katherine Johnson, Dorothy Vaughan, Mary Jackson, and (later, from the 1960s through the 1990s) Christine Darden have only recently garnered recognition for their work.

While most of these notables received formal educations, there were many others who never had the opportunity to grace the halls of the academy, but who nonetheless had formidable knowledge of the medicinal properties of plants and herbs, or had unusual insight into the habits of animals and insects, or knew the movements of the constellations from years of observation. They were also scientists, though uncelebrated.

But in addition to using their intellect, the African-descended also contributed to science through their bodies, often without their consent and even by way of deceit. The experience of Henrietta Lacks, a poor tobacco farmer who in 1951 died of cervical cancer just months after its diagnosis, is a primary example. Succumbing to the disease at Baltimore's Johns Hopkins Hospital at the age of thirty-one, the cancerous cells of this mother of five were removed – without the authorization of the family – and unlike any other similar cancerous tissue, continued (and continues) to live, doubling every twenty to twenty-four hours. Nicknamed "HeLa" in memory of her first and last name, these cells have since served as the basis for research in the battle against cancer, leukemia, influenza, Parkinson's disease, hemophilia, and so on, her unfortunate circumstances having been transformed into a global blessing. Millions of people have received health benefits from the study of her cells, while millions of dollars in profit now line the pockets of a few. Predictably, the family of Henrietta Lacks, who was buried in an unmarked grave, has yet to receive a comparable level of compensation.

Given the stages of both medical science and Henrietta Lacks' cancer, her life could not be saved. But just the opposite was true in another part of the South, around the same time, when in 1932 hundreds of black sharecroppers were enrolled by the U.S. Public Health

Service in a study at Tuskegee University in Alabama. Responding to fliers promising a "Free Blood Test; Free Treatment, By County Health and Government Doctors," 600 men participated in the study, although 399 of them were unaware that they had already contracted syphilis. In exchange for free "medical" treatment, free burial insurance, and meals, all 600 were told they were being treated for "bad blood," a catch-all phrase in common use at the time covering a variety of illnesses. Originally intended to last only six months, the study would actually continue for another forty years until 1972, when a whistleblower made it public. By that time, at least forty spouses had also contracted the disease, and nearly twenty of their children were born with it. This means that for forty years, government officials made and affirmed the decision to allow the disease to progress for the purpose of monitoring it. What makes the "experiment" particularly egregious is that penicillin was identified as a viable treatment for the disease in 1945, yet none of these men were ever administered it. Consistent with a long history of repression and neglect, what happened at Tuskegee helps to explain general African American distrust of government.

The use of black subjects for scientific experimentation was not confined to the United States, nor was it limited to the living, as there was quite a market for black cadavers in medical schools and similar institutions, a practice reaching back to slavery. In eighteenth-century Jamaica, for example, Dr. John Quier's experiments on enslaved individuals included exposing pregnant women and newborn babies to smallpox. In both the US and Brazil, prison inmates, disproportionately black, have been used in a variety of scientific and social investigations. These approaches are contradictory in that they concede a common humanity, yet they are informed by the myth that black people do not physically suffer in the same way, or to the same extent as whites, a conviction dating back to slavery. Lamentably consistent with such views, twenty-first-century studies report that black patients are half as likely as whites to be prescribed pain medication, as contemporary physicians continue to mistakenly believe that blacks do not experience as much pain as whites; or that their skin is thicker; or that their blood coagulates more quickly. History and contemporary practice concur in their low regard for black life, whose pernicious results include health care disparities as well as an impacted self-perception among blacks.

Efflorescence

Regarding cultural production in the African diaspora, the plastic arts, music, dance, and literature were tightly interwoven with labor and politics, reflecting as well as influencing. Whatever the political circumstances, black folk have consistently lived in strikingly beautiful and uniquely innovative ways. In the beginning of the twentieth century, however, black artists, writers, and musicians began to experience a notoriety previously unknown by their ancestors. The "discovery" of black aesthetics had the effect of intensifying cultural production, otherwise referred to as a renaissance. We should not approach the phenomenon uncritically. Black intellectuals debated the purpose of black cultural production, and whether it should always have redeeming social value and be of use in the overall struggle to "uplift" the poor and oppressed. Further complicating black art were questions relating to white patronage, and whether the latter was merely supportive or more intrusive. Issues of authenticity were also present, as the relatively privileged, in some instances, sought to interpret for a white audience the experiences of the downtrodden. Twin considerations of white patronage and class difference therefore raise the question: How representative of the black masses was the cultural work of a small black elite?

We can begin this discussion in Harlem, where the early twentieth-century arrival of immigrants from the English-, French-, and Spanish-speaking Caribbean merged with that of blacks migrating from the American South to create an ambiance of extraordinary energy. The rise of the UNIA and the NAACP invigorated the black community, as did other organizations whose leaders addressed throngs of listeners from their stepladders on Harlem's various street corners, charging the air with an expectancy that looked to move beyond the legacies of slavery to a new day. Harlemites vigorously debated alternative visions of the future, thrilled with the thought that they could at least dream a better future, a world in which increasing emphasis was placed on similarities between the African-descended rather than differences (see Figure 18).

It was in such a context that the Harlem Renaissance began to flourish, spanning the 1920s and early 1930s, having been slowed by the depression of 1929. Also referred to as the New Negro Movement – to underscore the fact that the phenomenon was by no means limited to New York City, but instead took form in a number

FIGURE 18 Children playing in Harlem, 1925. Bettmann / Getty Images.

of cities – the movement stressed that a different kind of black person was emerging out of the shadows of the past, a person much more assertive and demanding of her rights. Black writers in particular achieved recognition during this period, benefiting from a growing American interest in urban life and social challenges.

For a number of scholars, the Renaissance began with Jean Toomer's *Cane* (1923), an excursion into issues of race from which Toomer later took a detour in his life, opting to explore mysticism instead. Jessie Fauset, who supported Toomer's development as a writer, was herself a major figure of the period, serving as literary editor of the *Crisis* from 1919 to 1926. Like Toomer, Fauset's *There is Confusion* (1924) and *Plum Bun: A Novel Without a Moral* (1929) both examine interracial questions, in particular the plight of light-skinned blacks who sought to "pass" for white – the theme of the so-called tragic mulatto. Fauset also played a role in the rise of Langston Hughes, often referred to as the "Poet Laureate of the Negro Race." Author of "The Negro Speaks of Rivers," Hughes published *Weary Blues* in 1926 and *Not Without Laughter* in 1930, demonstrating his versatility as both poet and novelist. *The Big Sea*, his 1940 autobiography, is an important source for what is known about the Renaissance. Countee Cullen was also a poet of tremendous talent, publishing *Color* in 1925, containing his most famous poems, "Heritage" and "Incident." The second black person to win a Guggenheim Fellowship, he followed *Color* with *The Ballad of the Brown Girl* and *Copper Sun*, both in 1927. Though ending in divorce in 1930, his 1928 marriage to Du Bois' only child Yolande demonstrates the interconnectedness of the period's black intelligentsia, as well as the challenges and struggles Cullen faced as a person with same-sex desire.

James Weldon Johnson had been active prior to the emergence of Jean Toomer. Secretary of the NAACP for a time, Johnson published *Fifty Years and Other Poems* in 1917, followed in 1922 by *The Book of Negro Poetry*. His *Autobiography of an Ex-Coloured Man* was reissued in 1927, the same year that *God's Trombones* appeared, in which the oratorical style of the black preacher was poeticized (and immortalized). Perhaps the most recognized figure of the Renaissance, Johnson was later joined in prominence by the celebrated Zora Neale Hurston, whose insight into the lives and culture of the black peasantry and working class, particularly her depiction of women and their struggles in black southern communities, is exemplified in such works as *Jonah's Gourd Vine* (1934) and *Their Eyes Were Watching God* (1937). An anthropologist, she also studied African-based religions in the American South and Haiti; *Tell My Horse* (1937) remains an important discussion of the latter, while her autobiographical work, *Dust Tracks on a Road* (1942), is a reflective as well as stinging critique of American policies.

In 1925, Alain Locke published a major compilation of nonfiction prose called *The New Negro*, and among those who would become prominent later, but who participated in the Renaissance at an early age, was Sterling Brown, whose 1932 collection of poetry, *Southern Road*, was a significant landmark. In addition to editing the works of others, Du Bois contributed to the literary movement through his own creative writing, including *The Quest of the Silver Fleece* (1900), *Darkwater* (1920), and *Dark Princess: A Romance* (1928).

Writers from the Caribbean were also among the leaders of the literary outpouring; Nella Larsen was possibly among them, as her mother may have come from the Caribbean. Her novels *Quicksand* (1928) and *Passing* (1929), however, correspond more closely to issues raised in the work of Jessie Fauset. More clearly fitting this category was the Jamaican Claude McKay, who in 1924 published the classic *Home to Harlem*. He was joined by Eric Walrond, from British Guiana, who worked for a number of black journals before publishing his *Tropic Death* in 1926. As writers explored connections among African-descended populations and Africa's meaning for the diaspora, tensions sometimes developed; McKay, for example, became alienated from black American intellectuals. In spite of this disaffection, or perhaps because of it, his contributions to the creation of a diasporic intellectual network were enormous, as he maintained a lively correspondence with North American and Caribbean thinkers during his stay in Europe from 1922 to 1934. In 1929, McKay would publish one of the most important novels of the period, *Banjo*, which depicts the social, cultural, and political interplay of West Indian and West African dockworkers in Marseilles, France. For his part, Walrond would help to publish the writings of René Maran (born in Martinique of French Guyanese parents) in *Opportunity*, a journal of the Urban League, for whom Walrond worked at one point. Mention of *Opportunity* allows for the general observation that black periodicals of the day, including Garvey's *Negro World* and Du Bois' *Crisis*, were instrumental in promoting the literary renaissance, regularly publishing short works of fiction as well as poetry.

In addition to creative writers, New York City was either home or way station for a constellation of other black intellectuals and artists, including the prominent sociologist E. Franklin Frazier, political activist and organizer Hubert Harrison, journalist J.A. Rogers, and bibliophile Arthur (Arturo) Schomburg, the last three from St. Croix, Jamaica, and Puerto Rico, respectively. Arna Bontemps occupied several stations as poet and novelist (for example, his 1936 *Black Thunder*), but he was also a researcher and scholar. All of these people lived at a time when the artwork of Henry Ossawa Tanner enjoyed great notoriety in Europe and the Americas, the sculpture of Meta Warrick Fuller was critically acclaimed, and the artwork of Aaron Douglas was attracting ever-widening attention. Black film companies such as the Lincoln Motion Picture Company, established in 1916, and that of Oscar Micheaux, created in 1918, sought to counter the racist depictions of the film industry. Blacks in the theater and musicals included Paul Robeson's 1924 leading role in Eugene O'Neill's *All God's Chillun Got Wings*, and the 1921 debut of *Shuffle Along*, written and produced by Eubie Blake, Noble Sissle, Aubrey Lye,

and F.E. Miller. All of these activities were enlivened by the music of
the period, jazz (to be discussed). New York City, Chicago, New
Orleans, Kansas City, and several other sites experienced the music,
but Harlem as the focal point of concurrent movements was exceptional, certainly a cultural capital.

Paris was another. North American and Caribbean blacks relocating to the city included North American soldiers who chose to
remain in France at the end of the First World War. A number of
musicians alighted as well, either passing through or electing to settle
in the Montmartre section of the city, the center of the black American expatriate community. Paris, for much of the twentieth century,
served as a refuge for black Americans seeking to escape virulent
American racism, a place where the appreciation of jazz allowed
musicians to make a living. No doubt the greatest examples of such
expatriates were Sidney Bechet and Josephine Baker. Bechet, a pioneer in a jazz form closely associated with New Orleans, went back
and forth between the United States and France until he finally
settled in the latter in 1950, and where he died nine years later. In
contrast, the dancer, singer, and actor extraordinaire Baker arrived
in Paris in 1925 and remained there for most of her life until her
death in 1975, having acquired French citizenship in 1927 while later
serving the French Resistance in the Second World War. In addition
to Claude McKay, writers and intellectuals who spent significant
time in Paris included Anna Julia Cooper (the first African American
to achieve the doctorate at the Sorbonne), Langston Hughes, Jessie
Fauset, Nella Larsen, Alain Locke, and Countee Cullen. Henry
Ossawa Tanner was the most illustrious black artist living in Paris,
but also studying in France was sculptor Augusta Savage, known for
her *Lift Every Voice and Sing*; Nancy Elizabeth Prophet, who worked
in stone and wood, producing *Head of a Negro* and *Congolaise*; Hale
Woodruff, perhaps best known for his *Amistad* murals in the
Talladega College Library (in Alabama); Palmer Hayden, whose
paintings of everyday life are represented in *The Janitor Who Paints*;
and Aaron Douglas, regarded as the "Dean" of black painters. His
work graced the *Crisis*, as it also illustrated James Weldon Johnson's
God's Trombones. Douglas was deeply influenced by African art, and
it was in France, ironically, that these artists were exposed to such
art, the animating source of Cubism's genius. Like Paul Robeson,
they traveled to Europe to either discover or develop a more intimate
relationship with African culture.

In contrast to the way English-speaking black musicians and intellectuals may have been received in France, less distinguished persons from Africa and the French-speaking Caribbean, though needed for their labor, nonetheless met with hostility and rejection. As colonial subjects, their relationship to France was very different, and that colonial relationship sparked the rise of *négritude*, a movement largely consisting of French-speaking and French-writing individuals who, like their Harlem Renaissance counterparts, tended to be elites relative to their countrymen. Négritude writers posited the idea that people of African descent throughout the world possessed an essence distinguishing them from non-Africans, a difference that was expressed culturally. They further sought to explain the reasons why blacks were nearly everywhere under European domination, and they found their answer in their concept of négritude or "blackness." Briefly, négritude maintains that the African-descended seek a harmonious rather than exploitative relationship with their environment; that they are warm, sensual, and artistically creative, and therefore susceptible to the ruthless. Needless to say, not all in Africa or the diaspora subscribed to such views, and many rejected them outright. Nonetheless, négritude was an important concept whose influence remains discernible. One might begin a consideration of négritude with the aforementioned René Maran, who in 1921 published the highly sensual novel *Batouala*, winner of that year's prestigious Prix Goncourt. *Batouala* is controversial as it seems to reflect views of equatorial Africans from the perspective of a colonial officer from the Caribbean. But a general distaste for colonial rule was shared by most, including students studying in Paris from Africa and the Caribbean, who began organizing when sisters Paulette, Jane, and Andrée Nadal of Martinique held weekly literary salons from 1929 to 1934. Persons from Africa, the Caribbean, and North America met (usually on Sundays) to discuss art and politics, and to dance. In 1929, Paulette Nadal and the Haitian dentist Leo Sajous started a monthly publication in both French and English entitled *Revue du Monde Noir*, in which writers from all over the diaspora and Africa were featured. The *Revue* folded in less than a year, but was replaced by *Légitime Défense*, published by another group of students from Martinique. In 1935, students began the journal *L'Etudiant Noir*, and among them were those who would become leading intellectuals. Léopold Senghor, prolific writer and future president of Senegal, was a participant, as was Aimé Césaire of Martinique, who in 1939 published the highly

FIGURE 19 Nicolás Guillén, Afro-Cuban poet and editor of *Mediodía*, Madrid, Spain, September 1937. Photographs and Prints Division, Schomburg Center for Research in Black Culture, The New York Public Library, Astor, Lenox, and Tilden Foundations.

influential *Cahier d'un retour au pays natal* ("Notes on Return to My Native Land") an anticolonial classic that also presented the concept of black cultural unity. Other négritude writers included Jacques Roumain, Léon G. Damas, Étienne Léro, and Birago Diop.

In tandem with négritude and the New Negro movement, Spanish-speaking artists developed what was called *negrismo*. African Cuban poet, writer, and journalist Nicolás Guillén is a prominent example (Figure 19), whose works celebrate African beauty while depicting black struggle over the centuries. His 1929 collection of poems, *Cerebro y Corazón* ("Brain and Heart"), was a major contribution and signaled his lifelong commitment to social and political change. Guillén was joined in the negrismo movement by poet Luis Palés Matos of Guayama, Puerto Rico, whose 1937 *Tuntún de pasa y grifería* ("Drumbeats of Kink and Blackness") also focuses on race. That Palés Matos was phenotypically "white" drew criticism, and his subsequent poetry reflects different issues. African Cuban poet and journalist Marcelino Arozarena Ramos was a third major voice in the

literary movement, but perhaps the quintessential artist of the period
was the Cuban painter Wilfredo Lam. Born of a Chinese father and a
mother of African, European, and indigenous ancestry, Lam's work
developed an intense engagement with African themes, perhaps owing
to both his background and his personal participation in *santería*.

Suggestions for Further Reading

Much of what is contained in this chapter is related to suggested materials for
Chapters 5 and 6, as works often venture into multiple periods and subjects. In
addition to both these aforementioned publications and the numerous works
referred to in the text, a good place to learn more about migrations is Irma
Watkins-Owens, *Blood Relations: Caribbean Immigrants and the Harlem Com-
munity, 1900–1930* (Bloomington and Indianapolis: Indiana University Press,
1996), a book that also moves into early twentieth-century Harlem and
Marcus Garvey. It can be complemented by Lara Putnam, *Radical Moves:
Caribbean Migrants and the Politics of Race in the Jazz Age* (Chapel Hill:
University of North Carolina Press, 2004); and Winston James, *Holding Aloft
the Banner of Ethiopia: Caribbean Radicalism in Early Twentieth-Century America*
(London and New York: Verso, 1998). World war is a critical context for
many of the issues discussed, for which an excellent work is John H. Morrow,
Jr. and Jeffrey T. Sammons, *Harlem's Rattlers and the Undaunted 369th Regi-
ment and the African American Quest for Equality* (Lawrence: University of
Kansas Press, 2015), and Richard S. Fogarty, *Race and War in France: Colonial
Subjects in the French Army, 1914–1918* (Baltimore: Johns Hopkins University
Press, 2012). Concerning indentured Africans, see Monica Schuler, *"Alas,
Alas Kongo": A Social History of Indentured African Immigration into Jamaica,
1841–1865* (Baltimore: Johns Hopkins University Press, 1980), and Maureen
Warner-Lewis, *Guinea's Other Suns: The African Dynamic in Trinidad Culture*
(Dover, MA: Majority Press, 1991).

Labor movements, national and international, are covered in such works as
Minkah Makalani, *In the Cause of Freedom: Radical Black Internationalism from
Harlem to London, 1917–1939* (Chapel Hill: University of North Carolina Press,
2011); Robin D.G. Kelley, *Hammer and Hoe: Alabama Communists during the
Great Depression* (Chapel Hill: University of North Carolina Press, 1990);
Harry Haywood and Gwendolyn Midlo Hall, *Black Communist in the Freedom
Struggle: The Life of Harry Haywood* (Minneapolis: University of Minnesota,
2012); and Joe William Trotter, Jr., *Black Milwaukee: The Making of an
Industrial Proletariat, 1915–1945* (Urbana: University of Illinois Press, 1985).
Trotter has also edited a useful volume on migration in *The Great Migration in
Historical Perspective: New Dimensions of Race, Class and Gender* (Bloomington:
Indiana University Press, 1991).

A gendered, intersectional approach is well done in Erik S. McDuffie, *Sojourning for Freedom: Black Women, American Communism, and the Making of Black Left Feminism* (Durham, NC: Duke University Press, 2011), as well as in Carol Boyce Davies, *Left of Karl Marx: The Political Life of Black Communist Claudia Jones* (Durham, NC: Duke University Press, 2007), and in Gerald Horne, *Race Woman: The Lives of Shirley Graham Du Bois* (New York: New York University Press, 2002). On club women, the standard work of reference is Evelyn Higginbotham, *Righteous Discontent: The Women's Movement in the Black Baptist Church, 1880–1920* (Cambridge, MA: Harvard University Press, 1993), but also see Paula Giddings, *When and Where I Enter: The Impact of Sex and Race on Black Women in America* (New York: William Morrow, 1996); and Brittney Cooper, *Beyond Respectability: The Intellectual Thought of Race Women* (Champaign: University of Illinois Press, 2017). Cheryl Higashida's *Black Internationalist Feminism: Women Writers of the Black Left, 1945–1995* (Champaign: University of Illinois Press, 2013) is also germane, though it focuses on subsequent periods. Relating labor and political developments in the United States through the mid-twentieth century is Penny M. Von Eschen, *Race Against Empire: Black Americans and Anticolonialism, 1937–1957* (Ithaca, NY and London: Cornell University Press, 1997).

In *Freedoms Given, Freedoms Won: Afro-Brazilians in Post-Abolition São Paulo and Salvador* (New Brunswick, NJ: Rutgers University Press, 1998), Kim D. Butler provides insight into both labor developments and African-based religions in her discussion of Brazil. This can be read together with J. Lorand Matory, *Black Atlantic Religion: Tradition, Transnationalism, and Matriarchy in the Afro-Brazilian Candomblé* (Princeton, NJ: Princeton University Press, 2005); Philip A. Howard, *Changing History: Afro-Cuban Cabildos and Societies of Color in the Nineteenth Century* (Baton Rouge: Louisiana State University Press, 1998) and *Black Labor, White Sugar: Caribbean Braceros and Their Struggle for Power in the Cuban Sugar Industry* (Baton Rouge: Louisiana State University Press, 2015); Michael G. Hanchard, *Orpheus and Power: The Movimento Negro of Rio de Janeiro and São Paulo, Brazil, 1945–1988* (Princeton, NJ: Princeton University Press, 1994); Melina Pappademos, *Black Political Activism and the Cuban Republic* (Chapel Hill: University of North Carolina Press, 2011); and Tomás Fernández Robaina, *El negro en Cuba, 1902–1958: Apuntes para la historia de la lucha contra la discrimininación racial* (Havana: Editorial de Ciencias Sociales,1990).

There is substantial literature on the Harlem Renaissance. One can begin with such classics as Arna Bontemps, ed., *The Harlem Renaissance Remembered* (New York: Dodd, Mead, 1972), and Nathan Huggins, *Harlem Renaissance* (New York: Oxford University Press, 1971). There is also the meticulous scholarship of Arnold Rampersad, *The Life of Langston Hughes*, vols. 1 and 2 (New York, Oxford University Press, 2002); David Levering Lewis, *When Harlem Was in Vogue* (New York: Knopf, 1981); and Philip S. Foner, *American*

Socialism and Black Americans from the Age of Jackson to World War II (Westport, CT: Greenwood Press, 1977).

Regarding négritude, see Janet G. Vaillant, *Black, French, and African: A Life of Léopold Sédar Senghor* (Cambridge, MA: Cambridge University Press, 1990); Gary Wilder, *Freedom Time: Negritude, Decolonization, and the Future of the World* (Durham, NC: Duke University Press, 2015); Trica Danielle Keaton, T. Denean Sharpley-Whiting, and Tyler Stovall, eds., *Black France/ France Noire: The History and Politics of Blackness* (Durham, NC: Duke University Press, 2012); Dominic Thomas, *Black France: Colonialism, Immigration, and Tramsnationalism* (Bloomington: Indiana University Press, 2006); Manthia Diawara, *In Search of Africa* (Cambridge, MA: Harvard University Press, 1998); Édouard Glissant, *Caribbean Discourse: Selected Essays*, trans. J. Michael Dash (Charlottesville: University of Virginia Press, 1989); James Arnold, *Modernism and Négritude: The Poetry and Politics of Aimé Césaire* (Cambridge, MA: Harvard University Press, 1981); Gregory Mann, *Native Sons: West African Veterans and France in the Twentieth Century* (Durham, NC: Duke University Press, 2006); Femi Ojo-Ade, *Leon Gontran-Damas: The Spirit of Resistance* (London: Karnak, 1993); Jennifer Ann Boittin, *Colonial Metropolis: The Urban Grounds of Anti-Imperialism and Feminism in Interwar Paris* (Lincoln, Nebraska: University of Nebraska Press, 2010); and Léopold Senghor, *Négritude, arabisme et francité: réflexions sur le problème de la culture* (Beyrouth: Éditions Dar al-Kitab Allubnani, 1967). Tyler Stovall's *Paris Noir: African Americans in the City of Light* (Boston and New York: Houghton Mifflin, 1996), although primarily concerned with black Americans in Paris, also discusses négritude, as does Michel Fabre, *From Harlem to Paris: Black American Writers in France, 1840–1980* (Champaign: University of Illinois Press, 1991). Finally, Brent Hayes Edwards centers a global black experience in France in *The Practice of Diaspora: Literature, Translation, and the Rise of Black Internationalism* (Cambridge, MA: Harvard University Press, 2003).

One could focus on any number of influences in the Harlem Renaissance, and the Garvey phenomenon was certainly one. Edited by Amy Jacques Garvey, *Philosophy and Opinions of Marcus Garvey*, 2 vols. (New York: Arno Press, 1968–9) is a classic distillation of his views. For context, see Jeffrey Babcock Perry, *Hubert Harrison: The Voice of Harlem, 1883–1913* (New York: Columbia University Press, 2008); Adam Ewing, *The Age of Garvey: How a Jamaican Activist Created a Mass Movement and Changed Global Black Politics* (Princeton, NJ: Princeton University Press, 2014); Tony Martin, *Race First: The Ideological and Organizational Struggles of Marcus Garvey and the Universal Negro Improvement Association* (Dover, MA: Majority Press, 1986); and Rupert Lewis, *Marcus Garvey: Anti-Colonial Champion* (Trenton, NJ: Africa World Press, 1988). Robert A. Hill, Barbara Bair, Tevvy Ball, and Erika A. Blum have edited primary documents relating to the Garvey movement in *The Marcus Garvey and Universal Negro Improvement Association Papers*, 9 vols.

(Berkeley: University of California Press, 1983–). For works linking Garvey with related movements in the Caribbean, particularly Rastafari, see Horace Campbell, *Rasta and Resistance: From Marcus Garvey to Walter Rodney* (Trenton, NJ: Africa World Press, 1987), and Robert A. Hill, *Dread History: Leonard P. Howell and Millenarian Visions in the Early Rastafarian Religion* (Chicago and Kingston: Research Associates School Times Publications/Frontline Distribution International and Miguel Lorne Publishers, 2001). A cutting-edge work on Rastafari that connects the movement to subsequent developments in East Africa, but nonetheless provides an excellent introduction to Rastafarianism, is Monique Bedasse's *Jah Kingdom: Rastafarians, Tanzania, and Pan-Africanism in the Age of Decolonization* (Chapel Hill: University of North Carolina Press, 2017). An excellent tome on the Nation of Islam is Claude Andrew Clegg III, *An Original Man: The Life and Times of Elijah Muhammad* (New York: St. Martin's Press, 1997); but also see Michael A. Gomez, *Black Crescent: African Muslims in the Americas* (Cambridge: Cambridge University Press, 2005).

Women played major roles in the Garvey movement, and elsewhere. See Michelle Ann Stephens, *Black Empire: The Masculine Imaginary of Caribbean Intellectuals in the United States, 1914–1962* (Durham, NC: Duke University Press, 2005); Ula Yvette Taylor, *The Veiled Garvey: The Life and Times of Amy Jacques Garvey* (Chapel Hill: University of North Carolina Press, 2002); Barbara Bair, "Pan-Africanism as Process: Adelaide Casely Hayford, Garveyism, and the Cultural Roots of Nationalism," in Sidney Lemelle and Robin Kelley, eds., *Imagining Home: Class, Culture and Nationalism in the African Diaspora* (London and New York: Verso, 1994); Adelaide M. Cromwell, *An African Victorian Feminist: The Life and Times of Adelaide Smith Casely Hayford, 1868–1960* (Washington, DC: University Press, 1986).

Regarding W.E.B. Du Bois, see Arnold Rampersad, *The Art and Imagination of W.E.B. Du Bois* (New York: Shocken Books, 1990); Manning Marable, *W.E.B. Du Bois: Black Radical Democrat* (Boston: Twayne, 1986); and David Levering Lewis, *W.E.B. Du Bois: Biography of a Race, 1868–1919* (New York: H. Holt, 1993) and *W.E.B. Du Bois, 1919–1963: The Fight for Equality and the American Century* (New York: Holt, 2000). On C.L.R. James, see Anthony Bogues, *Caliban's Freedom: The Early Political Thought of C.L.R. James* (London and Chicago, 1997); Bogues, *Black Heretics, Black Prophets: Radical Political Intellectuals* (New York: Routledge, 2003); and Paul Buhle, *C.L.R. James: The Artist as Revolutionary* (London and New York: Verso, 1988).

Works that bypass the nation-state in their analyses of anticolonial struggle include the foundational W.E.B. Du Bois, *The World and Africa: An Inquiry Into the Part Which Africa has Played in World History* (New York: International, 1965); C.L.R. James, *A History of Pan-African Revolt* (Washington, DC: Drum and Spear, 1969) 2nd ed., revised; Cedric J. Robinson, *Black*

Marxism: The Making of the Black Radical Tradition (Chapel Hill: University of North Carolina Press, 1983); and P. Olisanwuche Esedebe, *Pan-Africanism: The Idea and Movement, 1776–1963* (Washington, DC: Howard University Press, 1982).

Finally, literature on blacks, science, and the social and political implications includes Margot Lee Shetterly, *Hidden Figures: The American Dream and the Untold Story of the Black Women Mathematicians Who Helped with Space* (New York: William Morrow and Co., 2016); Rebecca Skloot, *The Immortal Life of Henrietta Lacks* (New York: Crown Publishing, 2010); Wini Warren, *Black Women Scientists in the United States* (Bloomington: Indiana University Press, 200); Kenneth R. Manning, *Black Apollo of Science: The Life of Ernest Everett Just* (New York: Oxford University Press, 1983); John P. Jackson and Nadine M. Weidman, eds., *Race, Racism, and Science: Social Impact and Interaction* (New Brunswick, NJ: Rutgers University Press, 2005); Stephen Jay Gould, *The Mismeasure of Man* (New York: W.W. Norton and Co., 1996), revised ed.; Ibram X. Kendi, *Stamped from the Beginning: The Definitive History of Racist Ideas in America* (New York: Nation Books, 2016); Ivan Van Sertima, *Blacks in Science: Ancient and Modern* (New Brunswick, NJ: Transaction Books, 1983). The Tuskegee Experiment is discussed in James H. Jones, *Bad Blood: The Tuskegee Syphilis Experiment* (New York: Free Press, 1993), revised ed.; Susan M. Reverby, *Examining Tuskegee: The Infamous Syphilis Study and Its Legacy* (Chapel Hill: University of North Carolina Press, 1981); Harriet A. Washington, *Medical Apartheid: The Dark History of Experimentation on Black Americans from Colonial Times to the Present* (New York: Doubleday Books, 2007). Additional studies of note include Daina Ramey Berry, *The Price for Their Pound of Flesh: The Value of the Enslaved, from Womb to Grave, in the Building of a Nation* (Boston: Beacon Press, 2017); Jim Downs, *Sick from Freedom: African-American Illness and Suffering during the Civil War and Reconstruction* (New York; Oxford University Press, 2012); Londa Schiebinger, *Secret Cures of Slaves: People, Plants, and Medicine in the Eighteenth-Century Atlantic World* (Stanford: Stanford University Press, 2017); Olivia Gomes da Cunha, *Intenção e Gesto; pessoa, cor e a produção cotidiana da (in)diferença no Rio de Janeiro, 1927–1942* (Rio de Janeiro: Arquivo Nacional, 2003).

III

Empire's Dismantling and the Third Wave (since 1945)

CHAPTER 8

Movement People

Movement has long been a principal characteristic of the African diaspora. The period 1945 to 1968 was an important era of "movement," a term that, in contrast to involuntary transatlantic transfers and reluctant labor migrations, came to signify organized campaigns to reverse the legacies of slavery and discrimination. Black people were indeed on the move, fighting racism and colonialism globally. In concert with each other and the aspirations of the similarly downtrodden, the period witnessed the persistence of a defiance made manifest with the first slave revolt, the continuing quest for the full free.

The period after the Second World War period created new conditions for freedom's struggle. Nazi Germany's defeat discredited racism and brought empire under increasingly unfavorable light. Returning African veterans further fueled anticolonial protests, adding to the costs of maintaining colonies. Europe, seat of colonial power in Africa, was superseded by the United States and the Soviet Union as the two world superpowers, neither with territorial claims in Africa. The new Cold War facilitated anti-imperial struggle while transforming parts of Africa into an East–West theater of conflict. Egypt's Gamal Abdel Nasser took power in 1952 and ended British military control of the Suez Canal in 1956, the year of Sudan's independence. In fact, the 1950s saw a number of African colonies held by the British, French, and Belgians achieve a generally peaceful transition to independence, in contrast to the more turbulent transition in Kenya from

1952 to 1963. With the exception of Zimbabwe, Namibia, and South Africa, the rest of the continent became independent by 1975, although often via war.

Africa's independence movement took place concurrently with parallel developments elsewhere, especially in India and China, and was also unfolding at a time of tremendous unrest in the United States, the Caribbean, and Latin America. The imagination of the African diaspora was especially captured by five developments in Africa: Ghana's independence under Kwame Nkrumah in 1957; the bloody struggle of Jomo Kenyatta and the Kenyan Land and Freedom Army (the so-called Mau Mau) against the British, culminating in Kenyan independence in 1963; Congo's independence (1960) and the assassination of its first prime minister, Patrice Lumumba (1961); the Algerian War (1954–62), a particularly grim, intense struggle against the French; and the ongoing anti-apartheid campaign in South Africa. Like Senegal's Léopold Senghor, many anticolonial leaders had studied in Europe and the United States, and had been influenced by Garvey, Du Bois, Padmore, and others. This was true not only of Nkrumah, who envisioned a United States of Africa as a part of his pan-Africanism, but also Nnamdi Azikiwe, who also studied at Lincoln University and the University of Pennsylvania, and had Nkrumah as a student while teaching in Ghana. Azikiwe (or "Zik") became Nigeria's president in 1963 and the father of Nigerian nationalism, a pragmatic leader and unifier of disparate groups. As such, the dawn of African independence included illumination from the diaspora, and the effect of simultaneous conflict in Africa and the diaspora were closer cultural and political links between the two.

For Africa and its diaspora, the end of the Second World War presented very different opportunities, which Africans and their descendants would seize to reconfigure their realities. In so doing, a third diasporic wave took (and continues to take) form, characterized by both anticolonial ideological currents and the relocation of substantial numbers of African nationals to Western countries. There they would encounter the descendants of the preceding, second diasporic wave, with varying effects and implications. These matters are explored in the current chapter with a view toward developments in the Americas, followed by an African-centered perspective in Chapter 9.

Freedom and Fire

Technological advances, especially in mass media, were important components of American social movements of the 1950s and 1960s. Often mobilizing university students, social protest formed around various issues, including the Vietnam War, the feminist movement, and LGBTQ rights, which together with the civil rights and black power movements are referred to by some scholars as the New Left. This is a broad umbrella term, under which were those who maintained a more classic Marxist orientation and support for labor, and those who rejected it. With respect to the feminist movement, this was the beginning of its second wave, wherein women's sexuality, domestic violence, sexual assault, and reproductive rights were a focus, but in which equality in all spheres was the goal. Black women in particular began to distinguish themselves, perhaps best represented by the Boston-based Combahee River Collective, led by black feminists, many of whom were queer, who from 1974 to 1980 addressed the unique challenges of simultaneous interlocking systems of oppression. This exploration of the ways in which gender, race, class, and sexuality are multiply configured and experienced would develop into the powerful analytic of "intersectionality," adopted and expanded by legal scholar Kimberlé Crenshaw in the late 1980s. These and other differences between more conventional and radical feminists would be mirrored in the schism between those leading the struggle for civil rights and the advocates of black power. Broadcast nightly on television for all to see, the civil rights and black power movements exposed America's principal fault line, the fundamental divide of race, and would preoccupy much of American domestic policy for the remainder of the century.

Racial segregation suffered serious assault in the US military during the Korean War, when black and white troops began fighting in integrated units. The US Supreme Court overturned the 1896 *Plessy v. Ferguson* ruling (that found racial segregation constitutional) with its 1954 *Brown v. Board of Education* decision, and the steady surge of southern blacks north and west saw some modification in discriminatory employment and housing practices. Black participation in the franchise was increasing, and by 1954 the House of Representatives included three black men – Adam Clayton Powell, Jr. of New York,

Charles Diggs, Jr. of Michigan, and William Dawson of Illinois. But such modest gains far from characterized the experience of a growing number of blacks trapped in rapidly expanding urban ghettoes; indeed, Chicago politicians, as an example, planned the construction of vast, high-rise housing projects on its south side to minimize the amount of land a swelling black population would otherwise require. Unemployment, inadequate housing, substandard education, and restricted access to quality health care resulted in rising crime and festering resentment. Both in the North and South, black folk were catching hell.

Organizations such as the Congress of Racial Equality (CORE), founded by Bayard Rustin and James Foreman in 1942, pioneered nonviolent protest against discrimination in public accommodations, and the successful Baton Rouge, Louisiana bus boycott of 1953 preceded the more famous 1955 bus boycott in Montgomery, Alabama, a nonetheless crucial campaign ignited by the refusal of Rosa Parks, a member of the NAACP, to yield her seat to a white man. The strategy of CORE and the NAACP was to fight both in the courts and in the marketplace, making discrimination illegal and costly. A 1956 Supreme Court decision declared Alabama bus segregation laws unconstitutional, and signaled the emergence of twenty-seven-year-old Dr. Martin Luther King, Jr., who had led the bus boycott while pastoring Dexter Avenue Baptist Church. He soon founded the Southern Christian Leadership Conference (SCLC) to challenge segregation throughout the South, and in so doing exemplified an Africanization of Christianity in that he drew deeply from the well of black experience to fashion religion into an implement of liberation.

That Ghana's independence and congressional passage of the Civil Rights Act both occurred in 1957 was no coincidence. The Act, establishing a commission to help defend black voting rights while monitoring abuse of their civil liberties, reflected increasing awareness within the US government that its treatment of African Americans now carried international significance. But the struggle was far from over, as President Eisenhower evinced little interest in enforcing the Act. Black students pressed the issue by launching the sit-in movement, beginning in Wichita, Kansas in 1958, but bursting onto the national scene in February of 1960, when four students attending North Carolina A&T in Greensboro, North Carolina, sat at a lunch counter and were refused service. Sit-ins, involving black and white students, erupted all over the South that spring and summer, only to be followed by CORE's Freedom Rides in 1961, involving students using public transportation to test interstate antidiscrimination laws. The Student Nonviolent Coordinating Committee (SNCC), newly formed with the encouragement of NAACP veteran Ella Baker, also contributed freedom riders, but SNCC and SCLC met with stiff opposition in Albany, Georgia in 1961, followed in 1963 by the brutality of city commissioner of public safety Bull Connor in Birmingham, Alabama.

Albany and Birmingham were setbacks, but on August 28, 1963, the March on Washington drew hundreds of thousands, the highlight of which was King's "I Have a Dream" speech. W.E.B. Du Bois had died in Ghana the day before, perhaps a symbolic passing of the torch. For all of their differences, King and Du Bois shared a powerful critique of American capitalism and imperialism, emphasizing their concern for the working classes of all races. King's detractors within the black community included black conservatives, especially high-profiled ministers, who were either reluctant to challenge the status quo in such a confrontational manner, or whose opposition was informed by personal animus toward this young upstart from Georgia. This was especially true in northern cities, where such prominent leaders as Rev. Joseph H. Jackson of Chicago (president of the National Baptist Convention, USA, Inc.) and Rev. Adam Clayton Powell, Jr. of New York (former pastor of Harlem's historic Abyssinian Baptist Church and member of the House of Representatives from 1945 to 1971) very much resented King (mimicking the resistance of prior established leadership to Marcus Garvey). At one point, Powell went so far as to threaten to publicly (and falsely) claim that Dr. King and Bayard Rustin were in a sexual relationship; Rustin was openly gay.

Yet other black leaders would eventually oppose King's goal of racial integration and embrace of nonviolent protest and civil disobedience, and would brand him an accommodationist who principally sought white acceptance and inclusion into the American mainstream. Any serious review of King's writings and speeches, however, would acknowledge that his vision of a nonracist America was directly related to his call for a redistribution of resources and eradication of poverty. Like Anna Julia Cooper, King was one of the few to make connections between imperialism, industrialism, and domestic policy, calling for an end to corporate greed and the Vietnam War.

The history of the civil rights movement is often written with an emphasis on leaders, especially men. But the movement was borne by the labor of women who cooked and sold chicken dinners, answered the phones, ran the endless errands, and cleaned up after the meetings, yet marched in the streets as well as helped to plan strategy. As for leaders, Fannie Lou Hamer joined Ella Baker as one of the most electrifying, male or female, in her capacity as co-founder of the Mississippi Freedom Democratic Party and powerful orator. Ann Moody, activist in SNCC, CORE, and the NAACP; Daisy Bates, leader of the movement in Little Rock, Arkansas; and Jo Ann Robinson, co-founder of the Montgomery Improvement Association, are just a few of the other prominent movement women.

In response to the March on Washington in August of 1963, the death of four little black girls in the bombing of a Birmingham church that September, and the assassination of President Kennedy in November, President Johnson signed into law the Civil Rights Act of 1964, comprehensive legislation targeting discrimination in public housing, accommodations, education, and voting. This was a critical moment in the dismantling of Jim Crow, which in effect constituted the reimagination of the American Negro as an American citizen. Enraged resistance to such reforms in Selma, Alabama led SCLC and SNCC to organize a march from that city to Montgomery, and on "Bloody Sunday," March 7, 1965, state troopers viciously assaulted some 600 marchers on Selma's Edmund Pettus Bridge. On August 4, Johnson again responded with the Voting Rights Act of 1965, but by then the pattern was clear: before the federal government would act, participants in the civil rights movement had to first make enormous sacrifices in blood and resources.

Dr. King would shift his efforts to include discrimination in the North, but he was beginning to have trouble containing the rise of black radicalism – what he would call "this marvelous new militancy." A careful reading of his later writings and speeches reveals his own frustration with intractable racism. Many within the black community, while deeply respectful of King, were beginning to question his approach. A rifle shot ended the challenge to his leadership on April 4, 1968. The perennial threat of "hot summers," having exploded in Watts, Los Angeles in 1965, erupted into multiple conflagrations in both the immediate aftermath of King's assassination and the ensuing summer. Over one hundred cities were scorched from several days of rioting, looting, and burning; some have yet to recover.

King was in communication with the larger world and was supportive of anticolonial struggles, but he is rarely associated with pan-
Africanism, most likely due to his universal appeal, his commitment
to nonviolence, and his engagement with ideas not primarily concerned with the diaspora, perhaps most notably those of Mahatma
Gandhi. Malcolm X, a King critic for part of his life, was on the other
hand the quintessential pan-Africanist, the very embodiment of the
diaspora. In accepting the Nation of Islam's teachings while in prison,
Malcolm was in some ways returning to his origins, as his parents were
Garveyites. That his mother was from Grenada also meant he shared a
bond with the diaspora beyond the rhetorical. He turned away from
a life of crime and became the Nation of Islam's most public and
articulate spokesman, an ardent advocate of black nationalism and a
student of the broader black world. In keeping with the Nation of
Islam's principles, Malcolm rejected King's vision of an integrated
America, calling instead for racial separation. Malcolm viewed nonviolence as counterintuitive and ineffective, a position from which
he never wavered. However, Malcolm would renounce the racialism
of the Nation of Islam once he split with that organization and
embraced orthodox Islam in early 1964. At that time, he made the
Pilgrimage to Mecca, after which he returned to Africa to meet with
heads of state, activists, and students. Having previously visited Egypt
and Saudi Arabia in 1959, he spent nearly half of 1964 in Africa and
the Middle East.

It was Malcolm who repeatedly raised the issue of American
involvement in the assassination of Lumumba, and who kept the
plight of Congo and other African nations in the forefront of his
followers' consciousness. He consistently spoke out against apartheid
in South Africa, while supporting the anticolonial struggle in Kenya
and elsewhere. In imitation of the Organization of African Unity, he
would create the Organization of Afro-America Unity. While events in
Africa were high on his agenda, Malcolm was also careful to address
developments involving the African-descended in Latin America, the
Caribbean, and Europe. It was his ambition to coordinate the struggle
for freedom in the United States with those in Africa and the diaspora,
and to that end he extended his offer of help to Dr. King and others in
the civil rights movement. Cautious for the most part, civil rights
leaders were in the process of organizing a meeting between
King and Malcolm two weeks before the latter's assassination on
February 21, 1965.

Malcolm's brilliance and uncompromising fearlessness had a profound impact, and served as the modern basis for the black power movement. Frustrated with the incremental pace of progress, many in the black community began to de-emphasize integration as a realistic or even desirable goal, instead focusing on developing the economic and political clout of African American communities. Stokely Carmichael, Trinidadian-born, may be the best example of a former SNCC member who, under the influence of Malcolm's philosophy, rejected nonviolence and began to speak of revolution. Later changing his name to Kwame Toure and repatriating to Guinea, it was Carmichael who coined the phrase "Black Power!" Influenced by the rapidly changing political environment, Huey P. Newton and Bobby Seale founded the Black Panther Party for Self-Defense in Oakland, California in 1966; the following year, the Black Power Conference in Newark, New Jersey, in which writer and scholar Amiri Baraka (Le Roi Jones) played a vital role, called for an independent black homeland on US soil.

The Black Panther Party (BPP, officially abbreviated in 1968) was a response to both national and local challenges. The former included intensified questioning of nonviolent civil disobedience, the aforementioned assassination of Malcolm X, the growing protest movement against the Vietnam War, and a massively unpopular military draft. Locally, tensions were running high in California's Bay Area (and elsewhere), as incidents of police harassment and brutality escalated. Presaging the twenty-first century's Black Lives Matter Movement, Newton formed patrols to monitor the police, and as California was an open-carry state, Newton did so with fully loaded shotguns and other firearms. Partially inspired by the self-defense philosophy and black panther motif of Alabama's Lowndes County Freedom Organization, as well as by Louisiana's Deacons for Defense and Justice – begun in 1964 to defend civil rights workers from white vigilantes – the BPP publicly brandished weapons while arrayed in black leather jackets and black berets, a performance of virility the Oakland police viewed as a provocation.

In further articulating their objectives, in 1967 the Panther Party adopted a ten-point program that called for sweeping changes in education, employment, housing, crime, and the criminal justice system, while continuing to rail against police brutality. Quickly expanding throughout the US and reaching as far as Great Britain and Algeria, the BPP began free breakfast and health care programs,

as well as after-school and summer educational programs, known as
"liberation schools," in the inner cities. Fred Hampton, leader of the
Panther chapter in Chicago, earned the community's respect and
admiration, no easy task as the party's Marxist-informed rhetoric,
conveyed by way of its widely circulating newspaper, was far too
radical and dangerous for many. Fred Hampton and fellow party
member Mark Clark would be assassinated in December of 1969 by
authorities in an early morning raid. We return to this event in
Chapter 9, as it critical to understanding the election of the first
African American president of the United States some forty
years later.

The symbols and speech of the BPP were fueled not only with
defiance, but also with high levels of testosterone. For at the end of
the day, the Black Panthers were thoroughly masculinist in word and
deed, as black manhood was very much at stake for many. Even so,
and consistent with the experience in the civil rights movement, black
women were highly participatory in the BPP, and by 1970 comprised
well over half of the membership. Women leaders would include
Kathleen Cleaver and Erika Huggins, and in some locales women
headed the chapters. Angela Davis was even a member for a brief
period in 1968, the party's sexism a major reason for her exit. During
Huey Newton's exile to Cuba from 1974 to 1977, Elaine Brown would
serve as the BPP's first chairwoman. Notwithstanding these examples,
the party would battle with phallocentrism throughout its existence.

The BPP would suffer internal schisms, particularly between David
Hilliard and Eldridge Cleaver; some of these differences were driven
by principle, others by competing egos. The BPP would also experience conflict with other black organizations, most famously the US
(United Slaves) organization, a black nationalist formation led by
Maulana (Ron) Karenga in Los Angeles, resulting in a number of
fatalities and injuries, including the death of Panther Bunchy Carter, a
former leader of LA's Slauson street gang.

Paralleling the BPP were the Young Lords (officially the Young
Lords Organization), originally a Chicago street gang that developed a
political consciousness in concert with the times. The transformation
took place in 1968 under the leadership of José Cha Cha Jiménez, and
though chapters would be established in a number of cities, Chicago
and New York City would serve as the principal hubs. In conversation
with the BPP's ten-point plan, the Young Lords' eventual thirteen-
point platform (originally there were only ten points) was

pan-Hispanic ("We want self-determination for all Latinos"), unapologetically nationalist (regarding Puerto Rico), and decidedly socialist. As was true of the BPP, women comprised a significant proportion of the Young Lords, as much of 40 percent of the membership, but as was also the case with the BPP, women faced significant chauvinism within the party, notwithstanding its public advocacy of gender equality. In becoming the organization's Minister of Economic Development, Denise Oliver-Vélez would represent its highest-ranking woman. Other prominent figures would include Angela Lind Adorno, Marta Chavarría, Pablo Yoruba Guzmán, and Felipe Luciano.

A related organization was the Black Liberation Army (BLA), possibly formed after disgruntled Panthers left the BPP following Eldridge Cleaver's ousting in 1971. Until 1981, the BLA engaged in "armed struggle" against government and police targets, as well as drug dealers. Assata Shakur and Geronimo Pratt (Geronimo ji Jaga) may be its most famous members, with the former, convicted of murdering a state trooper in a 1973 shootout on the New Jersey Turnpike, escaping from prison and finding political asylum in Cuba in 1979. As committed to revolutionary change were the Weathermen, a faction of the Students for a Democratic Society (SDS), a mostly white, Marxist-informed group originally formed on the University of Michigan's Ann Arbor campus in 1969.

The end of the Vietnam War in 1975 was certainly an important reason for the decline of many radical organizations, but another, arguably more important, was the FBI's creation of the Counter Intelligence Program in 1967, most (in)famously known by its acronym COINTELPRO. This initiative targeted a variety of dissident groups, including civil rights and black power organizations, and employed a variety of means to weaken and ultimately destroy these groups, including fomenting divisions within and between groups, as well as harassment, arrests, feeding news outlets with false information, and of course, assassination. Conflict within the BPP was mirrored by a major split between the Chicago and New York City branches of the Young Lords in 1970. As a result of COINTELPRO and other political and social dynamics, the BPP as well as the Young Lords were no longer viable by 1982 (though the Young Lords would reinvent themselves and participate in Chicago politics). Perhaps emblematic of their descent was the demise of Huey Newton himself, who in 1989 was killed in a drug purchase gone awry. A "New Black

Panther Party" was formed in 1989, but without the authorization or support of surviving BPP leaders.

Developments in the Caribbean, Latin America, and Europe

From the 1960s onward, many Caribbean colonies achieved independent status, paralleling events in Africa and Asia. Developments in these different parts of the world were akin to mirror images, as ten British territories in the Caribbean established a political union – the West Indies Federation – in 1958. Led by Barbados, Jamaica, and Trinidad and Tobago, the other members were Antigua, Dominica, Grenada, Montserrat, what was then St. Kitts-Nevis-Anguilla, St. Lucia, and St. Vincent.

As the Federation was still part of the British Empire, London appointed a governor general to head it, but consistent with global anticolonial sentiment, West Indian leaders moved rapidly to acquire more autonomy, establishing federal institutions and seeking to assert greater control over their economies. As was true of Africa and Asia (and Cuba), these were heady times led by such veritable giants as Eric Williams of Trinidad and Tobago, Norman Manley and Alexander Bustamante of Jamaica, and Grantley Adams and Errol Walton Barrow of Barbados. Meanwhile, the efforts of Cheddi Jagan of British Guiana (formed in 1831 from the Dutch colonies of Essequibo, Berbice, and Demerara) paralleled those of the Federation.

With its capital in Trinidad and Tobago, the Federation pursued a magnificent vision of political and economic union, but the challenges of coordinating federal policy, the imbalances in economic viability among the various territories, and arguably the considerable egos of such eminent leaders proved too powerful to overcome in combination. The issue of more economically advanced territories sharing their resources with those less advantaged was a major challenge, and when the matter was put to a vote in 1961 in Jamaica, the latter withdrew from the Federation, declaring its own independence in 1962. Trinidad and Tobago would do the same that year, and the Federation came to an end, having survived four years (1958 to 1962). Guyana would also become independent in 1966, but even so, the need for regional economic coordination among otherwise sovereign states continues to be reflected in CARICOM (the Caribbean Community), formed in 1973 (with Guyana and Haiti as members).

The particular context within which Trinidad and Tobago debated Federation was partially informed by a US occupation lasting from 1941 and 1947, the result of an agreement with Britain giving the US two military bases (Chaguaramas and Cumuto) in the midst of world war. The ensuing Cold War (between the US and the Soviet Union) would especially inform the region's geopolitics, further rocked by revolution in Cuba that began in 1953 and culminated in Fidel Castro's coming to power in 1959. The Caribbean was therefore a central theater in simultaneous global dramas.

All of these developments would impact migratory activity, though in some contrast, Trinidad's petroleum and natural gas resources would distinguish it from the rest of the region. Outside of Trinidad, local economies saw agribusiness steadily replace plantations, increasing emigration pressures on the unemployed. In addition to New York, Toronto, Paris, and London, such emigrants journeyed to Caribbean cities as well as to rural areas. Haitians and Dominicans followed the earlier pattern of migrating to the US and Canada, where they continued to be joined by American southerners in cities, and by Central Americans picking fruit, harvesting vegetables, and working as domestics. Migrant workers often did not come to stay, but rather to save enough money to create better conditions for themselves and their families back home.

While pockets of English-speaking blacks have influenced ideas about race in places like Costa Rica and Nicaragua, US empire in the Americas was perhaps a greater factor in that it exported a model of racism contributing to conditions in which the African-descended had the least education, occupied the lowest economic levels, and were without political power. Their plight can be difficult to discern in Latin America, where many cultures do not acknowledge the existence of discrimination, or even race, citing the high rate of miscegenation and mixed marriages as proof.

Race in the Dominican Republic highlights the extent to which it is an arbitrary and politicized concept, and is significantly conditioned by Haiti; the fear of being mislabeled a Haitian lead many to undervalue their African heritage. Sixty percent of the country is of mixed ancestry, but those of the upper class are classified as white, illustrating the principle that class "whitens" throughout Latin America, while the 12 percent of "purer" African ancestry are invariably poor.

The idea of a color-blind "Cuban race" has been contested, as African Cubans were the worst educated, eking out an existence in rural backwaters or as unskilled laborers in urban areas. Their situation remained unchanged under Fulgencio Batista, himself of partial African ancestry, who assumed power in 1933 when Cuba was the playground of US elites (casinos, etc.). Although controversial, there is no gainsaying that after coming to power via armed revolution in 1959, the education, health care, and living conditions of African Cubans improved dramatically under Fidel Castro (d. 2016).

In Mexico, the 1.2 percent of the population (some 1.4 million) who in 2015 self-identified as Afro-Mexican are mostly descendants of maroons, with a number of "Afro-mestizo" communities lining Mexico's Gulf and Pacific coasts, particularly within the Costa Chica region of Guerrero state. Reference to African Mexicans as Afro-mestizos underscores the general Mexican self-description as mestizo (of Spanish and Native American ancestry), while connoting that the African component is a generally unacceptable part of the meld. Indeed, the African Mexicans themselves, until the recent rise of tourist interest, emphasized their mestizo heritage due to the devaluation of both indigenous and African identity.

The theme of the invisible African also emerges in South America's southern cone. Argentina is the best example, where significant numbers of Africans imported through the eighteenth century seemingly "disappeared" by the end of the nineteenth. Black participation in frequent wars, their horrendous living conditions, and Argentina's nineteenth-century policy of importing Europeans to whiten the population (in concert with Brazil's efforts) helps to explain the decline, plummeting from 30 percent of the total population in the early nineteenth century to less than 2 percent by 1887. However, remaining African Argentinians continued their mutual aid societies and newspapers, their numbers arguably augmented by the early twentieth-century arrival of Cape Verdeans. Living in a country proud of its distinctive "whiteness," African Argentinians have lived under considerable duress. Paraguay's African-descended population was similarly decimated by incessant war; by the mid-twentieth century, most were actually descendants of blacks from Uruguay called Cambá Cuá ("place of the blacks" in Guaraní, their adopted language). Rural and few in number, their land has been the target of government appropriation since the 1940s. Uruguay was home to another beleaguered, small community who in 1936 started their own Partido Autóctono Negro (Native Black Party) to agitate for inclusion, an attempt resisted by a government that repressed the African music and dance of *candombe*. As for Bolivia, the tiny number of African-descended, concentrated in the Yungas provinces, have continued with such African-influenced practices as *el rey negro*, crowning a king every year in a ceremony similar to those in New England and the Caribbean during slavery.

Venezuela's racial history of the nineteenth and early twentieth centuries resembles that of Argentina, while its subsequent history approaches that of Cuba. African Venezuelans descend from distinct groups and historical moments; they are the descendants of the enslaved, the hispanicized progeny of late nineteenth-century Caribbean immigrants, and Guyanese blacks maintaining their own culture. While acknowledging the African presence, Venezuelan leaders believed it was inferior, and like Brazil and Argentina set upon a policy of whitening that also called for blacks to surrender their African heritage in hispanicization. Before 1945, most blacks were uneducated and suffered significant discrimination, and were far from acceptable to the Venezuelan elite. After 1945, however, the party Acción Democrática took power, extolling the triple heritage of Venezuela (African, European, Native American), and referring to Venezuelans as a *café con leche* (brown-skinned) people, a concept that included the African contribution. The African-descended have since experienced some amelioration of their conditions, with more employment, improved education, and movement of individuals into positions of leadership.

A popular understanding of race in Brazil has been heavily influenced by the work of sociologist Gilberto Freyre, who in the 1930s made the deceptively persuasive argument that Brazil, because of its large African-descended population and extensive racial miscegenation, was a racial democracy, and that race was not an impediment to the individual. Since the 1950s, however, scholars like sociologist Florestán Fernandes have been busy debunking racial democracy as a myth. Brazilians of African descent have historically been disproportionately poor and uneducated, achieving significant status only as star athletes and entertainers. Attempts to address these deficiencies included cultural responses, and in 1944 the *Teatro Experimental do Negro* was created by one of the most important of all African Brazilian intellectuals, Abdias do Nascimento. The absence of organization among blacks following the Second World War, however, combined with a repressive military regime from 1964 to 1985, meant that more intense political activity did not commence until the 1970s.

As for Europe, two principal sites for the African diaspora have been Britain and France. Though Africans have been in Europe since antiquity, enslaved Africans began arriving in England in the sixteenth century. By the late eighteenth century, there were as many as 10,000 of them enslaved in Britain (often called "blackamoors"), mostly in London, Bristol, and Liverpool, a major port in the slave trade. Black seamen became fixtures in the various ports, where they played leading roles in labor struggles. Early twentieth-century England would boast a small black community numbering in the thousands, but subsequent immigration of colonial subjects from Asia, Africa, and the Caribbean, in response to the labor and sol-diering needs of two world wars, significantly augmented their numbers. Following the 1948 arrival of the SS *Empire Windrush* (to be discussed), Caribbean labor continued to arrive in the 1950s to assist in the rebuilding of Britain's postwar economy, but a grow-ing black presence had the effect of increasing white resentment, xenophobia, and violence animated by fears of economic competi-tion. Racial antagonisms helped to shape a black culture, or set of black cultures in Britain, emphasizing ties between, Africa, and Asia, and the Caribbean.

Developments in France were analogous. With expansive territorial claims in both North and West Africa, the Caribbean, and the Indian Ocean, France has long been acquainted with people of African descent, boasting one of the most important writers of the nineteenth century – Alexandre Dumas, author of *The Three Musketeers* and *The Count of Monte Cristo*; Dumas' father, born in Saint-Domingue, was the son of an African-descended mother. France's subsequent conflict with Algeria has profoundly impacted race relations in France, and the experience of the North African immigrant, originally recruited to fill labor needs, has been the most critical of all. Anti-North African sentiment in France was inflamed by not only the end of the Second World War and the reclamation of jobs by white Frenchmen, but by the Algerian Revolution. Islam is an important dynamic, as North Africans are highly integrated into the Muslim world. However, North Africans also acknowledge ties to the non-Muslim African world, the best example of which was their embrace of Martinican Frantz Fanon. A psychiatrist and participant in the struggle against the French in Algeria, his 1963 publication *The Wretched of the Earth* helped to popularize the Algerian Revolution throughout the African diaspora, establishing it as a model for subsequent revolts.

Xenophobia has since been on the rise in France, with North and West Africans as the main targets.

Since the Second World War, African and African-descended populations have registered appreciable numerical levels throughout Europe. Italy, Portugal, Spain, the Netherlands, and Germany (via American troops) all have recognizable black populations, often owing to very different historical circumstances. Even Russia has a black history, which includes the servants of Peter the Great (d. 1725) and other czars. Such great Russian personalities as poet and playwright Alexander Pushkin had direct ties to Africa, as his great-grandfather Abram Hannibal (d. 1781), a major general in the Russian army, was possibly Ethiopian or Eritrean. Imperial Russia's interest in Africa was largely confined to Ethiopia, due to their similar Christian orthodoxies and the strategic location of the latter. Soviet Russia would become a magnet for African university students and visiting black intellectuals, including Claude McKay, Langston Hughes, George Padmore, W.E.B. Du Bois, Paul Robeson, and Harry Haywood, a leading activist and international figure in the Communist Party who in 1978 wrote *Black Bolshevik: Autobiography of an Afro-American Communist*. They saw in the Soviet Union an alternative model to the pervasive racism of the West.

Cultural Innovations

In the North America of the 1950s and 1960s, blacks were openly embracing their African heritage while pushing for full equality as Americans. Full lips, nappy hair, and dark skin, once despised, were now celebrated, while such descriptors as "colored" and "Negro" were rejected for "black" and "Afro-American." Long neglected in textbooks as unworthy of formal study, the history and culture of Africa and African Americans began to appear in schools and universities around the country, a concession to growing student demand and new geopolitical realities. In the 1960s and 1970s black studies programs were inaugurated on majority-white campuses, corresponding to modest increases in the numbers of black college students, while the curricula at such historically black colleges and universities as Spelman, Morehouse, Fisk, Dillard, Morris Brown, and Howard, among others, were infused with African-related content.

In resonance with the call for black power was the black arts movement, led by such writers and poets as Amiri Baraka, who

published *Preface to a Twenty-Volume Suicide Note* in 1961, and wrote
and produced *Dutchman* in 1964, founding the Black Arts Repertory
Theatre/School that same year; Gwendolyn Brooks, celebrated author
of such works as *A Street in Bronzeville* (1945), *Bronzeville Boys and
Girls* (1956), *The Bean Eaters* (1960, in which can be found the previ-
ously published "We Real Cool"), and *In the Mecca* (1968); Sonia
Sanchez, whose period plays and poetry include *Sister Son/ji* (1969),
Home Coming (1969), and We *a BaddDDD People* (1970); Haki Madhubuti (Don Lee), founder of Third World Press in 1967 and author
of *Don't Cry, Scream* (1969); Mari Evans, renowned poet of *Where is
All the Music?* (1968) and *I Am a Black Woman* (1970); and Nikki
Giovanni, poet and essayist whose first works, *Black Feeling, Black
Talk* (1968) and *Black Judgement* (1969) established her as a critical
voice. Many were more radical than James Baldwin, whose novels and
social commentary *The Fire Next Time* (1963) are often hailed as
emblematic of the period. Baldwin had been in dialogue (and competition) with Richard Wright, whose *Native Son* (1940) and *Black Boy*
(1945) identified him as a major writer and thinker. Even so, Ralph
Ellison's *Invisible Man* (1952) remains one of the more profound
analyses of race in America.

African American expatriation to France resurfaces with mention
of Wright and Baldwin. The former lived in Paris from 1947 until his
death in 1960, and his writings from the period suggest an evolving
view of race. Baldwin arrived in Paris in 1948, often returning to New
York until the period 1957 to 1963, when he remained in the US as a
participant/observer in the civil rights movement while exploring race
and homosexuality in such novels as *Go Tell It On the Mountain* (1953)
and *Giovanni's Room (1956)*. Chester Himes, author of *Cotton Comes to
Harlem (1965)*, part of a detective series featuring protagonists Grave
Digger Jones and Coffin Ed Johnson, also relocated to France in 1953
(though he would move again to Spain, where he died in 1984).

While in France, African American writers came into contact with
French-speaking black intellectuals, including Alioune Diop, director
of the journal *Présence Africain,* and Ousmane Sembene, author and
film maker. Senghor and Césaire remained the leaders of the black
Francophone elite, and cooperated with Wright and others to form the
Congress of Negro Artists and Writers in 1956, a critical meeting of
some sixty delegates from twenty-four countries, among whom were
Mercer Cook, a scholar of black literature, and Horace Mann Bond, a
major figure in higher education and civil rights. Influenced by the

philosophy of négritude, the gathering discussed matters of race, colonialism, and culture, and contributed to a decolonization effort in dialogue with such non-African intellectuals as Jean-Paul Sartre and Albert Camus.

Caribbean intellectuals in addition to Césaire played a large role in conceptualizing global Africa following the Second World War. Édouard Glissant of Martinique laid the theoretical foundations for "Caribbeanness," a response to négritude that emphasizes multiple influences in Caribbean life and culture. His first novel, *La Lézarde* ("The Ripening," 1958), was followed by a series of works whose critique of négritude is echoed in the poet and writer Derek Walcott (d. 2017) of St. Lucia, whose initial *In a Green Night* (1964), followed by *Dream On Monkey Mountain* (1970), garnered attention to what would become a phenomenal career of literary production. But perhaps the consummate intellectual-activist was Trinidadian Eric Williams, whose *The Negro in the Caribbean* (1942) was followed two years later by the classic *Capitalism and Slavery* (1944). These books, so critical to understanding the Western world, came out of a diasporic context, as Williams taught at Howard University between 1939 and 1948. He would go on to serve as Trinidad and Tobago's prime minister from 1962 to 1981, dying in office.

In addition to black literature and scholarship, connections within the African diaspora were facilitated through the music and dance. Indeed, diasporic musical genres would proliferate throughout the twentieth century, engaging and borrowing from each other as well as non-African traditions. In the US, the sorrow songs and field hollers and spirituals of slavery, all having their roots in African musical traditions, slowly gave way in the late nineteenth century to a profusion of musical expressions. There was continuity of idiom and form, but the content changed. Work songs would be epitomized by ballads concerning black folk hero John Henry, but like other black folk music remained largely unknown outside the African-descended community. The creation of the Fisk Jubilee Singers in 1867, one year after the founding of Fisk University in Nashville, Tennessee, began to change this, as the group toured the United States and Europe, introducing their spirituals and folk songs and inspiring the development of similar groups. Black minstrel groups, sometimes known as Ethiopian minstrels, also toured the country and indeed the world in the last quarter of the nineteenth century with their ballads and comic songs. Black minstrelsy would give way, in turn, to vaudeville, with an expanded repertoire that included operatic scenes and arias.

While some black minstrel troupes were able to expand the genre, minstrelsy on the whole has impeded the progress of the African-descended all over the world. The first minstrel show began on the slave ship, when Africans were forced to dance and sing and efface their suffering. Then, in New York City as early as 1843, whites in black face found a way to commercially benefit from the caricaturing and belittling of slaves and ex-slaves. This brand of live entertainment, otherwise known as the "coon show," quickly became very popular (Mark Twain was an ardent fan). In 1926, two white men began a radio show called *Sam n' Henry*, which became *Amos and Andy* in 1928. Its popularity was such that in 1951 a television version using black actors was launched. Black protest led to its cancellation in 1953, but reruns in syndication remained until 1966. The film industry's projection of the coon worldwide has not only facilitated white racism, but has also led to misunderstandings between diasporic communities, as blacks outside of the US have also been exposed to the stereotype of the shiftless, scheming, absurdly ridiculous "nigger." The trajectory and legacy of minstrelsy has yet to end, but there is an alternative tradition of serious black theatrical performance, with partial roots in the founding of the African Grove Theatre in New York City in 1821. There, at the corner of Mercer and Bleecker Streets, tragedies, ballets, and operas were performed by blacks, the most famous of whom was Ira Aldridge (1807–67), an internationally acclaimed Shakespearian actor, touring Europe as far as Russia.

The entire point of minstrelsy was to display the black body as spectacle, an object of ridicule with exaggerated features and mannerisms that communicated cultural maladroitness and innate inferiority. Viewed as a childlike creature suspended between the realms of true human beings and lesser animals, the black body was simultaneously the object of white longing and loathing, and as minstrelsy developed, there also emerged yet another theater in which the black female body became the site of a collective white gaze. Saartjie "Sara" Baartman, a South African Khoikhoi woman born in 1789, would be sold into slavery and transported to Cape Town, from where she would sail to England and Ireland in 1810. There, gawkers paid to have a closer look at her buttocks and general form. Larger audiences from all over Europe gathered in London's Piccadilly Circus to see this South African woman, now advertised as the "Hottentot Venus," appear on stage in a significant state of undress, in a cage. In 1814, she would go on to Paris, where she was similarly exhibited, at times virtually naked, by an animal trainer who purchased her. The subject of intense interest on the part of French scientists, she was only twenty-six years old when she died, impoverished, in 1816. A plaster cast of her body was made, her brain and genitalia both preserved and displayed at the Musée de l'Homme. By the direct intervention of Nelson Mandela, her remains were eventually returned from France to South Africa in 2002. The story of Baartman is emblematic of a Western world both drawn to and repulsed by a black sexuality considered excessive, if not monstrous. Such perceptions continue to inform ideas about who and what is beautiful, and who and what is not.

Minstrels employed music, but musical innovation went far beyond minstrelsy. The rise of the "jig piano" in the late nineteenth century, a style in which the left hand takes the place of foot-stomping and the right hand delivers syncopated tunes similar to those of the banjo and fiddle, was the basis of ragtime, a genre made famous by Scott Joplin (d. 1917). The term "rag" was synonymous with dance, and ragtime emerged at a time when the cakewalk, a dance of plantation and ultimately African origin, was in vogue. Meanwhile, the blues and the spirituals were being popularized, the distinction between them essentially one of content rather than form. Sacred music was sung through much of the twentieth century by "lining-out," where the leader verbalizes the next "Dr. Watts" line (an apparent reference to the English minister Isaac Watts, composer of many popular hymns before his death in 1748), to be repeated by the congregation in a slow imploring of the heavens. The blues, focusing on the tragedies and disappointments of the individual (rather than the group), is laced with humor and irony, its ultimate objective the easing of the human condition. While its origins go back to an undetermined past, the blues were first popularized by W.C. Handy's 1912 published composition *Memphis Blues*, followed two years later by his *St. Louis Blues*. By the early 1920s the blues had become the preserve of black female vocalists, including Mamie Smith, Bessie Smith, and Ma Rainey. Georgia-born Thomas Dorsey, who toured with Ma Rainey from 1923 to 1926, relocated to Chicago, where he created gospel music through the incorporation of the blues into the sacred. Mahalia Jackson, whose voice became the clarion sound of gospel, became associated with Dorsey in Chicago, while the Clara Ward Sisters, also affiliated with Dorsey, became the first gospel group to sing at the

Newport Jazz Festival in 1961. There were many other gospel legends, including Alex Bradford and James Cleveland, who also had Chicago connections.

The early decades of the twentieth century also saw the development of black brass bands throughout the country, especially in New Orleans, where black and "colored" creole bands competed in "cutting" or "bucking" contests. Out of this interaction came Buddy Bolden, regarded by some as the "father" of jazz. In New York City, James Reese Europe organized a dance band and invented the fox trot and turkey trot in the process, and during the First World War took an army band to Europe where he, along with other such bands, introduced the music. By 1918, the term "jazz" was common currency, and was played as dance music by both black and white bands. Learned through listening to others, jazz came to be characterized by a high degree of improvisation; a call-and-response relationship between two instruments (or solo instrument and ensemble) that derived from the blues; breaks in which the soloist is featured; riffs or short phrases repeated by the ensemble; and scatting, where vocalists often imitated instruments. What follows makes reference to specific recordings, but they represent only a fraction of a vast body of work.

Great jazz innovators include "Jelly Roll" Morton, whose integration of blues, ragtime, and jazz qualifies him as the "father" of the solo jazz piano and, for some, the first true jazz composer, publishing his *Jelly Roll Blues* in 1915; Louis Armstrong, whose genius in playing the trumpet and distinctive singing qualifies him as the premier jazz soloist, after whom so many have modeled themselves; King Oliver, a mentor of Louis Armstrong who launched King Oliver's Creole Band in Chicago in 1922 following the start of his career in New Orleans; Mary Lou Williams, viewed by some as the "First Lady of Jazz," having profoundly influenced the Kansas City sound as a pianist, composer, and arranger while serving as sidewoman for major bands; Fats Waller, pianist and composer best known for his 1929 *Ain't Misbehavin'*; Duke Ellington, master composer of an unparalleled orchestral style that, assisted by the pianist-composer Billy Strayhorn, resulted in more than 3,000 compositions, including *Mood Indigo, Sophisticated Lady, Tell Me It's the Truth, Come Sunday* (a blend of jazz and sacred music), and *Take the A Train*; Lester "Prez" Young, melodic alto saxophonist who played with a number of legends, including Billie Holiday, and whose style would influence many; Ethel Waters, whose early career as a blues singer included such hits as *Down Home Blues* and *Oh, Daddy*; Count Basie, whose band incorporated the Kansas City jazz sound into a style copied by many, producing such recordings as *April in Paris*, *Lester Leaps In*, and *Jumping at the Woodside*; Billie "Lady Day" Holiday, a lyricist whose unforgettable vocal quality produced *God Bless the Child* as well as *Strange Fruit*, an attack on lynching and American racism; and Ella Fitzgerald, whose range, articulation, and scatting were incomparable, as evidenced in such classics as *Lady, Be Good* and *How High the Moon*.

Mention of Mary Lou Williams underscores the fact that although black women were prominent in blues and jazz as vocalists, they were also musicians of note. The piano was often the instrument of choice, as demonstrated by the careers of Chicago's Lil Hardin Armstrong and New Orleans' Emma Barrett in the 1920s. But Dolly and Dyer Jones (daughter and mother) were trumpeters, and women playing instruments other than the piano often played in all-women bands. In the 1930s, the pattern of women pianists playing with otherwise male bands and non-pianist female musicians playing in all-women bands became more familiar, the latter perhaps best exemplified by the Harlem Playgirls. The outbreak of the Second World War saw more women incorporated into previously male bands by necessity, but such groups as the International Sweethearts of Rhythm, who played before African American soldiers stationed in Europe, continued to perform in all-female ensembles.

The sounds of blues, gospel, and jazz were popularized during the interwar period by the mass production and distribution of "race records," aimed at black consumers but enjoyed (and studied) by whites as well. With the end of the Second World War came a new era in jazz – bebop – led by such giants as trumpeter Dizzy Gillespie, composer of such standards as *Salt Peanuts* (1942) and *A Night in Tunisia* (1942); saxophonist Charlie "Bird" (or "Yardbird") Parker, whose *Now's the Time* (1945) and *Parker's Mood* (1948) heralded his genius; and pianist Thelonious Monk, a maverick whose unconventional approach to music can be sampled in *Round Midnight* (1947), as well as in his subsequent *Misterioso* (1958) and *Straight No Chaser* (1967). In part a rebellion against swing, dominated in the 1930s by white musicians Benny Goodman, Tommy Dorsey, and Gene Krupa, bebop joined a flatted fifth of the scale to already existing "blue" or "bent" notes, and was characterized by complicated polyrhythms, dissonance, and irregular phrasing, to which dancing became difficult.

Cool jazz followed next, led by Miles Davis, his minimalist technique exemplified in *Birth of the Cool* (1949–50). Hard bop ensued, as such artists as tenor saxophonist Dexter Gordon (*Our Man in Paris*, 1963) and drummers Max Roach (who together with Clifford Brown recorded *Study in Brown* in 1955) and Art Blakey (*Hard Bop*, 1956) attempted to move the music back to an earlier period when it connected with the audience. The late 1950s and 1960s also saw the rise of avant-garde or free jazz, led by saxophonist Ornette Coleman, whose 1959 album *The Shape of Jazz to Come*, followed by his 1960 *Free Jazz* signaled a new musical direction; saxophonist John Coltrane, who catapulted to fame with his 1959 *Giant Steps*, followed (after other recordings) by perhaps his best-known work, *A Love Supreme* (1964); and bassist Charles Mingus, a composer of enormous talent whose repertoire includes *Pithecanthropus Erectus* (1956), *Mingus Ah Um* (1959), and *The Black Saint and the Sinner Lady* (1963). The music became exploratory, decoupled from fixed chord progressions and tonality, in many ways in concert with the turbulence of the times. As was true of jazz since its inception, these artists all played with each other at various points in their careers, in ever-shifting configurations.

An important example of interconnections within the African diaspora was the rise of Afro-Cuban jazz in New York. Led by the great Machito, the African Cuban percussionist, Afro-Cuban jazz (also known as Cubop) was based on African-derived, 6/8 polyrhythms that developed into the *clave* pattern. This form of jazz enjoyed an intimacy with dance, as it was associated with mambo, cha-cha, and guaguancó (a subdivision of rumba), all African-based dances. African-derived musical instruments, such as the conga and *batá* drums and *shekerés* (calabash gourds) are fundamental to the music, and are also associated with *orisha* worship. Cuban-born Celia Cruz would draw upon similar sources to help fashion salsa, a five-note, two-bar rhythm also organized around *clave*. Two other African-based dances, the tango and samba, would disseminate from Uruguay-Argentina and Brazil, respectively, and would impact dance around the world. Puerto Rican legend Tito Puente (who recorded the classic *Oye Como Va* in 1963–4) played in both Machito's band and that of Fernando Álvarez, along with Tito Rodríguez. Their music, influenced by the African rhythms of *bomba* and *plena* in Puerto Rico, would affect Dizzy Gillespie, who also incorporated North African, West African, and Middle Eastern elements into his work. Such influences were also embraced by Yusef Lateef, a master of multiple reed instruments; Pharoah Sanders, who plays various saxophones and flutes, and is famous for *The Creator Has a Masterplan*; the learned pianist and composer Randy Weston (d. 2018); and McCoy Tyner, long-time pianist for John Coltrane. A number of these artists, such as Randy Weston and Max Roach, are also descendants of Caribbean immigrants, adding to the complexity of their sound. The African diaspora was therefore connecting in important ways in New York City and elsewhere.

African American musical distinction was not confined to jazz, gospel, and the blues, but was achieved in every genre and expression. Concert artists such as Roland Hayes, Paul Robeson, and Marian Anderson received acclaim from the 1920s to the 1950s, while operatic prima donna Leontyne Price soared to prominence in the 1950s and 1960s. Jessye Norman, in turn, began devoting her talents to opera in the mid-1970s. Likewise, black dance was not limited to church sanctuaries and dance halls. The black concert dance troupe began in the 1930s, most famously led by Katherine Dunham's Ballet Nègre. Dunham, a student of diasporic dance forms, especially those of Haiti, drew upon folk music for her performances, and laid the foundation for the Alvin Ailey American Dance Theater in 1958, followed by Arthur Mitchell's Dance Theatre of Harlem in 1966, the first black classical ballet company in the US.

Black dance troupes relied upon black composers and various forms of black music for their performances. Black music produced in the United States, in turn, became popular around the world not only because of its power, but because of technology. Recordings and radio programs emanating from the US would enjoy an advantage over those musical forms not similarly promoted. This was especially true of rhythm 'n' blues, a phrase gaining currency in 1949, and soul music, the term of the 1960s. Motown Records, founded in Detroit by Berry Gordy in 1959, signed such artists as Smokey Robinson and the Miracles, Martha Reeves and the Vandellas, Diana Ross and the Supremes, the Temptations, Aretha Franklin, Stevie Wonder, and Marvin Gaye. Motown had a distinct urban sound, combining rhythm 'n' blues and gospel with driving beats consonant with the social protests of the time. In some contrast to Motown was the distinct sound of Stax Records out of Memphis, with its more bluesy, gritty, rural quality exemplified by Otis Redding, Johnny Taylor, and Booker T. and the M.G.'s. As such, the Stax sound was not unlike that of James Brown, the "godfather of soul," who stressed racial pride in some of his music. Motown and Stax were complemented by a musical style coming out of Philadelphia, a smooth rendering led by Kenny Gamble, Leon Huff, and Thom Bell. But perhaps no artist expressed the tenor of the times better than Nina Simone, Sam Cooke, and Curtis Mayfield of the Impressions, whose political discourse was straightforward, unapologetic, and soul stirring.

The political connotations of North American soul music were matched and perhaps exceeded by Trinidadian calypso (or kaiso). Introduced to the broad American public by the Andrews Sisters' 1944 recording *Rum and Coca-Cola* and further popularized by Harry Belafonte's 1956 album *Calypso* featuring the "Banana Boat Song," calypso in fact goes back to the African-born presence in Trinidad, the calypsonian the descendant of the griot turned chantuelle, who rose to prominence through annual competitions at Carnival. The first calypso recording was made in 1914, and by the 1930s such artists as Atilla the Hun, Roaring Lion, and Lord Invader (*Rum and Coca-Cola*'s original recorder) were prominent. Lord Kitchener emerged in the 1940s and dominated calypso through the late 1970s, together with the Mighty Sparrow, who first achieved acclaim with his 1956 hit *Jean and Dinah*, celebrating the removal of US troops from Trinidad. The 1940s also saw the rise of pan, or steel drum, another distinctly Trinidadian form. By the late 1970s, calypso was declining in popularity, and was eclipsed by soca, a more up-tempo, less politicized version of calypso led by such artists as Lord Shorty (later Ras Shorty I). Calypso remains current and is a major vehicle of sociopolitical commentary, while soca has been infused with influences from Indian culture, Jamaica, hip-hop, and French and Spanish cultures resident in the island, resulting in chutney soca, dancehall soca, ragga soca (soca and reggae), rapso (soca and rap), parang soca, and so on. These forms are paralleled in the French-speaking Caribbean by *zouk*, a sound divided into dance (*chire zouk*) and more mellow expressions (*zouk love*).

Jamaica had its own version of calypso, called mento, that in the 1950s mixed with North American rock 'n' roll to form ska. Ska was the major Jamaican musical form by the mid-1960s, but by then the slower beat of rock steady had also taken hold, popularized through Prince Buster's *Judge Dread*. By the end of the 1960s, reggae had begun to make an impression, with its Rastafarian spirituality, critique of government, and lament of poverty. Toots and the Maytals, along with Jimmy Cliff, were early artists, but the genre became an international phenomenon through Bob Marley. His first group, the

Rudeboys, later became the Wailers and included Peter Tosh and Bunny Wailer. In 1973, the group became Bob Marley and the Wailers with the addition of Rita Marley, Marcia Griffiths, and Judy Mowatt. The 1972 release of Marley's first album, *Catch A Fire*, together with the premier of the film *The Harder They Fall* starring Jimmy Cliff, launched reggae into a global orbit. In stark contrast to the political and spiritual dimensions of reggae, the more bawdy and libidinous music of dancehall would begin as early as the 1940s, but would explode in the 1970s.

Black music from the Caribbean, Latin America, and the US traveled the world over, and has been a major influence since the Second World War. In places like Britain, Caribbean forms have mixed with African genres to create new profusions, while in the US these influences would eventually give rise to hip-hop. In the African continent, diasporic musical forms, with their basis in earlier African traditions, were reintegrated into the work of such artists as Fela Anikulapo Kuti, born in Abeokuta, Nigeria in 1938. Joining a highlife band in 1954, he launched what he called Afro-beat in 1968, a convergence of West African music with jazz (and a little bit of James Brown). Fela was more diasporically influenced than his fellow countryman, King Sunny Ade and his African Beats, who perform a genre known as Juju. Like Marley, Fela was an outspoken critic of Nigerian despotism, and a proponent of pan-Africanism, but his own political ambitions were silenced by death in 1997. South African Hugh Masekela (d. 2018), the "father of African jazz," was similarly influenced by his political surroundings. Exiled in 1961, he came to the US and began experimenting with novel musical expressions, producing his 1968 hit, *Grazing in the Grass*. He would be married (for two years) to fellow South African Miriam Makeba, the quintessential vocalist, whose exile from South Africa began in 1963. In turn, her subsequent, ten-year marriage to Kwame Ture (Stokely Carmichael) further underscores the interconnectedness of the African diaspora and its common struggles.

Of course, music and dance are intimately associated with Carnival, a mélange of African and European elements that often takes place prior to the Lenten season. Discussed in Chapter 6, Jonkonnu, Pinkster, and Kongo-related festivals may have facilitated infusions of African elements into Carnival, which otherwise traces to medieval Europe, if not ancient Rome's Bacchanalia and Saturnalia. Other examples are Crop Over in Barbados in late July to early August;

June and July festivals in Santiago de Cuba; the Grenada Carnival in the second week of August; Carabana in Toronto in early August; and London's Notting Hill Carnival in late August. Invariably, Carnival provides an opportunity for a variety of African-based cultural expressions, from the samba schools and "blocos Afros" (drummers, in the hundreds) of Brazil to the steel bands of Trinidad. New Orleans has its version in Mardi Gras, but Carnival in Trinidad is rivaled only by its counterparts in Rio de Janeiro and Salvador, Bahia. Carnival has reinforced cultural affinities throughout the diaspora.

With Carnival and music come food. African cuisine accompanied Africans throughout the diaspora, constituting its own widespread dispersal. Examples of foodways transferred from Africa to the Americas include rice, black-eyed peas, okra, and palm oil, called *dendê* in Brazil (probably from the Angolan term *ndende*). Akee, a red tropical, bland-tasting fruit consumed in Jamaica, is also of West African origin. Large white yams were brought to Brazil and other parts of the American southern hemisphere, but in the US they were replaced by sweet potatoes and yellow or orange yams. Peanuts, originating in South America, were first brought to Africa by the Portuguese and then reintroduced to the Americas via the slave trade as goobers (from *nguba* of West Central African origin). Transferred African cooking techniques included deep oil frying, fire roasting, steaming in leaves, and boiling in water to produce soups and stews. Spicy seasoning, such as hot sauces and pepper sauces, was used everywhere. Certain foods remain associated with African deities, so that in Brazil the *orisha* Ogun, god of metallurgy, prefers black-eyed peas, roasted yam, and *feijoada*, a mixture of black beans and smoked meats that has become Brazil's national dish. *Acarajé*, a popular snack in Brazil, is derived from the Yoruba bean fritter *akará* and associated with Yansã, goddess of cemeteries and whirlwinds. Rum, a sugar by-product and therefore a major factor in black enslavement in the first place, is not from Africa, but is associated with African labor in the Caribbean and remains an important regional beverage. Local and regional preferences have followed the African-descended in their various migrations since slavery's end, from Caribbean cuisine in North America to soul food prepared by North American musicians working in Paris. Not all of these preferences have been the healthiest, some contributing to a disproportionately elevated incidence of high blood pressure, heart disease, and cancer.

A final realm within which the diaspora interacted culturally was sports. Baseball, international amateur competitions, and boxing have been major arenas for fans of all colors and nationalities, as they are especially important to groups struggling to prove their worth. Baseball, segregated through the first half of the twentieth century, is perhaps the most significant vehicle through which diasporic communities learned of each other. Professional black teams were formed as early as the 1880s, and included the Philadelphia Orions, the St. Louis Black Stockings, and the Cuban Giants. Through 1920, black teams "barnstormed," traveling from town to town, playing any team the town could assemble, of any color. The Negro National League (NNL) was founded in 1920, followed by the Eastern Colored League in 1923. The NNL was revived in 1933 after folding two years earlier, featuring such legends as Cool Papa Bell, Satchel Paige, and Josh Gibson. It was during this period that Cuba, Mexico, and the Dominican Republic emerged as premier baseball venues, as white and black teams could compete in these countries during the winter. But in addition to playing in Latin America, American black teams had also been playing Latino teams since 1900, and in 1910 the Cuban All-Stars were an important part of black baseball, evolving into the New York Cubans in 1935 – only the Indianapolis Clowns had as many Cuban, Puerto Rican, Dominican, Mexican, and black American players. The New York Cubans won the Negro World Series in 1947, fielding such greats as Luis Tiant, Sr. and Martin Dihigo of Matanzas, Cuba. Jim Crow baseball came to an end with the Brooklyn Dodgers' signing of Jackie Robinson that same year (see Figure 20).

In addition to baseball, the participation of black athletes in other sports has also been a source of pride for fans around the world. This was certainly the case in 1957, when Althea Gibson became the first black tennis player to win the Wimbledon tournament. Her example has been emulated more recently by Venus and Serena Williams, sisters born in 1980 and 1981, respectively, who together have amassed a combined thirty Grand Slams in tennis (and counting).

International competition also include football's (or soccer's) World Cup, the Pan-American Games, and the Olympics. While fostering international relations as a whole, such competitions have played a vital role in promoting an awareness of the African diaspora through the emergence of black athletes. Concerning the World Cup, probably the most famous example is Pelé, the "black pearl" who in 1958 led Brazil to the championship at age seventeen. Scoring some 1,280 goals in 1,362 games, he was officially declared a national treasure in Brazil.

FIGURE 20 Group portrait of the Cincinnati Clowns baseball team with manager and business manager, 1940s. Photographs and Prints Division, Schomburg Center for Research in Black Culture, The New York Public Library, Astor, Lenox, and Tilden Foundations.

As for the Olympics, there are numerous examples to choose from, as the gathering of athletes every four years has exposed the world to the existence and excellence of black athletes from the Caribbean, Latin America, Europe, Africa, the Middle East, and the US. That black athletes competed from North America and the Caribbean came as no surprise, but the rise and dominance of black athletes elsewhere, especially Cuba and Brazil, has been a revelation to many. Certainly, Jesse Owens winning four gold medals at the 1936 games in Germany was a historic watershed, and following a young Cassius Clay's (later Muhammad Ali) victory in the light heavyweight boxing division in 1960, everyone took notice of the dominance of Cuban heavyweight Teófilo Stevenson in 1972 and 1976. More recently, Jamaica's Usain Bolt has electrified the world as an eight-time gold medalist over eight years, and is the fastest human being to have ever lived.

Black athletes are under enormous pressure as their race's "representatives" to live as models of decorum, and to avoid political controversy. But the 1960s changed all that, as athletes began to

politicize the Olympics and register their solidarity with freedom movements around the world. The medal ceremony for track stars Tommie
Smith and John Carlos at the 1968 Mexico City Games, at which the
two raised their gloved fists and lowered their heads at the singing of
the American national anthem, remains emblematic of the tensions
of the period. In 1976, thirty African countries boycotted the games in
protest against South African apartheid, a decision actively supported
by tennis star Arthur Ashe, who won the US Open in 1968.

Professional boxing has arguably been the most glamorous of the
various categories, and if the discussion is limited to heavyweights
after Joe Louis (champion 1937–48), there is no question that
Muhammad Ali (d. 2016) was the paradigmatic champion of the
entire diaspora, a man whose appeal transcended sports, an eminently
political figure whose conversion to Islam, announced immediately
after his defeat of Sonny Liston in 1964, catapulted him into rarified
atmosphere. Perfecting a pugilistic style featuring circular dance and
uncanny speed, his principled refusal to fight in Vietnam, his suffering
the removal of his championship title, and his pan-Africanist perspective endeared him to millions all over the world. His identification
with Africa reached its zenith with his reclamation of the title in the
1974 "rumble in the jungle" against George Foreman in Congo (then
Zaire), his overall career underscoring the vital role of international
sport in the rise of the contemporary African diaspora.

Suggestions for Further Reading

The second half of the twentieth century would see the emergence of literature
seeking to treat the African diaspora as a unitary field of analysis, otherwise
referred to as the Black Atlantic. Arguably principal among these is Paul
Gilroy's *Black Atlantic: Modernity and Double-Consciousness* (Cambridge, MA:
Harvard University Press, 1995). A number of edited volumes have been
produced among these works, including Joseph E. Harris, ed., *Global Dimensions of the African Diaspora* (Washington, DC: Howard University Press,
1982); Darlene Clark Hine and Jacqueline McLeod, eds., *Crossing Boundaries:
Comparative History of Black People in Diaspora* (Bloomington: Indiana
University Press, 1999); and Sheila S. Walker, ed., *African Roots/American
Cultures: Africa in the Creation of the Americas* (Boston: Rowman and Littlefield,
2001). One of the better, co-authored syntheses is Michael L. Conniff and
Thomas J. Davis, *Africans in the Americas: A History of the Black Diaspora*
(New York: St. Martin's Press, 1994). A work examining the linkages between
liberation struggles not yet mentioned is Imanuel Geiss, *The Pan-African*

Movement: A History of Pan-Africanism in America, Europe, and Africa, trans. Ann Keep (New York: Africana, 1974). An important article reviewing the historiography of the Diaspora is Tiffany Ruby Patterson and Robin D.G. Kelley, "Unfinished Migrations: Reflections on the African Diaspora and the Making of the Modern World," *African Studies Review* 43 (April, 2000: 11–45).

Concerning Africans and their descendants in Europe, in addition to the sources listed in Chapter 7, also consider David Northrup's useful *Africa's Discovery of Europe: 1450–1850* (New York and Oxford: Oxford University Press, 2002); Winston James and Clive Harris, eds., *Inside Babylon: The Caribbean Diaspora in Britain* (London: Verso, 1993); James Walvin, *Making the Black Atlantic: Britain and the African Diaspora* (London and New York: Cassell, 2000); Tahar Ben Jelloun, *French Hospitality: Racism and North African Immigrants*, trans. Barbara Bray (New York: Columbia University Press, 1997); Allison Blakely, *Russia and the Negro: Blacks in Russian History and Thought* (Washington, DC: Howard University Press, 1986) and *Blacks in the Dutch World: The Evolution of Racial Imagery in a Modern Society* (Bloomington: Indiana University Press, 1993); Adam Lively, *Masks: Blackness, Race and the Imagination* (London: Chatto and Windus, 1998); and Inongo-Vi- Makomé, *La emigración negroafricana: tragedia y esperanza* (Barcelona: Ediciones Carena, 2000). There is also a wonderful collection of visuals in the multivolumed *The Image of the Black in Western Art* (Cambridge, MA: Menill Foundation, Inc. and Harvard University Press, 1976–89).

The civil rights and black power movements in the United States have engendered a great deal of research. Just a few include Barbara Ransby, *Ella Baker and the Black Freedom Movement: A Radical Democratic Vision* (Chapel Hill and London: University of North Carolina Press, 2003); Robyn C. Spencer, *The Revolution Has Come: Black Power, Gender, and the Black Panther Party in Oakland* (Durham, NC: Duke University press, 2016); Kay Mills, *This Little Light of Mine: The Life of Fannie Lou Hamer* (New York: Dutton, 1993); Chana Kai Lee, *For Freedom's Sake: The Life of Fannie Lou Hamer* (Urbana: University of Illinois Press, 1999); Belinda Robnett, *How Long? How Long? African-American Women in the Struggle for Civil Rights* (New York and Oxford: Oxford University Press, 1997); Taylor Branch, *Parting the Waters: America in the King Years, 1954–63* (New York: Simon and Schuster, 1988), and *Pillar of Fire: America in the King Years, 1963–65* (New York: Simon and Schuster, 1998); and Vincent Harding, *There is a River: The Black Struggle for Freedom in America* (New York: Harcourt Brace Jovanovich, 1981). On Malcolm X, a critical source remains *The Autobiography of Malcolm X, with the Assistance of Alex Haley* (New York: Grove Press, 1965). But also see Manning Marable, *Reinvention of Malcolm X: The Biography* (New York: Viking, 2011); John Henrik Clarke, ed., *Malcolm X: The Man and His Times* (New York: Macmillan, 1969). An accessible work examining Malcolm X and Martin

Luther King, Jr. is James H. Cone, *Malcolm and Martin and America: A Dream or a Nightmare?* (Maryknoll, NY: Orbis, 1991). Read it with Lewis V. Baldwin and Amiri YaSin al-Hadid, *Between Cross and Crescent: Christian and Muslim Perspectives on Malcolm and Martin* (Gainesville: University of Florida Press, 2002). Literature on feminism's second wave would include Estelle Freedman, *No Turning Back: The History of Feminism and the Future of Women* (New York: Ballantine Books, 2003); Nancy F. Cott, *The Grounding of Modern Feminism* (New Haven, CT: Yale University Press, 1989); Rory C. Dicker, *A History of U.S. Feminisms* (Berkeley: Seal Press, 2016), revised ed.; Alice Kessler-Harris, *In Pursuit of Equality: Women, Men, and the Quest for Economic Citizenship in 20th-Century America* (New York: Oxford University Press, 2003).

Of course, there is voluminous work on black music. One of the most important publications on the topic is Le Roi Jones (Amiri Baraka), *Blues People: The Negro Experience in White America and the Music that Developed from It* (New York: William Morrow, 1963), but not far behind are Eileen Southern and Josephine Wright, *Images: Iconography of Music in African-American Culture, 1770s–1920s* (New York: Garland, 2000), and Samuel A. Floyd, Jr. *The Power of Black Music: Interpreting Its Music from Africa to the Americas* (New York: Oxford University Press, 1995). A reliable general source is Eileen Southern, *The Music of Black Americans: A History* (New York: W.W. Norton and Co., 1997), 3rd ed. Regarding women in jazz and the blues, see Angela Davis, *Blues Legacies and Black Feminism: Gertrude "Ma" Rainey, Bessie Smith, and Billie Holiday* (New York: Pantheon Books, 1998); Farah Jasmine Griffin, *If You Can't Be Free, Be a Mystery: In Search of Billie Holiday* (New York: Free Press, 2001); D. Antoinette Handy, *Black Women in American Bands and Orchestras* (Metuchen, NJ: Scarecrow Press, 1999), 2nd ed.; Sherrie Tucker, *Swing Shift: "All Girl" Bands of the 1940s* (Durham, NC: Duke University Press, 2000). Also see Su'ad Abdul Khabeer, *Muslim Cool: Race, Religion, and Hip-Hop in the United States* (New York: New York University Press, 2016); Robyn D.G. Kelley, *Thelonious Monk: The Life and Times of an American Original* (New York: Free Press, 2009); Stanley Crouch, *Kansas City Lightning: The Rise and Times of Charlie Parker* (New York: HarperCollins, 2013).

On minstrelsy, see Eric Lott, *Love and Theft: Blackface Minstrelsy and the American Working Class* (New York: Oxford University Press, 1993); Yuval Taylor and Jake Austen, *Darkest America: Black Minstrelsy from Slavery to Hip-Hop* (New York: W.W. Norton and Co., 2012); Stephen Johnson, ed., *Burnt Cork: Traditions and Legacies of Blackface Minstrelsy* (Amherst: University of Massachusetts Press, 2012); Annemarie Bean, James V. Hatch, and Brooks McNamara, eds., *Inside the Minstrel Mask: Readings in Nineteenth-Century Blackface Minstrelsy* (Hanover, NH: Wesleyan, 1996); William J. Mahar, *Behind the Burnt Cork Mask: Early Blackface Minstrelsy and Antebellum American Popular Culture* (Urbana: University of Illinois Press, 1998).

For more on Saartjie "Sara" Baartman, see Natasha Gordon-Chipembere, ed., *Representation and Black Womanhood, The Legacy of Sarah Baartman* (New York: Palgrave Macmillan, 2011); Zine Magubane, *Bringing the Empire Home: Race, Class and Gender in Britain and Colonial South Africa* (Chicago: University of Chicago Press, 2003); Clifton Crais and Pamela Scully, *Sara Baartman and the Hottentot Venus: A Ghost Story and a Biography* (Princeton, NJ: Princeton University Press, 2010); Bernth Lindfors, *Early African Entertainments Abroad: From the Hottentot Venus to Africa's First Olympians* (Madison: University of Wisconsin Press, 2014); Shula Marks, ed., *Not Either an Experimental Doll: The Separate Worlds of Three South African Women* (Bloomington: Indiana University Press, 1988); Christina Sharpe, *Monstrous Intimacies: Making Post-Slavery Subjects (Perverse Modernities)* (Durham, NC: Duke University Press, 2010); T. Denean Sharpley-Whiting, *Black Venus: Sexualized Savages, Primal Fears, and Primitive Narratives in French* (Durham, NC: Duke University Press, 1999).

The literature on the BPP and the Young Lords continues to expand. Begin with Curtis J. Austin, *Up Against the Wall: Violence in the Making and Unmaking of the Black Panther Party* (Fayetteville: University of Arkansas Press, 2006); Robyn C. Spencer, *The Revolution Has Come: Black Power, Gender, and the Black Panther Party in Oakland* (Durham, NC: Duke University Press, 2016); Bryan Shih and Yohuru Williams, eds., *The Black Panthers: Portraits from an Unfinished Revolution* (New York: Nation Books, 2016); Elaine Brown, *A Taste of Power: A Black Woman's Story* (New York: Pantheon Books, 1992); David Hilliard and Lewis Cole, *This Side of Glory: The Autobiography of David Hilliard and the Story of the Black Panther Party* (Boston: Little, Brown, and Co., 1993); Assata Shakur, *Assata: An Autobiography* (Chicago: Lawrence Hill Books, 2001); Joshua Bloom and Waldo E. Martin, Jr., *Black Against Empire: The History and Politics of the Black Panther Party* (Berkeley: University of California Press, 2013); Miguel "Mickey" Melendez, *We Took to the Streets: Fighting for Latino Rights with the Young Lords* (New York: St. Martin's Press, 2003); Iris Morales, *Through the Eyes of Rebel Women: The Young Lords, 1969–1976* (New York: Red Sugar Cane Press, 2016); Darrel Wanzer-Serrano, *The New York Young Lords and the Struggle for Liberation* (Philadelphia: Temple University Press, 2015); Darrel Enck-Wanzer, *The Young Lords: A Reader* (New York: New York University Press, 2010); Michael Abramson, et al., *Palante: Young Lords Party* (New York: McGraw Hill, 1971).

On West Indian Federation, see Colin Palmer, *Eric Williams and the Making of the Caribbean* (Chapel Hill: University of North Carolina Press, 2008), *Freedom's Children: The 1938 Labor Rebellion and the Birth of Modern Jamaica* (Chapel Hill: University of North Carolina Press, 2014), and *Cheddi Jagan and the Politics of Power: British Guiana's Struggle for Independence* (Chapel Hill: University of North Carolina Press, 2010); and Eric D. Duke,

Building a Nation: Caribbean Federation in the Black Diaspora (Gainesville: University Press of Florida, 2016). Trinidad's occupation is discussed in Harvey R. Neptune, *Caliban and the Yankees: Trinidad and the United States Occupation* (Chapel Hill: University of North Carolina Press, 2007). Concerning calypso, reggae, and related music, see Njoroge Njoroge, *Chocolate Surrealism: Music, Movement, Memory, and History in the Circum-Caribbean* (Jackson: University Press of Mississippi, 2016); Kwame Dawes, *Natural Mysticism: Towards a New Reggae Aesthetic in Caribbean Writing* (Leeds: Peepal Tree Press, 1999); Chuck Foster, *Roots, Rock, Reggae: An Oral History of Reggae Music from Ska to Dancehall* (New York: Billboard, 1999); Lloyd Bradley, *This is Reggae Music: The Story of Jamaica's Music* (New York: Grove Press, 2000); J.D. Elder, *From Congo Drum to Steelband: A Socio-Historical Account of the Emergence and Evolution of the Trinidad Steel Orchestra* (St. Augustine, Trinidad: University of the West Indies, 1969); Donald R. Hill, *Calypso Calaloo: Early Carnival Music in Trinidad* (Gainesville: University of Florida Press, 1993); Rudolph Ottley, *Women in Calypso* (Arima, Trinidad: self-published, 1992); Louis Regis, *The Political Calypso: True Opposition in Trinidad and Tobago, 1962–1987* (Barbados: University of West Indies Press and Gainesville: University of Florida Press, 1999); and Keith Q. Warner, *Kaiso! The Trinidad Calypso: A Study of the Calypso as Oral Literature* (Washington, DC: Three Continents Press, 1992).

You can read about blacks in film in Manthia Diawara, ed., *Black American Cinema* (New York: Routledge, 1993); Donald Bogle, *Toms, Coons, Mulattoes, Mammies, and Bucks: An Interpretive History of Blacks in American Films* (New York: Bloomsbury Academic, 2016), 5th ed.; Michael T. Martin, ed., *Cinemas of the Black Diaspora: Diversity, Dependence, and Oppositionality* (Detroit: Wayne State University Press, 1996); Karen Ross, *Black and White Media: Black Images in Popular Film and Television* (Cambridge, MA: Polity Press, 1996), and Michael T. Martin, ed., *Cinemas of the Black Diaspora: Diversity, Dependence, and Oppositionality* (Detroit: Wayne State University Press, 1995).

The list is long concerning blacks in sports. Examples of serious scholarship include Gerald L. Early, *A Level Playing Field: African American Athletes and the Republic of Sports* (Cambridge, MA: Harvard University Press, 2011); Jeffrey Sammons, *Beyond the Ring: The Role of Boxing in American Society* (Urbana: University of Illinois Press, 1988); Muhammad Ali, *Muhammad Ali Unfiltered* (New York: Simon and Schuster, 2016); and Kenneth Shropshire, *In Black and White: Race and Sports in America* (New York: New York University Press, 1996).

Global Africa in the Era of Mandela and Obama

The last quarter of the twentieth and first two decades of the twenty-first centuries have witnessed extraordinary global change, all of which have directly impacted Africa and its diaspora. This second half of the diaspora's third wave saw ever greater numbers of African-born persons coming into contact with the African-descended by way of accelerated migration to North America and Europe. In addition to the cultural production of elites and ideological treatises of scholars, therefore, black people from both sides of the Atlantic, numbering in the millions, were now actually meeting each other, sharing the same living, work, and social spaces.

This complex process has been unfolding within multiple contexts. With regard to geopolitics, a major development was the demise of the Soviet Union under Mikhail Gorbachev in December of 1991, resulting in the reinvention of Russia under Boris Yeltsin. The general view is that the Soviet Union's dissolution also brought the Cold War to an end, though tensions with the United States and western Europe have waxed and waned ever since. The future of these relations is uncertain, but many theorists maintain that the Soviet Union's fall, representing the failure of the largest experiment in socialist policies the world has ever known, also signaled modernity's end and the transition to postmodernity. To be sure, there are a variety of ways to understand modernity, with Chapter 4 privileging the emergence of new economic relations, made possible by the transatlantic slave trade, as a useful way of understanding modernity's meaning.

Consistent with this approach is the apparent diminution of Marxism as a viable option for developing nations, and an arguable consequence of this development is the de facto rise of neoliberalism. Neoliberalism is a concept often used to convey a reliance on free market forces – privatization, deregulation, devaluation of currencies, etc. – as the primary mechanism to resolve a society's challenges. That is, neoliberalism represents the state's disinvestment in social policies aimed at ameliorating poverty and inequality, and results in the reduction of the state's role in such sectors as education and health care. From the perspective of those who embrace neoliberalism, the lack of progress registered in certain developing nations is not the fault of the market, but rather the poor choices made by its political and economic leadership. Neoliberalism has had serious implications for struggling African (and non-African) countries, as such international agencies as the World Bank and the International Monetary Fund (IMF) have made the adoption of one or more of these fiscal policies a condition for receiving aid.

At the same time, perhaps the most illustrative and successful example of developments since the mid-twentieth century is the rise of China and its eventual adoption of "state capitalism," by which the state owns and directs, or otherwise invests in major privately owned enterprises while employing Western management techniques. Though controlled by the Communist Party, China also allows for smaller private enterprise, and as a result of its policies China has emerged as a leading economic power, exercising its unique brand of capitalism.

China's rise has been accompanied by its more assertive military and political presence, especially in the Pacific Rim, but also by an increase in its population, with critical implications for Africa. In brief, China's population has doubled since 1964, growing from nearly 700 million to more than 1.4 million in 2018. That population needs energy and food, and Africa is second only to the Middle East in supplying China with oil (mostly from Angola, Congo, and South Sudan). The Chinese government has therefore been very aggressive in offering various African states assistance with infrastructural projects in exchange for African resources. China's posture of non-interference in African domestic politics has greatly facilitated Sino-African relations, with commerce between China and Africa increasing some 700 percent in the 1990s alone. Having surpassed the US as Africa's largest trade partner in 2009, China launched its "One Belt and One Road" strategy in 2013, by which it seeks to enhance Chinese goods and influence via massive investments in ports, roads, rail, and other infrastructural projects, connecting with world markets via the Persian Gulf, the Mediterranean Sea, and the Indian Ocean. In 2014, China set aside $40 billion to create the Silk Road Fund, recalling its predecessor established some 2,000 years before. As a consequence of both its needs and its expansive aims, China has progressively integrated a substantial proportion of Africa into its orbit, leading some observers to express apprehension about a "second colonialism" in Africa. This concern acknowledges African economic growth as a result of commercial ties to China, but at the same time fears that Chinese loans and investment may compromise the sovereignty of African countries; China loaned over $86 billion to various African states between 2000 and 2014.

All of these transformations have taken place within a general context of globalization, and as is true of modernity and postmodernity, globalization means different things to different people. As societies have exchanged goods and information over transcontinental distances since antiquity, some scholars reject the idea that globalization is anything new. But if transcontinental activity is not the principal feature of globalization, the growing integration of markets, together with an ever-accelerating pace and volume of activity that increasingly eliminates the constraints of time and space, thereby connecting an ever-expanding proportion of the world's population, is certainly something new. This acceleration is made possible by rapidly evolving technology that speeds up physical travel, and in combination with advances in the electronic transfer of information, results in the virtual collapse of time and space. We are now able to "inhabit" multiple spaces, instantaneously and simultaneously, all around the world.

Yet another context for understanding the unfolding of Africa and its diaspora has been the rise of a powerful critique of Western empire. The unraveling of colonial power from the mid-twentieth century through the demise of the Cold War toward century's end – which at its heart was a contestation over industrialization and labor, who controls the latter, who benefits from it, what political apparatus best facilitates that control, etc. – laid bare political and economic disadvantages in those parts of the world long associated with Islam.

Throughout Africa, the Middle East, and beyond, complex intellectual debates over Islam's relationship to the West and traditions such as democracy, often seen as representative of Western culture, have resulted in a wide range of positions, from those who see perfect compatibility between Islam, representative government, and capitalist orientation, to those who posit a fundamental, unbridgeable conflict in values and the absence of complementarity. The complicated nature of these debates can be lost on those outside of these communities, such that simplistically labeling those critical of the West as "radicals" and "jihadists" is less than productive. Though difficult, even uncomfortable, this topic is important in understanding the politics of contemporary Europe, where African Muslims, as well as Turks and others, have experienced and continue to encounter enormous challenges.

Finally, in addition to critiques of Western empire are the very real, challenging circumstances faced by far too many African women, men, and children every day. Poverty, unemployment, the lack of a viable future, as well as political repression, instability, and devastating wars have all contributed to waves of immigration to Europe and elsewhere, in search of asylum and a life. This is a tragic, human saga that, in addition to questions over the assimilability of Muslims into Western culture, has thoroughly roiled contemporary European politics. We will return to this matter, the most recent epoch in colonialism's aftermath, resulting in this related but different dimension of the African diaspora.

The Fight Against the Portuguese in Africa

One objective of this study has been to demonstrate how the consciousness of diaspora is achieved; that is, we have endeavored to identify the mechanisms by which disparate communities of African descent are able (or choose) to see themselves as participating in related experiences and circumstances that can be explained by a common background and comparable histories. The circulation of various cultural forms, including music and literature and iconic figures and moments in sport, has already been discussed. So too have such political pivots in global history as the 1896 Battle of Adwa and the US civil rights movement.

Along these same lines, the struggle for independence from Portuguese colonial rule in Guinea-Bissau, Angola, Mozambique, São Tomé and Príncipe, and Cape Verde was a defining moment for diasporic consciousness. Waged between 1961 and 1974-5, it would not only ultimately prove successful in Africa, but it would also result in Portugal's Carnation Revolution and a new government in Lisbon. In contrast to a relatively peaceful transition from colonialism to independence in a number of African countries, the fight against the Portuguese in Guinea-Bissau, Angola, and Mozambique was open warfare, involving guerrilla movements and active combat between armies. The Portuguese had long been involved in what would become Angola and Mozambique, trading in human captives and interfering in domestic affairs since the fifteenth century. Such a long history cannot be recapitulated here, but suffice it to say that in the 1930s a new, right-wing authoritarian government came to power in Lisbon, the *Estado Novo*. Tensions, also informed by anticolonial developments elsewhere in Africa and Asia, eventually led to Angola's insurgency, and spread to the other Lusophone African territories. In Angola, the União dos Povos de Angola (UPA, Union of Peoples of Africa) began attacking white farmers in 1961, and in 1962 Eduardo Chivambo Mondlane, who studied at Oberlin College before earning a PhD in Sociology at Northwestern University, launched a new, multiethnic movement called the Frente Revolucionária de Libertação de Moçambique (FRELIMO, the Revolutionary Front for the Liberation of Mozambique). Mondlane, assassinated in 1969, would be replaced by the charismatic Samora Machel the following year. But it was Amílcar Lopes Cabral, an intellectual, theorist, poet, and author, who occupied the imagination of many when he started the Partido Africano da Independência da Guiné Bissau e Cabo Verde (PAIGC, the African Party for the Independence of Guinea-Bissau and Cape Verde) in 1963, and who most successfully challenged the Portuguese militarily, training his soldiers in Ghana with Kwame Nkrumah's permission. Cabral would be assassinated in 1973.

Relative to other Portuguese-claimed territories in Africa, Portuguese settlement in Angola was substantial, constituting over 5 percent (some 335,000 in 1974) of the total population. Angola also boasted a relatively robust economy (led by oil, mining, and coffee), so that Portugal made every effort to stave off independence movements. In Angola, those movements were divided into the Movimento Popular de Libertação de Angola (MPLA, the People's Movement for the Liberation of Angola) under Agostinho Neto; the Frente Nacional da Libertação de Angola (FNLA, the National Liberation Front of Angola, formerly the UPA) under Holden Roberto; and the União Nacional para a Independência Total de Angola (UNITA, the National Union for the Total Independence of Angola) under Jonas Savimbi. These different groups represented both ideological splits as well as ethnic divides, and under Savimbi, the mostly Ovimbundu soldiers of UNITA would align with South Africa's white regime while making secret agreements with Lisbon and receiving aid from the Americans under President Ronald Reagan. In Guinea-Bissau, Angola, and Mozambique, the Portuguese fielded over 61,000 soldiers against no more than 33,000 armed insurgents. When the wars ended and these countries achieved their independence under Neto in Angola (succeeded by José Eduardo dos Santos in 1979), Samora Machel in Mozambique, and Luís Cabral (Amílcar Cabral's half-brother) in Guinea-Bissau, some 550,000 Portuguese settlers responded by returning to Portugal in a mass exodus. Samora Machel would marry Graça Machel in 1975, but died in a suspicious airplane crash in 1986. Graça Machel would later wed Nelson Mandela in 1998, who by then was president of South Africa.

Because of the Marxist orientation of a number of these leaders and organizations, their efforts were viewed as part of the Cold War, and therefore often opposed by Western governments. But leftist organizations in the West, including so-called black radicals, followed the conflict with the Portuguese with great interest. As many were Marxists, they often understood anticolonial struggle as class-based warfare against global capitalism, but this did not mean they did not also view these freedom struggles as connected to African-descendant populations around the world. And whether one privileged class or race, nothing was more electrifying than the entry of Cuba into the conflict.

From the early 1970s, Cuba sent hundreds of advisors to help FRELIMO in Mozambique, having previously sent small contingents of soldiers to fight in Algeria, Libya, Guinea, and elsewhere in Africa. Cuban advisors and doctors also assisted PAIGC in Guinea-Bissau throughout its fight for independence, while in 1977 some 16,000 Cuban soldiers fought alongside Ethiopia's Mengistu Haile Mariam, arguably a major blunder as Mengistu was widely condemned as a tyrant.

But it was in Angola that Cuban presence was most powerfully felt. With Portuguese rule ending and just before Angola's official

independence, Fidel Castro decided to intervene in a growing inter-
necine conflict between the MPLA's Agostinho Neto and Savimbi's
white South African-backed UNITA, sending 36,000 troops in
November of 1975. In March of 1988, the Cubans defeated the white
South African army at the Battle of Cuito Cuanavale, having deployed
some 52,000 soldiers to Angola that year. Altogether, over 337,000
Cubans served in Angola, and at least 4,300 died there. Cuban
involvement proved crucial, as negotiations following Cuito Cuanavale led to the New York Accords in December of that year, by which
not only did white South Africa agree to withdraw its forces from
Angola by the following year, but it also agreed to a process that
eventually issued in an independent Namibia (the former German
colony of South West Africa) in 1990. Cuba was also to withdraw by
1989, but exigencies led to it remaining in Angola until 1991.

Why did Fidel Castro get so involved with Africa? To be sure,
socialism's global fight against capitalism was a key factor. But that
was not the lone reason, as there was, from the beginning of Castro's
time in power, a conscious identification with black people. In what
survives as an iconic moment in diasporic history, in September of
1960, four months before the US would sever ties with Cuba, Castro
visited the United Nations in New York City, and ending up staying at
the Hotel Theresa in Harlem. There he played host to Malcolm X and
possibly Jackie Robinson, along with such visitors as Egypt's Gamal
Abdel Nasser, India's Nehru, and the USSR's Nikita Khrushchev.
Staying in the cultural center of black America made a powerful
statement, but Castro was after all Cuban, from a land with its own,
large black population. In 1975, in a speech delivered in Havana,
Castro repeated words he has been quoted as saying many times:

> And now it is Angola that is the source of friction. The imperialists seek to
> prevent us from aiding our Angolan brothers. But we must tell the
> Yankees to bear in mind that we are a Latin-American nation and a
> Latin-African nation as well. African blood flows freely through our veins.
> Many of our ancestors came as slaves from Africa to this land. As slaves
> they struggled a great deal. They fought as members of the Liberating
> Army of Cuba. We're brothers and sisters of the people of Africa and
> we're ready to fight on their behalf![1]

---

[1] From the speech "We Shall Defend Angola and Africa!" in Fidel Castro, Cuba and
Angola: Fighting for Africa's Freedom and Our Own (Atlanta, GA: Pathfinder Press,
2013), pp. 31–4.

As Castro is one of the most controversial figures of the modern period, especially as it concerns his domestic policies, these words could be read with a healthy dose of skepticism. But in places like southern Africa, Castro is revered for his support of the anticolonial struggle. More than just words, he laid it on the line with material and living support. And when combined with such efforts as Cuba's decades-long policy of providing medical care at minimal cost throughout the Caribbean, it is a challenge to argue against the conclusion that, whatever his true motives may have been, Castro's policies very much connected Africa to its diaspora in the most tangible of ways.

Dismantling South African Apartheid

As the foregoing discussion indicates, the fight against the Portuguese in southern Africa was directly connected to struggles in South Africa, so that generally speaking, these wars represented regional alliances among culturally distinct white populations, trying to salvage their privilege and power against the legitimate demands of native Africans. To be sure, there is a long history of European occupation and settlement in what would become South Africa, and following Portuguese involvement in West Central Africa in the fifteenth century, the Dutch East India Company (VOC in Dutch) would establish a settlement at Table Bay in 1652, the beginning of Cape Colony. The mostly Dutch settlers, along with a lesser number of Germans and French Huguenots, would soon expand into the Western Cape interior at the expense of the autochthonous Batwa (or Basarwa or "San," hunter-gatherers) and the Khoikhoi (pastoralists). Following several wars, the devastation of smallpox, and the plundering of their cattle, the Khoikhoi were essentially reduced to slavery in both status and economic function by 1750. In fact, by the end of the century South Africa had imported some 26,000 enslaved persons from such places as Madagascar, Mozambique, Dahomey, and Angola, along with those from India and Indonesia. In the age of the transatlantic slave trade, South Africa was a net importer of slaves. The inevitable intermixing between these various groups would serve as the basis for South Africa's so-called Coloured population.

The British would initially seize Cape Colony in 1795, with control over the territory changing three times before British consolidation in

1814. The British victory triggered the migration of the Dutch out of Cape Colony and into what would become the independent Boer (Dutch for "farmer") states of Natal, Transvaal, and Orange Free State, within which gradually evolved an Afrikaner identity and the Afrikaans language, derived from Dutch origins. The term Afrikaner signifies "African," thereby signaling a claim on South Africa's land and resources. But if the Afrikaners were the "Africans," who then were the Batwa and the Khoikhoi, or the indigenous, Nguni-speaking communities of the Zulu, Xhosa, Swazi, and Ndebele; or the Sotho, Venda, and Tsonga? The answer is that they would be categorized as "Bantu," a strategy aiding Afrikaner appropriations. Zulu lands, for example, were taken by the Voortrekkers, Dutch and German farmers fleeing British control of Cape Colony. Theirs is a history of glorified violence akin to the American West, exemplified by as many as nine wars fought over a hundred-year span against the Zulu and Xhosa (the Wars of Dispossession, alternatively referred to by white expropriators as the Kaffir or "Nigger" Wars, 1779 to 1879), highlighted by the 1838 Battle of Blood River and the decimation of the Zulu in Natal, where so many are said to have died that the nearby Ncome River ran red with their blood. The famous Zulu leader Shaka had been assassinated ten years prior by his two half-brothers, with one of them (Mpande) fighting on the side of the Voortrekkers. Afrikaners would celebrate the Blood River as providential, proof that God had given them the land.

The discovery of diamonds and gold at Kimberley and Witwatersrand in the 1870s and 1880s, deep in the interior of Afrikaner republics, attracted British capital along with mining technology. The ensuing mining revolution and its unbelievable wealth would result in war between the British and the Afrikaner republics, with the latter surrendering in 1902, making way for the establishment of the Union of South Africa in 1910.

Though the British won the fighting, the Afrikaners would win the war of ideology, a war of attrition, so that the national elections of 1948 saw the victory of the Afrikaner-based Nationalist Party (NP). The NP immediately implemented the policy of apartheid, or "separateness," an ever-evolving sum of legislation proscribing the integration of Africans and Indians into the South African mainstream. With its obvious analogy to Jim Crow segregation in the United States, apartheid would consist of an elaborate system whereby black South Africans were deemed "citizens" of such "Bantustans" as Transkei, Ciskei, Bophuthatswana, and Venda, as opposed to being citizens of South Africa. Corresponding to this political fiction were pass laws by which the presence of black workers, upon whose labor South Africa was highly dependent, could be regulated. Marriage between races was prohibited, residential and business segregation mandated, educational objectives and expenditures were racially differentiated, and so forth. Apartheid laws were extensive and became torrential, seeking to control all aspects of African and Asian life. Rather than a relic of the past, apartheid was a most modern, sophisticated system of racial discrimination and domination, the law of the land from 1948 to 1994.

It was against such a well-conceived scheme of racial oppression that the anti-apartheid struggle was waged. To be sure, racial discrimination had existed as early as the seventeenth century in Cape Colony, and even under the British, black, Asian, and mixed race (Coloured) communities suffered significant discrimination. Apartheid, however, was far more thoroughgoing – a sort of segregation on steroids; its defeat would require substantial sacrifice as well as international collaboration.

A number of organizations would challenge the racist South African regime, including the African National Congress (ANC, founded in 1912 as the South African Native National Congress and renamed the ANC in 1923). As a multiracial organization, the ANC initially focused on trade unionism, after which it began peacefully contesting racial discrimination through court filings, protests, and deputations sent to the British government in London – so-called passive resistance. The effectiveness of passive resistance had been demonstrated by Mohandas (Mahatma) Gandhi (born in 1869, but lived in South Africa from 1893 to 1914), but in contrast to the Indian community in South Africa, African passive resistance campaigns were brutally repressed. With the founding of the ANC Youth League in 1943 and its alliance with the South African Communist Party in 1946, the ANC expanded its strategic repertoire by emphasizing pan-Africanism, stressing that African nationalism must be led by Africans. In adopting the 1949 "Programme of Action," the ANC Youth League escalated its activities through boycotts, strikes, civil disobedience, and other strategies of non-cooperation with the state. The 1952 Defiance Campaign further saw the combined efforts of Africans, Indians, Coloureds, and progressive whites against apartheid laws, while the 1955, multiracial Congress of the People resulted in the Freedom Charter – its blueprint for a democratic and inclusive South African society. The Freedom Charter would for many years remain the principal response to the rise of the NP in 1948. The hostile reaction of Afrikaners to the Freedom Charter, together with ANC internal disagreements, eventually led to the formation of the Pan-Africanist Congress (PAC) under Robert Sobukwe in 1959.

The Sharpeville Massacre took place the following year, an event that would forever change the nature of the anti-apartheid movement. Sixty-nine peaceful, unarmed demonstrators, protesting the pass laws, were killed by police. This atrocity, combined with the banning of the ANC and PAC, led the former to conclude that there was a need to accelerate the struggle through sabotaging government facilities but avoiding human casualties. A wing of the ANC, Umkhonto we Sizwe ("Spear of the Nation") formed the next year under the co-leadership of Nelson Mandela. Arrested in 1963 and convicted of conspiring against the South African state in 1964, Mandela would spend the next twenty-seven years in prison on Robben Island, along with other political prisoners. Many deaths, imprisonments, and assassinations would ensue, none capturing more international attention than that of Steve Biko, leader of the Black Consciousness Movement, an initiative informed by the immediate circumstances, the writings of Martinican Frantz Fanon, and the American black power movement. Biko would die within three weeks of his arrest in 1977, having been severely beaten. In 1978, AZAPO (the Azanian People's Organization) was launched, embodying many of his ideas.

The struggle against apartheid clearly resonated with African Americans, who were all too familiar with American-style segregation. Indeed, the connections between the blacks of South Africa and the US go as far back as 1920, when the Phelps Stokes Education Commission (the Phelps Stokes Fund had been founded in 1911) began establishing schools for blacks in South Africa (and elsewhere) based on the Tuskegee model; that is, schools emphasizing vocational and agricultural training as opposed to the liberal arts. This approach would dovetail perfectly with South Africa's "Bantu education" policy, which expressly called for lower levels of investment and education for black South Africans. Civil rights and black power leaders followed the fight against racism in South Africa very closely; Dr. King spoke out repeatedly against apartheid, as did the leaders of SNCC and CORE throughout the 1960s, while the TransAfrica

Forum, an advocacy organization founded in 1977 by Randall Robinson, had as one its main objectives the dismantling of apartheid.

Although African Americans closely identified with South Africa's struggles, they were not the only participants in the anti-apartheid struggle. Many persons and groups, of all racial backgrounds and throughout many countries, were deeply involved in organized resistance. Jamaica and India were the first countries to declare a trade embargo against South Africa in 1957, and together with other Caribbean countries and the UK remained supportive of the anti-apartheid movement throughout. Other supporters included Sinn Féin, the political wing of the Irish Republican Army (IRA), Egypt's Gamal Abdel Nasser, and the Palestinian Liberation Organization under Yasser Arafat. In fact, Mandela received his first military training in 1961 from the Algerian National Liberation Front (FLN), whose fight with the French was nearing its end, while the IRA trained ANC soldiers in Ireland. More importantly, the so-called Frontline States in southern Africa – Angola, Mozambique, Tanzania, Zimbabwe, and Zambia – served as sites of training as well as refuge for the ANC throughout the struggle against apartheid, particularly after the defeat of the Portuguese in 1974–5. In fact, Lusaka, Zambia served as the headquarters for the ANC for much of its existence when it was banned in South Africa in 1960, until the ban was lifted in 1990.

The fight against apartheid crystalized in the 1980s with divestment and disinvestment movements across Europe and the US, and on American university campuses these efforts were often led by white students, along with labor union leaders. In the US, mounting pressure on government and business culminated in the 1986 Comprehensive Anti-Apartheid Act, a series of sanctions enacted against the wishes of President Ronald Reagan, who had publicly opposed the legislation before Congress overrode his veto. The US and Israel had become isolated in their support of a racist regime, so that the American action was apartheid's death knell. Nelson Mandela (or Madiba, a title of affectionate respect), freed from prison in 1990, became South Africa's first black elected president in 1994.

In sum, the anti-apartheid movement had the effect of uniting the entire African continent, from North Africa to southern Africa, turning the attention of many in the diaspora to the continent as well. Mandela's release and rise to power was celebrated as a victory for many all around the world, as it was the consequence of an international struggle waged over many years, mirroring his "long walk to freedom." As such, the fight against apartheid was arguably the most critical mechanism by which the African diaspora became more closely knit.

Further African Migration to the West

The defeat of apartheid of South Africa toward the end of the twentieth century represented the end of white political domination in Africa. The era of colonialism was officially over. But these struggles also unfolded in conjunction with the relocation of Africans to Europe and North America. With respect to the latter, this represented an entirely new experience in that it would bring Africans face-to-face, in substantial numbers, with the descendants of Africans. The ancestors of the latter had made the transatlantic voyage in chains, very much against their will. The question of how their progeny may continue to be related to Africa has been a matter of much debate, with opinions ranging from a relationship of little significance to an insistence on viable connections, and all manner of positions in-between. But in striking contrast to those Africans transported in chains since the fifteenth century, twentieth-century Africans landed in Europe and the Americas with their cultures and family ties largely intact. They continued to speak their languages, enjoy their own cuisine, and maintain relations with their native lands. They left Africa for different reasons – educational opportunities, political instability, economic exigency – and while their relocation may have been a matter of necessity, most did not suffer the debilitating process of severance from their origins and families. The rest of this chapter explores how this later diaspora, part of this third wave, has interacted – or not – with the descendants of the second wave.

To be sure, the primary catalyst for relocation to (and within) the West was in response to wartime labor needs. As discussed in Chapter 7, both Africans and West Indians were fully participatory in the world wars. But Europe also needed labor in the postwar period, with North Africans, whose identification as Arabs masks the fact that they are also Africans, among the largest group to meet the demand. By 1954, some 200,000 Algerians had arrived in France; by 1975, the population of both the Algerian-born and their descendants had grown to 700,000; and by 2008, out of a total French population of 64 million, some 10 percent were of North African heritage. By that same year, those of sub-Saharan African descent, who had also come to France to meet war-induced labor shortages, comprised 3.5 percent of that country's total population.

While Africans (from both North and West Africa) were migrating to France following the Second World War, West Indians were simultaneously arriving on European shores. The story of Caribbean immigration invariably begins with the 1948 voyage of some 492 Jamaicans aboard the SS *Empire Windrush*, arriving in Great Britain seeking work. From 1951 to 1971, the West Indian population in England (from a number of Caribbean islands) alone grew exponentially, from 15,000 to 304,000. By 2011, 595,000 people in the UK were of Caribbean ancestry, compared with 989,000 "black Africans," together comprising about 3.3 percent of the overall population.

France and Great Britain may boast the largest African descendent communities in Europe, but Africans and their progeny can be found throughout much of Europe. French-speaking immigrants from Guadeloupe and Martinique also migrated to France, particularly during the economic crisis of the 1960s. Similarly, blacks from Curaçao, Aruba, and Suriname migrated to the Netherlands in the 1970s and 1980s, either fleeing their fears of political instability, or in response to economic crisis, while a number of Africans from Angola, Mozambique, Guinea-Bissau, Cape Verde, and São Tomé and Príncipe relocated to Portugal following independence in those countries in 1974–5. Likewise, Somalis, Eritreans, and Ethiopians moved to Italy as a consequence of that country's political involvement in the Horn of Africa. In 1970, the number of "legally" migrating Somalis in Italy was 472, compared with 376 Eritreans and Ethiopians; by 1995, there were 17,400 such Somalis, compared with 14,000 Eritreans and Ethiopians in 1993.

Though originally recruited for their labor, Africans and the African-descended have everywhere been subject to discrimination, evidenced by squalid living conditions and limited opportunities. In places like France, their difficulties have been compounded by religion, as the vast majority of North Africans as well as those from what would become Senegal, Benin, Ivory Coast, Guinea, Niger, and Mali are Muslim. Europe, then, constitutes a critical site within which respective waves of African diasporic formation have been meeting.

Similar developments have been underway in the United States and Canada. Regarding the latter, significant migration from the Caribbean began with the 1962 Canadian Immigration Act, whose specific banning of overt racial discrimination resulted in some 64,000 "arrivants" from the Caribbean. Within a year or two, nearly 13 percent of all immigration to Canada came from the Caribbean, a rate that would fall to 6 percent between 1979 and 1996 with changes to immigration eligibility. Up until that time, most English speakers came from Jamaica, Trinidad and Tobago, Barbados, and Bermuda, and together with those from Haiti, Martinique, and Guadeloupe mostly settled in the urban centers of largely French-speaking Quebec and predominately English-speaking Ontario, with the vast majority of Haitians living in Montreal, Quebec. By 2006, Caribbean-related populations were enumerated as follows: over 231,000 were from Jamaica, over 102,000 from Haiti, some 61,000 hailed from Guyana, and nearly as many (over 58,000) from Trinidad and Tobago. Variegated as opposed to homogeneous, they continue to celebrate their culture in such large festivals as Carifête in Montreal and Caribana in Toronto, while waging battles against racism through a variety of national and local organizations. Their challenges include higher levels of unemployment, slightly lower percentages with university degrees, and overrepresentation in jails and prisons.

African immigration to Canada has been relatively late, growing from less than 0.3 percent of the total immigrant population before 1950, to about 2 percent by 1970. Political instability in Africa explains much of its immigration to Canada in the 1970s and 1980s, with persons fleeing Uganda, Angola, Mozambique, Zimbabwe, and South Africa. However, this "African" migration largely consisted of Asians (Uganda), Portuguese and British (Angola, Mozambique, Zimbabwe), and "non-blacks" from South Africa, thus considerably complicating the definition and parameters of "African" identity. Arguably, these so-called Africans were able, or chose, to exit the continent precisely because of their non-African origins.

Canada's 1978 Immigration Act opened the door to greater immigration by allowing Canadian citizens to sponsor close relations. Africans from Uganda, Kenya, Ethiopia, Zimbabwe, and South Africa especially benefited. By 2001, some 48 percent of all blacks migrating to Canada were African-born, consistent with a trajectory from 45,215 Africans in 1981, to nearly 275,000 in 2006, concentrated in Ontario, Quebec, British Columbia, and Alberta; nearly 78,000 French-speaking Africans live in Quebec alone. In some contrast with Caribbean communities and with the general Canadian population, those with direct ties to Africa are overrepresented in academic achievement, with over 25 percent boasting university degrees and over 41 percent having some level of post-secondary education. Nonetheless, African unemployment rates mirror those from the Caribbean in its overrepresentation, a testament to a similar experience with racial discrimination.

With respect to the United States, African (legal) immigration has essentially doubled every ten years from 1970 through 2013. There were 1.9 million African-born persons living in the US in 2013, representing 4.4 percent of the total immigrant population, more than twice the 881,000 who arrived in 2000, which in turn was ten times the number (some 80,000) in 1970. In fact, Africans were the fastest-growing sector of the immigrant population from 2000 to 2013, and in reaching a total of 1 million people between 2000 and 2010, were more than double the number of Africans trafficked via the transatlantic slave trade to what would become the US. These numbers were made possible by the Refugee Act of 1980, facilitating flight from such conflict zones as the Horn of Africa; and the 1990 Immigration Act, which instituted a lottery system designed to increase numbers from underrepresented countries.

African refugees have come from Somalia, Sudan, Eritrea, Ethiopia, and the Democratic Republic of the Congo, but in the aggregate most Africans in the US are from Nigeria, Ethiopia, Egypt, Ghana, and Kenya, accounting for almost 50 percent of the African-born population in 2013. Africans are more likely to settle in the South (38 percent) or North East (27 percent), than in the West (18 percent) or Midwest (17 percent). Like most other immigrant groups, African settlement patterns are largely influenced by earlier "arrivants" who, having established themselves, are then able to assist those arriving subsequently. With that said, there are also unexpected patterns that suggest the formation of enclaves: for example, Ethiopians make up the largest African immigrant group in South Dakota, followed by Sudanese and Somalians, and altogether Africans are nearly 30 percent of South Dakota's foreign-born population. There is a similar development in Minnesota, where Africans, led by Somalians, comprise 21 percent of the total immigrant community there.

The 1.9 million African-born persons living in the US in 2013 is essentially the same as the 1.83 million from the Caribbean (excluding Cuba and Dominican Republic) recorded for 2014. But the total numbers obscure arguably much more significant figures: there were 706,000 Jamaicans, 628,000 Haitians, and 220,000 from Trinidad and Tobago. In other words, while the African total population is larger, they hail from an entire continent that is quite diverse; whereas some 85 percent of the Caribbean immigrant population comes from only three countries. The potential influence of these three communities is therefore considerable. But of course, Cuba and the Dominican Republic are also significantly African-descended, and they are also Caribbean countries, and when the number of immigrants from these countries is included (1,173,000 and 998,000, respectively), the Caribbean total of 4 million is double that of Africa. As US citizens, Puerto Ricans are not immigrants.

Compared with conventionally defined African Americans, African- and Caribbean-born persons living in the US are far more likely to have college degrees, and less likely to live in poverty. For example, two-thirds of Nigerians have college degrees, while Africans as a whole are more likely to hold advanced degrees than others. Many of those degrees are from US universities, where they and their children, along with West Indian and Afro-Latinx students, have entered what can be a fraught conversation concerning just who is a "black" student. Indeed, two-thirds of Harvard's black students are either African- or Caribbean-born, or their descendants, corresponding to about 41 percent for all Ivy League schools in 2007.

The capacity to live in Europe or North America, yet remain vitally connected to Africa by way of culture and family ties, coupled with opportunities to regularly visit the continent and even maintain multiple domiciles in Africa and outside of it, has led to the rise of what some call the "Afropolitan" – relatively young, well-educated Africans who navigate multiple worlds in pursuit of their careers. It is a privilege the second wave of Africans, secured in chains, did not have.

That African- and Caribbean-born persons and progeny may fare better than conventionally defined African Americans does not shield them from American racism. Some assert that Africans, unless they grew up in South Africa or Kenya with their large settler-derived populations, are not necessarily unaware of "race" as an everyday social reality until they relocate to the West. If true, they experience a rude awakening. Though relatively better educated, their employment opportunities, access to quality healthcare, and overall life options are still affected by racism's structural limitations. And they are just as subject to the edge of the American judicial system's sword – the police. Examples garnering national and international attention include the case of Abner Louima, who underwent untold suffering

when in 1997 he was unjustifiably arrested, brutalized, and violated
with a broomstick in Brooklyn, New York. He was Haitian. Two years
later, in 1999, four police officers fired forty-one shots at unarmed
Amadou Diallo in the Bronx, New York, killing him with nineteen
bullets after mistakenly identifying him as a rape suspect. He was from
Guinea.

It is therefore clear that the African diaspora's second and third
waves differ in substantial ways, yet one of the most striking examples
of their collective potential was the election of Barack Hussein
Obama, sworn in on January 22, 2009 as the 44th president of the
United States. Far from the conventional definition of an African
American, Obama's mother was a white woman from Kansas, his
father an academic from Kenya. He lived in Indonesia from ages
6 to 10, returning to Hawaii (where he was born) to live with white
maternal grandparents through high school. By his own admission, he
struggled with his sense of identity, and writes that *The Autobiography
of Malcolm X* helped him to understand the black experience. In other
words, he learned through books how to think and conduct himself as
a black male in American society.

President Obama had no direct connection whatsoever to the
second diasporic wave – he was not the descendant of slaves, his
foremothers knew nothing of Jim Crow and segregation, his people
knew nothing of the lash and the hatred of the mob, or the degradation
of centuries of racism. In his first term as a US senator from Illinois,
he entered the 2008 Democratic primary as a decided underdog to the
vaulted Hillary Clinton machine, senator from New York. After winning the January 3 Iowa caucus, he lost the January New Hampshire
primary to Clinton, as expected. The pundits began to write Obama
off as an ephemeral sensation who could not possibly stand up against
the Clinton juggernaut, and many high-profile blacks fell in line to
back Senator Clinton. Polling data from around the country revealed
that Clinton had considerable black support, as they were unfamiliar
with Obama. The Michigan and Nevada primaries came next, and
Senator Clinton won them both, at which point she seemed unstop-
pable. Next up was the South Carolina primary, with the Clinton
machine already hard at work wooing voters and buying the support
of black preachers. The situation looked grim for the Obama camp.

And then something amazing happened. Something awe-inspiring.
African Americans, sons and daughters of the soil, whose parents and
grandparents and great-grandparents had borne the heat of the day and

knew first hand the depth of American racism, rose up and made a collective decision. Gathering in barbershops and hair salons and performing their own caucuses, they discussed the candidates' merits. Down in the deep South – where family connections are of such great significance that, upon introducing yourself, you are likely to get a series of questions regarding who your father and grandmother are, and where you attended school, and whether you are related to cousin Bertha – down there, a collective decision was made that went far beyond a few misstatements made by former President Bill Clinton. Black people listened to Barack Obama, and they heard a familiar cadence. They studied how he conducted himself, and they recognized a familiar gait. They took note that he had married Michelle Obama, a brilliant, equally educated black woman from Chicago's Southside. And they concluded that, wherever his father was from, here before them was an extraordinarily capable individual who was just as black as they were. Led by African American women, they forded the divide of doubt, and they embraced the senator from Illinois. Obama would receive nearly 80 percent of the black vote on January 26, giving him a commanding 55 percent of the total. Black South Carolinians stood up that day, and their example was soon followed in Georgia, Alabama, and Mississippi. Northern blacks, for all of their sophistication and cosmopolitanism, would remain torn in their loyalties between Clinton and Obama, but down in the deep South, black folk made a profound verdict about Mr. Obama's candidacy. They embraced him as one of their own, demonstrating a capacity to understand that they are connected to persons and communities whose specific background may differ, but with whom they share a wide expanse of experiences and values. In embracing a son of Africa, African Americans also reconnected in some ways with Africa itself. Fittingly, it was in the South that the diaspora's potential as a conceptual framework of commonality and coalition was vividly and remarkably demonstrated. In retrospect, it was South Carolina that proved to be the turning point in the Obama campaign, when and where black people saw themselves in Barack Hussein Obama. He would go on to win 95 percent of the black vote in the general election against Senator John McCain. Ninety-five percent.

★ ★ ★

Barack Obama would serve two terms as president of the United States, from 2008 until 2016. And though certain of his policies would be criticized by some of the very black folk who elected him (which is entirely appropriate), he remains a much-beloved figure. His Ivy League education and political ascendancy, along with those of his spouse Michelle, are testaments to what is possible, and he clearly benefited from the goodwill of many different constituencies, not just blacks. It is difficult to argue that their success does not represent substantial social progress in the US with respect to race relations, though this must be tempered with continuing disparities in employment, wealth, education, healthcare, and black overrepresentation in the judicial system. That same overrepresentation can be observed in Brazil, the UK, France, etc. Class distinctions are certainly a factor. But whether originating in the second or third waves, African-descended persons often share similar experiences with racial discrimination. Like the slave trades and slavery, these ongoing forms of racial injustice form the very bridges over which disparate black communities often find each other.

Suggestions for Further Reading

On the struggle against the Portuguese and Cuba's involvement see David Birmingham, *Empire in Africa: Angola and its Neighbors* (Athens: Ohio University Press, 2006); Linda M. Heywood, "Angola and the Violent Years 1975–2008: Civilian Casualties," *Portuguese Studies Review* 19 (2011); W. Martin James III, *A Political History of the Civil War in Angola: 1974–1990* (Piscataway, NJ: Transaction Publishers, 1992); Lars Rudebeck, *Guinea-Bissau: A Study of Political Mobilization* (Uppsala: Scandinavian Institute of African Studies, 1974); Patrick Chahal, *Amilcar Cabral: Revolutionary Leadership and People's War* (Cambridge: Cambridge University Press, 1983); Edward George, *The Cuban Intervention in Angola, 1965–1991* (New York: Frank Cass, 2005); Piero Gleijeses, *Conflicting Missions: Havana, Washington, and Africa, 1959–1976* (Chapel Hill: University of North Carolina Press, 2011).

The literature on South Africa and the anti-apartheid movement is extensive. One can begin with Leonard Thompson, *A History of South Africa* (New Haven, CT: Yale University Press, 2014), 4th ed.; Clifton Crais and Thomas V. McClendon, eds., *The South Africa Reader: History, Culture, Politics* (Durham, NC: Duke University Press, 2013); John C. Eby and Fred Morton, *The Collapse of Apartheid and the Dawn of Democracy in South Africa, 1993* (Chapel Hill: University of North Carolina Press, 2017); Steve Biko, *I Write What I Like* (Chicago: University of Chicago Press, 2002); Mark Mathabane, *Kaffir Boy: An Autobiography* (New York: Free Press, 1998).

On African immigration to the West, and West Indian immigration to Europe, see Taiye Selasi, "Bye-Bye Babar," *Lip #5 Africa* (March 3, 2005);

Isidore Okpewho, "Introduction: Can We 'Go Home Again'," in Isidore Okpewho and Nkiru Nzegwu, eds., *The New African Diaspora* (Bloomington: Indiana University Press, 2009); Tahar Ben Jelloun, *French Hospitality: Racism and North African Immigrants* (New York: Columbia University Press, 1999); Margarita Cervantes-Rodriguez, Ramon Grosfoguel, and Eric H. Mielants, eds., *Caribbean Migration to Western Europe and the United States: Essays on Incorporation, Identity, and Citizenship* (Philadelphia: Temple University Press, 2009); Paul Gilroy, *'There Ain't No Black in the Union Jack': The Cultural Politics of Race and Nation* (Chicago: University of Chicago, 1991); Bill Schwarz, *West Indian Intellectuals in Britain* (Manchester: Manchester University Press, 2004); Ceri Peach, *West Indian Immigration to Britain: A Social Geography* (Oxford: Oxford University Press, 1968); Somini Sengupta, "Heat, Hunger and War Force Africans onto a 'Road of Fire'," *New York Times* (December 12, 2016) www.nytimes.com/interactive/2016/12/15/world/africa/agadez-climate-change.html?ref=world; Ben Taub, "The Desperate Journey of a Trafficked Girl," *The New Yorker* (April 10, 2017) www.newyorker.com/magazine/2017/04/10/the-desperate-journey-of-a-trafficked-girl; "At Least a Million Sub-Saharan Africans Moved to Europe since 2010," Pew Research Center Global Attitudes and Trends (March 22, 2018), www.pewglobal.org/2018/03/22/at-least-a-million-sub-saharan-africans-moved-to-europe-since-2010/; Monica Anderson, "African Immigrant Population in U.S. Steadily Climbs," Pew Research Center Fact Tank – News in the Numbers (February 14, 2017), www.pewresearch.org/fact-tank/2017/02/14/african-immigrant-population-in-u-s-steadily-climbs/; Niraj Chokshi, "How the American Electorate is Changing," *New York Times* (November 25, 2016) www.nytimes.com/2016/11/25/us/politics/how-the-american-electorate-is-changing.html.

The discussion of Barack Obama's tenure as president of the United States is just beginning. See Barack Obama, *Dreams from My Father: A Story of Race and Inheritance* (New York: Broadway Books, 2004); Ta-Nehisi Coates, "My President Was Black: A History of the First African American White House and of What Came Next," *The Atlantic* (January/February 2017) www.theatlantic.com/magazine/archive/2017/01/my-president-was-black/508793/.

Epilogue

The twenty-first century finds communities of the African diaspora poised to assume far greater control over their circumstances and futures. African-descended populations around the globe, from the Americas to Europe to Africa, even to Asia, are more politically and economically empowered than ever before, or at least since the seventeenth century. They occupy every rung of government and business, while continuing to exhibit brilliance in the arts and sports.

The progress achieved through long struggle against colonialism and the vestiges of slavery is threatened, however, by a powerful nativist resurgence in the West that unmistakably resonates with the most virulent forms of racism, xenophobia, sexism, and homophobia. Often undistinguishable from white nationalism, this nativism at times draws inspiration from Nazi ideology. This sort of tribalism has fueled the rise of right-wing political parties all over Europe as well as the United States, and their ultimate success is a distinct possibility.

As this study has demonstrated, racism has been a fixture of the human condition for centuries. This most recent iteration, however, is to an extent a response to the so-called illegal immigration of the African, the Latina/o, and the Muslim (with some checking all three boxes), who are at times perceived to be an existential threat to the West's economic welfare, if not to "civilization" itself. Driven by political upheaval in the central Islamic lands and the absence of viable futures elsewhere, the "sans papiers" of Africa and Latin America often become the "sans abri," and are largely unwanted throughout the northern hemisphere. In a desperate struggle to survive, individuals and whole families spend exorbitant sums to travel thousands of miles, over land and sea, to begin anew. If most become undocumented through overstaying their visas in the US (though enough have undertaken coyote-led, treacherous voyages), the motivations for their journeys are not unfamiliar to those who embark upon rickety, unseaworthy boats organized by equally exploitative human traffickers of the Mediterranean. Thousands have perished along the way, while the survivors live precariously, in the shadows. Young African women are particularly exploited, forced into prostitution in many European cities.

With respect to the African diaspora, the plight of the undocumented cuts both ways. To be sure, there are African-descended citizens of various northern hemispheric countries who are as opposed to "illegal" immigration as the most conservative elements of the society, and who do not "identify" with the plight of the undocumented. But there are also those who see themselves in the undocumented, and rally to their defense.

In fact, the perception of social and economic injustice is a powerful mechanism by which disparate African-descended communities have made common cause. Perhaps there is no greater evidence of this than the Black Lives Matter (BLM) movement. Originally organized in 2013 by Alicia Garza, a queer African American woman, African American "queer activist" Patrisse Cullors, and Nigerian-descended Opal Tometi, these women launched BLM via social media with the hashtag #BlackLivesMatter, in response to police harassment and brutality and the deaths of Americans Trayvon Martin, Eric Garner, Tamir Rice, Mike Brown, Mya Hall, and Sandra Bland. With chapters around the world, BLM is now a global phenomenon that enjoys support from all segments of various societies, including those that are non-black. Whether it is in France, Germany, the UK, or the US, instances of social injustice and police brutality are now correlated, knitting the diaspora even more closely. Meanwhile, the list of those unjustifiably killed by paramilitary forces, on a seemingly daily basis, continues to grow.

Transformations in information technology certainly facilitate the BLM movement, and in the post-apartheid era, as opposed to before it, it is not so much the epic development that knits together diasporic communities as much as cultural diffusion by way of these rapidly changing technologies. And it is by means of these impressive innovations in the spread of information that fashions and hairstyles have also disseminated, such that black folk separated by tremendous distances can instantaneously study and mimic and refashion each other's somatic and sartorial splendor. Scientific and technological advances are equally making information about the human genome ever more accessible, including discoveries about origins in Africa and elsewhere, and as individuals submit DNA tests to learn more about themselves, they invariably identify that much more with those origins.

But there is arguably no more important channel by which communities meet than hip-hop music. Unfolding in both connection and tension with a third (and for some theorists fourth) wave of feminism in which individuality, intersectionality (which understands the human experience as a varying distillation of gender, class, race, and sexual preference), body positivity, and sexual fluidity are emphasized and sexual violence is targeted, hip-hop has been a global phenomenon since the beginning of its "Golden Age" in the mid-1980s. Highly generational in orientation, it effectively provides the framing, language, and symbols through which younger generations reflect on common struggles. To be sure, hip-hop has greatly impacted all races, ethnicities, and religions around the world, not just black folk. Even so, its origins in the black world are the basis for a particular resonance within that world, especially as it addresses, in many different languages, the impoverishment, unemployment, poor education, inadequate healthcare, and lethal levels of police brutality disproportionately borne by African-descended communities.

We cannot know how the African diaspora will continue to unfold. But this third wave, in which large numbers of African-born persons are increasingly in contact with the African-descended, may well represent a moment of transformation. The African in Europe and North America could prove to be the very bridge over which the descendants of slaves reclaim what was believed to be unrecoverable.

Index

Abbasid caliphate, 37, 44
Abbott, Robert (United States), 210
Abena (queen mother in Jamaica), 149
'abīd, 43
abolition and abolitionism
  British Empire, 135, 151
  Caribbean, 166–167
  feminism and, 162
  Haiti, 165
  Iran and Turkey, 56
  Latin America, 109, 163, 166, 168, 170
  North America, 135, 161–163, 167–168
  racism and, 124
  repatriation movement and, 163–165
abortion and birth control, 137
absconding, 146, 148
Abū Dulāma (poet), 53
Accompong (Jamaican maroons), 150
affranchis (Saint-Domingue), 104–105
African National Congress (ANC), 272–274
African Service Bureau, 205
Afro-beat, 254
Afrocentrism, 10
Afropolitans, 279
Aḥmad Bābā, 38
Akan (ethno-linguistic group), 77, 97
  in Jamaica, 97, 129, 149–150
  revolts involving, 149–152
Akhenaton, 14. See also Egypt, Nubia
Aksum, 28. See also Ethiopia
al-Andalus. See Iberia.
Aldridge, Ira (United States), 247

Alfinete, O (Brazil), 210
Algerian War, 230, 243
'Alī b. Muḥammad (leader of Zanj revolt), 42
Ali, Muhammad (Cassius Clay), 257–258
Ali, Noble Drew, 199
aliyah, 29
Almohads, 43, 45
Almoravids, 43–45
Alvin Ailey American Dance Theater, 252
amaros (repatriated Africans to Sierra Leone), 165
American Civil War, 134, 168–169, 173
American Colonization Society, 164
American Federation of Labor, 193
American Negro Labor Congress, 193
American War of Independence, 123, 134, 157, 161, 164, 167, 169
  and revolt in Bahia, 153
Anderson, Marian, 252
Andrada e Silva, José Bonifácio de (Brazil), 163
Angel Gabriel Riots, 173
Angola
  Cuba and, 269
  independence movements, 267–268
  martial arts, 153
  Portuguese settlement, 267
  slave capture and export, 69, 79, 81
  slave mortality, 80
Anomabu (Gold Coast), 70
'Antara, 51

Antigua.
  British arrival, 96
  maroons in, 130
  peasantry, 187
  revolt, 149
antislavery literature, 162
apartheid, 235, 258, 270–275
Aponte Rebellion, 168
Apprenticeship (British Caribbean), 167, 171
Arawak, 132
Argentina (and race), 241
Armstrong, Lil Hardin, 250
Armstrong, Louis, 249
Arthur (slaver), 82
Artisans' Philanthropic Union Beneficent Society (Brazil), 194
  as financiers of sugar cane trade, 66
Asante, 77
Asantehene, 77
Ashe, Arthur, 258
asiento, 69, 110, 151
Askia al-ḥājj Muḥammad Ture, 35, 40
Associated Colored Employees of America, 193
Association of Afro-American Steam and Gas Engineers and Skilled Workers of Pittsburgh, 193
Assyrians, 21
Atilla the Hun, 253
Atlanta University, 175, 203
Augustine of Hippo, 30
Averroës, 46
Avicenna, 46
Azikiwe, Nnamdi ("Zik", Nigeria), 206, 230

Bahia (Brazil), 71, 96
  maroons in, 128
  Muslim revolts, 152–153
Baker, Ella (United States), 233
Baker, Josephine, 219
Baldwin, James (United States), 245
Ballano (revolt leader in Panama), 125
Bambara (ethno-linguistic group), 56
bananas, 190
Bandera, Quintín (Cuba), 169
Banneker, Benjamin, 211
Baraka, Amiri (Le Roi Jones), 236, 244
Barbados
  British arrival in, 96
  destination of the *James*, 81

mortality in, 100
peasantry, 187
slave numbers, 96
slave rebellions, 151, 173
workers on Panama Canal, 189
Barbers' Union Beneficent Society (Brazil), 194
Barnett, Ida B. Wells, 202, 204
barracoon (slave trading phase), 79–83
Barrett, Emma, 250
baseball, 256
Basie, Count, 249
Bates, Daisy (United States), 234
Bathsheba, 26. *See also* Queen of Sheba
Baton Rouge bus boycott, 232
bauxite, 187, 190
Bayen, Malaku, 198
Bechet, Sidney, 219
Belafonte, Harry, 253
Bell, Cool Papa, 256
bella, 55
Benin, Bight of.
  context for transatlantic trade, 73–74, 76
  source for transatlantic trade, 70, 82
  source of captives, 70, 82
    Jamaica, 97
    North America, 113
    Saint-Domingue, 103
    Trinidad, 98
Berbers, 42, 44, 46, 55
Beta Israel, 28–29, 198. *See also Falasha*, Ethiopia
Biassou, Georges (Saint-Domingue), 155
Bible, 4, 15, 21, 23–26
  Africans in, 23
  Egypt and Nubia in, 21–23
  influence on African experience, 21
  Queen of Sheba, 26–28
  slavery in, 21, 25
Bilali (Sapelo, Georgia), 116
Birmingham church bombing, 234
Black Caribs (St. Vincent), 132
Black Codes (United States), 174
Black Liberation Army (BLA), 238
Black Lives Matter movement, 285
black minstrelsy, 246–248
Black Panther Party, 236–239
"black poor" (Britain), 164
Black Power Conference (United States), 235

black power movement (United States), 231, 236, 273

Black Sea, 65

Blake, Eubie (United States), 218

Blakey, Art, 251

"Bloody Sunday" (Selma), 234

blues music, 248–249, 252

Blyden, Edward W. (St. Thomas), 201

Bôa Morte sisterhood, 196

Bogle, Paul (Jamaica), 169, 173

Bolívar, Simón, 166

Bolivia, 242

Bolt, Usain, 257

Bom Jesus das Necessidades e Reden ção dos Homens Prétos (Good Jesus of the Needs and Redemption of Black Men), 197

Bond, Horace Mann (United States), 245

Bonny (Bight of Biafra), 70, 79

Bontemps, Arna (United States), 218

bori (spirit-possession cults in Muslim areas), 139–143

boricua (native population of Puerto Rico), 108

Bornu, 36

Bouchet, Edward A. (United States), 212

Bowler, Jack (United States), 159

boxing, 258

bozales (unacculturated Africans), 108

Brazil
    abolitionism, 163, 170
    culture, 144, 153, 251, 255–256
    Golden Law, 170
    maroon communities, 127–128
    medical experiments, 214
    race and racism, 153, 191, 194–195, 210–211, 241–242
    repatriation from, 165
    Rio Branco Law of 1871, 170
    slave exports, 109
    slave import volumes, 70, 95
    slave revolts, 152–153
    slavery in, 96
    sugar production, 69, 107
    urbanization, 191
    See also Bahia

Britain, 18. See United Kingdom.

Brooke, Edward (United States), 175

Brooks, Gwendolyn (United States), 245

Brotherhood of Sleeping Car Porters and Maids (Pullman Porters), 193

Brown University.
    and slavery, 118

Brown v. Board of Education, 231

Brown, Clifford, 251

Brown, Elaine, 237

Brown, John (United States), 161

Brown, Sterling (United States), 217

Bruce, Blanche K. (United States), 175

brutality.
    in Caribbean, 100
    in Saint-Domingue, 107

Bussa (revolt leader), 151

Butler Riots (Trinidad), 194

Byzantine (eastern Roman) Empire, 65

cabildos (fraternal organization in Cuba), 165, 197

Cabinda (West Central Africa), 70

Cabral, Amílcar Lopes (Guinea-Bissau), 267

Cabral, Pedro (Portugal), 67

cacao. See cocoa.

Calabar (Bight of Biafra), 70

calypso music, 253

Canada
    abolitionism, 135
    migration to, 276

Candaces, 15, 27, 30

candomblé (traditions), 196

Cape Castle (Gold Coast), 70

Cape Colony, 270–272

Caribbean, 96–99
    abolition of slavery, 166–167
    Apprenticeship, 167, 171
    labor strikes, 171, 173
    migration to and from, 187, 189–190, 276
    post-independence, 239–240
    revolts, 149
    slave economies, 99
    slave import volumes, 70

Caribs, 69, 132

carnival, 254–255

Carthage, 18

Carver, George Washington (United States), 211

Castro Alves, Antônio Frederico de (Brazil), 163

Castro, Fidel, 269

Catherine of Austria, 92
Catholic Church, 140–143
Cayenne, 98
cédula (Trinidad), 98
Central Sudan, 36
Césaire, Aimé (Martinique), 220
Charles X of France, 181
Charleston, 145, 148, 157
Chicago, 192
Chicago Defender, 210
China
    investment and influence in Africa,
        264–265
    state capitalism, 264
Chinese "coolies" (Cuba), 111
Christianity, 28–31, 72, 92, 141, 153, 159,
    195, 232
Civil Rights Acts, 232, 234
civil rights movement, 5, 178, 180, 208,
    210, 231–232, 234–238, 245, 273,
    283
Clarim da Alvorada, O (Brazil), 210
clave (musical pattern), 251
Cleaver, Kathleen, 237
Cliff, Jimmy, 253–254
cocoa.
    Saint-Domingue, 105
    Trinidad, 98
    Venezuela, 108
Code Noir (French slave codes), 107,
    140–142
coercion, 87, 91, 100, 102, 138–139
coffee, 98–99, 104, 106, 110, 155, 267
    Jamaica, 98
    Saint-Domingue, 105
    Trinidad, 98, 102
COINTELPRO program, 238
Cold War, 206, 229, 240, 263, 265, 268
Cole, Rebecca J. (United States), 212
Coleman, Ornette, 251
Colombia, 108, 125, 166
colonos (European immigrants to Brazil),
    192
Coltrane, John, 251–252
Columbus, Admiral Diego, 124
Combahee River Collective, 231
Congo
    and revolt in Bahia, 153
    independence, 230
    See also West Central Africa
Congress of Industrial Organizations, 193

Congress of Racial Equality (CORE), 232
convince (worship of Christian deity,
        veneration of African and maroon
        spirits), 195–196
Cook, Mercer (United States), 245
Cooke, Sam, 253
Cooper, Anna Julia (United States), 201,
    219, 233
Cordoba, 46–47
Cornish, Samuel (United States), 162
cotton.
    North America, 113–114, 118
    Saint-Domingue, 105
    Trinidad, 98
Council on African Affairs (CAA), 206.
        See also Robeson, Paul
Court (Antigua revolt leader), 149
Crenshaw, Kimberlé, 231
creole languages, 98, 106, 139–143
crioulos (Brazilian-born), 153, 196
"crows of the Arabs", 53
Crummell, Alexander (United States),
    201, 203
Cruz, Celia, 251
Cuba
    abolitionism, 168, 170
    African independence movements and,
        269–270
    early African importation estimates to,
        68
    English occupation of, 109–110
    free blacks, 111
    Guerra Chiquita, 169
    independence struggle, 168–169, 179
    La Escalera, 169
    maroons, 126
    patronato, 169
    peasant population, 187
    plantation system, 109–111
    post-slavery conditions, 179
    race and racism, 165, 169, 179–180
    revolts, 168–169
    Saint-Domingue and, 155
    slave mortality, 111
    slave numbers, 68, 110 111
    slave origins, 110
    slave trade, 70, 109–110, 114
    sugar industry, 107, 110, 157
Cuban All-Stars, 256
Cuban Independent Party of Color, 241
Cuban Liberation Army, 126, 169, 179

Cuban Revolutionary Party, 180, 187
Cudjoe (Jamaican maroon leader), 129
Cuffe, Paul (United States), 165
Cuffy (revolt leader in Jamaica), 150
Cugoano, Ottobah, 167
Cullen, Countee (United States), 217, 219
Cush (Kush), 14, 24. *See also* Nubia

Dahomey, 73, 152, 270. *See also* Benin
Dalits ("untouchables"), 56
Damas, Léon G., 221
Damnation Oath, 149
Dan, lost tribe of, 29. *See also Beta Israel*
dates (produced in Sahara), 42
Davis, Angela, 237
Davis, Miles, 251
Davy, Captain (of Scotts Hall, Jamaica), 149
Delgado, Martín Morúa (Cuba), 180
Demerara Rebellion (1823), 151
Dessalines (Saint-Domingue), 156
dhow, 36
Diallo, Amadou, 280
Dihigo, Martin, 256
Dillard University, 244
Diop, Alioune, 245
Diop, Birago, 221
Diop, Cheik Anta, 10
Dismal Swamp, 134
domestic service, 50, 92
Dominican Republic, 102, 188, 240
Dorsey, Thomas, 248
Dorsey, Tommy, 250
Douglas, Aaron (United States), 218–219
Douglass, Frederick (United States), 9, 116, 162, 201
Drake, St. Clair, 9
"dreads" (hair locking), 198
Drew, Charles, 212
Du Bois, W. E. B. (United States), 9, 203, 230, 233
Dumas, Alexandre, 243
Dunham, Katherine, 252
Dunkley, Archibald, 198

East Africa, 36–37
Egypt
    'abid army, 43
    ancient civilization, 13–14, 45
    Biblical references, 21–23, 25
    Christianity in, 30

Graeco-Roman world and, 18
    ḥājj of Mansa Mūsā, 38
    Islam in, 33
    Jesus in, 26
    medieval period, 30
    modern state, 229
    race and, 12
    Roman conquest, 18
    trade, 34, 38
    twenty-fifth dynasty, 14
    See also Nubia
Elizabeth (slaver), 87
Ellington, Duke, 249
Ellison, Ralph (United States), 245
Emancipation Act (British Caribbean), 166–167
Emancipation Proclamation (United States), 168
embranquecimento ("whitening"), 191
engagés, 102
Equiano, Olaudah, 85, 162, 167
Estenoz, Evaristo (Cuba), 211
Ethiopia.
    Aksum, 28
    Arabian peninsula, 50
    Christianization, 27
    Italian invasion, 198
    Jewish *Beta Israel*, 28–29, 198
    Kebra Nagast, 27
    Solomonid dynasty, 27–28
    Zagwe dynasty, 28
Ethiopian World Federation, 198
Etudiant Noir, L', 220
eunuchs, 23, 29, 37, 41, 43, 49
Evans, Mari (United States), 245
Ewe (ethno-linguistic group), 73

Faboulé, Francisque (Martinican maroon leader), 130
Falasha, 28. *See also* Beta Israel
families, 139–142
Fanon, Frantz, 243
Fatiman, Cécile (Saint-Domingue), 155
Fauset, Jessie (United States), 216, 219
First Maroon War (Jamaica), 128, 130
First Nations societies (North America), 67–68, 70, 90, 103, 127, 132
Fisk Jubilee Singers, 246
Fisk University, 175, 203, 205, 244
Fitzgerald, Ella, 250
Florida, 69, 133–134, 176, 190

"flying Africans", 146
Fon-Ewe-Yoruba cultures, 73
Fonseca, Luís Anselmo da (Brazil), 163
food, 255
Foreman, James, 232
Fort Blount (Florida), 134
Fort Mose (Florida), 133–134
Fourteenth Amendment (United States), 174
France
  abolition of slavery, 155
  African American culture and, 245–246
  colonial possessions, 102
  culture, 220
  Haitian "independence debt", 181
  migration to, 190, 219, 243, 275–276
  Muslim encroachment, 44
  race and racism, 105, 244
  Saint-Domingue and, 154, 157
  sugar cultivation, 107
  sugar industry, 105
Francois, Elma, 207
Frazier, E. Franklin (United States), 218
Freedmen's Bureau, 174
Freedom Rides, 233
Freemasonry, 200
FRELIMO, 267–268
French Revolution, 123, 154
Fugitive Slave Act, 135
Fulani (ethno-linguistic group), 77
Fuller, Meta Warrick, 218
Futa Jallon, 38, 77–78

Gabriel (Guadeloupe maroon), 130
Galen, 46, 54, 158
Gama, Vasco da, 37, 66
Gambia, 81. See also Senegambia
Garifuna (or Garinagu), 132. See also Black Caribs
Garnet, Henry Highland (North America), 162, 201
Garrido, Juan, 68
Garrison, William Lloyd (United States), 162
Garvey, Amy Jacques, 204
Garvey, Marcus, 202–203, 230
Garza, Alicia, 285
Genoa, 65
gens de couleur, 104–105, 155
Georgia, 113, 133–134, 158

Gezo, 73
Ghana (ancient empire), 33, 44
Ghana (modern state), 165, 204, 230, 232, 267
Gibson, Althea, 256
Gibson, Josh, 256
Gillespie, Dizzy, 250–251
Giovanni, Nikki (United States), 245
Gladstone, John, 151
Glissant, Edouard (Martinique), 246
globalization, 265
gnawa, 55
gold
  mining, 68–69, 95, 271
  trade in, 13–14, 33, 35, 66, 77
Gold Coast. 70–71, 77–79, 98, 113, 129, 143
Gómez, Juan Gualberto (Cuba), 180, 211
Gonzalez de Léon, Juan, 68
Goodman, Benny, 250
Gordon, Dexter, 251
Great Dying, 68
Greece (Classical), 15–19
Grenada, 98
Grigg, John and Nanny, 151
Guadeloupe, 98, 131
Guanches (of Canaries), 66
Guerre Nègre, 173
Guerrero, Vicente "El Negro" (Mexico), 166
Guillén, Nicolás (Cuba), 221
Guyana (formerly British Guiana), 135, 172–173, 187, 218, 239, 277
Guianas. See Suriname

"Habshis", 48, 56
Haile Selassie I of Ethiopia, 197
Haiti, peasantry, 187
Hamer, Fannie Lou, 234
"Hamitic Curse", 24. See also "Table of Nations"
Hampton Institute, 175
Handy, W.C. (United States), 248
Hannibal, Abram (Ethiopian?), 244
haraṭīn (Morocco), 55
harems, 40
Harlem Playgirls, 250
Harlem Renaissance, 215
Harrison, Hubert, 218
Harvard University, 118, 201
Hatshepsut, 14. See also Egypt, Nubia

Hausa (ethno-linguistic group), 35, 56, 78, 152
Hausaland, 36
Haward, Bartholomew, 84
Hayden, Palmer, 219
Hayes, Roland, 252
Haymarket Square riots, 193
Haywood, Harry (United States), 244
Hebrews, 13, 22
Hemings, Sally (North America), 139. See also Jefferson, Thomas
Henri-Christophe (Saint-Domingue), 155
Herodotus, 17, 57
Hibbert, Joseph (Jamaica), 198
hijra, 51
Himes, Chester (United States), 245
hip-hop music, 286
Hispaniola
    division of, 102
    early African importation estimates to, 68, 107
    indigenous Taíno, 68, 124
    See also Dominican Republic, Haiti
Holiday, Billie, 249
Homer, 27
hoodoo, 195. See also voodoo
"hot summers" (United States), 234–235
Howard University, 175, 205, 244, 246
Howell, Leonard Percival (Jamaica), 197
Huggins, Erika, 237
Hughes, Langston (United States), 216, 219
Hurston, Zora Neale (United States), 217

Iberia.
    Islam in, 43–46
    Muslim architecture, 46
    Muslim technological contributions to global travel, 46
    Reconqista, 65
    "rediscovery" of European knowledge in, 46
Ibibio (ethno-linguistic group), 74
Ibn Rushd, 46
Ibn Sīnā, 46, 54
Igbo (ethno-linguistic group), 74, 76, 143, 159
Ilê do Axe Opô Afonjá, 196
Ilê Iyá Nassô, 195–196
    images of Africans in Islamic world, 54

India, Delhi Sultanate, 48
India, Islam in, 48
indigenous. See Native Americans
    indigoinfanticide
ingenio (sugar mill), 108–109, 124
insurrection, 152. See aslo revolt
International Sweethearts of Rhythm, 250
Iran, 47–48, 56
irmandades (brotherhoods), 165, 196
Isaiah (prophet), 21
Isis (Egyptian goddess), 19
Islam
    Asia Minor, 48
    central Sudan, 36
    East Africa, 36–37
    Iberia, 43–47
    Indian subcontinent, 47
    pilgrimage, 37
    slavery, 38–43
    West Africa and, 33–36
    Western culture and, 266
Italian city states, 65
Ivonet, Pedro, 211

Jāḥiẓ, 53
Jackson, Mahalia (United States), 248
Jamaica.
    as Akan preserve, 98
    British arrival in, 96–97
    destination for those from Bight of Biafra, 98
    economy during slavery, 98
    maroons in, 128–129
    Morant Bay Disturbances, 173
    music, 253
    slave numbers, 97–98
    smallpox experimentation, 214
    Spanish in, 97
    sugar production as affected by Haitian Revolution, 107
James (slaver), 82
James, C. L. R. (Trinidad), 205–206
Jamestown, 111
Janissaries (servile army), 42
Japan, 200
jazz, 249–252, 254
Jean-François (Saint-Domingue), 155
Jefferson, Thomas (United States), 139, 158–159, 164
"Jêjes" (Aja-Fon-Ewe), 152, 195–196
Jenne, 35

Jews, 2, 24, 28–29, 66, 198
jihād (holy war), 39–40
Jim Crow laws, 178, 180, 189, 234, 256, 271, 280
jinn (disembodied spirits), 56
Johnson, James Weldon, 217
Jones, Claudia, 207
Jonkonnu festival, 143–144
jornaleros (day wage workers), 111
Juan Latino, 93
juju, 254
Juka (Djuka), 136
Just, Ernest E., 212
Jula (merchants), 35

kalunga, 73
Kanem, 33, 36
Kano, 36
Katsina, 36
Kebra Nagast (holy book), 27–28, 198
Kenu, John, 143
Kenya's Land and Freedom Army ("Mau Mau"), 198, 230
Kenyatta, Jomo, 205–206, 230
Kharijism, 44
Kimpa Vita, Dona Beatrice, 72. *See also* Kongo, West Central Africa
King Sunny Ade, 254
King, Jr., Martin Luther, 232, 234
Kislar Aghā (head Ottoman eunuch), 41
Knights of Labor, 193
Kongo, 72. *See also* West Central Africa
Korean War, 231
Krupa, Gene, 250
kumina (worship form), 195, 197
Kuti, Fela, 254

labor movements, 192–194
Lacks, Henrietta, 213
ladinos, 108, 124
Lam, Wilfredo (Cuba), 222
Larsen, Nella, 217, 219
Las Casas, Bartolomé de (friar), 108
Lateef, Yusef, 251
Latimer, Lewis (United States), 212
Le Maniel (Saint-Domingue), 131
Leeward maroons (Jamaica), 128, 149
Légitime Defense, 220
Leite, José Correia, 210
Léro, Etienne, 221
Liberdade, A (Brazil), 210

Liberia, 164
Lincoln, Abraham (United States), 164, 168
loas, 73
Locke, Alain (United States), 217, 219
Lord Invader, 253
Lord Kitchener, 253
Louima, Abner, 279
Louis, Joe, 258
Louisiana, 113, 115, 134, 175–176
Louisiana Purchase, 102, 110
Louverture, Toussaint (Saint-Domingue), 125, 155
Love, Robert (Jamaica), 205
Luanda (West Central Africa), 70
lucumí (religion), 197
Lumumba, Patrice (Congo), 230, 235
Lusius Quietus, 18
Luxorius, 18
lynching, 100, 178, 190, 250

Maceo, Antonio (Cuba), 169, 180
Machito, 251
macumba (religion), 197
Madeira, 66–67, 69, 92
Madhubuti, Haki (Don Lee), 245
Mai Idrīs Alooma, 36
Makandal, François (Saint-Domingue), 131
Makeba, Miriam, 254
Makeda, 27–28. *See also* Queen of Sheba
Malagasy, 78, 129
Malcolm X, 235, 280
malê revolt (Bahia), 152–153, 191
Mali (ancient), 35, 90
Malik Ambar (India), 48
mamlūks (servile army), 42
Mandela, Nelson, 248, 268, 273–274
Mansa Mūsā, 35, 38, 46
Mansur, al-, 45–46
manumission, 39, 51, 92–93, 166, 169
Maran, René, 218
March on Washington, 233–234
maréchaussée (in Saint-Domingue), 105
Marley, Bob, 253
maroons
  Antigua, 130
  Brazil, 127. *See also* Palmares
  Cuba, 126. *See also* palenques
  Guadeloupe, 130
  Guianas, 135

Hispaniola, 124
Jamaica, 128–129
Martinique, 129–130
North America, 133–134
Saint-Domingue, 131
Martí, José (Cuba), 179
Martinique, 98, 129–130
Maryland, 113
Masekela, Hugh, 254
Mas'udī, al-, 54. *See also* Galen
Matos, Luis Palés (Puerto Rico), 221
Mauritania, 55
Mayfield, Curtis, 253
McCoy, Elijah, 211
McKay, Claude (Jamaica), 218–219
Medici, Alessandro de, 93
Menelick, O (Brazil), 210
Menelik, 27–28
mento, 253
Meroë, race and, 16
Meroë (Nubian kingdom), 14, 16–17, 30
Mexico, 67–68, 166, 241, 256, 258
Micheaux, Oscar (United States), 218
mid-Atlantic colonies/states.
  number of blacks
    slaves in, 112–113
Middle Passage, 69, 79, 81, 86, 141
Midrashim, 26
Mighty Sparrow, 253
migration.
  Brazil, 192
  Caribbean, 187, 189–190, 276
  France, 190, 219, 243, 275–276
  Great Migration, 190
  North America, 189–190, 276, 278–282
  undocumented migrants, 284–285
  United Kingdom, 190, 243, 276
  women, 189
Mingus, Charles, 251
Mitchell, Arthur, 252
Moïse (Saint-Domingue), 155
Moncada, Guillermo (Cuba), 169, 179
Mondlane, Eduardo, 267
Montserrat, 96
Moody, Ann (United States), 234
Moody, Harold (Jamaica), 205
Moore, Ruth Ella, 212
Moorish Science Temple of America.
  See also Ali, Noble Drew
Moors, 45
Morehouse College, 244

Morelos, José Maria (Mexico), 166
Moret Law (Spain), 170
Moret, Segismundo (Cuba), 168
Morocco, 55, 198, 200
Morris Brown College, 244
mortality estimates, 69, 80, 83, 85–86,
    100, 111
  description of, 79
Morton, "Jelly Roll", 249
Moses, 25
Motown records, 252
Mozambique, 79, 267–268, 270, 274,
    276–277
Muḥammad (founder of Islam), 33, 51
Muhammad, Elijah (United States), 199
Muhammad, W. D. Fard (United States),
    199
Mūlāy Ismā'īl, 40, 43, 45
music
  blues, 248–249
  calypso, 253
  early African American, 246
  hip-hop, 286
  Jamaican, 253
  jazz, 249–252, 254
  "race records", 250
  ragtime, 248
mutual aid societies, 200
myalism (employing spiritual powers for
    good), 195

Nabuco, Joaquim, 163
naciones (nations, Cuba), 197
nações (nations, Brazil), 195, 197
Nadal, Paulette, Jane, and Andrée
    (Martinique), 220
"Nagôs" (Yoruba), 152, 196
Nanny (Jamaica maroon leader), 129
Nanny Town (Jamaica), 128
Napata (Nubian kingdom), 14
NASA, 212
Nasser, Gamal Abdel (Egypt), 229
Nation of Islam, 199–200, 235
National Association for the
    Advancement of Colored People
    (NAACP), 37, 204
National Urban League, 204
Native Americans, 80. *See also* First Nations
nativism, 284
Nefertari, 220
negrismo, 221

négritude, 5, 219–220, 246
Negro National League, 256
Negro World, 95–96
Nevis, 264
New England, 112
New Testament, 26, 30
New York City, 113, 119, 151–152, 190,
    198, 206–208, 215, 218, 237–238,
    247, 249, 252, 269
  migration to, 189
  revolts in, 151–152
Nicaragua, 204, 230
Nimrod, 25
Nkrumah, Kwame, 204, 209, 230, 267
Noah, 24–25 .
Noël, 131
Norman, Jessye, 252
North Africa.
  Christianity in, 29–30
  Islam in, 33
North America
  black population by 1860, 113
  black slaveholders, 117
  black-owned property, 117
  captives from Bight of Benin, 113
  captives from Bight of Biafra, 113
  captives from Gold Coast, 113
  captives from Senegambia, 113
  captives from Sierra Leone, 113
  captives from West Central Africa, 113
  "clustering", 114
  differentiation among enslaved,
      116–117
  domestic slave trade, 114
  early African presence, 111–113
  enslaved population, 114–115
  "free" blacks, 116–117
  literacy among enslaved, 116
  maroons in, 133–135
  Muslims in, 116
  pre-Columbian African presence, 90
  Slave Codes, 114, 116
  various skills of the enslaved, 115
  white slaveholders, 113–114
  See also United States, Canada
Nova Scotia, 150
Nubia, 14–15
  Biblical references, 21–23
  Christianity in, 29
  Egypt and, 13
  women, 13

Obama, Barack, 5, 280–281
Obbah (or Aba, revolt leader in Antigua),
    149
obeah (spiritual manipulation), 129, 137,
    195
Oliver, King, 249
Olympic Games, 256
Olympius (black athlete), 18
O'Neill, Eugene (United States), 218
orishas (gods), 197, 251
Othello, 93
Ottoman Empire. 41–42, 48–49, 56, 93,
    249
Ovando, Nicolás de, 108, 124
Owens, Jessie, 257

Padmore, George (Trinidad), 205–206,
    230
Paige, Satchel, 256
palenques (maroons), 125, 127
Palmares, 127
pan (steel drum), 253
Pan-African Congresses (and W. E.
    B. Du Bois), 204–205
pan-Africanism, 201–202, 205, 230, 235,
    254, 272
Panama.
  early revolts in, 125
  introduction of American Jim Crow,
      189
  Panama Canal, 188–189
  Senegambian presence in, 108
"Panama money", 189
Paraguay (and race), 241
Paraguayan War, 170
pardo (as a mixed race category), 111, 191,
    196
Paris, 219
Park, Mungo, 80
Parker, Charlie "Bird", 250
Parks, Rosa, 232
partus sequitur ventrum, 140
patois. *See* creole languages
Patrocínio, José do (Brazil), 163
Paul (Saint-Domingue), 155
Pelé, 256
Pernambuco (Brazil), 69, 96, 127
petroleum, 187, 190
Pinchback, P. B. S. (United States), 175
Pineda, Policarpo (or Rustán, Cuba), 169
Pinkster (holiday), 143–144

Pinnacle, the (Jamaica), 198
plaçage, 138
plantations.
  Caribbean and North American, 99
  Saint-Domingue, 102, 106
Plessy v. Ferguson (United States), 178, 231
poisoning (Saint-Domingue), 131
Poitiers, Battle of, 44
Ponce de Léon, 69
Portugal, 91, 267–268, 277
  African imperialism, 37, 69, 266–270
  African population, 244, 276
  Brazil and, 69, 94, 128
  Christian reconquest (1267), 65
  circumnavigating Africa, 66
  enslaved population, 91–92
  gold trade, 66
  Madeira and, 66, 69, 92
  Palmares and, 33, 127
  slave trade, 66, 69, 79, 91
    abolition, 170
    Indian Ocean, 66
  See also Iberia
Pratt, Geronimo, 238
prêto (black), 191, 196
Price, Leontyne, 252
Prince Buster, 253
Progresso, 210
Prophet, Nancy Elizabeth, 219
Prosser, Gabriel (United States), 159
provision grounds (Saint-Domingue),
  106–107
Puente, Tito, 251
Puerto Rico.
  early African presence in, 108
  early revolts in, 125
Punic Wars, 18
Pushkin, Alexander, 244

Quakers, 161
Queen of Sheba, 23, 26–28
Quier, John, 214
quilombo (or *mocambo*, maroon), 128.
  See also Palmares

race and racism, 284
  ancient Egypt, 11
  Brazil, 153, 191, 194–195, 210–211,
    241–242
  Central America, 241
  contemporary nativism, 284

Cuba, 110–111, 179
  defined, 11
  European views, 124
  Graeco-Roman Antiquity, 15
  Iberian peninsula, 46
  Islam and, 50–51, 54–55
  Latin America, 240–241
  Mexico, 241
  Qur'ān, 50
  Saint-Domingue, 102, 105
  South America, 241–242
  United States, 176, 212, 240
ragtime, 248
Rainey, Ma (United States), 248
Ramos, Marcelino Arozarena, 221
Randolph, A. Philip, 193, 202
Rastafarianism, 197–198, 253
ratios.
  male-to-female in Caribbean, 99
  male-to-female in Saint-Domingue, 106
Rebouças, André Pinto (Brazil), 163
Reconstruction (United States), 174–178
  "forty acres and a mule", 175
  Radical Reconstruction, 176
  Reconstruction Act of 1867, 175
  Southern Homestead Act of 1866, 176
Red Summer of 1919, 192
religion.
  African influences in Americas, 195
  and resistance, 139–141
  renewed African religions in Americas,
    195, 197
  transformation of Christianity, 195
Renaissance period, 91–94
repatriation movements, 163–165
resistance to slavery, 136–148
Revels, Hiram R. (United States), 175
revolts, 149
  aboard slavers, 84, 124
  Antigua, 149
  Bahia, 152–153
  Brazil, 151–153
  circum-Caribbean, 149
  Demerara (Guiana), 151
  Jamaica, 149–150
  New York City, 151–152
  North America, 157–161
  Saint-Domingue, 155
  seventeenth- and eighteenth-century
    Latin America, 125
  sixteenth-century Latin America, 125

Revue du Monde Noir, 220
Ricard, Cyrian (Louisiana), 117
rice, 77, 113
Rigaud (Saint-Domingue), 157
Rillieux, Norbert (United States), 212
Roach, Max, 251–252
Roaring Lion, 253
Robeson, Paul (United States), 93, 206, 218, 252
Robinson, Jackie, 256
Robinson, Jo Ann (United States), 234
Rogers, J. A. (Jamaica), 218
Rome (Classical), 15–19
Roosevelt, Franklin D., 212
Roumain, Jacques, 221
Russia, 243
Russwurm, John (North America), 162
Rustin, Bayard (United States), 232

Saba (Yemen), 27
Saint-Domingue
    captives from Bight of Benin, 102
    captives from West Central Africa, 70, 102
    economy during slavery, 105–106
    engagés in, 102, 105
    labor, 106
    life expectancy of enslaved, 105
    market activity, 106
    maroons in, 131
    numbers of enslaved in, 102, 105
    plantations in, 103
    provision grounds in, 106–107
    relative wealth of, 102
    See also Haiti, Hispaniola.
Ṣāliḥ al-Fulānī, 38
salsa (dance and music), 251
"salt-water" blacks, 100
San Martin, José de (South America), 165–166
Sanchez, Sonia (United States), 245
Sánchez, Ventura (Cuba), 126
Sanders, Pharoah, 251
santería (religion), 196, 222
Santo Domingo, 102. *See also* Hispaniola, Dominican Republic
Santos, Arlindo Veiga dos (Brazil), 210
Santos, Eugenia Anna dos (Aninha), 196
São Paulo, 96, 170, 191, 210

São Tomé, 68
Sapelo (Georgia), 116
saqāliba, 39–40
Saramaka, 136
saros (repatriated Africans), 165
Savage, Augusta, 219
Schomburg, Arthur (Puerto Rico), 218
science, 211–214
    black scientists and engineers, 211–213
    experimentation on black subjects, 213–214
Scott, Emmett J., 192
"seasoning", 100
"secret societies", 77. *See also* Sierra Leone.
Sembene, Ousmane, 245
Seminole Wars, 134
Seminoles, 133
Senegambia.
    context for transatlantic trade, 78
    source for those in revolt in Hispaniola, 125
    source of captives for Costa Rica, Panama, Hispaniola, Puerto Rico, 108
    source of captives for North America, 113
Senghor, Léopold (Senegal), 220, 230
Senhor dos Martírios ("Lord of the Martyrs"), 197
Septuagint, 24
Serra y Montalvo, Rafael (Cuba), 180
Seville, 47, 92, 94, 126
Shakur, Assata, 238
Shango (religion), 197
sharecropping (United States), 176
sharī'a (Islamic law), 39
"Siddis", 56
Sierra Leone.
    resettlement site for recaptives, 164
    site of those resettled from Trelawny War, 150
    source for transatlantic slave trade, 71
Siete Partidas (Spanish laws that include slave codes), 140–143
Sika Dwa, 77
Simon of Cyrene, 26
Simone, Nina, 253
Sissle, Noble (United States), 218
sit-in movement (United States), 232
ska, 253
Slave Codes (North America), 114

slave trade.
  Atlantic, 64, 69
    abduction and transport to coast,
      78–80
    European nations involved, 69
    mortality rates, 80, 86
    origin of slaves, 70–78
    sale and purchase in Africa, 82
    scope of trade, 67–70
    slave ships, 81–82
  domestic North American, 114
  Iberian peninsula, 91–92
  Islamic, 37
  Old World, 37–38, 64
  transatlantic trade "abolished" in
    North America, 113, 161
slavery.
  Brazil, 96
  British-claimed Caribbean, 99, 102
  economic development of Americas
    Europe, 118–119
  Islam and, 39–40
  Islamic world
    eunuchs, 41
    military slaves, 42–43
    slave labor, 42
    status of slaves under *sharī'a*, 39
    women and children, 40
  North America, 111–118
  Ottoman Empire, 40, 56
  Renaissance Europe, 91–94
  Saint-Domingue
    Spanish-claimed lands, 107–111
slaves, humanity of, 64
smallpox, 214
Smith, Bessie (United States), 248
Smith, Mamie (United States), 248
Smith, Tommie, 258
soca (music), 253
soccer (sport), 256
social Darwinism, 124
Society for the Protection of the Needy
    (Brazil), 194
Solomon, 23, 26–28
Solomonid dynasty, 28. *See also* Ethiopia
Songhay (ethno-linguistic group), 56
Songhay (imperial state), 35–36, 38, 40
South Africa, 206, 230, 258, 268–275,
    277, 279
South America.
  captives from West Central Africa, 70

South Carolina.
  captives from West Central Africa, 113,
    157
  early African presence in, 112
south-east Africa, 71, 78, 110
southern Arabia.
  domination by African powers, 27
Southern Christian Leadership
    Conference (SCLC), 232. *See also*
    King, Jr., Martin Luther
southern Europe.
  Africans in, 16, 19
Spelman College, 244
sports, 255–258
St. Augustine (Florida), 133–134
St. Jan (slaver), 82
St. Kitts (St. Christopher), 96
St. Lucia, 98
St. Vincent.
  Vox Populi Riots, 173
Stevenson, Teófilo, 257
Stono Rebellion, 133, 157
Stowe, Harriet Beecher (United States),
    162
Strayhorn, Billy, 249
Student Nonviolent Coordinating
    Committee (SNCC), 233
suffragette movement, 162
sugar cane.
  Barbados, 96, 110
  Brazil, 107, 128, 191
  Caribbean, 97–98, 100, 103, 105, 107,
    109, 188, 190
  Central America, 108, 189
  Cuba, 107, 109–110, 157, 179
  France, 107
  Iraq, 42
  Madeira, 67
  Mediterranean, 66
  North America, 114–115
  Peru, 109
  Saint-Domingue, 105–107, 155
  South America, 69, 95, 108–109
  trade, 112
Suhaym (poet), 35
suicide, 146
"surgeons", 86
Suriname, 135, 276
Swahili (ethno-linguistic group), 36–37, 78
Swahili coast, 36–37, 49
syphilis, 214

"Table of Nations", 24–25
Tabot (Ark of the Covenant), 27–28
Tackey (Antigua revolt leader), 149
Tackey (Jamaica revolt leader), 149
Talladega College, 219
Talmud, 25
Tanner, Henry Ossawa, 218–219
tennis, 256
Thirteenth Amendment (United States),
    168
Thousand and One Nights, 42, 53–54
Tiant, Sr., Luis, 256
timber, 187
Timbuktu, 35, 38
Tiye, 14. *See also* Egypt, Nubia
tobacco, 96, 110, 113, 130, 213
Tobago, 149, 173, 187, 207, 239, 246,
    277, 279
    Belmanna Riots, 173
Tometi, Opal, 285
Toomer, Jean (United States), 216
Toots and the Maytals, 253
Tosh, Peter, 254
trade, East Africa, 36
Trelawny Town (Jamaican maroons), 150
Trelawny Town War, 150
Trinidad.
    British seizure of, 98
    cédula, 98
    free and colored smallholders, 99
    French in, 98
    numbers of enslaved, 98
    percentage from Bight of Benin, 98
    percentage from Bight of Biafra, 98
    percentage from Gold Coast, 98
    percentage from West Central Africa, 98
    under Spanish, 98
Trotter, Monroe, 204
Truth, Sojourner, 162
Tuareg, 35, 37, 42
Tubman, Harriet (North America), 135
Tula (revolt leader in Curaçao), 154
Tulun, Ahmad, 43
Ture, Kwame (Stokely Carmichael,
    Trinidad), 254
Turkey, 48. *See also* Ottoman Empire
Turner, Nat (United States), 160
Tuskegee Airmen, 192
Tuskegee syphilis experiments, 214
Twelve Tribes of Israel, 198
Tyner, McCoy, 252

Umar b. Said (United States), 116
Umayyad (caliphate), 37, 44
umbanda (Brazil), 197
United Fruit Company, 189
United Kingdom, 243, 276
    abolition of slave trade, 161
    African diaspora, 243
    Caribbean and, 102
    Caribbean imports, 102, 105
    colonial soldiers, 192
    culture, 208, 254
    Marcus Garvey and, 203
    migration to, 190, 243, 276
    music, 254
    repatriation movements, 164
    textile industry, 119
United States
    culture, 244–253
    migration to, 189, 278–282
    postwar social movements, 231–239
    Public Health Service syphilis
        experiments, 213
    See also American Civil War, American
        War of Independence, Jim Crow
        laws, North America
Universal Negro Improvement
    Association, 202–203, 208,
    215
uprisings, 152. *See also* revolts
urban ghettoes, 232
urbanization.
    Brazil, 191
    United States, 190
Uruguay, 241

Vasconcelos, Mario de (Brazil), 210
Venezuela, 108, 125, 166, 188, 242
Venice, 65, 93
Vermejales, Los (Jamaican maroons), 128
Vesey, Denmark (United States),
    158, 159, 201
Vietnam War, 168, 231, 233, 236,
    238
Virgin Islands.
    American purchase, 188
Virginia.
    and captives from Bight of Biafra, 113
voodoo (or *vodu* or *vodun*),
    and Cécile Fatiman, 154
    and François Makandal, 131
    influence upon Christianity, 195

Wailer, Bunny, 254
Walcott, Derek (St. Lucia), 246
Walker, David (United States), 9, 160
Walker, Madam C. J., 212
Waller, Fats, 249
Walrond, Eric (British Guiana), 218
Washington, Booker T., 192, 203
Waters, Ethel, 249
Weathermen (revolutionary group), 238
West Africa.
    domestic slave trade in, 36
    gold trade, 33
    Islam in, 33
West Central Africa, 73
    as source of captives
        Cuba, 110
        North America, 113
        Saint-Domingue, 103
        South Carolina, 157
        Trinidad, 98
West Computers, 213
West Indies Federation, 239–240
Weston, Randy, 252
white terrorist organizations (United
    States), 178
Whydah (Bight of Benin), 70, 73
Williams, Daniel Hale, 212
Williams, Eric (Trinidad), 90, 118, 207,
    246
Williams, Henry Sylvestre (Trinidad), 205
Williams, Mary Lou, 249–250
Williams, Venus and Serena, 256
Wilson, Isaac, 87
Windrush (ship), 243, 276
Windward Coast, 79. *See also* Sierra
    Leone
Windward maroons (Jamaica), 128, 149
women
    absconding, 148
    agricultural labor, 65, 72, 77, 100, 106,
        112
    ancient world, 13, 15, 18, 23
    Caribbean, 100, 102
    commercial activity, 106, 145, 172
    domestic service, 40, 50, 65, 92

    in Islamic societies, 38, 40, 48, 52
    leadership, 30, 127, 149, 196
    manumission petitions, 169
    maroon communities, 131
    migration, 189
    music, 250
    political activism, 162, 207–209, 234,
        237–238, 285
    rape and sexual exploitation, 40–41, 83,
        100, 138, 231, 285
    reproductive issues, 137–139
    scientific work, 212
    secret societies, 78
    slave transport, 83
    soldiers, 192
    status in African societies, 75, 77
Woodruff, Hale, 219
Woods, Granville T., 212
Woodson, Carter G. (United States), 9
world war
    African American participation, 192
    and migration in US, 190
    diasporic participation, 192
Wright, Richard (United States), 245

Xenophanes, 17

Yale University, 118
Yemen, 27, 50
Yoruba, 73, 78, 132, 152, 165, 196–197,
    238, 255
Yoruba (ethno-linguistic groups), 73
Young Lords, 237–238
Young, Lester "Prez", 249
Young, Roger Arliner, 212
Yūsuf b. Tāshīn, 43

Zagwe dynasty, 28. *See also* Ethiopia
Zambos Mosquitos, 132
Zanj, revolt of, 42, 53, 160
Zanzibar, 42
Zephaniah, 23
Zheng He, 37
zouk, 253
Zumbi (of Palmares, Brazil), 127